THE CERTIFICATE LIBRARY

THIS SERIES of books has been designed to cover the various syllabuses of the Ordinary Level Examination for the General Certificate of Education. The books are equally suitable for all students who wish to improve their standards of learning in the subjects of the various volumes, and together they form an invaluable reference library.

The Editor of each book is an experienced Examiner for one or more of the various Examination Boards. The writers are all specialist teachers who have taught in the classroom the subject about which they write; many of them have also had experience as Examiners.

Each volume is comprehensive and self-contained and therefore has far more than an ordinary class textbook: each has a full treatment of the subject; numerous illustrations; questions on the chapters with answers at the end of the book; and a Revision Summary for each section of the book.

These summaries give the information in a concise and compact way so that examination candidates may easily revise the whole contents of the book—they can soon see how much they readily know, and how much they have forgotten and need to study again. The facts in these summaries serve, therefore, as a series of major pegs upon which the whole fabric of the book hangs.

Advice is given on answering the examination paper and there are questions of examination standard together with suggested answers.

Series Executive Editor
B. E. COPPING, B.A.HONS.

THE CERTIFICATE LIBRARY

★ ★ ★

EUROPEAN HISTORY

Edited by

C. EMMOTT, B.A., B. Litt.

Headmaster, Hales Owen Grammar School

Contributors:

J. H. ROWSELL, M.A.

Senior History Master, Hales Owen Grammar School

B. S. MILLICAN, M.A.

Senior History Master, Hessle High School

and

C. EMMOTT

THE GROLIER SOCIETY LIMITED

LONDON

First published 1965
Reprinted 1968

Made and printed in Great Britain by
Odhams (Watford) Ltd., Watford, Herts

PREFACE

A KNOWLEDGE of the course of European History is of increasing importance today at a time when a united Western Europe may be a distinct possibility. The various examining boards include the study of European History in their history syllabuses, with alternative schemes, within which a sufficiently wide selection of material must be taught to give a student a reasonable choice of questions to answer in the examination.

A prescribed syllabus may expect from the examinee an outline knowledge of the whole period dealt with in this volume, or it may allow for special attention to be paid to no more than two centuries. The principle of selection adopted in this volume has been to concentrate attention upon major political topics, and knowledge of European economic or literary or cultural history must, if required by a particular board's syllabus, be sought elsewhere. Moreover, space has been largely devoted to the years after 1648, as these years seem to be most popular with examination candidates.

History is not a matter of dates—it is a matter of movements among peoples, either in ideas, ways of life, peaceful progress or violent wars and revolutions, and no book of European history would be complete without illustrations of the people of the times and maps to show the changing face of Europe throughout the centuries.

C. EMMOTT

CONTENTS

CONTENTS

Coloured Illustrations and Maps

EUROPE AT PEACE

*Two views of
Rheims Cathedral
at different
times of its
history.*

EUROPE AT WAR

CHAPTER 1

DAWN OF MODERN TIMES

THERE are in history no clean breaks. Historical development is a continuous stream; the events of one era have their origins in the past and their influence upon the years that are to come. When historians speak of the centuries before the sixteenth as the Middle Ages and thereafter of Modern Times, they do not imply that history stopped and started again; these terms are used to make study easier, grouping together those years when methods of government and man's way of life seem to follow different patterns.

European society in the Middle Ages was dominated by the Church. The Pope, as head of the Church, claimed to be superior to all earthly rulers. No king was lawfully instated until he had been crowned and anointed by the Church, and what the Church had given him, it could remove, if it deemed fit. The Church courts, with a supreme court of appeal in Rome, claimed the right to try certain cases in preference to the king's court and through its courts the Church could direct the lives of men. Medieval culture too was strongly influenced by the Church. While scholars wrote about theological problems and painters and sculptors chose religious subjects, scientists, fearing death, shunned the disclosure of findings contradicting the teachings of the Church authorities. The strongest political force was the Emperor and under him and the rulers of lesser states men had their appointed places, either as local magnates or as workers, the latter paying in produce and service for the order and justice which was maintained by the former. The acquisition of wealth, and thus progress up the social scale, was impossible.

In the fifteenth and early sixteenth centuries, the power of the Pope and of the Emperor was shattered and man's way of life changed by four movements: the Renaissance, the Voyages of Discovery, the Rise of National States, and the Reformation.

The Renaissance

The term Renaissance, if literally translated, is confusing, since "rebirth" suggests a new beginning, which we have already seen is impossible in history. The term is used, however, in a wider sense to indicate the many results of the revival of Greek and Roman studies in fifteenth-century Italy.

During the fourteenth century Greek was studied by a few scholars in Italy and their number was increased by the scholars who fled from

9

Constantinople, when that city was attacked by the Turks in 1453. Libraries and monasteries were ransacked for old Greek manuscripts hitherto forgotten; the thoughts and ideas found in them and in Latin manuscripts that had been previously neglected, caused the scholars to drop medieval philosophy and theology, which had little to do with life on this earth, and to become aware of the great power of mankind. From the fact that Earth and Mankind rather than Heaven and God became the main objects of their study they are called humanists.

The new learning arose in Italy, partly because of the close association of the country with the life of ancient peoples and because Italy had, in the city states, retained the ancient form of government, but mainly due to the fact that many rulers of these states, especially in Rome, Florence and Milan, took an interest in the movement and, being rich, were generous patrons to the scholars and artists.

Literature and Painting

The earliest literary work which may be said to have been inspired by the spirit of the Renaissance is the *Divine Comedy* of Dante, which was written in Italian rather than the customary Latin, but here its relationship with the movement ends, for its religious subject is medieval in character. This was followed in the fourteenth century by the Italian love poems of Petrarch and the prose of Boccacio, the first short story writer of the modern world. Writers, however, were not prolific in their output during the Renaissance period. It is to the painters that we must look for the greatest evidence of the movement.

Under the patronage of the Medici rulers, the city of Florence produced a great series of painters. One of the earliest was Massacio, whose work heralded the arrival of a new style of painting. Massacio gave his pictures a three-dimensional appearance by employing the mathematician's knowledge of perspective and marking in highlights and shadows. At the same time his own knowledge of anatomy enabled him to make his figures more realistic. In the work of Gozzoli we see the beginnings of a breakaway from the ecclesiastical influence. When commissioned to decorate the chapel of a local palace with an illustration of the Epiphany story, he in fact painted a picture of a Florentine procession in fancy dress and one of the wise men was unmistakably Lorenzo de Medici, the commissioner of the painting. Such a liberty with a biblical subject would have been unthinkable in the Middle Ages and it led men to paint pictures which were not of religious subjects at all. The works of Botticelli illustrate this difference. He put on to canvas the ideas of the poets and scholars of the Medici court. Two of his most famous pictures, *The Spring* and the *Birth of Venus*, depict classical myths.

The high water mark of Renaissance achievement in painting is to be found in the famous trio of Florentine painters, Da Vinci, Michelangelo and Raphael. The career of the former provides an excellent illustration of the great versatility of the artists of this era, a characteristic most remarkable to us in these days of intense specialization. In addition to painting, Da Vinci took an interest in music, sculpture, architecture, mechanics, physics, astronomy, anatomy, hydraulics and engineering. He prophesied the possibility of steam engines and in one of his notebooks were found sketches for flying machines! His greatest gift in painting was his ability to portray emotion and character in his subjects. The best examples of this are the faces he painted—that of the *Mona Lisa* and those of the disciples in his painting, the *Last Supper*.

Michelangelo was first and foremost a sculptor. Despite this he also achieved greatness as a painter and an architect. When summoned by the Pope to paint the ceiling of the Sistine Chapel, he protested violently at being pressed into the trade of a painter. The Pope, however, insisted and in doing so helped to provide us with the largest and greatest of Renaissance paintings. This and other work of Michelangelo is characterized by perfectly proportioned and beautiful figures; the sculptor's eye for form and detail manifest in paint.

The last of the trio, Raphael, had not the creative genius of the other two; his greatness lay in his ability to pick out the best techniques in the work of his contemporaries and to develop them. He was in his day an immensely popular artist; there were many orders for his paintings and thus his output was enormous.

The works of the Florentine artists reached a perfection that seemed impossible to excel. One field, however, that they had not really explored was the improvement of colour. This was to become the province of the Venetian painters, of whom the greatest was Titian. His works include frescoes for churches, illustrations of the classics and above all portraits of the famous, including the Emperor Charles V; all are remarkable for the brilliance of their colour and for a vitality unknown in medieval art.

Sculpture and Architecture

Before the fifteenth century, sculptors thought only in terms of creating a bodily representation of their subjects; Renaissance sculptors set out to give their images life and individuality. Two statues by Donatello, *St. John the Baptist in the Wilderness* and *Mary Magdalene at the foot of the Cross* show real passion and sorrow. The same ability to express emotion may be seen in Michelangelo's representation of *Christ being taken down from the Cross*. Other statues, such as the classical figures of Verrocchio, are meticulous in their detail of the human body. Through accurate detailing of muscle and sinew, Verrocchio was able to capture in stone the strength of his subjects.

Among the early architects of the Renaissance period is Brunelleschi. He spent many years in Rome discovering exactly how the Romans constructed their buildings. He then returned to his native Florence and was responsible for the building of the great dome of its cathedral. A landmark in the history of architectural achievement, it is 140 feet in diameter and 120 feet high. It became the pattern for the famous dome of St. Peter's in Rome and the dome of London's St. Paul's. The building of St. Peter's in Rome marks the highest achievement of Renaissance architecture. Its foundations were laid according to the plans of Bramante and when he died the work of completing it was ultimately entrusted to Michelangelo, who designed the dome. Michelangelo and his predecessors used the techniques and forms of the Roman architects and the results of their work are more exciting and interesting than the creations of the later Renaissance designers who merely copied the Greek and Roman styles.

Influence of the Italian Renaissance

It has been seen how the return to the study of Greek and Roman manuscripts led the Italian artists and scholars to adopt different styles and techniques in their work. The spirit which brought this about, however, was not confined exclusively to Italy. Through the agency of merchants and the increased availability of books and pamphlets, resulting from the invention of printing, the spirit soon travelled north of the Alps. In Europe it was to have many and far reaching effects. It also encouraged the men who set sail on the voyages of discovery and was an aid to those who were working to set up national states.

Birth of Modern Science

One important aspect of the Renaissance was that from the methods of enquiry, comparison and experiment, which it used, came the basis of modern scientific research. A notable example of this is to be seen in the development of the science of astronomy. Men of the Middle Ages had accepted the theory of the Egyptian astronomer Ptolemy. He had maintained that the earth stood in the centre of the universe encased in a number of crystal spheres. The passage of the sun, moon and other heavenly bodies round it was explained by the fact that they were attached to these spheres. The Polish scientist Copernicus, after years of study, came to the conclusion that the earth travelled round the sun and itself revolved every twenty-four hours. He published his ideas in 1543, but they were not immediately accepted since the earlier theory had become closely associated with men's religious beliefs. Nevertheless, Copernicus' theory of the solar system, with some alterations made by Brahe and Kepler in the sixteenth century and Galileo in the seventeenth, is the one that is still used today.

Ink sketch by Leonardo da Vinci of one of his inventions: this war machine took the place of four men on a battlefield.

The Voyages of Discovery

Men's knowledge of the land masses of the world at the beginning of the fifteenth century was very slight indeed. They knew of little more than those countries which surrounded the Mediterranean Sea; a fact of which we are reminded by its classical name, the middle of the earth. They had some ideas about China from the stories brought back by Marco Polo, a thirteenth-century travelling merchant, but they did not even suspect the existence of America. The majority of people believed that the world was flat and those who were convinced that the world was round were of the opinion that if one travelled for two or three days from the western shores of Europe, one would arrive in China.

There were three factors which inspired men to set out on voyages of discovery at this time. First, the Renaissance spirit of enquiry made men inquisitive about what existed in unknown parts of the earth's surface. Also, scientific discoveries of these years reduced the terrors of sailing in unknown seas. The compass and the astrolabe were in common use and men learnt to determine latitude by the stars.

Second, there was the need for the discovery of new routes to the East, since, after they had captured Constantinople in 1453, the Turks imposed heavy duties on merchandise passing through the city. This meant that goods carried by the overland route from the East had to be sold for a very high price in Europe in order to regain the tax. A sea route to the East, then, would bring a reduction in prices and goods would be available to more people.

13

Third, new markets in the East were also required. Eastern luxuries such as silks, carpets and spices were in great demand and the markets supplying them were asking for payment in silver. On account of this the silver reserves of Europe were gradually being drained away. Men hoped to find markets where they could exchange goods for goods instead of goods for silver.

The first voyages were made by the Portuguese, who were inspired by one of their rulers, Prince Henry the Navigator. He did much to prepare the way, before his death in 1460, by making maps of the west coast of Africa and by studying the science of navigation. In the course of finding out more about Africa, the Portuguese hoped to convert the Africans to Christianity and to improve their own trade. In 1486 Bartholomew Diaz sailed down the west coast of Africa and rounded the Cape. Once in the Indian Ocean he ran into heavy seas and violent storms, and mindful of stories that it always rained fire and brimstone in that ocean, he turned back. Ten years later Vasco da Gama, after rounding the Cape, sailed up the east coast of Africa to Mombasa, across the Indian Ocean and landed at Calicut, thus opening up the first sea route from Europe to India. He was not well received by the Arabs, who had the monopoly of trade in that area.

Discovery of the New World

In the meantime Columbus, a Genoese sailor, with financial backing from Ferdinand of Spain sailed across the Atlantic in 1492 and landed in the Bahamas. To his dying day he believed that he had reached India by sailing

The Doge's Palace in Venice—an eighteenth-century painting by Canaletto.

to the west and thus he called the islands the West Indies. Some years later Amerigo Vespucci discovered that here was a whole new continent and it was ultimately named after him.

In 1494, in order to prevent disputes between Spain and Portugal over the ownership of these newly-discovered lands, Pope Alexander VI intervened and by the Treaty of Tordesillas decreed that the Spanish should have all to the west of an imaginary line drawn 370 leagues west of the Cape Verde Islands; all to the east could be claimed by Portugal.

After the turn of the century the acquisition of new lands gathered speed. While Alfonso Albuquerque took Malacca and Goa for the Portuguese (1514), Cortes conquered Mexico for Spain (1519), and Pizarro added Peru to the Spanish acquisitions in 1532.

In the meantime the English had not been disinterested spectators in the movement. In 1496 Cabot, commissioned by Henry VII, took Newfoundland and Labrador. These acquisitions did not bring anything like the wealth to England that had been gained by Spain and Portugal from territories they had won. After this English energies were devoted to the attempt to find a north-eastern route to India. In the course of this Chancellor was able to establish a trading route with Muscovy in 1555.

The achievements of the discoverers had widespread effects on Europe. They increased the wealth and importance of those countries on the western seaboard of Europe and weakened those around the Mediterranean, when the trade routes were removed from that sea to the Atlantic.

Second, they created changes in the finances of Europe. The large amounts of gold and silver imported from America meant that there was soon more money available in Europe. For the merchant this was excellent, for it meant that his trade was increased and he became richer; for the poor, however, it was not so good for prices rose and made them even poorer.

Third, they meant that there were more eastern luxuries available in the markets of Europe together with new products from America, such as tobacco, potatoes and sugar.

Finally they encouraged men to improve the design of ships. The days of the oared galleys built high out of the water to ease the work of boarding parties in war were passing away. Such vessels were being replaced by others narrower and lying lower in the water, features which made them immeasurably faster and more easily manoeuvred.

Rise of National States and Decline of Feudalism

The most powerful ruler in the Middle Ages was the Emperor. He was the supreme overlord of the rulers of the three hundred small states which covered the area of modern Germany. Some of the holders of the office looked forward to the day when they might, as the Pope did in religious affairs, command the whole of Europe. Any likelihood that this dream would become a reality was scotched by the rise, at the beginning of the sixteenth century, of strong national states. Examples of such states are England, Spain and France.

Strong national states arose when the kings were able to increase their power and unify the country under their command. The feudal system of the Middle Ages was a disruptive force, as the first allegiance of many men was not to their king, but to the overlord who gave them their land in return for labour and military services. If the need arose the tenant would fight for the lord against his king. This close bond between lord and tenant was broken when the increased use of money enabled the latter to pay for his land in money instead of service. Thus a force of disunity was gone. From the ranks of these rent-paying tenants there arose a new merchant middle class, which was prepared to support to the full a strong monarch who would promote trade by maintaining peace.

We have seen then that the increased use of money and the rise of the middle class played an important part in the development of national states. Among other factors which contributed was the introduction to Europe of gunpowder. The revived study of Roman law also played its part. From it men learnt that the King's Will was law. Finally, there were contributory circumstances peculiar to different countries. For instance, in England the development was influenced by the desire of the people to place themselves under one strong ruler in order that they might enjoy peace after thirty years of chaos and uncertainty during the Wars of the Roses. In France, the people were united during the Hundred Years War in their efforts to remove the English from their country. Finally in Spain unity was born of a common desire to remove the Moors from the country and by the marriage of the rulers of two of the more influential states, Ferdinand of Aragon and Isabella of Castile.

QUESTIONS

1. Why is the end of the fifteenth century regarded as marking the beginning of the modern period in European history?

2. Describe and explain the importance of the voyages of (*a*) Columbus; (*b*) Vasco da Gama.

Renaissance canal barge

architecture of Renaissance Italy

soldier of the condottieri

burning of heretics
in Florence

costumes

LIFE IN ITALY IN THE FIFTEENTH CENTURY

Suleiman's janissaries

Battle of Lepanto, 1570

Moorish architecture in Spain

Moorish costume

THE MOSLEMS IN EUROPE

CHAPTER 2

THE ITALIAN WARS

ENGLAND, France and Spain were developing, at the end of the fifteenth century, into strong national states. Such development did not take place in Italy, which was to remain for a further four centuries deeply divided. This division kept Italy weak, a weakness which encouraged other nations to attack her. Such an attack was made in 1494, the opening date of our period, by Charles VIII of France. The conflict, which he then began, lasted intermittently until 1559. In this chapter we are concerned with the first twenty years of the conflict; an era which is of immense importance in European history, on account of the changes it brought about in many countries and institutions.

Political Disunity

The Italians had inherited from their classical forbears the system of city states. As a result, Italy was not a nation, but a collection of separate states. National patriotism was non-existent, a man's first loyalty was to his city. The governments of the various states pursued their own policy without concern for national interests. This led not only to their failure to unite in a common cause, which made Italy incapable of resisting foreign invasion, but to inter-state competition so fierce on occasions that they even called in foreign aid to help them overcome their rivals.

Furthermore the power of the leading states was so evenly balanced that no one of them was in a position to force all to unite. If any state did appear to be growing more powerful than the rest, its neighbours were never slow to form a league against it.

The leading states were Milan, Venice, Florence, the Papal States and Naples.

Milan, since 1447, had been ruled by the Sforza family, and when our period opens Ludovico Sforza, who had seized power during the minority of his nephew, Gian Galeazzo Sforza, was in command. This usurpation and the fact that the Orleanist branch of the French Royal family claimed to be the heirs of the Visconti Dukes were to be an important factor in the coming wars.

By virtue of her maritime activities, Venice was the most powerful of the states. Her lucrative trade was built upon her possession of trading bases in the East. As well as her trading prowess Venice had an efficient system of government. This was centred on the *Doge*, or chief magistrate. Under him there was a series of administrative councils and a legislating senate.

In earlier centuries the Venetians paid little attention to the affairs of Italy for they were primarily concerned with their trading empire, but as this was decreased by the advance of the Turks, in the fifteenth century, they began to take a part in Italian politics.

Florence came under the influence of the great banking family, the Medici. This family substituted a Council of Seventy, all their own nominees, for the existing republican machinery and they kept themselves in power by attracting the support of the working class.

Florence, on account of the generosity of the Medici to the artists, played a prominent part in the Renaissance. She also produced in Savonarola and Machiavelli two outstanding personalities of the age.

If any one cause were to be singled out as more responsible than the others for the continued disunity of Italy, it would be the papacy. For the popes of this era were particularly jealous of their temporal, or worldly, power and any movement which looked like bringing unification to Italy and thus decreasing that power met with their resolute opposition. Furthermore, any one who dared to attack the Papal States risked encountering, because of religious allegiance, the opposition of a great section of the European community. On the other hand the papal entry into politics did much to harm the reputation of the office and this was to give added strength to the movements towards schism in the Church.

Naples was in every way much inferior to the other states. In the thirteenth century Naples was ruled by the French and Sicily by the Spanish, but in the fifteenth they were united under Spanish rule. The French, however, never forgot their association with the Neapolitan throne and their desire to regain that throne was to be yet another factor in the outbreak of the wars.

Further Causes of the Italian Wars

There were other factors in addition to the political weaknesses of Italy which encouraged countries to invade her. First, the Italians were neither fond of, nor capable in, the arts of war. Consequently they did not possess a strong national army. They preferred to hire mercenaries or *condottieri* to fight for them. These men made poor soldiers as they were unwilling to fight hard for fear of being killed. Furthermore they were untrustworthy, prolonging fights to earn more money and not being above changing sides if they were offered a higher fee. Thus no one invading Italy had to fear strong opposition.

Secondly, Italy, being one of the richest countries of Europe, was attractive as a source of loot, doubly so when it is remembered that this would consist mainly of treasures of the Renaissance.

A third consideration was the fact that the Pope lived in Italy. At the beginning of the sixteenth century his pronouncements still influenced the great majority of European people; thus to hold power in or near Rome could be a valuable asset to a ruler.

Finally, it should be noted that Italy became the battleground of France and Spain for both were fearful lest the other become a predominant power there and thus dangerously upset the balance of power in Europe.

Charles VIII's Invasion of Italy, 1494-95

In 1494, Ludovico Sforza, the usurper in Milan, invited Charles VIII of France to join him in an attack on the kingdom of Naples. As an excuse for this attack the French King's claim to the Neapolitan throne was to be used. Charles was flattered by the invitation and set out for Italy.

From the first the campaign was more like a bank holiday outing than a military manoeuvre, for the young and irresponsible King of France found it impossible to curb his enthusiasm for tournaments and dancing and his army lacked training and equipment. When Charles' army reached Florence, Piero de Medici was forced to come to terms with Charles, promising him financial aid and the use of some of his fortresses during his stay in Italy. The people of Florence were humiliated and banished Piero, but this made no difference to Charles, who was already assured of a number of supporters from Florence. He moved into the Papal States, and making great show of the fact that the conquest of Naples would give him a starting point for a new crusade against the infidel, Charles received the submission of Pope Alexander VI and the promise of the use of further fortresses.

So without striking a blow, Charles reached his objective and in Naples things were made just as easy for him. When Alfonso heard that the French were approaching, he fled to Sicily, and with the craven submission of her ruler the resistance of Naples came to an end.

Charles found no difficulty in taking Naples, but to hold it was to prove a far more arduous task. He had lost the support of Ludovico. Following the mysterious death of his nephew, Ludovico assumed legal control of Milan and he no longer required Charles to distract the attention of the King of Naples from his state. Also, Ludovico was not the only person who began to worry about the growing Italian power of the King of France. Against this potential menace an alliance was soon formed, not only of Italian rulers; Maximilian of Austria and Ferdinand of Spain were both ardent supporters of the League of Venice now formed against him.

At one moment the conqueror of Naples, Charles found himself in the next all but trapped in his newly acquired domain. Leaving a few troops to garrison

21

the fortresses of Naples, Charles quickly rushed northwards only to find his route across the Apennines blocked by an army of the League at Fornova. Disease, desertion and the need to leave troops in Naples seriously depleted Charles' army and he should have been easily defeated. Luck, however, was on his side and dissensions among the allies gave him an undeserved victory and a safe passage back to France.

French blood and money had been expended in Italy and Charles had nothing to show for it, but the campaign demonstrated to the rest of Europe the lack of loyalty among the Italian states and the inability of her armies to fight, thus encouraging people to invade her. It also marked the beginning of Franco-Spanish rivalry in Italy, which was to last for over sixty years.

Louis XII's Invasion of Italy, 1499-1515

Despite his predecessor's lack of success there, Louis XII was not slow to seize the opportunity of taking the French army to Italy again. He came to terms with the Venetians and between them they were to capture Milan. The task appeared very easy as Ludovico was without allies and the *condottieri*, on whom he relied for fighting, were far from trustworthy.

With a twofold attack on the state, the French threatening from the east and the Venetians from the west, Milan was soon taken. Ludovico fled for help to Maximilian of Austria. In the following year he returned at the head of 20,000 troops and this number was daily increased by anti-French supporters who came to join them. Unfortunately for Ludovico, at the last minute the Swiss *condottieri* in his army refused to fight against their fellow countrymen in the French army, with the result that he lost the battle of Novara in 1500. Louis was therefore confirmed in his tenure of Milan.

After his success in Milan Louis was in a strong position. He had captured one of the major states; of the others Florence and Venice were his allies and the papacy was neutral. If he could take Naples, Italy would be his. To make an attack on Naples would undoubtedly bring him into conflict with Ferdinand of Spain, whose family also had interests in the kingdom. Accordingly by the Treaty of Granada in 1500 Louis came to an arrangement with Ferdinand. They were to join forces to capture the kingdom and then share the spoil between them. The first part of the agreement was quickly executed; the Spanish and the French soon had Naples in their grasp. It was not long, however, before the victors squabbled over their prize. In this Louis was at a distinct disadvantage, for whereas Ferdinand could bring unlimited supplies through the island of Sicily, the supply lines from France were impossibly long. Louis felt that it would be prudent to give up the struggle and he left the kingdom to the Spanish.

For some time the eyes of European rulers had been cast with antagonism upon the state of Venice. This was due in part to the success of her commercial

Ludovico Sforza, Duke of Milan, called "Il Moro" (the Moor) because of his dark complexion.

Girolamo Savonarola: his attempts at reform in Florence resulted in his death.

ventures and also to the fact that she had been prepared to give her loyalty to anyone ready to pay. The ill-feeling towards Venice culminated in the formation, with papal approval, of the League of Cambrai in 1508. The League's objective was the total destruction of Venetian power and among its members were Ferdinand, Louis and Maximilian.

Formation of the Holy League

By joining the League, Louis was deserting an erstwhile ally, and one who had given him great assistance in the taking of Milan, but he wanted Milanese land, with which he had rewarded the Venetians, for himself. The army of the League, in which the French predominated, overthrew the Venetians at the battle of Agnadello in 1509. The power of the Venetians was broken and, save for a temporary revival, they were never to be a predominant state in Italy again. In the long run the wisdom of Louis' participation in the League of Cambrai is suspect. He was becoming too strong in Italy for the comfort of other powers and not least the papacy. Julius II now decided to devote his energies to clearing Italy of her foreign occupants. To this end he combined in 1511 with Spain, England and Venice to drive out the French. On account of its papal leadership, the League was known as the Holy League. In the first encounter of this new conflict the French were victorious at the battle of

23

Ravenna in 1512, but their leader, Gaston de Foix, was killed—an irreplaceable loss. After this the League used Swiss soldiers to drive the French from Milan and the state was given back to the Sforza family. French efforts to recapture the state ended in defeat at Novara in 1513.

For all his activities in Italy, Louis had no more to show at the end than Charles VIII.

Francis I in Italy, 1515-16

Francis I was determined to succeed where Louis had failed and he lost no time, on coming to the throne, in renewing the French claim to Milan and setting off for Italy.

The League remustered its men but at the battle of Marignano the French artillery triumphed. Once again Milan was under French domination. Nor did Francis allow things to rest there. He gained from the papacy the right of the French church to enjoy a considerable degree of independence. Later, after the death of Ferdinand of Aragon he came to terms with Charles V at Noyon in 1516. By this Treaty he surrendered the French claim to Naples and in return received Spanish recognition of the French tenure of Milan.

Effects of the Italian Wars

On Italy. In Italy itself the wars had the effect of prolonging the disastrous disunity and she remained until the nineteenth century no more than a "geographical expression."

The wars compelled the papacy to take a direct part in international intrigue for the protection of its territory. This aroused the resentment of several groups in Europe and helped to foster the schism in the universal Church.

On Spain. So far as Spain was concerned the Treaty of Noyon was no more than a truce; it was inevitable that the conflict would be resumed. It was, and Spain missed the opportunity of developing lands in the New World which her sailors had won for her.

On France. While after Noyon, France had Milan to show for her troubles, she was eventually to lose it. On the face of it she appears to have been a heavy loser, but ultimately, while successive rulers were busy making France into a strong state, they were at a considerable advantage having no Italian possessions to worry about.

On the Empire. The Emperor Maximilian had intervened in the wars and involved the Empire, and while Charles V was fighting in Italy, in his dual capacity as Emperor and King of Spain, the Imperial princes seized the opportunity to gain greater independence. The power that they gained helped to keep Germany disunited until the nineteenth century.

In general. The wars, then, condemned Italy and Germany to disunity for four hundred years, assisted with the rise of France, prevented Spain from seizing her opportunities and helped to destroy the reputation of the papacy. Further they allowed the Turks a free hand in their conquests in eastern Europe and possibly by bringing several hundred "visitors" to Italy helped to speed up the spread of the spirit of the Renaissance.

Some Personalities of the Period

Alexander VI (1431-1503), who took office in 1492, was undoubtedly the most corrupt and worldly-minded pope of the Renaissance period. While he was in power, the papacy sunk to the lowest depths of degradation. He had spent a considerable sum bribing the cardinals to vote for him and once installed in the Vatican he sold positions in the Church to the highest bidder, in order to recoup his losses.

Despite the requirement of celibacy for men in his profession, Alexander was the father of a number of children. The existence of these did not embarrass him in the slightest and far from concealing them, he did all within his power to see them well established.

Caesar Borgia. The most famous of them was Caesar Borgia, who was appointed by his father to maintain good order and loyalty among the subjects of the Papal States. He carried out his duties with such thoroughness that all stood in awe of him, eventually his own father. His methods were quite unscrupulous, opponents had to be removed at all costs and by any means.

Caesar may well have entertained ideas that on his father's death, if he was not elected Pope, he would continue to rule the papal territory as a secular state. The chance of putting the plan into practice was missed, for in 1503 father and son were taken ill together having, by accident, tasted a poisoned sweetmeat intended for a wealthy cardinal. Alexander died and Caesar was too ill to seize power.

Girolamo Savonarola (1452-98) was brought up in a courtier household and destined by his parents for a career in medicine. As a boy, he found great enjoyment in reading and writing and he was repelled by the way of life he saw around him. Eventually, at the age of twenty, he left home and joined the monastery of St. Domenico at Bologna. On account of the preaching ability which he developed, he assumed an important place in the history of Italy, at the end of the fifteenth century.

In 1491 he was made prior of St. Mark's in Florence and he attracted vast congregations to hear his sermons. These conveyed two messages to his hearers. He demonstrated the urgent need for reform within the church and he warned the Florentines of the terrible consequences that would come to Italy as judgement for her people's sins.

When Charles VIII invaded Florence, Savonarola was drawn into politics. He welcomed the French as the scourge of God, whose coming he had prophesied. After Piero de Medici had been expelled he played an influential part in the republican government that was established by the pro-French party. Through it he attempted to bring about moral reform in Florence. New laws which were introduced against gambling, horse racing, blasphemy and, above all, against more innocent pastimes such as public carnivals, were extremely unpopular.

His attempts at moral reform in Florence brought Savonarola a number of opponents. Others blamed him for the French alliance and for allowing Charles VIII to advance through Florence without opposition. Finally, he incurred the wrath of the Pope by his continual references to the need for reform within the church. Alexander VI, who was guilty of most of the abuses against which Savonarola preached, could tolerate it no longer and so he excommunicated him. At the same time he threatened to place Florence under an interdict, if the rulers did not silence Savonarola.

In 1498 his opponents triumphed and Savonarola was hanged for treason and then his body was burnt as being that of a heretic.

Nicolo Machiavelli (1469-1527). The career of Savonarola shows us politics closely allied with religion; that of Machiavelli shows religion and politics completely separated.

Machiavelli was a republican Florentine, who went into exile on the restoration of the Medici. In exile he wrote a book, known as *The Prince*, outlining his political ideas, He argued that what Italy needed was unity and the expulsion of the foreigner. This could only be achieved under the rule of a powerful despot. It seemed to Machiavelli that the only way such a despotism could be created was by force, fraud and other unscrupulous means, and in these circumstances he maintained they would be justified. In fact, he denied that a personal code of morality was applicable to the statesman; he praised the work of Caesar Borgia, whom he regarded as a model ruler, and taught that any action which made for the security or aggrandisement of the state was justified by its end. Such views were typically modern; medieval politics had been essentially religious.

QUESTIONS

1. Give an account of the political condition of Italy in 1494.
2. Outline the part played by Charles VIII and Louis XII in the Italian wars.

CHAPTER 3

EARLY CAREER OF CHARLES V

BY THE year 1519, despite the fact that he was still two years from attaining his majority, the Emperor Charles V was ruler of the largest block of territory that had been seen since the fall of the Roman Empire. The concentration of so vast an area of land in the hands of one man may be said to have started in 1477, when Charles the Bold of Burgundy was succeeded by his daughter Mary. Mary married Maximilian of Austria, and retained the Netherlands. Her son Philip married Joanna, the daughter of Ferdinand and Isabella of Spain, and the child of this marriage, later Charles V, inherited the Netherlands at the age of six when his father died in 1506.

Upon the death of his grandfather ten years later, Charles acquired Spain and all its possessions. The kingdoms of Aragon and Castille having been united at the end of the fifteenth century by the marriage of Ferdinand and Isabella, Spain was now an important power. Although Ferdinand disliked the idea of so much land being accumulated in the hands of one man, he feared the predominance of France more, and therefore left everything to his grandson Charles.

As it was traditional for the chief member of the Hapsburg family to be elected Emperor, when Charles' grandfather Maximilian died in 1519 Charles succeeded him as ruler of Austria, and was duly elected head of the Holy Roman Empire.

Character of Charles V

Charles, who had inherited so much land and was to become the central figure in European history, was not handsome. His looks were marred by his protruding lower jaw, which was a feature of the Hapsburg family. This not only disfigured him, but also distorted his speech, giving people the impression that he was dull and stupid; an opinion which was intensified by his lack of linguistic ability. French, his native language, he never spoke fluently; he had been King of Spain for two years before he knew any Spanish, and his Latin and German were poor.

What Charles lacked intellectually, however, he made up in physical ability; he was a good horseman, a keen fencer and, save for a life-long fear of mice

27

and spiders, a man of considerable courage. It is often the case that the best in people is brought out by responsibility and here Charles was no exception. Contemporary critics believed that he would never be equal to the task that had been thrust upon him. As Emperor, however, he showed enormous powers of perseverance, a strong devotion to duty and above all an indefatigable energy.

Charles' position was far from strong. His scattered possessions, differing in race, language and customs, made a strong centralized government out of the question. His main assets were Spain and the Netherlands, for they provided him, though unwillingly, with money and soldiers. The remainder of his territories were real liabilities. In the Empire, for instance, the power of the princes left him with little authority and these rulers were constantly seeking to increase their independence. The threats of the Turks on the eastern borders made the Austrian lands a considerable source of trouble and Turkish piratical attacks on the coasts were a menace also to Charles' Italian possessions.

Charles Consolidates his Position in Spain

Charles had been King of Spain for eighteen months before he set foot in Spain in 1517; when he did so he was unenthusiastically greeted. This initial dislike was aggravated when it was realized that he was unable to speak Spanish and that he had arrived surrounded by a group of Flemish advisers, on whom he intended to bestow the best paid posts in the government and the Church.

Before long, matters were further complicated by Charles' decision to stand for election as Holy Roman Emperor. The Spaniards did not feel that this was in Spain's best interests, but Charles refused to listen to Spanish views and sent large sums of money to Germany for the purpose of bribing the electors. Strangely enough, much of this money had been given to him by the *Cortes*, or parliaments, of Castille in exchange for a pledge that in future all important political and clerical posts in Spain would be filled by Spaniards. Charles gave his word, received the money and then left his Flemish tutor, Adrian of Utrecht, as his representative when he set off for the Empire.

Charles left the country just as a revolt of the *Communeros*, or townspeople, broke out. It was led by the citizens of Toledo, who were soon joined by inhabitants of other towns, members of the nobility and representatives of the church. The rebels set up a *Junta*, and this they claimed, rather than the regent and his council, was the legal government of Spain. Once in power, the *Junta* demanded that all foreigners should be excluded from office, that the *Cortes* should meet more frequently and that Charles should return to Spain and live there permanently. This could have been a dangerous moment for Adrian, but he was saved, not by his own action, but by that of the rebels.

For the *Junta* suddenly attacked the privilege of the nobility, thereby transforming what had been a revolt against the crown into a class war. In this the nobility proved too powerful, the revolt was quashed and Charles' cause triumphed without his presence or assistance.

Charles and the Imperial Election

The power of the Emperor of the Holy Roman Empire (corresponding roughly in area to modern Germany) was rapidly deteriorating, due to the increase in power of the rulers of the small internal states. The position of Emperor was elective, not hereditary. In 1519 there were three contestants for the title, Charles, Francis I of France and our own Henry VIII. Of these, Henry was very much an outsider and the real competition lay between Charles and Francis. Both of them were prepared to offer enormous bribes to the electors and it seemed that the victor would be the man who could raise the largest sum of money. In this case, Francis would have been the favourite, but Charles' German connections eventually won him the day and he was duly crowned in 1520.

The Diet of Worms

In the following year, Charles called his first diet, or meeting of the heads of the various states. It met at Worms and on account of its association with the affairs of Martin Luther, which will be described later, won itself an important place in history. Religion, however, was not the only item on the agenda. The princes were hoping to increase their power while Charles sought greater financial and military resources.

Before the election, in his effort to attract votes, Charles had suggested that a council, representing all the states, should take charge of imperial affairs whenever he was absent. At the Diet, the princes asked for such a council to be permanent and that it should make decisions whether Charles was out of the country or not. It was finally laid down that a council of regency should exercise authority during Charles' absence, but even then decisions on important issues were to be his alone.

Renewal of the Franco-Hapsburg Italian Conflict, 1521-29

Charles' disappointment at being kept short of men and money was intensified by the fact that, following the imperial election, war between himself and Francis was inevitable, not solely because the latter was jealous of the success of his rival, but rather because he grew anxious on being encircled by Hapsburg territories. And Francis was furious that the Spanish still held Navarre, despite the fact that, at the Treaty of Noyon in 1516, they had promised to return it.

Francis, being in a better position for war than Charles, was the first to strike a blow. His strength lay in the fact that his territory was compact, united and loyal, and his absolute power assured him of free and unquestioned use of the country's resources.

War began with the French invasion of Navarre, which Francis took but was unable to hold due to the treachery of his best general, the Duke of Bourbon. In 1525 Francis was captured at the battle of Pavia while trying to recapture Milan, and before being released he was forced to renounce all claims to Italy and the Netherlands, and to sign Burgundy over to Charles.

The moment he arrived back in Paris, Francis absolved himself from his promises which he claimed were made under compulsion. Charles' difficulties with Francis were made worse by the formation of the Holy League of Cognac in 1526, under the leadership of the Pope, and expressly intended to curb the power of the Emperor. The original members of the league were Florence and Venice, and Francis and Henry VIII soon joined. In addition to this, Charles' unpaid troops in Italy set upon the city of Rome in 1527 and devastated it more thoroughly than did the barbarians of the early Middle Ages. Lastly, a Turkish advance threatened the borders of Hungary.

In 1528 war broke out again and Charles' position in Italy went from bad to worse. Finally, all that remained in his hands were Milan and Naples. In the former, the garrison was starving, while the latter was jointly surrounded by the French army on land, and the Genoese fleet, under Andrea Doria, at sea.

Luckily for Charles, Doria and Francis had a financial disagreement, and the admiral offered his services to Charles in exchange for the independence of the Genoese republic. Charles agreed, and the French siege was lifted. French troops also met defeat at Milan during the battle of Landriano in 1529.

Both sides, weary of fighting at this point, signed the Peace of Cambrai in 1529. Charles no longer insisted upon Burgundy, but required Francis to give up all claims to Italy and the Netherlands. As the undisputed master of Italy, Charles received the Crown of Italy and the Imperial Crown of Rome from the Pope. This was the last Italian coronation of a Roman Emperor.

QUESTIONS

1. Explain how Charles V acquired the various territories over which he ruled.
2. Account for (a) the renewal of the Italian wars in 1521; and (b) the ultimate failure of Francis I.

CHAPTER 4

THE LUTHERAN REFORMATION

THE Reformation, leading to the breaking away of certain groups from
the Universal, or Catholic, Church, did not originate, as is popularly
supposed, with the career of Martin Luther. For at least three centuries
before his time people had been trying to alter customs and practices in the
Church which they believed to be wrong. Several of the popes had tried to
make changes and for this purpose nine councils had met, at various times,
but they had failed to agree as to what changes were necessary and how they
should be carried out. As a result nothing had been done.

Weaknesses in the Church

The need for reform grew greater and the Church became less capable of
helping itself. Its head, the Pope, gradually assumed the position of an Italian
prince. Hence to be Pope became the ambition of many an up-and-coming
Italian nobleman, with the result that unsuitable men were frequently
appointed. These men had no interest in religion and their principal objectives
were to regain the money, which they had spent on their election campaign,
and to increase the luxuries of their position. Both objectives demanded an
increase in papal taxation levied on the people of Europe, who in turn became
more hostile to the Church.

In addition to the failings of the papacy, there was a great need for reform
among the clergy, who had become lazy and corrupt. Some priests were
guilty of pluralism, the practice of holding two or more Church appointments
at the same time and usually not performing the duties in any; others committed the sin of simony, offering money in return for being appointed to a
good position, while some, by marriage, broke their vows of celibacy.

At the same time, the wealth of the Church tended to attract the wrong kind
of men into the monasteries. Far from being the great centres of learning,
which they had been in the Middle Ages, they became places of sloth and
ignorance, where the rules of the order were not obeyed and over-indulgence
in food and drink was not uncommon.

Erasmus

The decline in clerical standards did not go unnoticed. With the exception,
however, of Savonarola, no one in Italy said much about it. North of the

Alps criticism was far more frequent. Here, scholars began to study critically the early Greek manuscripts of the church and found many mistakes in the Latin translations, upon which much of the church's teaching was based. The Dutchman Erasmus, forerunner of Luther, was the most famous of these scholars. The relationship between these two men is often summed up in the phrase—"Erasmus laid the egg which Luther hatched."

Erasmus published, in 1516, his edition of the Greek Testament, accompanied by a new Latin translation with notes and commentary. This gave the scholars their opportunity and they soon passed it on to the ordinary people by translating it into different national languages.

But Erasmus never wanted to overthrow the Church. He frequently appealed to the Pope to remove the abuses within it, but to no avail. When Luther and his followers began to use more violent methods to press the Pope to take action, Erasmus was most distressed and tried to stop them. He prophesied, quite correctly, that Europe would witness a long series of bitter wars if the Church became divided, but he failed to realize that attacks in pamphlets and appeals to the popes would not induce them to remove abuses, and that only the hostile attack of a movement like Luther's could do so.

Martin Luther

Luther was born at Eisleben in 1483. While at university, he was overcome by the terrible fear that he would never be righteous enough to go to Heaven. He entered a monastery and began to read St. Augustine, from whom he derived that idea that a simple faith in God alone was necessary for man's salvation. This is known as the doctrine of Justification by Faith. There was no necessity for a priest as an intermediary between God and man, for every man who had faith was his own priest.

All these new ideas did not mean that Luther had broken away from the Catholic Church. This moment was to come in 1517, after he had taken up the appointment as Professor of Theology at the University of Wittenberg. It was in that year that a monk named John Tetzel arrived in the town selling indulgences in aid of the building of St. Peter's. His arrival was to be the turning point in Luther's career and in the history of modern Europe. The teaching of the Catholic Church said that the sinner must not only be sorry for his sins, confess them to a priest and obtain absolution, but he must also undergo a penance or punishment. This latter could be avoided by obtaining an indulgence, i.e. undertaking some good deed or paying a sum of money. Over the course of time the second alternative was so constantly abused that some people were of the opinion that forgiveness of sins might be obtained by merely paying a sum of money. It was this state of affairs to which Luther was so hotly opposed, and the presence of Tetzel selling indulgences on his own doorstep roused him to action. He drew up ninety-five theses—or reasons

Erasmus in his study, a portrait by Holbein. Desiderius Erasmus (1466?-1536) advocated a return to a simpler Christian doctrine. Because of this he had a great influence on the leaders of the Reformation. Erasmus spent five years in England, where he taught Greek at Cambridge University.

—why he considered the sale illegal and nailed them to the door of the church in Wittenberg, thereby challenging Tetzel to a public debate.

At this juncture Luther had absolutely no idea of breaking relations with the papacy. But the great interest which was shown all over the Empire in his attack on indulgences led him to an attack on the position of the papacy and finally to queries about the teaching of the Church. He strongly maintained that the truth of religion did not depend upon the tradition of the Church, but only upon the words of the Bible. He suggested that the monasteries should be dissolved, queried the need for so many Saint's Days, reduced the sacraments of the Church to two, Baptism and Holy Communion, and maintained that priests should be allowed to marry.

Leo X could eventually stand it no longer; in 1520, he condemned Luther's writings and excommunicated him. Expulsion from Church membership did not worry Luther and, in order to show his complete disregard for the severest penalty which the Pope could impose, he burnt the Pope's bull, or letter, publicly in the market place of Wittenberg.

Charles V and the Reformation

The Pope called upon the Emperor to take action. Charles summoned the offender to appear before the Diet at Worms in 1521. Luther was ordered to withdraw all that he had written against the Pope's authority, but he refused to do so, unless he could be proved wrong in scripture. For this open defiance the Emperor had only one answer: Luther was outlawed from the Empire.

This ban was impossible to enforce, for the Elector of Saxony, one of the most powerful princes of the Empire, took Luther "under his wing" and hid him, for a time, in Wartburg Castle. As a "guest" here, he whiled away the hours translating the Bible into German.

Because the Empire was not a unified state, the Emperor lacked sufficient power to crush the Lutheran movement. The subordinate rulers within the Empire joined the Lutherans simply because they saw in so doing a means of increasing their own independence.

Instead of concentrating on the overthrow of Lutheranism after the Peace of Cambrai, Charles went back to war with Francis. In 1526, because Francis was using the Lutherans within the Empire against him, Charles agreed at Diet of Spires in 1526 that each ruler must settle what religion was to be followed within his own realm.

Three years later, after military success in Italy, Charles issued a second decree from Spires enforcing the ban on Luther. Luther's followers drew up a formal protest and were henceforth called Protestants.

The Emperor now called for a formal statement of the Protestant point of view. The composition of this document was entrusted to Philipp Melancthon, and when it was published in 1530 as *The Confession of Augsburg* it showed how far removed the new Church was from the old. Charles immediately condemned it, but was unable to use force as he was fighting Francis in the west and the Turks in the east. To protect themselves, the Protestants formed the League of Schmalkalden, 1531, and Charles arranged a truce with them in 1532 stating that no one should be persecuted for his religious opinions.

Protestantism appeared doomed in 1547 when, freed from fighting France by the death of Francis I, Charles defeated the League at Mulhberg. But while awaiting the decree of the Great Council called by the Pope, Charles was taken completely by surprise by an intrigue of Maurice of Saxony against him. He fled to Italy, and returned only with the death of Maurice.

By this time Charles was ready for peace, and drew up terms at a diet held at Augsburg in 1555. These allowed the ruler of each state to decide whether the religion of his state would be Lutheran or Catholic. This religious division of the Empire paved the way for the wars prophesied by Erasmus, and showed Charles' complete inability to halt the Reformation.

QUESTIONS

1. In what ways was the Catholic Church in need of reform at the beginning of the sixteenth century?
2. Write an account of the career of Luther.

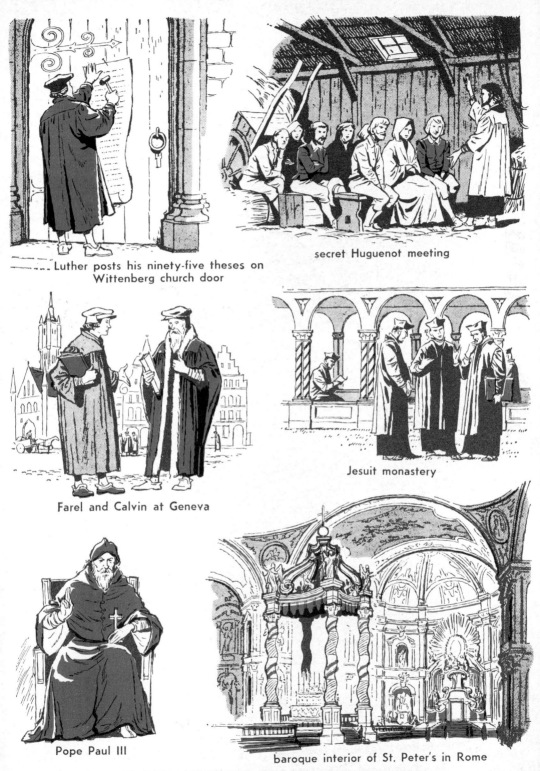

Luther posts his ninety-five theses on Wittenberg church door

secret Huguenot meeting

Farel and Calvin at Geneva

Jesuit monastery

Pope Paul III

baroque interior of St. Peter's in Rome

REFORMATION AND COUNTER-REFORMATION

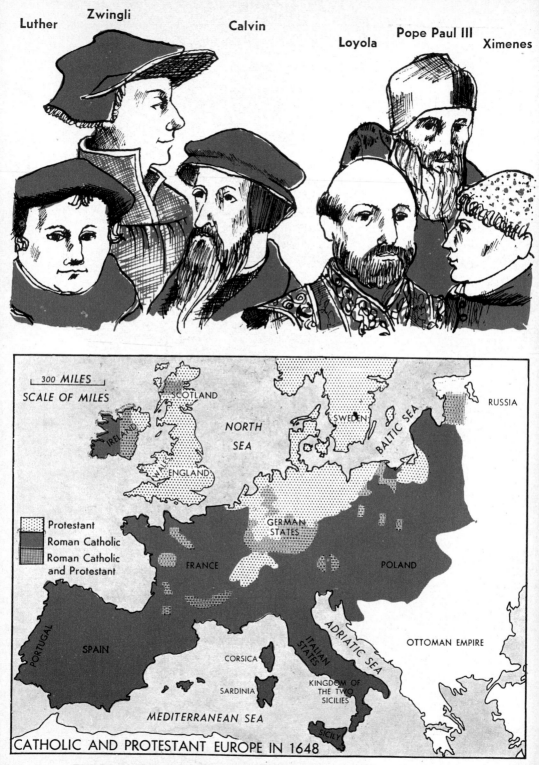

Luther Zwingli Calvin Loyola Pope Paul III Ximenes

300 MILES
SCALE OF MILES

SCOTLAND
RUSSIA
NORTH SEA
SWEDEN
BALTIC SEA
IRELAND
ENGLAND
GERMAN STATES
Protestant
Roman Catholic
Roman Catholic and Protestant
FRANCE
POLAND
PORTUGAL
SPAIN
CORSICA
ITALIAN STATES
ADRIATIC SEA
OTTOMAN EMPIRE
SARDINIA
KINGDOM OF THE TWO SICILIES
MEDITERRANEAN SEA
SICILY

CATHOLIC AND PROTESTANT EUROPE IN 1648

PERSONALITIES AND PLACES IN THE RELIGIOUS STRUGGLE

CHAPTER 5

LATER CAREER OF CHARLES V

W E have seen, through a study of Charles' early career, some of the many problems which faced him when he assumed control of so large an area of territory and how these problems prevented him from providing an effective barrier to the spread of the Protestant Reformation in the Empire. Now, through a study of Charles' later career, we shall see how these problems eventually became too much for him to bear so that, when he realized that he could never master the situation, he abdicated and divided his possessions between his son, Philip, and brother, Ferdinand.

Charles and the Turks (1529-35)

In 1520, under their able leader Suleiman, the Turks had taken Belgrade, and six years later they invaded Hungary after the battle of the Mohacs. The Hungarian king was slain, and Suleiman declared Zapolya, a Hungarian nobleman faithful to himself, as the new king. Charles, who wished to see his brother Ferdinand on the throne of Hungary, engineered the overthrow of Zapolya. Suleiman promptly reinstated him and laid siege to Vienna. Charles was too heavily committed elsewhere in Europe to use force against Suleiman, but the citizens themselves rose to the occasion and drove the Turks back. But for decades to come, Turkish influence in Hungary was a menace to the Austrians. The Turks were also an important maritime threat, and although the Turkish fleet was smaller than that of Spain and Venice combined, it was a more efficient fighting force. Under Barbarossa, a Greek ex-pirate whom Suleiman had appointed to lead his fleet, the Turks seized Tunis in 1533. The entire western Mediterranean was threatened. Charles, regarding himself as a great crusader, set sail for Tunis with a large force in ships bearing banners of the crucified Christ. His eventual victory in Tunis, 1535, aided by a rising of Christian slaves in the city, added greatly to his prestige. The Turks continued to menace the Mediterranean, but Charles was momentarily hailed as a saviour.

Renewal of Hostilities with Francis I (1529-44)

The Peace of Cambrai, which had brought peace between Charles and Francis in 1529, did not maintain it. The moment for a further outbreak of hostilities was never far away. After three years of indecisive fighting, the Pope mediated the Truce of Nice, 1538. This only preserved peace for four years. Francis could not rest while Charles possessed such strong advantage in Italy. In 1541 the continuing Turkish menace provided Charles with an excuse to attack the Turkish stronghold of Algiers. His attack was unsuccessful, and Francis meanwhile allied himself with the Turks. He won a victory at Cerisolles, but before he could take Milan from Charles he ran out of money and his mercenary troops deserted.

By the Treaty of Crespy in 1544 Charles came to terms with Francis, who gave up his claims to Milan and the Netherlands. After this, Francis was too ill to renew the conflict but his son Henry II was prepared to take up the struggle where his father had left off.

After the Diet of Worms, it will be recalled, an edict was issued, banning Luther and his works from the Empire and limitations were imposed upon the power of the council of regency, which was to take charge of affairs when Charles V was out of the country. Of course, the edict proved quite futile. Luther remained in the Empire and his works were widely read, and the limitations upon the authority of the council were hotly opposed by the princes. These sequels to the pronouncements of the Diet are significant because they indicate the trend of events for the rest of the reign. On the one hand, Charles wished to be the complete master of the situation, but had neither the financial nor the military resources to make people do as he wanted, while, on the other, the princes, thoroughly jealous of their power, were determined to resist any efforts on the part of the Emperor to curtail it.

Charles' preoccupation with Francis I and later the Turks kept him away from the Empire for long periods after the Diet of Worms. During his absence, in 1522, the knights under Franz von Sickingen rose against the nobility, and two years later the peasants rose against their landlords. The suppression of both these social outbreaks, on account of Charles' absence, was undertaken by the princes. They used it to increase their own power and to discredit the council of regency.

The spread of Lutheranism horrified Charles both because it ran contrary to his religious beliefs and because it threatened a division in his Empire.

Charles at the Pinnacle of his Power (1545-50)

The last years of the 1540s saw Charles at the peak of his power. The deaths of both Francis and Henry VIII removed the major threats to his Empire, and the Sultan, who wanted peace with the west while he carried out an attack on Persia, concluded a treaty with Charles in 1545.

By 1545, too, Charles' position in Spain was much stronger. During his first visit to the country, he had, as we have seen, been insecure and unpopular, but circumstances and an increase in his own powers of statesmanship, helped him to triumph here to such an extent that, as we shall see, though not a Spaniard by birth, he came to regard the country as the most important of all his possessions and when he had divested himself of all his responsibilities, it was to Spain that he retired to spend the last years of his life. The circumstances which brought about this transformation were due to the failure of the revolt of the *Communeros* and the growth of his reputation among the Catholic Spanish; a result of his having been brought into conflict with the heretical Protestants and the infidel Turks. Aspects of policy responsible for this change of heart, among the Spanish, were Charles' eventual readiness not to appoint foreigners to posts of power or influence in the country. His only remaining problem was the political ambition of the princes of his Empire and the spread of Lutheranism among them.

Final Years of Charles (1550-58)

Throughout his extensive reign over his even more extensive dominions, Charles looked forward to the day when he would rule supreme over a peaceful Europe. He came as near to the realization of this ambition as he was ever going to do when he triumphed at Muhlberg in 1547. After this victory the tide of success turned against him, things went from bad to worse and, in a growing fit of despair, he made up his mind to abdicate and divide his territories between his relations.

The rapid change in the fortunes of Charles at this time was brought about, in the first place, by the defection of Maurice of Saxony, the hero of his victory, to the side of the princes. Secondly, the most Catholic King of France, Henry II, was not above making a Protestant alliance, when there were advantages to be gained by doing so. Thus he sent men and money to Maurice and, when the latter died, he entered into agreement with the Protestant princes, whereby in return for his help he should receive Metz, Verdun and Toul, three small, yet strategically important states on the borders of France and the Empire. Henry, then, was proving as much a thorn in the flesh to Charles as his father, Francis, had been.

In addition to the activities of Maurice and Henry II, Charles' despair was brought on by the renewed activities of the Turks in the Mediterranean. This was the last straw and he at once began to put into operation plans for abdication, which he had been considering for some years. In the Hall of the Golden Fleece at Brussels on 25 October, 1555, he formally resigned the Netherlands to his son Philip. This was carried out amid tears from both Charles and his audience, for he never forgot his Flemish origin and among the Flemish he was well beloved. At the beginning of the following year, Spain and the Italian possessions were also handed to Philip. In the same year, he handed over his imperial authority to his brother Ferdinand, who was formally elected Emperor two years later, in 1558.

Charles V (reigned 1519-58). *Francis I (reigned 1515-47).*

In September 1556 he set sail from Flushing, on what turned out to be the last of many journeys. It took him to Spain, where he was installed in a small house on the estate of a monastery near San Yuste. Here, surrounded by paintings by his favourite artist Titian, he tinkered with clocks and studied maps, while waiting anxiously for couriers, who kept him in constant touch with the affairs of Spain. He would not listen to his doctor, who advised him not to eat such vast quantities of rich food, and this greed brought him to his death in September 1558.

It remains for us to consider whether this extraordinary character, who was the dominant figure in the history of Europe in the first half of the sixteenth century, was a great ruler. Historians, over the ages, have come to the conclusion that he was not great. He is very easy to condemn, for despite the vast power and wealth that he had at his command, his achievements were negligible. It is perhaps fairest to view him as a man who was attempting to carry out what he believed to be his duty, but whose plans and methods were old-fashioned in the age during which he ruled. He tried to uphold the old medieval idea, whereby the Pope and Emperor held spiritual and temporal power in Europe respectively. Times, however, were changing and the power of the Pope was being challenged by the growing strength of Lutheranism and the old imperial idea by the rapidly developing spirit of nationalism.

QUESTIONS

1. Describe the progress of the Turkish power in Europe during the reign of Charles V.
2. State why Charles V was driven to abdicate and the arrangements which he made for the future government of his dominions.

CHAPTER 6

THE ZWINGLIAN AND CALVINIST REFORMATIONS

AT THE very time that Luther's movement was thriving on the difficulties of the Emperor another movement, quite independent of it, was beginning in Switzerland under the leadership of Ulrich Zwingli.

Zwinglianism

Zwingli preached against indulgences and pilgrimages but without the violence of Luther. He hoped simply to ridicule them out of existence. The turning point in his career came in 1523, when his sixty-six theses outlining his ideas for improvement in the Church formed the basis of a series of city council debates. In these he insisted, as had Luther, on the sole authority of the Bible to determine religious problems. He also agreed with the German reformer's idea of justification by faith. In addition he rejected many features of the Catholic faith such as the papacy, priests, Mass, confession, pilgrimages, monasteries and indulgences. He won the full support of the council, who gave him a free hand to do as he wished with the Church in Zurich. As a result great changes were made, Mass was abolished, church ornaments were put away, frescoes on the walls of churches were covered with whitewash and the relics of saints, displayed for veneration, were buried. These changes were far more sweeping than those which had been made by Luther in the German Church; thus in outward appearance the two movements appear to differ widely, but in their teaching they were in fact very similar.

Zwingli and Luther

The teaching of Luther and Zwingli differed in only one important aspect: they disagreed in their views of the Mass or Holy Communion service. Neither party believed, as do the Roman Catholics, in transubstantiation, i.e. that the bread and wine, when blessed by the priest, are turned into the body and blood of Christ. Luther taught that the bread and wine, when blessed, do not change but become the vehicle of both the divine and human aspects of Christ's personality. The elements of the sacrament thus, after being blessed, embody the real presence of Christ. This teaching is misleadingly known sometimes as consubstantiation. Zwingli, on the other hand maintained that no change takes place at all and that the service is purely commemorative. By blessing bread and wine and handing it round to the congregation, the priest is merely recalling the similar action of Christ in the Upper Room on the night before He died.

Supporters of the reformed Churches were very anxious that Luther and Zwingli should come to an agreement, for a split in their movement would make them so much weaker. Philip of Hesse went so far as to arrange a meeting between the two men, at Marburg in 1529. Here both men, while remaining perfectly friendly, refused to move from their own contentions and thus there appeared in the Protestant Church a permanent division.

In the meantime in Switzerland the Church of Zwingli began to grow and it was eventually accepted by all except five of the Swiss cantons. The two parties, Catholic and Protestant, grew jealous of one another and war became inevitable. It finally broke out in 1531 and the Catholic cantons at once proved superior. Not only were the Zwinglians defeated but their leader, who had followed them into battle as chaplain, was killed at Kappel. In the peace which terminated hostilities in 1531, it was agreed that each canton was free to decide which religion it would follow, and that preachers of one faith must not enter districts where the other was practised.

Calvinism

The work which was begun by Zwingli at Zurich, was later paralleled by John Calvin in Geneva.

Calvin was born, in 1509, at Noyon in France. His father was secretary to the bishop there and he determined to use his association with the Church to give his son every possible advantage in life. Thus at the age of twelve young Calvin was given charge of a parish; he could not, of course, undertake the work, but he received the income of the post. Some of the money thus obtained was used to pay another man to do the work, while the remainder went to pay for Calvin's education. The irregularity of placing a boy in such a post was excused on the grounds that he was in any case preparing to follow the vocation of a priest. Suddenly, however, Calvin's father had the idea that the law offered better prospects than the priesthood and the boy's studies were immediately switched from theology to law. Calvin did not like studying law, but he tolerated it until his father's death in 1531, when he changed, yet again, this time to a study of literature.

In 1532, Calvin announced that he had experienced a sudden conversion. Details of this he never disclosed, but it resulted in his severing connections with the Catholic Church and moving to Switzerland, since France was no longer safe for people who declared themselves to be Protestants.

Four years later, in Basle, he published *The Institutes of the Christian Religion*. This was an outline of his ideas of religion. Originally written in

Latin, it was soon translated into other languages. The French edition was dedicated to Francis I, in an unsuccessful attempt to convert him to the reformed doctrines. Over the years the book became the basis of the Calvinist faith.

Calvin and Luther

In many respects Calvin's teaching was similar to that of Luther. Both men insisted upon the sole authority of the Bible in determining the answers to religious disputes and problems, and both believed in justification by faith. But whereas Luther was prepared to accept everything which was not specifically forbidden in the Bible, Calvin accepted only those things which were, in his opinion, specifically mentioned. While Calvin looked upon God as the fearful and majestic King of the Old Testament, Luther regarded Him in the New Testament light as the God of Love. In his teaching about the communion service Calvin taught that the power of the body and blood of Christ was spiritually present in the consecrated elements providing they were received in faith.

One idea, peculiar to Calvin's teaching, is that of predestination. Though Calvin agreed with Luther that salvation is by faith, he maintained that not everyone will be saved, but only those who have already been predestined or chosen by God. This is diametrically opposed to the belief in free will, which maintains that man is free to behave as he will on this earth, and in accordance with the way in which he behaves, he will be chosen for Heaven or Hell. It should be noted that the idea of predestination is Luther's doctrine of salvation by faith taken to its logical conclusion, a reflection of Calvin's legal training. If man's salvation depends on God, and in no way upon his own behaviour, since the mind of God is eternal and unchangeable, it must follow that each person is predestined to salvation or damnation and nothing he does can alter his spiritual fate.

Calvin in Geneva

Calvin maintained that it was the duty of the elect to make men moral, to fashion their own communities and eventually the world in accordance with God's Will. His own opportunity to refashion a community came in 1536. He was travelling in Switzerland, and made a stop at Geneva; as things turned out, he was to remain there, with one brief intermission, for the rest of his life.

The reformer there, William Farel, persuaded the reluctant Calvin to stay and help him refashion the city into a model Christian community. How very different the course of modern European history would have been, had not the persuasive powers of Farel been so strong!

Calvin and Farel were such harsh disciplinarians that after two years the people of Geneva had had enough and they turned the two men out of the city. There followed three years of complete chaos in Geneva until at length, in 1541, the city council besought Calvin and Farel to return from Strasbourg, whence they had fled.

Back in Geneva Calvin established a system of government known as a theocracy; in it the rulers in religious matters were also the rulers in the day-to-day affairs of the city. Government was exercised by a consistory of twelve clergy and twelve laymen; this body imposed a series of laws, formulated by Calvin from his interpretation of the Bible. In addition to those matters ordinarily regulated by the law, laws relating to church attendance, behaviour, dress, amusements, and luxuries were also included. Thus women were imprisoned if their dresses were too gorgeous, no plays were allowed save those with scriptural subjects, and musicians remained in the city only if they promised not to play dance music. Those who refused to comply with the regulations were handed over to the magistrates to be dealt with. In fact his Church in Geneva was as intolerant of other faiths and as ready to persecute them as the Roman Church had ever been!

Calvin is the third and the most important of the three men who were responsible for establishing a reformed faith alongside the established Catholic Church. Erasmus prepared the ground, Luther broke with the papacy, then Calvin established Protestantism as a strong, militant and invincible faith. His teaching spread from Geneva and spurred on Protestant communities to struggle fiercely for religious freedom: the Dutch Protestants in the Netherlands, the Huguenots in France and the Presbyterians in Scotland, to name but a few. He gave to the reformed Churches a creed, theology and organisation quite as definite as that of the Roman Church and this enabled it to withstand the strong and persistent attempts, known as the Counter-Reformation, of the Roman Church to regain that which had been lost.

QUESTIONS

1. Compare the teachings of Luther with those of Calvin.
2. Write an account of the career of Calvin and show why it was important in the history of the Reformation.

CHAPTER 7

THE COUNTER-REFORMATION

BY 1560 the new faiths, born of the Reformation, had triumphed in Holland, Switzerland, Scotland, Sweden and some states of the Empire: in England and France they had strong followings and only in Spain and Italy could they be said to have made no headway at all.

The success of these creeds can be attributed to three major factors. In the first place, there was the poor quality of the popes and clergy. Secondly, the hierarchy of the Church was divided as to how the attacks of Protestantism should be confronted. In the end, the more moderate factions seeking a compromise were overcome by the extremists. Lastly, there was never complete co-operation between the various Catholic states and the papacy.

The Catholics realized that before they could stem the tide of Protestantism, they would have to find abler popes, insist on a better-behaved clergy, and decide upon a united policy. The process by which they put their house in order is known as the Counter-Reformation.

The inspiration and model for this movement was Spanish. Towards the end of the fifteenth century, in other words before the Protestant movement was fully under way in Europe, the Spanish Church had been reformed, in order to help it in its conflict with those members of the Moslem race who had settled in the country and were known as the Moors. The leader of the movement was Cardinal Ximenes; he set out to extirpate, or remove, heresy from the country and to improve the morals and the education of the clergy. He brought all the religious orders under the control of the secular authority and the monks were required to observe the rules of their order so rigidly that many fled the country. In a remarkably short space of time Spain became a model Catholic country and this success encouraged men, at a later date, to try the schemes in other countries.

Early Agencies of the Counter-Reformation

Early in the sixteenth century three groups sprang up, who had in common a determination to reform the Church. In 1517 an unofficial society of priests met in Rome. They wished, by joining together for discussion and worship, to improve their spiritual lives, and among them was Cardinal Caraffa, the future Pope Paul IV. The group attracted the attention of Pope Paul III, who entrusted them with the preparation of a report on the Church. This report stated, with great thoroughness, the need for internal reform and was so outspoken on the subject of papal behaviour, quality of bishops, and the condition of monasteries that it was never published.

The Theatines, founded in 1524, wished to improve the quality of the ordinary clergy. At the same time the Capuchins, a reformed branch of the Franciscans, attempted to attract scholars into the priesthood. Both the last groups were peaceful, in contrast to the Jesuits.

The Jesuits

Ignatius Loyola, the founder of the Jesuits, was a Castillian nobleman, a member of a very ancient aristocratic family. He was a man of tremendous personality, a born leader and organizer and had a determination to excel in whatever he set out to do. His career as a soldier was cut short when he was crippled in both legs by a shot from a cannon. During a long period of convalescence, he spent his time reading the lives of saints; it left him with a determination to devote the rest of his life to the service of Christ. Realizing that he lacked sufficient learning to become a leader in religious circles, he sought to remedy matters by entering the University of Paris and it was here that his movement was founded.

In 1534, Loyola and his companions took the customary vows of monks, namely poverty, celibacy and obedience to the Church. They now prepared to set out for Jerusalem and convert the heathen. The political situation, however, was against them; they were held up in Venice and while waiting they changed their plans; they would fight the Protestants in Europe instead of the heathen in Jerusalem. This change was endorsed by Paul III, who issued a Bull, in 1540, which officially founded the new order. It was to be a military company fighting against the forces of heresy. Like other groups of soldiers they took their name from their Captain and were known as the Society of Jesus, or the Jesuits.

Influence of the Jesuits

Loyola was very careful in his selection of recruits. They had to be men devoted to the cause, of high intellectual standing and prepared to be obedient to Loyola, as leader of the order, who in turn promised absolute obedience to the Pope. Through the excellence of their preaching they gained many converts. They also founded many colleges and schools, at which there was a great demand for places, for the standard of teaching was incomparably the best in Europe. In these institutions, the Jesuits not only produced first-rate priests for succeeding generations, but they had under their influence, at a most receptive age, the children of some of the best families in Europe, and they could rely on the majority of them remaining good and zealous Catholics for the rest of their lives. Jesuits were also to be found in the courts of the kings and the princes. As the father confessors to these rulers, they undoubtedly played a significant part in the politics and diplomacy of Europe. There were in fact few countries where their influence was not felt in some measure and the strenuous efforts made by Protestant rulers to exclude them bear testimony to Jesuit efficiency.

Council of Trent

The Church also needed a precise outline of its beliefs and policies, and these were laid down at the Council of Trent.

For several years a succession of popes had, for obvious reasons, ignored the pleas of Europe for a council to discuss the abuses of the Church. Such a council could not be put off indefinitely, however, and, in 1537, Paul III summoned a council to meet at Mantua; its meeting was delayed by the outbreak of war between Charles V and Francis I and it eventually opened in 1545, at Trent, a city in Austria on the Italian border.

At the opening of the first session, the Pope, dreading an attack on his authority, played for time by introducing a lengthy and unnecessary discussion on procedure. This resulted in a triumph for him, since it was decided that the bishops and not the representatives of the nations present should vote. This put the council quite literally in his pocket, as there was a majority of Italian bishops, and none dared vote against him because they depended on him for extra favours to supplement the very poor salaries which they earned.

After the dispute over procedure came a discussion, not on reform, for

Italian seventeenth-century engraving of the Council of Trent.

which all had been clamouring, but on the teaching of the Church. Two important decisions were reached; tradition and the Bible were to have equal authority in directing the course of the Church and the doctrine of justification by Faith was condemned. These decisions meant that a compromise with the Protestants was no longer to be considered and did much to strain the relations between the Pope and the Emperor, who saw in a union of the Catholics and the Protestants the only chance of solving his political problems.

In a tense atmosphere, the council next turned to discuss reform. A rule was introduced requiring bishops to live in their sees and make proper visitations of the churches under their command. It was clearly going to be ineffective since bishops who did not wish to obey would obviously be excused by means of a papal dispensation. Its greatest achievement was to strain the relations between Pope and Emperor to such an extent that the former's representatives brought the session to a close by advising the removal of the council to Bologna, whither the Emperor forbade his bishops to follow.

The next session was called in 1551 by Julius III. At this, the teachings of Luther, Zwingli and Calvin about communion were all condemned, making any compromise with the Protestants still further out of the question. The final session of the council took place in 1562 and it continued the work of drawing up a precise statement of Catholic beliefs.

The council was, in the first place, a clear victory for the papacy. Secondly, by laying down quite clearly what its people were to believe and how they were to behave, the council obviously did much to strengthen the Catholic Church, but at the same time it did much to ensure that the breach between the Catholics and the Protestants would be permanent.

The Inquisition

The most formidable attack made on the Protestants was the revival of the medieval Inquisition. It had been successfully revived in fifteenth-century Spain to crush the heretics, but it was not then under papal control. In 1542, it was revived in Italy with the papal blessing. Its victims were subjected to a long and wearying trial before the Grand Inquisitor, during the course of which they might be encouraged to swear away their beliefs. If they refused, they were handed over to the officers of the secular government for punishment, and were frequently burnt alive at the stake. Hundreds of people suffered at the hands of the Inquisition, and their deaths, and the manner of them, have ever since been used as a grave reproach to the Catholics by their opponents. In their defence, however, it should be remembered that the Inquisitors did not work with vicious intent, but in the sincere conviction that by encouraging men to renounce their heresy they were doing them a service.

As an instrument of the Counter-Reformation, the Inquisition failed, for by

Heretics going to the stake during the Inquisition.

demonstrating that the Protestant faith was something for which people were prepared to give their lives, it gave it added strength.

Achievements of the Counter-Reformation

The Counter-Reformation bred, and was conducted through its latter stages by, a series of reformed popes. These were men who put their religious duties above all other considerations. Paul III led the way; not only did he give his blessing to the foundation of the Jesuit movement and the Inquisition, but he drew up an *Index of Prohibited Books*. These Catholics were not to read, because they contained opinions contrary to their faith. Later in the century, Paul IV reduced papal taxation, prohibited the sale of clerical positions and introduced measures to prevent bribery in the Church courts. In short, honest government of the Church superseded finance as the primary interest of the papal court. Pius V is an example of a man who put religious principles before political wisdom and excommunicated Elizabeth of England in 1570. Above all, these reformed popes set a personal example, which was soon copied by Catholic priests generally, and thus brought a long-needed improvement in the standard of the clergy.

The publication of a new catechism, in 1566, and the reform of the Missal did much to foster unity among Catholic people and gave them a clear indication of the way in which they were expected to conduct their lives.

Also, in order to make the worship more impressive and so tempt the people back, the movement brought an increase in ceremonial to the services of the Church. The effect of this was considerably enlarged in the new baroque churches, with their theatre-like settings, and by the richness of Palestrina's music.

As a result of the Counter-Reformation, Protestantism was prevented from spreading and it was stamped out in Spain, Italy, Poland, much of Germany, the southern Netherlands and nearly all France. That the Counter-Reformation was not a complete success may be attributed to a variety of factors.

In the first place the real force of the movement was launched too late; had it come fifty years earlier, before Protestantism had made headway among the peoples of Europe, the chances of its total victory would have been immeasurably greater. Then, too, against Lutheranism alone, Catholicism might have triumphed, but the highly organized, militant Protestantism of Calvinism opposed it with an invincible front.

The narrow definition of Catholic beliefs at the Council of Trent turned many from membership of the Catholic Church. It lost supporters also because Catholic rulers used the Counter-Reformation as a disguise for their aggressive policies. For example, Philip II of Spain used it as a partial excuse for an attack on England and for his treatment of the people of the Netherlands; while in the second half of the sixteenth century it was in part responsible for the civil wars in France and in the next century for the Thirty Years' War in Germany. Still further support was lost for Catholicism through the association of Catholics with the assassination of Henry III and IV of France, and William the Silent, and the part they played in the many conspiracies against Elizabeth, the Massacre of St. Bartholomew and the Gunpowder Plot.

Despite all these factors, however, the real reason for the incomplete success of the Counter-Reformation is to be seen in the fact that it was an international movement rowing against the tide of the ever-strengthening spirit of nationalism.

QUESTIONS

1. Outline the career of Ignatius Loyola and the aims and achievements of the organization which he set up.
2. Account for the limited success of the Counter-Reformation.

CHAPTER 8

PHILIP II OF SPAIN

THE birth of an heir in 1527 to Isabella, Empress of Charles V, was a signal for much rejoicing in Spain. The excitement was sadly dampened, however, by the news from Italy that the imperial forces had sacked the city of Rome and were holding the Pope prisoner. The gossips were soon saying that the coincidence of these events was a sure sign that the young boy was destined to be a bane to the papacy in years to come and in this prophecy there proved to be more than an element of truth. Indeed, not only was the papacy to feel the power of his presence, but also the other rulers of Europe, for he was to become as much the central figure of European politics, in the latter half of the sixteenth century, as his father had been in the first.

The affection in which Spain held Philip increased when he married his cousin, Maria of Portugal. On the threshold of success, however, tragedy overcame Philip, a pattern which was to be repeated with monotonous regularity throughout the reign. Two years after the marriage Maria died, while giving birth to a son, Don Carlos. He was sickly, puny and physically deformed; early in life he showed signs of insanity which were intensified by a brain operation. Subsequently he revealed an increasing dislike of his father, whom he threatened to murder. His disappearance from the scene in 1568 is veiled in mystery; some have accused Philip of murdering him, but there is no circumstantial evidence to prove it. Not until Philip's fourth marriage to Anna of Austria was the Spanish succession assured.

For his second bride, Philip took England's Queen Mary. This was no love match, for the ageing Tudor queen was skinny, sickly and unattractive. In any event, this diplomatic marriage arranged by Philip's father was short-lived and unsuccessful. Married to Philip in 1554, Mary died in 1558.

Philip had a far better start, as a ruler, than his father had had forty years earlier, when, as an inexperienced young man of nineteen, Charles had become King of Spain and Emperor. Philip was nearer thirty and well instructed in the art of government, when his father invested him with the Spanish Italian possessions, the Netherlands, Spain and the Spanish New World, country by country, over the space of three years, before finally abdicating.

Philip also inherited the Franco-Spanish feud, which, it will be recalled, had been raging intermittently over the preceding sixty years. In this, Philip permitted the Spanish army one further burst of glory with victories over the French at St. Quentin and Gravelines and then brought the proceedings to a close by the Treaty of Cateau Cambresis, 1559, which allowed a mutual exchange of recently acquired territories and was sealed by the third marriage of Philip, to Elizabeth of Valois, the fourteen-year-old daughter of the French king.

Having concluded the Treaty of Cateau Cambresis, Philip, after a brief visit to the Netherlands, returned to Spain, and with this homecoming his personal rule there may be said to begin.

Philip's Character

Unlike his own son, Philip had a great respect for his father and he tried to model himself upon him. So closely did he copy the gravity and dignity of his father, that he was never seen to smile in public. This, coupled with the fact that he never allowed himself to be moved by the feeling of others, led people to think that he was unnaturally cold and reserved, but the genuine affection revealed in letters to his daughters belies this idea. His stature was slight; his face, with its white complexion brought about by lack of exercise, had more pronounced Hapsburg features than his father's, and his eyes, perpetually red ringed, bore witness to the hours he spent poring over books and papers. The excessive vitality of the father was not apparent in the son; Philip was prepared to let others lead his armies, while he stayed at home, an action which earned him, unjustly, a reputation for cowardice.

Like Louis XIV, Philip refused to delegate responsibility. He believed in the Divine Right of kings, and acted as his own chief minister. As a result of his inability to distinguish between relevant and trivial matters, his government was paralysed by slowness. Moreover, because he wished to establish the supremacy of Spain in Europe, Philip was involved in constant wars, which his father had advised him to avoid. The resulting burden on the tottering Spanish treasury contributed to the decline of Spain in the seventeenth century. Philip's final aim was the promotion of the Catholic cause in Europe, an aim which he never allowed to override his other two ambitions if a conflict between them arose.

The Moriscoes and Turks

Those members of the Moslem religion who settled in Spain were known as the Moors; those whom the efforts of the Spanish Church managed to convert to Christianity were dubbed Moriscoes. They were a peaceful people and were settled principally in the southern and eastern provinces of the country. It was feared that they might be in contact with the Turkish pirates in the Mediterranean. In 1566, Philip, spurred on by his anti-heresy campaign, declared that they must all learn Castillian within the space of three years,

country scene in 17th-century France

town scene in 17th-century France

TOWN AND COUNTRY IN SEVENTEENTH-CENTURY FRANCE

port of Amsterdam in the 17th century

interior of a Dutch home

agriculture in the Netherlands

Dutch burgher

ASPECTS OF DUTCH LIFE IN THE SEVENTEENTH CENTURY

after which the use of Arabic was to be forbidden. They were immediately to abandon their Moorish clothes, including the women's veils and they were to cease giving their children Moorish forenames. A revolt of the Moriscoes ensued which took Don John, Philip's half-brother, two years to suppress. The subsequent removal of the Moriscoes to one part of Spain to live in near-captivity was the prelude to their expulsion from the country (1609) and was also the cause of irreparable damage to the Spanish economy.

Equally destructive of an heretical race was Philip's attack on the Turks. In 1570 he joined the Pope and Venice in an anti-Turkish League. The services of Don John were again enlisted as a commander. The Turks were encountered off Lepanto, in the Gulf of Corinth, and, after four hours of fighting, they suffered their first defeat at sea. The battle is also memorable for being the last victory for the oared galley employing the medieval grappling iron and boarding party tactics. After Lepanto, the Turks made no further advances.

Philip's Foreign Policy, 1559-78

Philip's effort to quell the revolt in the Netherlands, described in the next chapter, not only had a disastrous effect upon his treasury, but brought him into conflict with two of the most unpredictable and most infuriating women, Catherine de Medici, the Queen Mother of France, and our own Elizabeth I. Both these women did their best to keep the revolt in the Netherlands going by surreptitiously sending support to the rebels.

Elizabeth, who had already refused to marry Philip, since she did not wish to become a Catholic, nor be dragged needlessly into his wars, saw the prolongation of the Netherlands revolt as an opportunity to keep him in check. While he was occupied in trying to suppress it, he would be unable to join France in a profitable offensive alliance against England.

Catherine sought to prolong the revolt because she did not wish either side to succeed. If the rebels, who were Protestant, triumphed, they would obviously send help to the Huguenots (the Protestant rebels in France) who were threatening her own position. On the other hand, if Philip won, with strong Spanish possessions on either flank, France would find herself gripped between the claws of a Spanish vice.

Of the two, Elizabeth was perhaps the most annoying ruler with whom Philip had to contend. Whenever he approached her about an issue, she was evasive, and despite his repeated protests English privateering against Spanish possessions and treasure fleets continued.

Philip's Foreign Policy after 1578

After 1578, Philip turned to the offensive. He had a first-rate adviser in Cardinal Granvelle and a sound diplomat in Mendoza. The Duke of Parma was incomparably the finest soldier of his age, while, as a naval commander, the Marquis of Santa Cruz had few equals. Despite this wonderful team, Philip's successes were negligible. In the first place, he would never accept the advice that all the Spanish strength should be focused on one theatre at a time. In addition, he had an inefficient navy, a slow government, and an empty treasury. Above all Philip underestimated the strength of England.

Nevertheless, Philip's first venture in this period was a triumph, though not a permanent success for Spain. In 1580 the throne of Portugal became vacant and at once Philip claimed it through his mother, who had been the eldest daughter of King Manuel. He enforced his claim with an army. Resistance was poor and the Portuguese were soon overcome. Philip was proclaimed king.

The entire Iberian peninsula was now under the rule of one sovereign and, in addition, Philip claimed the Portuguese dominions in America and India. It was a short-lived triumph, for within sixty years Portugal had once again achieved its independence.

The Armada: Its Causes

From his Portuguese triumph, Philip turned to an ill-fated attack on England. English sailors, famous among them Drake and Hawkins, were continuously attacking Spanish possessions and treasure fleets. Supplies and money for wages en route from Spain to her armies in the Netherlands were repeatedly taken in the English Channel and more infuriating than anything to Philip, Elizabeth continued to disclaim all knowledge of these events.

Throughout the year 1586, the shipyards and arsenals of Spain rang with the thud of hammers as Philip prepared for a gargantuan onslaught on England. If he required further incentive to go ahead with his plans, it came, in the following year, when Elizabeth consented to the execution of her cousin, Mary Queen of Scots. With Mary out of the way, Philip became the Catholic claimant to the English throne, now held by a heretic, from allegiance to whom the Pope had freed her Catholic subjects some seventeen years earlier by a Bull of Excommunication.

If the year 1587 brought Philip further incentive for attack, it also brought him a major setback when Sir Francis Drake, following the maxim that attack is the best means of defence, entered the harbour at Cadiz, set light to the galleons that were being prepared for the invasion and demonstrated the great superiority of the English warships over the Spanish. This daring adventure is referred to by historians as the "Singeing of the King of Spain's Beard." A more astute ruler than Philip would probably have learnt from this attack that his navy was not good enough for the project he had in mind and so cancelled it, but Philip obstinately proceeded with his plans.

The attack had a double motive, on the one hand, political, to quell a nation which was inflicting indignities upon his shipping, and on the other hand religious, to overthrow a heretic queen and bring her country back to Catholicism. It was the second motive which gave the Armada, as the attack was called, a crusading image in Spanish eyes. All the ships which took part were named after saints, mass was celebrated before the men embarked, and before they could go aboard they had to produce a certificate showing that they had recently confessed their sins and completed a penance. This did not make up for the enormous Spanish deficiencies in craft, ammunition and naval skills.

Failure of the Armada

From the outset the sailing of the Armada was dogged by misfortune. When the ships had hardly left the coast of Spain they were struck by a storm and forced to return for a refit. The details of the triumph of the English navy, under Lord Howard of Effingham with Drake, Hawkins and others in support, need not detain us here. Much is made of it being the victory of superior commanders and equipment, which it undeniably was, but the sheer stupidity of Philip's plan also played a large part in the Spanish defeat. He had in mind a military attack on England, not a naval battle. He despatched his ships with orders to sail to the Netherlands, collect more men and invade England. The thought that his ships might be

Philip II receives the news of the defeat of the Spanish Armada.

attacked on the journey by a fleet in the English Channel never appears to have entered his reckoning.

Later Spanish Attacks on England

The loss of the Armada, though disappointing to Philip, did not lead him to give up his plans for an attack on England. In 1595 Spanish sailors raided the Cornish coast and in the same year Philip sent aid to rebels in Ireland. Plans for a second Armada were only dropped when good opportunities developing in France averted his gaze elsewhere.

Philip's Intervention in France

In 1585, when the succession of a Protestant to the throne of France in the near future seemed likely, Philip came to an agreement with the French Catholic faction, by the Treaty of Joinville, that he and they should work together for the removal of heresy and the exclusion of the Bourbon (Protestant) line from the throne. When Henry of Navarre succeeded in 1589, hostilities broke out, but Philip made little headway. He lost a great deal of support when it was realized that he had his sights on the throne of France as well as on the removal of heresy. Later, when Henry, realizing that "Paris was worth a mass", became a Catholic, anti-Spanish feeling in France grew apace. Two years later, by the Treaty of Vervins in 1598, Philip was forced to surrender Calais and other Spanish holdings in north-western France, and to recognize the integrity and independence of France under Henry IV.

Estimate of Philip

Shortly after agreeing to terms at Vervins, Philip was struck down by a gruesome illness. He was carried to a monastery overlooking Madrid, and there for several weeks he lay dying. Here he probably mused over the events of his reign, his achievements, his disappointments, his unfulfilled ambitions and so on. What had he achieved? He had succeeded in making the Spanish monarchy absolute, and, with the notable exception of the Netherlands, he had kept his dominions free from heresy. On the other hand, however, he had failed to suppress the Dutch rebels and neither his war with England nor with France had been brought to a triumphant conclusion.

The fact that he assumed the role as champion of the Counter-Reformation coupled with his limited success has, on many occasions, made Philip an easy target for the arrows of Protestant critics. Yet entire responsibility for the decline of Spain in the seventeenth century cannot be placed upon his shoulders. The seeds of this were sown before Philip was born, when Charles was collecting his vast number of possessions. Since the Spanish temperament was completely unsuited to empire-building, the new possessions rapidly

Portrait of the Infanta Dona Margarita (a grandchild of Philip II) by the seventeenth-century Spanish court painter Velasquez. Notice the famous "Hapsburg jaw," which was well marked even in a young Hapsburg descendant.

became a liability. The lack of a sound financial policy and the slowness of the government's administration may have hastened the decline of Spain under Philip, but these factors were not the sole cause.

Finally, however we rate the personality of the King and his achievements, we should not forget that in Spain itself the years of his reign were a golden age—comparable in brilliance to that of the Elizabethan Age in England—a fact to which the writings of Cervantes and the paintings of El Greco bear witness.

QUESTIONS

1. What were the aims of Philip II and how far was he successful in achieving them?
2. Give an account of Philip II's attitude and policy towards the following: (*a*) The Moriscoes, (*b*) the Turks, (*c*) the Portuguese, (*d*) the French Catholic Section.

CHAPTER 9

REVOLT IN THE NETHERLANDS

O NE of the most important developments in the latter half of the sixteenth century was the emergence of the United Netherlands, generally called Holland, as a strong state.

During the Middle Ages, the seventeen provinces of the Netherlands, extending over modern Holland, Belgium and part of north-eastern France, were each ruled by their own overlord. One by one they came in time under the control of the Dukes of Burgundy and eventually through Mary of Burgundy they passed to the Hapsburg Charles V, her grandson. There was little unity among the states. Differences of origin, language, culture and temperament made them jealous of their own rights and customs and determined to retain their independence. The people of the seven northern provinces spoke Dutch, they were democratic in character and eventually adopted Calvinism. On the other hand, the southern provinces were populated with Flemish-speaking people, who were very conservative, ardently Catholic and for the most part loyal to Spain.

The Netherlands as a whole, despite disunity, was the most valuable Hapsburg possession. It was a natural centre of trade, and the Antwerp and Amsterdam banking houses were internationally famous. The south produced cloth, and the north, fish, and in addition the country was not culturally backward; Erasmus, it will be recalled, was a Dutchman, and in the paintings of the brothers Van Eyck can be seen the earliest signs of the Renaissance style outside Italy.

Charles V did what he could to centralize the government by a system of councils, but he respected the keen desire for independence on the part of the individual states. He proceeded with less caution against Protestantism, and thousands lost their lives because they contravened his edicts.

Despite his severity with the Protestants, Charles was well liked and admired by the people, because he was Flemish. At the same time, he had a great admiration for them and from their ranks he chose many to serve him, in various capacities, in different parts of Europe. This firm understanding between ruler and ruled led to prosperity and contentment, a happy state of affairs which was rudely shaken when his son, Philip II of Spain, took over when Charles abdicated in October, 1555.

Philip began his career in the Netherlands under the grave disadvantage of being a Spaniard, which won him instant unpopularity. Instead of seeking to win the friendship of the people he straightway set out to impose upon them the absolute and anti-heretical policies which he was pursuing in Spain. These, by cutting across the national pride, attachment to local freedoms and hatred of absolute rule so characteristic of the Netherlands, created a conflict which was to continue throughout Philip's life and beyond.

The leader of the Dutch struggle for independence and Philip's opponent was William, Prince of Orange. Ironically, William was not Dutch but German by birth, although he had inherited a considerable amount of land in the Netherlands. He derived his name from the minute state of Orange in southern France, which he never visited, and as a young man his military ability had won him the position of an officer in Charles V's army. His nickname "the Silent" was inappropriate and is said to have been earned by the silence he maintained, because of his desire for religious toleration, when told of Philip's desire to destroy all Protestants in the country.

Regency of Margaret of Parma, 1559-67

In 1559 Philip set up a regency in the Netherlands under his characterless half-sister Margaret. The council aiding her consisted of three Spaniards and two local men, William and Count Egmont, but it soon became evident that only the Spaniards were consulted and the independence of the Netherlands was being attacked.

Further opposition to Philip was excited, when he increased the number of bishops in the Netherlands from three to fifteen. In many respects, this was a wise and long-needed piece of reform, for three bishops could not be expected to administer the church with any efficiency. Philip's opponents, however, saw it as a means by which he could suppress heresy the more easily and strengthen his hold over the country.

Finally in April, 1566, Margaret was presented with a petition by some four hundred nobles from all parts of the country, setting forth their grievances and asking for immediate redress. Margaret promised to give serious consideration to the position, an action which encouraged one of her Spanish councillors to ask if she really feared these "beggars." This derisive description was at once seized upon and afterwards always used of those who opposed Philip's government.

While Philip's answer to the petition was awaited, religious riots broke out. Spurred on by Calvinist preachers, mobs invaded Catholic churches, smashed the statues, broke the windows and defaced the altars. They had gone too far. In addition to ruining innumerable works of medieval art, the rebels lost the support of many Catholics. While William, for fear of losing his life, fled to his estates in Germany, Philip determined to avenge the action.

Regency of the Duke of Alva, 1567-73

In 1567 the Duke of Alva arrived in the Netherlands with some 10,000 troops and orders to suppress the rebels. He immediately established a special court, officially known as the "Council of Troubles," but dubbed by the people the "Council of Blood"; it was founded to try all those people who had been in any way connected with the recent outbreaks. Before resigning as regent Margaret warned Alva of the dangers of proceeding in this way, but her advice was ignored. Farcical trials were held and people, often in large batches, were convicted on the slenderest evidence of paid informers.

Despite the criticism of the Pope and most of Philip's advisers the work continued and 18,000 people are said to have lost their lives through its agency.

During the course of this persecution the Counts of Egmont and Horn lost their lives. When William refused to return from exile, he was declared an outlaw and his lands were confiscated. This famous outlaw now proceeded to make a number of attacks on the country. The negligible achievement of these attacks mattered little; their importance lay in the fact that they led the way to resistance of a more effective nature.

Alva introduced a ten per cent tax on trade, the source of the nation's wealth, to pay for his régime. This crippling imposition was felt by all, Protestant and Catholic, and succeeded in uniting the people in opposition to Spain and brought them to the verge of revolt.

The first success of the revolutionaries was achieved by the so called "Sea Beggars." They were a group of Calvinists, who had fled for safety to England during Alva's persecution. Using English ports as a base, they attacked Spanish shipping in the North Sea and the English Channel. Since they were the naval counterpart of the soldiers who opposed Philip's régime in the Netherlands, they assumed the title of the "Sea Beggars." Elizabeth never discouraged their activities, but in 1572, after repeated representations from Philip, she ordered them to leave her shores. Accordingly a fleet of twenty-four of their ships sailed to Brille, at the mouth of the Meuse, took over the port and raised the flag of Orange. The struggle for Dutch independence had begun. One by one the towns of the north, with the exception of Amsterdam, joined the revolutionaries and the northern provinces elected William to be their stadholder or governor. He was invested with considerable powers and voted supplies for the conduct of the war.

The Duke of Alva, however, was not finished and he was still determined to reduce the Dutch to obedience. There thus followed a series of sieges, which were characterized by the increasing brutality of the Spanish army and a growing determination on the part of the Dutch never to surrender. The town of Naarden, for example, was mercilessly sacked and Alva was

Alva's statue dragged through the streets of Antwerp.

able to write with glee of the exploits of his soldiers in that "they cut the throats of the burghers and all the garrison and they did not leave a mother's son alive." The most famous of the sieges was that of Haarlem, which held out for seven months, until its inhabitants had eaten all available weeds, vermin and leather.

The initiative of the Dutch in opening their dykes and flooding the country, making life difficult for the Spanish army, finally saved them. In addition, the Spanish government grew short of money, and Philip recalled Alva at the end of 1573.

Regency of Requesens, 1573-76

Philip then sent as regent Don Louis de Requesens, a moderate man and a good administrator. He suppressed the Council of Blood, and soon came to terms with the southern provinces who were separated from William by a religious difference. The new regent's efforts to repeat his success in the north, however, were thwarted by William's insistence that there should be freedom of worship for all, that ancient privileges should be restored and that all foreigners should leave the country forthwith. Hostilities continued, and there occurred the notorious siege of Leyden. Determined not to submit, the inhabitants bore months of hardship with tremendous fortitude. When the wind was in a favourable quarter, William cut the dykes; the sea then covered the fifteen-mile strip between the coast and the town. As soon as the water was deep enough, the Sea Beggars sailed over it and forced the besiegers to flee.

A year after the relief of Leyden, Requesens died. Following his death, there occurred one of the most dreadful episodes in the whole struggle. The pay of the Spanish troops being in arrears, they broke out in revolt and decided to gain in plunder what they lacked in wages. No one was safe; no one was spared. Catholic and Calvinist, pro-Spaniard and Beggar suffered, as the soldiers burnt and pillaged where they felt inclined. The result of the outburst, aptly known as the Spanish Fury, was to unite the northern and southern provinces, previously separated by religious differences, in a common hatred of Spain.

The union brought about by the Spanish Fury was made stronger by the diplomatic skill of William. A meeting of representatives of both northern and southern provinces was held and they agreed to a treaty known as the Pacification of Ghent, 1576. This laid down that Philip should be recognized as the King of the Netherlands, but that William should govern in his name, while each province was free to decide upon its own religion and was not to persecute members of other creeds.

Regency of Don John of Austria, 1576-78

After a momentous interregnum, Don John of Austria, Philip's half-brother, and the popular hero of Lepanto, was sent to take charge of the Netherlands. A great dreamer, he is alleged to have entertained ideas of defeating the rebels, invading England and marrying Mary Queen of Scots. Yet he was also a realist. He readily saw that the union registered in the Pacification of Ghent, embracing Catholics and Calvinists, was extraordinarily flimsy. A little patience and it would soon be dissolved.

His first action was to win the confidence of the country, which he did by issuing the Perpetual Edict, 1576. This signified his agreement with the terms of the Pacification of Ghent. Holland and Zealand ignored it; they realized that it was only a cunning way of playing for time. Infuriated by their action, the regent seized Namur. It was an ambitious move; he was short of men and could never hope to hold it. William, however, was not in a position to take advantage. With the days of Spanish injustice behind them, the people no longer gave him their support. When reinforcements arrived, Don John started to make progress, but it was halted by his death.

Regency of the Duke of Parma, 1578-92

When Alexander Farnese, Duke of Parma, arrived to take over the country, he found that religious dissensions were rapidly removing the last shreds of the unity fostered by the Spanish aggression and recorded in the Pacification of Ghent.

Within a year the provinces of the south concluded with the new governor the Treaty of Arras in 1579 by which they agreed to support the Roman Church and accept Philip, on condition that the Spanish soldiers were removed and Flemish privileges respected.

Although he still yearned for a union of the entire country, after the Treaty of Arras William realized that it was an impossibility. Accordingly, he fell back on a smaller union of the seven northern provinces (Holland, Zealand, Utrecht, Gelderland, Friesland, Groningen and Overyssel). By the Union of Utrecht, 1579, they agreed to work together for the promotion of their religion and the defence of their liberties.

From henceforth, the two sections of the country went their separate ways. The southern provinces remaining loyal to Catholicism and Spain became the Spanish Netherlands. On the other hand, the northerners, who in 1581 renounced their allegiance to Philip, constituted the Dutch Republic. The latter development is of immense historical interest; it produced the first federal government of modern history. Under the agreement each of the seven states was to manage its own domestic affairs, but to submit its foreign and military policy to a common government. Here was a forerunner of the organization of the United States of America.

Assassination of William

The breakaway of the northern provinces annoyed Philip intensely. He declared William a traitor and offered twenty-five thousand gold crowns to any man who "would rid the world of this enemy of the human race." The result of the bribe was the assassination of William, in 1584, after several earlier attempts had been made on his life.

The movement for the independence of the Netherlands appeared to have been struck a mortal blow by the death of William. In the years following William's death, however, the union which he had created proved that it was too strong to be broken by the death of one man and the course of events served to make it permanent. In the first place, Philip became increasingly involved in quarrels with England and the Protestant groups in France and was unable to maintain a strong force in the Netherlands. Secondly, Maurice of Nassau, William's son, reorganized the Dutch army and inflicted several defeats on the Spaniards. Thirdly, in 1592, Parma died. Finally, the economic decline of Spain meant that the Dutch were soon in a position to challenge her commercial supremacy.

To his dying day, Philip refused to recognize the independence of the north, a policy which his son Philip III religiously followed. Finally, in 1609, worn out by the incessant hostilities, both sides agreed to a twelve-year

William the Silent, 1533-84.   *Duke of Alva, 1508-83.*

truce. After this the war continued, but peoples' attentions were distracted by the Thirty Years' War in Germany. At the end of this, in the terms of the Treaty of Westphalia, 1648, Spain was prepared to recognize the independence of the United Provinces.

The success of the Dutch was a severe blow to the power of Spain and the efforts of the Catholic Church to regain what it had lost; it marked the arrival of a new kind of state based upon the ideas of political and religious freedom, yet a state strong enough, despite its size, to cause plenty of trouble later for so strong a monarch as Louis XIV.

QUESTIONS

1. What were the causes of the revolt in the Netherlands? Why did the Dutch succeed in gaining their independence?
2. Trace the main stages in the Dutch struggle for independence against Spain.

CHAPTER 10

THE REFORMATION IN FRANCE

SOME years before Martin Luther nailed his theses to the door of the University of Wittenberg there appeared in France a group which bore a strong resemblance to the Lutheran movement. This group centred round the person of Jacques Lefèvre, a lecturer in the University of Paris. In 1512, he published a Latin translation of the Epistles of St. Paul with a commentary, which revealed his belief in the theory of justification by faith. Through the medium of preachers his ideas were soon spread over the southern regions of France, but they did not initiate a movement comparable in strength and importance with that of Luther's, since the political and social conditions, which did so much to stimulate the development of the German movement, did not exist in France.

Under Francis I, 1515-47

Since his mortal enemy, Charles V, was the champion of Catholicism, it was at first thought likely that the King of France would champion the Protestants. But Francis soon came to appreciate how detrimental to the unity of a country a religious difference could be, and with this realization came a determination to rid France of heretics. The burnings began, and the Parlement of Paris was enlarged by the addition of a Chambre Ardente (Burning Chamber).

It was during the years of these burnings that Calvin made a discreet exit from his native country to find a safer home in Switzerland. He did not, however, forsake the cause of Protestantism in France and in the pious hope that he might convert the king he dedicated the early additions of his "Institutes" to Francis.

Under Henry II, 1547-59

Henry II continued the policy of burning heretics, which his father had inaugurated. Indeed he advanced it with greater determination than his father and would have liked to see an Inquisition, on the Spanish model, introduced in France. His plans were blocked by the Parlement of Paris. The opposition was significant. It demonstrated that the burning of Protestants was strengthening, rather than eliminating, the creed; and that the new faith was gaining converts in high places. The Calvinists in France were called Huguenots, a title of obscure origin. Its adherents met secretly, and were drawn mainly from the upper and middle classes. Although Calvinism had found strongest support in the north of Germany and the Netherlands, in France it existed mainly in the south and west. The movement was so well organized, with its own self-government extending from local consistories to a national synod, and its members so determined, that it became obvious that attempts to destroy it could only end in war.

While the burnings were in full spate, Henry II was fatally, yet accidentally, injured while jousting in a tournament held to celebrate the marriage of his daughter, Elizabeth, to Philip II of Spain.

Henry's untimely death was the gravest misfortune for France. At a time when the country was rent by two rival factions and strong government was essential, Henry's legacy to France was four feeble sons, weak alike in mentality, morals, and physique. Such a situation led the way to jealousy and intrigue which accelerated the approach of the war.

Under Francis II, 1559-60

The reign of Francis is interesting, not so much for the person of the sickly, characterless, sixteen-year-old king, husband of Mary Queen of Scots, but for the development of factions, whose squabbles for power were destined, for the next forty years, to dominate the history of France.

We will begin with the Guise faction, since, through their close relationship to Mary Queen of Scots, they were to be the first to gain supremacy. They were by religion Catholic and dominated the eastern side of the country. Their leader was Francis, Duke of Guise, a soldier of considerable renown. The faction had strong support among the nobility, the hierarchy of the Church and the peasantry.

The western half of France was dominated by the Bourbons, who were, for the most part, a Protestant family. Anthony of Bourbon, their head, through his descent from Louis XI, was next in succession to the throne after Henry's sons. Always liable to change his alliances and his religion at a whim, he was most undependable and ill-fitted to gain support for a party. The leadership of the faction thus fell to his younger brother, Louis, Prince of Condé.

The third great family, the Montmorency, had considerable influence in the centre of France. It was another family of divided religious allegiance; its most important member was Gaspard de Coligny, Admiral of France, a Calvinist much respected for his sincerity. A man of high moral character and political wisdom, he stood, in many ways, head and shoulders above the other participants in the coming feuds, until he was foully murdered.

Having described the factions who were to compete in the approaching contest, we must now consider its leading promoter. This was Catherine de

Medici, Queen Mother of France, and regent for her puny brood. The behaviour of this masculine woman, fond of hunting and sundry male pursuits, has been variously described by historians. To paint her, as so many have done, in the blackest oils is perhaps unfair to a woman who was never seen in favourable circumstances, but only in a series of unenviable positions which brought out the very worst traits in her character.

In the court of her husband, Catherine had found herself a complete outcast. Finding other ladies more attractive, Henry ignored her and gave her no say in the government. It was natural for Catherine, at his death, to seize upon the regency as a source of power. She was now prepared to play her rivals off against each other in an effort to maintain her position.

The Florentine writer Machievelli, in his great treatise on politics, "The Prince" (dedicated, incidentally, to Catherine's father), had laid down that in the governing of states, the normal rules which determine what is right and what is wrong may be waived so long as the state is to benefit. Catherine was prepared to adopt these principles. Craft, intrigue and assassination became her favourite weapons, since she found them to be the most effective. Not only did she foment quarrels between her rivals and arrange for the deaths of her most persistent opponents, but she was prepared to instigate quarrels between her own children and weaken them by encouraging them in their debauchery.

Under Charles IX, 1560-74

While Francis reigned his wife's relatives, the Guise, had played a leading role in the government of the country. When he died, Catherine determined that she would suffer no further loss of power and went to great lengths to prevent it.

Catherine determined to weaken the Catholics by granting the Huguenots more favours. An edict of 1562 gave Huguenots legal status by permitting them free worship outside walled cities. This sparked off the contest for which France had waited.

Driving through the town of Vassy one day, the Duke of Guise heard singing and discovered a Huguenot service taking place in a barn. This was contrary to the edict, and in the ensuing struggle sixty people were killed. This was the beginning of the religious wars, destined to last throughout the century.

Early in the conflict both sides lost leaders. In 1562 Anthony of Navarre was killed at the siege of Rouen and in the following year the Duke of Guise was murdered by a young Huguenot, acting on the instructions of Coligny. The disintegration of both armies gave Catherine the opportunity to negotiate the Peace of Amboise in 1563. Her object here and in other subsequent treaties was not to end hostilities, an impossibility, but to prevent either side from gaining any undue advantage which might threaten her position.

The arrival of Alva in the Netherlands and his suspected love affair with Catherine was a signal for the outbreak of further hostilities, during which Condé made an unsuccessful attempt to kidnap the king. Two Catholic victories, in 1569, at Jarnac, where Condé was slain, and Moncontour, swayed the balance so strongly in their favour that Catherine once again intervened.

On this occasion, through the Peace of St. Germain, the Huguenots gained more favourable terms than at any other time. The number of towns where they could worship was increased to two in each of the twelve provinces, while four towns, including Montauban and La Rochelle, were assigned to them as fortified strongholds. In addition, they were not to be banned from any employment on account of their faith.

Coligny now called for an end to the squabbling so that France might offer a united front to the growing menace of Spain, and arranged a marriage between the king's younger sister Margaret and Henry of Navarre. Catherine was momentarily in favour as she felt that the marriage would destroy the power of the Guise, but before long it was the destruction of Coligny that was uppermost in her mind. She detested his influence over the king, and her efforts to remove him led to the most dreadful event of the era.

St. Bartholomew Massacre

In order to celebrate the marriage of Henry and Margaret, in August 1572, hundreds of Huguenots crowded into Paris, among them Coligny. Having failed in one assassination attempt against Coligny, in which Catherine feared her part might be discovered, she persuaded Charles that the Huguenots were his mortal enemies. Charles agreed to their destruction on condition that all of them were to be slain to avoid the possibility of repercussions.

As the bell tolled midnight, on the Eve of St. Bartholomew, a wholesale massacre of Huguenots in Paris began. Coligny was first to die, his end personally supervised by the Duke of Guise. In all, two thousand people were slain in the capital and a further ten thousand in other parts of the country. Of the leaders of the party only Henry and the young Prince of Condé escaped.

Outside France news of the massacre was variously received. Philip of Spain was overjoyed, and, it is said, smiled in public for the first and last time. Pope Gregory XIII struck a medal in honour of the event. Other rulers, however, Catholic and Protestant, were perturbed, since they felt that little good could be achieved by an action of this kind. They were right, for the massacre strengthened rather than obliterated the Huguenot movement in France.

Even Catherine realized that things had gone too far and she tried to appease the Huguenots by further concessions offered in the Peace of La Rochelle. For Charles, it was all too much; worn out by nightmares associated with the atrocities, he died within two years.

Richelieu Condé James I Tilly Maximilian Wallenstein

300 MILES
SCALE OF MILES

NORWAY

RUSSIA

ESTONIA

LIVONIA

SWEDEN

SCOTLAND

NORTH
SEA

DENMARK

BALTIC SEA

IRELAND

Spanish possessions
Austrian possessions
Church lands
Brandenburg-Prussia
Swedish dominions
Boundary of the Empire

WALES

ENGLAND

UNITED
PROVS.

MECKLENBURG

BRANDENBURG

POLAND

NETHERLANDS

HESSE

SAXONY

SILESIA

BOHEMIA

MORAVIA

ATLANTIC

OCEAN

FRANCE

SWITZ.

BAVARIA

AUSTRIA

HUNGARY

TYROL

MOLDAVIA

TRANSYLVANIA

WALLACHIA

OTTOMAN EMPIRE

BLACK
SEA

TUSCANY

CORSICA

PAPAL
STATES

ADRIATIC SEA

PORTUGAL

SPAIN

SARDINIA

KINGDOM OF
THE TWO
SICILIES

MEDITERRANEAN SEA

SICILY

EUROPE IN 1648 (TREATY OF WESTPHALIA)

MEN OF THE THIRTY YEARS' WAR, AND THE DIVISION OF EUROPE

Defenestration of Prague, 1617

Gustavus Adolphus at Lützen

Wallenstein and Tilly hold a conference

murder of Wallenstein

Battle of Rocroi

Peace of Westphalia, 1648

EVENTS IN THE THIRTY YEARS' WAR

Under Henry III, 1574-89

Under Henry III, a new era in the religious wars began, which was heralded by the rise of a new group, the Politiques, moderates who "preferred the repose of the kingdom and their own homes to the salvation of their souls." They were joined by the depleted ranks of the Huguenots, and because it seemed certain that Margaret's Protestant husband, Henry of Navarre, would succeed to the throne, they championed the monarchy. The Catholics, urged on by the Jesuits through the medium of the Holy League, a Guise faction organized in 1576, vehemently opposed the idea of a Huguenot king and enlisted the support of Philip II of Spain.

King Henry himself opposed the League, which by nominating Henry of Guise as the next king was tending to increase the power of the Guise at the expense of his own. Thus a new wave of hostilities began by a war usually known as the War of the Three Henries, after the three leaders Henry III, Henry of Guise, and Henry of Navarre. In 1588, on the Day of Barricades, the Parisians rose in support of the Guise and drove the king out of the city. Henry felt that there was only one course open to him, and accordingly had both the Duke of Guise and his brother murdered. Henry was soon to learn, however, as his mother had learnt before him, that the death of one man is insufficient to ruin a cause. The Catholics in France were now bitterly opposed to him.

With the Catholics against him, the king turned to the Huguenots for support. He promised them complete toleration and officially recognized Henry of Navarre as his successor. It was a strange sight to see one of the authors of the Massacre of St. Bartholomew preaching freedom of conscience for all men, but such radical changes of opinion were typical of the French statesmen of the time.

The collective military strength of Henry III and Henry of Navarre was immense and it seemed that they would easily crush the power of the League, but Parisians, who were staunchly behind the League, endured a long siege. During the course of this, a Dominican friar stabbed the king to death, feeling that it was a just reparation for the evil he had done. Henry of Navarre thus became, in 1589, Henry IV of France.

Immediately, Henry had to abandon the siege, because his army was seriously depleted by the withdrawal of those men who were prepared to support the hereditary king against the League only if that king was Catholic. His position, however, was not hopeless. Paradoxically, although the strength of the Catholic forces lay in Spanish support, this lost them the good-will of many Frenchmen who objected to Spanish interference. This objection was intensified when Philip began to think in terms of the French throne for himself. Other factors, which augured well for Henry, were his good looks and manly physique (which contrasted favourably with the debauched and effemi-

Massacre of St. Bartholomew's Eve: August 24, 1572.

nate image of his predecessors), his great ability as a soldier and, above all, the French desire for a strong king, who could bring an end to the wars.

Henry's obvious disadvantage was his religion, which made him a target for Spanish aggression and an enemy of many of his people. Although he had embraced Catholicism once, to save his life at the Massacre of St. Bartholomew, he was unwilling to desert his followers until he felt in a strong enough position to defend them. In 1593, when he felt this point had been reached, he was duly received into the Catholic Church. This put an end to Philip's grandiose schemes and forced him to recognize Henry as the undisputed King of France by the Peace of Vervins (1598). One by one the towns of France came over to Henry's side. Nine years after he had officially become king, Henry was firmly established on the throne and set about to heal the injuries France had suffered during the civil wars.

QUESTIONS

1. Describe the part played by Admiral de Coligny and Catherine de Medici in the religious struggle in France.
2. Explain the circumstances which led to the murder of Henry, Duke of Guise, and the alliance between Henry III and Henry of Navarre.

74

CHAPTER 11

FRANCE UNDER HENRY IV, 1598-1610

THE year 1598 was a turning point in the history of France. Henry had brought the civil wars to an end and he was now able to embark on a policy of reconstruction. Like our own Henry VII, who had faced a similar task a hundred years earlier, he was extremely successful. By his success, he laid the foundations for the ascendancy of France in the seventeenth century.

The deep affection in which Henry was held by his people was not only due to his good looks, gallantry, and successful policies, but to his intense patriotism. He has been described as the "most French king that France ever had." He was also loved because he was more accessible and approachable than other French kings had been. With little likelihood that he would ever become King of France, he had been brought up away from the court; thus he understood the people and their problems. He loathed the pomp and ceremony of court etiquette, which kept men at a distance from their monarch and in which his grandson, Louis XIV, was later to revel. His good looks, rather than his vulgar and peasant-like manners, attracted the ladies, but he never allowed his love affairs to become confused with affairs of state.

Henry's efforts to restore order and prosperity in France led him, in the first place, to a settlement of the religious controversy; in second place, to re-establish the power of the Crown; and then to improve the economy of France by attention to industry and agriculture, commerce and communications.

Settlement of the Religious Controversy

Henry owed it to the Huguenots to look after their interests in any arrangement which he introduced to solve the religious problems of the country. They had been, after all, victors in the war. That he was now a Catholic could not alter the fact that he owed his position on the throne to the loyal support which they had given him. Accordingly, one of his first actions was to issue the Edict of Nantes, 1598. The edict gave the Huguenots both civil and religious liberty, and the right of public worship in all places except Paris and its environs. This proviso was included on account of the difficulty of suppressing riots in the narrow and crowded streets.

It was further enacted by the edict that Huguenots were not to be excluded from holding public office on account of their faith, and their ministers were to enjoy the same rights and privileges as the priests of the Catholic Church. It set up special tribunals to hear cases in which Huguenots were involved. Other sources of grievance were removed by allowing them to hold their own synods and provincial political councils and to establish their own schools, colleges and hospitals.

To give the Huguenots a sense of security, as they had so often been granted concessions in the past only to have them removed later, the edict included the controversial clause which allowed them to keep La Rochelle and a hundred other towns as fortified strongholds, garrisoned at public expense.

Henry's edict stands out as a unique attempt to settle the religious problems of a country and as a landmark of toleration in an age which was essentially intolerant. In the event, it satisfied no one. As was to be expected, it was hotly opposed by the Catholics, who declared it to be too liberal and conclusive evidence of the insincerity of the king's conversion. More unexpectedly and indeed unjustifiably, it was condemned by the Huguenots, who felt that they had received too little. It is hard to believe that a party, which numbered less than a twelfth of the population, could seriously have expected more. As the years went by, it was the political and military aspects of the edict, rather than the religious privileges, that became the greatest bones of contention. They evoked jealousy amongst the Catholics, who had no comparable rights in these spheres, and doubts among men who felt that it was inadvisable for the Huguenot party to be put in the position of a state within the state. The history of the edict was to prove these people absolutely right. Under Henry, who was sympathetic to the Huguenots, it mattered little; Richelieu, however, as we shall see, found it necessary to remove the political privileges; while Louis XIV, in his fetish for political uniformity, repealed the edict in its entirety.

Restoration of Power to Crown and Improvement of French Economy

In order to regain the lost power of the Crown, Henry found it necessary to bribe some of the greater nobility, who held council seats and dominated the States General. Eventually, thirty-two million livres were spent in this way, more than the annual revenue of the Crown. In return for these favours, Henry demanded the individual's undivided loyalty.

Once Henry had put down the power of the nobility, he ruled as an absolute monarch. Throughout his reign, he never summoned the States General and he kept a close watch on the work of the law courts. The most representative gathering of the people that met, while he ruled, was the assembly of notables at Rouen in 1596 and its members did little else but inform the king of the grievances of the country.

For the task of rebuilding the shattered French economy, Henry enlisted the help of Maximilian de Béthune, Duke of Sully, whom he made super-intendent of finances. Sully was a Huguenot and unpopular at court; moreover he was austere and humourless while the king was jovial and warm-hearted, but nevertheless these two men between them formed an excellent team.

Financially, Henry and Sully not only inherited an empty treasury but a national debt of 350 million livres, which had been borrowed from foreign sources during the wars. The annual interest payable on the sum was 30 million livres, a figure only slightly less than the government's annual income. They also inherited a very poor system of taxation. The country was divided into sections and each of these was allotted to a tax farmer. The farmers were told how much was required in taxation from their areas and anything which they managed to collect over and above that sum they retained as a reward for their work. It is easy to see how the tax collectors worked under such a system, and it is not surprising to learn that less than one quarter of what was collected as taxation actually reached the treasury. The extortions of these men fell most heavily on the peasantry, since the nobles and clergy claimed exemption from taxation.

Much as he would have liked to do so, Sully made no sweeping changes in this system since they would have brought him into conflict with the nobility. Instead he contented himself with trying to improve it. First, he ordered the collectors to keep registers which had to be submitted annually for inspection. In this way, he was able to check fraud and see at a glance what money was available. Next, he examined the cases of all those who claimed exemption from taxation and removed the privilege from those who had merely assumed it during the wars. Beyond this, he laid down that no tax was to be collected unless it had been authorized by the king. Moreover, he ordered those people who had taken Crown lands to return them. Finally, he made reductions in

Duke of Sully, 1560-1641. *Henry IV (reigned 1589-1610).*

the amount of royal grants to individuals and generally made cuts in the expenses of the court.

Such was the success of Sully's measures that by 1610 the annual revenue was doubled and he was able to reduce the national debt by 100 million livres. In addition, he set aside a reserve of 30 million livres, which was stored in the Bastille.

Henry was also eager to repair the damage done by the wars to French agriculture. The nobles were forbidden to go trampling across peasant crops while hunting, and new methods of farming were introduced. The marshes were drained, and the peasants were protected from bandits. An edict was issued forbidding courts to seize farm implements as payment for debts, and the tax on grain exports was removed except in years of shortage, thus assuring the farmers of a good gain generally. Soon there was a surplus of good quality foodstuff for export.

The only area over which Henry and Sully disagreed was industry. Sully feared that agriculture would suffer by an increase in industry, but Henry felt that an advancement of industry was essential to a strong state. As a firm believer in the mercantilist theory, he wished to amass a larger surplus of bullion than any other nation. What better way of achieving this end than by manufacturing goods at home. Accordingly, he set out to do what he could to stimulate industrial growth. He took especial interest in the luxury trades, tapestries, carpets, glassware and pottery. To further the silk industry he ordered the planting of mulberry trees (to provide food for silkworms) in the south and west. Henry's policies in this direction did not meet with the same success as he achieved in other aims, due to the fact that his schemes were too restrictive and left no room for enterprise and initiative.

As good communications were essential for prosperity, many roads and canals were repaired or rebuilt during Henry's reign. Rivers were made navigable, and a better postal system was introduced. Henry also made commercial treaties with England and Holland, granted a charter to the French East India Company and sent Champlain on an expedition to colonize the shores of the St. Lawrence River. These ventures lacked the backing of Sully, who was more concerned with balancing his budgets than with spending money on far-sighted projects from which an immediate return could not be expected.

Henry's Foreign Policy

Despite the Peace of Vervins, Henry, throughout his reign, remained hostile to Spain, since he was apprehensive of the growing power of the Hapsburg family, whose combined territories completely encircled his kingdom. In his early years he sought to curb the danger by diplomacy. His greatest diplomatic triumph was the treaty which he concluded with the

Grisons in 1602, granting him the right to occupy the Valtelline, a valley which formed an important link in Hapsburg communications between the Spanish Milanese and southern Germany.

In 1609 the ruler of Cleves, Julich, and Berg, three small principalities in the Empire and controlling the lower Rhine, died without a direct heir. The Emperor sent an army to occupy the territory. An Imperial garrison so close to her borders was against the best interests of France, so Henry set out with his army to take over the states and hold them for the rightful heirs. At this point he was assassinated by François Ravaillac, a Catholic fanatic obsessed with the idea that Henry was an enemy of the Church.

In his memoirs, Sully credits Henry with a far more grandiose scheme for the destruction of the power of the Hapsburgs than the one that was thwarted by his untimely death. The plan, known as the Grand Design, was for a federation of European powers. It envisaged each power calling its own council to deal with purely internal matters, but submitting to one central council all major questions of European policy and administration. This council was ultimately to have brought about total disarmament in Europe.

If we accept the writings of Sully, then we must credit Henry with being the originator of an idea which, in different forms and at different times, has been tried, though unsuccessfully, as a means of bringing peace to Europe and the world. It is, however, now fashionable to disregard Sully's contention and to see the Design as an idea of his own which he attributed to Henry. For it seems a more likely product of his own imaginative mind than that of the very practical king.

The chaos and confusion which spread over the country after Henry's untimely death illustrates how much the strength of his régime depended on his personality. As we shall see in a later chapter, it was not long before many of his accomplishments were undone.

QUESTIONS

1. Outline the work of Henry IV and Sully in restoring order in France and in assisting the development of French agriculture and commerce.
2. State the main provisions of the Edict of Nantes and explain the importance of this settlement of religion in France.

CHAPTER 12

THE THIRTY YEARS' WAR

THE Thirty Years' War was in reality a series of four wars which on account of their close proximity are customarily considered as one. It began as a continuation of the struggle between Catholics and Protestants in the Empire, but it developed into the most widespread, bloodiest and protracted war that the western world had, up to that time, experienced. Commensurate with its magnitude and length were the far-reaching effects which it had upon the whole history of Europe.

The root cause of the war was the confusion, brought about by the division of the Empire at the time of the Reformation, and the subsequent ineffective measures to resolve it, drawn up by the Diet of Augsburg in 1555. The diet's settlement of the religious issue gave no recognition to Calvinism, yet throughout the latter half of the sixteenth century it was this form of Protestantism which continued to grow numerically. Again, it had been resolved by the Diet in 1555 that Church lands which had fallen into Protestant hands before 1552 were to be retained by the new owners. Land, however, which had passed into Protestant possession after 1552 was to be returned to its Catholic ownership. This so-called "Ecclesiastical Reservation" clause was subsequently interpreted in different ways by the two contending parties: the Catholics maintained that if a bishop became a Protestant, he must forfeit his land, but the Protestants declared that this was unnecessary if the priests of his diocese followed his example. Thus tempers were frayed. Actual war between the rival parties was averted for over sixty years, as no Emperor was sufficiently strong to lead the Catholic attack. Charles V's brother and successor, Ferdinand I, for instance, greatly weakened his position by distributing territory amongst the younger branches of his family; the feeble-minded Rudolf became completely insane and the ancient Mathias was totally incapable. This state of affairs was reversed by the arrival on the scene of two young nobles, who had been educated by the Jesuits and rose to power with a determination to further the work of the Counter-Reformation. One of them, Ferdinand of Styria, was to become Emperor, while the other, Maximilian of Bavaria, became leader of the "Catholic League" formed to oppose the Protestant "Evangelical Union" under the leadership of Frederick of the Palatinate, 1608.

Ferdinand saw in an anti-Protestant campaign a means of furthering the work of the Counter-Reformation and of unifying the Empire. He fused the internal religious struggles of the Empire with the Hapsburg policy of aggrandisement. Before it was over, this nominally religious struggle was to witness Catholic princes fighting against the Catholic Emperor and a Catholic country subsidizing a Protestant one to do likewise, through fear of an increase of Hapsburg power.

Bohemian and Palatinate War, 1618-23

The war began in Bohemia, home of the Czechs. Traditionally the Czechs elected their king, although they usually nominated the Emperor. When it became apparent that Ferdinand would succeed the childless Mathias, the Bohemian Protestants feared the withdrawal of the toleration granted them by the Emperor Rudolph's "Letter of Majesty."

Then, in 1617, it was rumoured that some of the councillors had been encouraging the king to withdraw the religious freedom. By way of revenge, several Protestants burst into the Royal Palace in Prague, seized two of the councillors and threw them out of the window, which was seventy feet above the ground. They were only saved from death because they landed on a dung heap. This incident is known as the "Defenestration of Prague," and is usually regarded as the first event of the war, although no fighting took place for a further two years.

The feeling of revolt, engendered by this incident, spread throughout the country. In 1619, when Ferdinand assumed the throne, the Czech army instantly deposed him and offered the crown to Frederick of the Palatinate.

Ferdinand at this point lacked an army, but soon received troops from Bavaria and Saxony on the promise that he would reward them for their services. His new army was placed under the leadership of an outstanding commander, Count Tilly.

In 1620 Tilly defeated the rebellious Czechs at the Battle of the White Hill and Frederick, derisively known as the "Winter King," on account of the short time that he had held the throne, fled to Holland. He must have regretted his decision to accept the kingdom of Bohemia, for in trying to defend it, he lost his own state as well.

Ferdinand was determined to take the fullest advantage of Tilly's victory. He turned first on Bohemia. He withdrew from the Czechs the right to elect their own king as well as many of their other political privileges. Next, those members of the nobility who had taken part in the revolt were executed and their lands used to reward his officers. Finally, in a determination to drive out all religious denominations other than Catholicism, he packed the country with Jesuit missionaries.

With Bohemia subjugated, Ferdinand vented his wrath upon the Palatinate. By 1623, after successful campaigns by Tilly and a Spanish army under Spinola, the whole territory was captured and duly assigned to Maximilian of Bavaria, who became its Elector. So ended the first war, with the Catholic-Hapsburg cause triumphant.

The Danish War, 1624-29

In the course of history, overwhelming triumphs have often proved a mixed blessing for the victors, on account of the jealousy they have incited in other powers. In this respect, the Hapsburgs of 1624 were no exception. Immediately, the fate of Frederick caused great anxiety amongst the Protestant princes in the Empire, and their common hatred of the Emperor drew them into a closer alliance than ever before. Then Cardinal Richelieu, who had just come to power in France, sought to embarrass the Hapsburgs by enlisting the services of Count Mansfeld and his mercenary army, on behalf of the Dutch, whose twelve-year truce with Spain was drawing to its close. Similarly, James I of England, who had long sought a Spanish marriage for his son, found him a French wife and declared war on Spain instead. Finally, Christian IV of Denmark entered the war, in order to prevent Ferdinand from gaining power in the north and threatening Danish possessions.

Surrounded by foes, Ferdinand found a valuable ally in Albert von Wallenstein. A Bohemian Protestant, who had been educated as a Catholic, Wallenstein had no strong religious convictions and cared for little save his own aggrandisement. A great military organizer and a wonderful strategist, he raised a private army in 1618, and helped to put down the Bohemian revolt. He now promised to gather a further army for the support of the Emperor, if he could have absolute control and levy compulsory contributions in the areas in which he served, to provide wages for his men. Soon he had a well-paid, well-disciplined army of 50,000 in the field, a force which, with the exception of that of Sweden, was the finest that was seen in the war.

The Danish war opened with a disastrous Protestant offensive. Count Mansfeld, who it was planned should attack from the east, was defeated by Wallenstein at Dessau, on the Elbe, as he marched south; and he died of tuberculosis while trying to reach Hungary. Meanwhile, Christian of Denmark, who came to the support of the Protestants in the north-west, was twice defeated at Lutter by the armies of Wallenstein and Tilly.

Although Wallenstein wished to use his victory to sweep across the northern states of Europe, Ferdinand wished to come to terms with Denmark. By the Treaty of Lübeck, 1629, he guaranteed the safety of Christian's lands provided that Christian did not enter the war again.

The Swedish War, 1630-35

Following the Treaty of Lübeck, two moves by the chief members of the Catholic League ensured that the war would continue. In the first place,

A contemporary engraving of a battle during the Thirty Years' War.

jealous of Wallenstein's success, apprehensive of his ambition and wearied by his continual exactions from their people, the League implored the Emperor to remove him. Ferdinand agreed to do this, and at the Diet of Ratisbon, 1630, Wallenstein was duly dismissed. Further, the League encouraged Ferdinand to exploit his recent victories over the Protestants for the Counter-Reformation. So by the Edict of Restitution, 1629, he ordered the return to the Catholics of all Church land taken since 1552. Had such a decree been enforced Protestant territorial supremacy in the north would have been lost. Clearly the Protestants could not accept this without a struggle and the dismissal of Wallenstein encouraged them to renew the war without any delay.

Gustavus Adolphus of Sweden entered the war at this point, both for religious reasons and through the fear that Imperial power in the north would ruin his trade. With the aid of Brandenburg and Saxony, and through the revolutionary use of artillery and troops, he defeated Tilly at the battle of Breitenfeld, 1631. This brought the triumph of the Protestant cause in the north. At Lechfeld, further south, Tilly was defeated and killed by Gustavus, who then seized Munich, but that was the height of his success.

Late in 1631 Ferdinand recalled Wallenstein to check this amazing advance. In 1632 the Swedish king was killed at Lützen while defending his supply lines, and his death reduced his army to the level of the others in the conflict. Two years later the Swedes were routed at Nordlingen, and the Protestants lost the Southern Empire.

Ferdinand dismissed Wallenstein at this point and came to terms with Saxony by the Treaty of Prague, and the land settlement gave the north to the Protestants and the south to the Catholics in 1635.

The French War, 1635-48

With the demise of the Swedes, it seemed that the war had come to a permanent end; but Richelieu of France saw in the continuation of the conflict the only hope France had of destroying the Imperial power of the Hapsburgs. Thus he sent a French army into the field. With the French and the Swedes on one side and the Austrians and Spanish on the other, the war dragged on for a further thirteen years. At first the French met with little success, but before Richelieu died in 1642, they had occupied Alsace. Then, in the following years, the Prince of Condé inflicted a severe defeat on the Spanish, at Rocroi, shattering the legend that their army was invincible. By 1647, the western defences of the Hapsburgs had collapsed and Ferdinand III, who had succeeded his father as Emperor, was forced to make peace. He negotiated with the opposing powers separately, first with the Germans and Swedes at Osnabrück, then with the French at Munster. The Spanish were not present at either of these meetings; they made a separate treaty with the Dutch, at this time, but their war with the French continued for a further seven years. Nevertheless, the other negotiations, which are collectively known as the Treaty of Westphalia, brought peace to the Empire and central Europe in 1648.

Treaty of Westphalia, 1648

From the religious aspect, the Treaty marked the utter failure of the Counter-Reformation to make Catholicism the universal faith of the Empire. By acknowledging the religious divisions of the Empire, the Emperor surrendered his last chance of re-establishing his central authority. Thus, from henceforth, the Empire ceased to exist in all except name. Its perpetual division was further ensured by granting the rulers of the various states the right to make treaties with outside powers. A clause stating that such alliances must not be made if they would injure the Emperor, was virtually meaningless. In fact, each state was now independent.

Among territorial readjustments brought about by the Treaty, the tenure of Maximilian of Bavaria in the Upper Palatinate was recognized, while Charles Lewis, son of the unfortunate Frederick, received the title of Elector and was restored to the Lower Palatinate.

Sweden obtained Western Pomerania, which Brandenburg had claimed, as well as the districts at the mouth of the Oder and the bishoprics of Bremen and Verden. Hence her dissatisfaction at the Treaty of Prague, in which she received no recognition of any kind for the part she had played, was appeased.

France gained the most, collecting the bishoprics of Metz, Verdun and Toul and, save for the city of Strasbourg, sovereign rights in Alsace. These latter were ill-defined and destined to be a source of trouble in later years.

Brandenburg, in addition to receiving Eastern Pomerania, was granted the bishoprics of Halberstadt, Minden, and Camin, together with part of the bishopric of Magdeburg.

Finally, Switzerland and the United Netherlands were formally recognized as independent states.

Historical Effects of the Treaty of Westphalia

The Treaty of Westphalia made changes as far-reaching in European history as those brought about by the Renaissance and the Reformation in the preceding century.

The power of the Emperor in Germany, which had been diminishing for many years, was now completely destroyed. The Hapsburgs did not lose their Imperial power completely, however, for it continued to exist in Austria and in the Kingdoms of Bohemia and Hungary.

While the power of the Emperor was eliminated in the centre of Europe, so also was that of the Pope. He was not consulted over the negotiations at Westphalia and when he violently condemned the treaty no one took any notice. With the passing of papal influence, the use of Canon, or Church, law in international agreements also disappeared and was gradually replaced by a code of international law.

In addition to marking the decline of the Empire and the Papacy the treaty also signalled the ascendancy of France, Brandenburg and Sweden.

Economic Effects of the War on Germany

For many years it was customary for historians, and especially those from Germany, to consider the war responsible for the wholesale destruction of the economy and land of Germany in the early seventeenth century. Such an impression is now held to be an erroneous generalization. It is doubtless possible to cite areas where incredible damage was done, either by the ravages of war or the plundering habits of Wallenstein's troops, but fighting did not take place in every locality.

The economy of Germany was at a low ebb by 1648, but we must account for it by other factors, in addition to the Thirty Years' War. To do so, we might consider two events of the sixteenth century, the dislocation of German agriculture by the Peasants' Revolt and the effect on German markets and banks of the discovery of America.

QUESTIONS

1. Why did the Thirty Years' War begin as a Bohemian revolt and end as a European war?
2. In what ways did the Treaty of Westphalia mark the end of an epoch in European history?

CHAPTER 13

FRANCE UNDER RICHELIEU, 1624-1642

THE premature death of Henry IV, in 1610, brought his nine-year-old son, Louis XIII, to the throne and left the affairs of the government in the hands of his widow, Marie de Medici. A woman of bloated appearance, few morals and less sense, she soon fell under the influence of the Spanish Ambassador and an Italian adventurer named Concinni. This trio set out to reverse the policies of the previous reign. A pro-Hapsburg foreign policy was adopted and an alliance with that family cemented by the marriages of Louis to Anne of Austria and of his sister, Elizabeth, to the future Philip IV of Spain. At home the brimming treasury which Henry had built up was squandered to curry favour with those whose interests the policies of Sully had attacked. Sully himself, his powers withdrawn, retired to the country and played no further part in governing the country.

The nobles recognized their opportunity for power and demanded that the States General should be summoned. They were joined by the Huguenots, who wished to secure their privileges under a Spanish-influenced government. Concinni acceded to their requests, but the States General, meeting for what was to be the last time before the revolution of 1789, proved hopelessly inefficient and was dismissed. With it went any form of united opposition to the government. The various factions went on voicing discontent, but without any power to back up their complaints. Concinni did what he could do to augment the jealousies and differences among these factions to weaken them still further, and gathered an able ministry about him, including the young Armand Jean Duplessis de Richelieu, Bishop of Luçon, who was in charge of foreign affairs and war.

Concinni's position remained strong until 1617 when the young king, emerging from adolescence, began to resent the control which his mother and her associates had over him. He struck at his mother's ministry. Concinni was assassinated and his wife was burnt as a witch; Richelieu, who narrowly escaped arrest, and the remainder of the ministers were dismissed, while Marie de Medici was made a virtual prisoner at Blois.

The young king found that his ministry was as bitterly opposed as that of his mother had been, only now opposition was centred round the alternative court at Blois. The return to a period of civil war seemed imminent. From such a catastrophe the French were rescued by Richelieu. He had returned to Luçon and from there had kept a careful eye on the French political scene. In 1619 he seized the opportunity of demonstrating his diplomatic skill and succeeded in reconciling mother and son; this in turn prevented civil war and won Richelieu a number of admirers. As a reward he was elevated to the cardinalate in 1622.

Richelieu was born in Poitou, the third son of a professional family with noble origins. Encouraged by his parents, he left a military academy to study for the priesthood, and soon became Bishop of Luçon.

Though Luçon was but a rung on the ladder of success to an excessively ambitious man, Richelieu took his duties there seriously. He spent a great deal of time converting the Huguenots and working in the poorer parts of the diocese.

There followed from Luçon, his membership of the Concinni ministry, his return to pastoral work, his part in healing the breach in the Royal family and finally his appearance, in 1624, as a member of the King's council, in which, as a cardinal, he took precedence over all.

Richelieu as First Minister, 1624-42

From 1624 until 1642, the history of France and the career of Richelieu are one and the same thing. This might suggest that his master, Louis XIII, was a nonentity, who allowed himself to be over-ridden, but it was not so. The situation came about because Louis was keener on hunting and having a good time than he was on affairs of state and, recognizing Richelieu's abilities, the king allowed him a free hand in the matter of ruling and rarely challenged his decisions. Thus the cardinal became the real successor of Henry IV in the development of the French monarchy.

Richelieu's policies were quite simple; he wished to make the power of the monarchy supreme in France and to make France predominant in Europe. The successful implementation of these simple policies was made more difficult by the plots devised by his enemies to remove the cardinal from office, but with his first-class intellect, his dominating personality, and his determination to succeed, he proved more than capable of dealing with these problems. Though by profession a priest, he made no secret of the fact that he was an ardent disciple of Machiavelli. In the business of government, he found the teachings of Christianity quite out of place. Deceit and fraud for the benefit of the state together with the punishment of innocent victims to deter would-be offenders were, to his way of thinking, permissible.

Richelieu versus the Huguenots and Nobility

The task of making the king supreme in France led Richelieu, in the first instance, to abolish the political and military rights of the Huguenots. He regarded their military power as a menace to national unity and as soon as he took office, he sought the opportunity to remove the danger. He did not have to wait long. In 1627 a revolt against the government broke out in La Rochelle and he went in person to direct a siege of the stronghold. By building an enormous dam across the harbour he foiled the English attempts at relief, and, in the following year, when two-fifths of the population had died of starvation, it was forced to surrender. Following up his victory, Richelieu forced the Huguenots, by the Peace of Alais, to dismantle the fortifications of their strongholds and relinquish their right to hold separate political assemblies (1629).

It should be noticed that in his dealings with the Huguenots, Richelieu made no effort to tamper with their religion or to prevent them from entering professions on account of their faith. History has shown how wise he was in this respect. For the Huguenots, well satisfied with their religious freedom, settled down as an industrious section of the population and later played a significant part in the growing prosperity of France.

Richelieu now turned his attention to the nobility, and by successive edicts he demolished many of their castles and forbade them to take part in private duels or wars. In 1637 he issued an edict increasing the power of local royal officials, or *Intendants*, seeking in this way to weaken the power of the nobles in local administration. The *Intendants* collected taxes, organized the militia and law courts, and generally maintained law and order. Due to the loyalty and efficiency of these middle-class officials, the nobles soon found themselves virtually excluded from active political life.

Richelieu achieved the unquestioned authority of the king at the cost of a great deal of popularity. The nobility were joined in their hatred of him by members of the court, including the Queen, the Queen Mother, and Louis's heir, all of whom were jealous of Richelieu's success and plotted against him. These plots were foiled by a vast army of spies and paid informers, who warned the cardinal in advance. The nearest his enemies came to achieving their purpose was on the "Day of Dupes," in 1630. Then, the two queens, encouraged by a nobleman called Mariallac, persuaded the King to dismiss Richelieu, but after the sudden appearance of the latter, he soon countered the order. Though the major conspirators in the plot were too high to be touched, Richelieu's treatment of the minor ones was typically severe; even people whose part was never proven went to the scaffold. It was actions like this which made the rule of the cardinal not only hated but positively feared, a situation which he found eminently satisfying!

Richelieu and Foreign Affairs

In foreign affairs, with French supremacy in mind, Richelieu returned to the anti-Hapsburg policy of Henry IV, which had been reversed by Marie

Richelieu watching the siege of La Rochelle.

de Medici. His first action was to try to regain the right to garrison the Valtelline, which Henry had attained through his treaty with the Grisons in 1601. Triumph in this project, however, was thwarted by a rebellion of the Huguenots. This necessitated the withdrawal of his army and ultimately forced Richelieu to accept a joint Franco-Spanish control of the pass. Such a settlement did not disrupt the vital links between the two sections of the Hapsburg family which it had been Richelieu's purpose to sever.

A revolt of the Huguenots also prevented Richelieu from sending a force to take Mantua when the ruler died. But he gained this strategic north Italian state by diplomatic means. By encouraging the Swedes to enter the Thirty Years' War, he forced the Emperor, who had occupied Mantua, to give it to the Duke of Nevers, a French claimant, according to the terms of the Treaty of Cherasco, 1631.

Richelieu's intervention in the Thirty Years' War was undoubtedly the cleverest and the most successful feature of his foreign policy. Although he never lived to see the final result, it was this intervention which was ultimately responsible for bringing France the final victory in her long struggle with the Hapsburgs, and making her the most important power in Europe.

At the end of 1642 bonfires were lit throughout France, not to celebrate the success of the country's intervention in the Thirty Years' War, but the death of the man who had brought it about. For, with the exception of du Tremblay, a Capuchin monk known as Father Joseph, whom he employed as a secretary, confidant and diplomatic emissary, Richelieu had no friends or admirers among his contemporaries.

Posterity has been kinder to the cardinal. He is not only hailed as a founder of French greatness in the seventeenth century, but as the man who prevented the return of a period of civil war and who, by reorganizing the army on a national scale, gave France the best military force in Europe.

On the other hand, posterity has not been so blinded by his success as to be unaware of his failures. Among these were his removal of every conceivable restriction on the authority of the crown. The power which he put in the hands of the monarch served well enough with a capable king, but became positively dangerous, as the history of the next century was to show, when wielded by men of lesser calibre.

Richelieu was equally ill-advised in his treatment of the nobility. By removing their responsibilities while allowing them to keep their rights, he left them as a class with privileges, which they in no way earned, a situation which helped to stimulate revolutionary feelings.

It was, however, in the economic sphere that the cardinal made his greatest blunders. So long as the money was there when he wanted to spend it, he was not concerned with the way it had been collected. He never realized that the methods of collection could be ruinous to the prosperity of the country. Thus, the old methods, with all the old abuses, remained and, at the time of his death, the revenue for the next three years had been estimated and spent in advance of collection. While the success of Richelieu helped to pave the way for the greatness of France in the seventeenth century, his failures were equally helpful in paving the way for the French revolution.

QUESTIONS

1. Describe the character of Richelieu and the measures he took to increase the power of the French monarchy.
2. Give an account of the foreign policy of Richelieu.

CHAPTER 14

THE RISE OF SWEDEN

ONE of the most amazing features of European history in the sixteenth and early seventeenth centuries was the swift rise to predominance of Sweden, under the guidance of the strongest members of the House of Vasa. In 1520 she was merely a dependency of Denmark, but in little over a hundred years the Protestant powers looked upon her as their champion, Cardinal Richelieu courted her alliance, and the entry of her army into the Thirty Years' War not only changed the nature of that conflict, but radically altered the course of history. It will be the purpose of this present chapter to account for Sweden's rapid development, while later it will be seen how lack of resources, among other things, led her to an equally speedy decline.

Origins of Swedish Power

At the beginning of the sixteenth century, Sweden was nominally under the rule of Denmark. This situation had existed since 1397 when, by the Union of Calmar, an attempt had been made to unite Norway, Sweden and Denmark under the Danish king. It was an uneasy alliance continually threatened by the demands of the Swedish nobility for independence. When Christian II became King of Denmark in 1513, he was determined to put the Swedish nobles in their place. In order to achieve this end, he allowed considerations neither of justice nor mercy to obstruct his path. Such a policy proved fatal. After the so-called Blood Bath of Stockholm, when all who opposed him were executed *en masse*, even his own countrymen turned against him and removed him from the throne. Taking advantage of this weakness in Danish rule, the Swedes revolted in 1523 and gained their independence. A subsequent meeting of the Swedish Diet nominated Gustavus Vasa, the revolutionary leader, as king. Thus a formidable line of Swedish kings was established.

Once enthroned Gustavus set out to strengthen his position. Any sign of opposition was harshly repressed. Thus, by the end of his reign, the Diet, formerly an assembly elected by the people, had become little more than a council of royal nominees. In addition to weakening the opponents of the royal power, Gustavus strengthened the monarchy considerably by declaring the Crown hereditary, thus removing the weaknesses to which an elective monarchy is always subject. Next Gustavus made a number of innovations to improve the prosperity of the country. Mines were opened to tap the natural resources, copper, silver and iron; industries were established and commercial treaties arranged with other states. A richer country meant a greater yield from taxation and thus a fuller treasury, and a wealthy treasury was essential for a state to become powerful.

It was not, however, only trade to which Gustavus looked in order to fill his exchequer. Like Henry VIII of England, he saw the property of the Church as a potential source of wealth and thus became one of the first monarchs to adopt the Lutheran faith. By the Recess of Vesteras, in 1527, the authority of the Pope in Sweden was abolished. It was forbidden to teach the Catholic doctrine in the country and the Catholic mass gave way to a Lutheran service. The King assumed the right to appoint the bishops and he licensed Lutheran preachers. Finally, the monasteries were suppressed and all Church lands were taken over by the state.

Briefly, it may be said that Gustavus Vasa established the Swedish monarchy and with trade and Protestantism as its major supports laid the foundations for his country's brief career as an important European power.

Interlude in Development, 1560-1600

Following the death of Gustavus the rise to predominance of Sweden was checked during the reign of his two elder sons and his grandson, Eric, John and Sigismund. None of this trio was able to command the same respect as Gustavus.

The arrogant, ill-tempered and mentally unstable Eric, by an unfortunate marriage and a habit of showering favours upon upstarts, made himself thoroughly unpopular with the nobility. Thus, at home, the years of his reign were a time of unrest.

Abroad, however, he was more successful and after varying fortune in a war with Poland and Denmark by the Treaty of Stettin he obtained Estonia, a province on the eastern shores of the Baltic. This was a valuable acquisition for it was the first step towards Swedish supremacy over the Baltic Sea and its valuable trade.

The unpopularity of Eric at home led eventually to his deposition, imprisonment and possible murder by poisoning. He was succeeded by his brother, John, a man of considerable learning, who had Catholic sympathies. He brought added complications to the affairs of Sweden in the coming decades, by marrying into the Polish royal family. In 1587 his son Sigismund became King of Poland and five years later succeeded also to the Swedish throne.

The eight years of Sigismund's rule were a time of incessant hostility between himself and the nobility. After he had taken Poland back into the fold of the Catholic Church, he attempted to do the same for Sweden, with

Gustavus Vasa proclaimed king at Stregnas in 1523.

disastrous results. He was eventually replaced on the throne of Sweden by his uncle, Charles, the youngest and most competent of the sons of Gustavus Vasa.

Sweden under Charles IX, 1600-11

Since he championed Protestantism and made no secret of his determination to make Sweden supreme in the Baltic, it was not long before Charles found himself encircled by hostile states. His nephew, Sigismund, who remained King of Poland after he had been forced from the Swedish throne, was undoubtedly his most bitter opponent. He still considered himself to be the lawful King of Sweden and paraded as the champion of the Counter-Reformation against Sweden's Protestant subjects. Charles was forced into war with him in order to defend Estonia. While he was thus engaged, he was attacked from the opposite direction by the Danes, under Christian IV, who had not forgotten that he too had a claim to the Swedish throne.

Charles left the completion of both his wars as a legacy to his son, Gustavus Adolphus. Nevertheless, he more than atoned for the burdens which he bequeathed in foreign affairs, by leaving a most orderly and well-run kingdom. From the beginning of his reign Charles had realized that the construction of a powerful state was imperative, if Sweden was to guard against the dangers which were threatening her on every side. To this end, he had curbed the power of the nobility and improved the system of administration. Through a law which banned Catholics from the throne, he had secured the country for Protestantism. Then, by encouraging trade, he had increased its revenue and used the new wealth to improve its defences, especially through the founding of a standing army.

Sweden under Gustavus Adolphus, 1611-32

In addition to being regarded by no lesser judge than Napoleon as one of the greatest generals the world has ever known, Gustavus Adolphus was one of the most attractive figures of his age. Abounding in personality and with innumerable talents, he was the kind of man who would have made his mark in whatever sphere of life he had been born. In addition to the fine physique, skill and daring, which made him a great warrior king, he possessed great intellectual gifts. He spoke several languages fluently and had a great knowledge and love of the arts, especially poetry and music. He was also a great idealist and unlike many idealists he had the ability and determination to put his ideas into practice.

As we saw earlier, it fell to the lot of Gustavus to complete the wars begun by his father. This he did with considerable success in the course of striving to achieve the ambition of "making the Baltic into a Swedish lake."

At his accession, the threat of Denmark appeared extremely dangerous, but Gustavus was able to counter a military and naval attack upon Stockholm. After this, the Peace of Knared, in 1613, brought the end of the war and the recognition of the Swedish right to pass through the Sound to the North Sea. Since this was her only outlet to that sea, such recognition was necessary for the prosperity of Sweden's trade.

Free from the fear of attack from the west, Gustavus was able to take advantage of the weakness, caused by a disputed succession, in Russia to send an army against her. Eventual success in this encounter led to the Peace of Stolbova in 1617, the Tsar admitting the right of Sweden to hold the provinces of Estonia, Livonia, Ingria and Karelia. This meant that Russia lost her access to the Baltic and that Sweden gained control of its entire eastern coastline.

Following his triumph against Russia, Gustavus turned his attentions to Poland, since Sigismund, while continuing to claim that he was the lawful King of Sweden, began to challenge Sweden's right to Estonia and Livonia. After a struggle lasting twelve years, the Polish forces were driven from Livonia and Gustavus began to advance along the coastline of the Polish province of Western Prussia. The war was eventually brought to a conclusion, in 1629, by the Truce of Altmark, in which Sigismund recognized the Swedish right to Estonia, Livonia and several ports in Western Prussia. The Truce was a great triumph for Gustavus. Not only had he strengthened the position of Sweden in the eastern Baltic and acquired a further source of revenue for her in the tolls and customs of the Prussian ports, but he had also freed himself to intervene in the Thirty Years' War. The military exploits of Gustavus in the Baltic territories, between 1611 and 1629, by affording experience for his army and helping to build up morale, undoubtedly played a great part in preparing Sweden for her momentous entry into the Thirty Years' War. Equally important, however, in this respect were the reforms and developments undertaken, at the same time, by Gustavus in Sweden.

Constitutional Reform

The most significant of these changes was in the position of the kingship itself. By accepting the Charter of 1612, Gustavus surrendered the right to rule on his own as an autocrat in the manner of his father. Instead he promised to govern with the advice of a select council, known as the *Riksrad* and over important issues to consult a representative assembly, known as the *Riksdag*. Far from weakening the power of the monarchy, the agreement actually strengthened it. For working together in close partnership the king and the institutions could be more certain of strong and continued support from the people, whom the latter represented, than the one-man governments had ever been.

Following the charter, a series of measures brought changes in both central and local government. At the centre the old hereditary offices were replaced by five specialized departments dealing with finance, royal correspondence, defence, foreign affairs and justice. The heads of these departments sat in the

Kronberg castle, Elsinore, Denmark, built after Sweden became independent from Denmark, and said to be the site of Shakespeare's Hamlet.

Riksrad, which thus became a kind of cabinet. Local government was improved by the division of the country into provinces, each with its own governor, who was responsible to the central authority for enforcing the laws, collecting taxes and so on. All these changes made the administration of the country so efficient, that Gustavus could absent himself for months at a time, during his campaigns, without fearing that he would find chaos on his return.

In order to finance his campaigns, Gustavus introduced measures to improve the prosperity and ultimately the revenue of the country. He founded new industries, such as glass and paper and did everything he could to increase the size of Swedish exports. In 1626 a South Sea Company to encourage trade with Africa, Asia and South America was founded, while three years later, a shipping company was formed for the purpose of building more craft.

So far we have seen, through the policies he followed at home and the successes he achieved abroad, what an important part Gustavus Adolphus played in the development of Swedish power. All this, however, should not be allowed to mask the fact that he was equally responsible for her decline. In particular the plan, faithfully completed by his successors, to turn the Baltic into a Swedish lake left the country with an Empire which it had neither the ability nor the resources to retain.

QUESTIONS

1. Describe the part played by Gustavus Vasa and Charles IX in the rise of Sweden.
2. Why and how did Gustavus Adolphus and Sweden take part in the Thirty Years' War?

REVISION SUMMARY

DAWN OF MODERN TIMES

REVOLT IN THE NETHERLANDS

CHAPTER 15

THE GLORY OF FRANCE, 1643-1715

LOUIS XIV was the child of a loveless marriage between the pious
Louis XIII and the flirtatious Anne of Austria. Born in 1638, twenty-three
years after his parents' marriage in 1615, he was to inherit at the tender age
of five the throne of France on his father's death in 1643. His mother was
made regent. Her first action was to appoint Cardinal Mazarin as her chief
adviser, and until his death in 1661 he was the real arbiter of France's destinies. He was to exercise a profound influence over the young king who looked
upon him more as a father, and over Anne who looked to him for the affection
denied her by her husband.

A Neapolitan by birth, a Frenchman by naturalization, Mazarin had been
marked out by his former master, Cardinal Richelieu, to continue the policy
of asserting the powers of the monarchy at the expense of the nobility.
Through subtlety and flattery, rather than ruthlessness, Mazarin succeeded
in continuing the trends of Richelieu's policy both in France and in Europe.

The Fronde

During Mazarin's early rule, the discontented nobles, whose political
power had been curtailed by Richelieu, rose in rebellion. The resulting civil
wars were called the *Fronde*, after the slings used by boys in hurling stones.
The Frondeurs wished to overthrow Mazarin, but after four years of fighting
(1649-53) Mazarin emerged victorious. The Parlement of Paris, which had
constituted the sole check on royal power through its partial control over
taxation, was overthrown. Drawing experience from this, Louis henceforth
never trusted the nobility, and as soon as he could he removed his court to
Versailles, where he was also out of reach of the Paris mobs.

Mazarin continued the trends of Richelieu's foreign policy, the aim of
which had been the reduction of the Hapsburg power, which threatened the
Bourbon monarchy of France. Mazarin followed up Richelieu's successful
intervention in the war by concluding the Peace of Westphalia of 1648, which
an earlier chapter has already examined.

Mazarin induced Cromwell, who for religious and economic reasons was
more kindly disposed towards France than towards Spain, to join France as
an ally.

An Anglo-French force seized Dunkirk and other fortresses in the Spanish Netherlands and thus induced Spain, exhausted by the long war, to conclude the Peace of the Pyrenees in 1659. Louis XIV was to marry Maria Theresa, the daughter of Philip IV. She was to renounce for herself and her children any claim to the Spanish throne, but this renunciation was conditional on the payment of a marriage dowry. This dowry was in fact never paid, and Louis was later to use this point in his claims to the Spanish Empire.

Two years later Mazarin died. Despite his unpopularity and avarice, Mazarin bequeathed to Louis XIV an unrivalled position both in France and in Europe. The nobility never again challenged the monarchy, while the Parlement of Paris was reduced to insignificance. Abroad, France through Mazarin's adroit diplomacy had succeeded in thwarting the Hapsburgs both of the Empire and Spain, and in extending France's boundaries and influence into the Empire.

Louis XIV—"Le Roi Soleil"

Mazarin's death marked the assumption of complete power by Louis XIV who henceforth until his own death in 1715, controlled the destinies of France and Europe.

Louis's fundamental political belief was based upon the theory of Divine Right: he had been educated in the conviction that God alone had chosen him to rule his subjects, and as he was only answerable to God for his actions, he was justified in the exercise of complete power. In the specimens of his boyish handwriting which have been preserved, one of the copy-book headings reads, *"L'hommage est dû aux rois: ils font tout ce qui leur plaît."*

To this office of king, Louis brought an insatiable desire for self-aggrandisement. Self-glorification and the prestige of France were both one and the same for he identified himself with the state. His emblem was the sun, implying that he was capable of lighting up and energizing the world. Louis impressed his contemporaries with his air of authority, his sense of justice, his knowledge of men, his sense of duty and his unflagging industry. Even his opponents like the Duc de Saint Simon commented that "Louis XIV was made for a brilliant court. In the midst of other men, his figure, his courage, his grace, his beauty, his grand mien, even the tone of his voice and the majestic and natural charm of all his person distinguished him till his death as the King Bee. . . ."

He took a real pride in the exercise of the art of kingship. Possessed of average mental ability, he worked long hours, planning his day methodically, interspersing meetings with his ministers with court ceremonials, and pleasures either of hunting, eating, attending comedies and operas, or in the company of one or other of his lady loves such as Louise de la Vallière or Mme de Montespan, but he never allowed pleasure to interfere with his duty.

Palace of Versailles

Anyone who has ever visited Versailles will have a deeper understanding of the implications of Louis's self-glorification. The magnificent palace of Versailles, which was copied by many princes, stood on the site of a château used by Louis XIV's father as a summer residence. In 1669, work on the new buildings that enveloped the old was started, and the palace was completed in 1710. In addition to Versailles, which was built for Louis XIV's court, two other palaces were built in the grounds, a small palace called Le Trianon for Mme de Montespan and the Palace of Marly for the king when he wished to retire from the court. Apollo, the chosen emblem of the "Sun King," other Roman gods and classical temples adorned the ordered beauty of the gardens which contained shrubs and trees from all parts of France. Long terraces and numerous artificial lakes with their fountains added to the beauty; but, in the task of diverting the waters to fill these, many thousands of workers perished from marsh fever. In this temple of self-glorification, surrounded by a hypocritical, fawning, idle and licentious set of courtiers, lived Louis XIV. Life was regulated by a strict court ceremonial. The day commenced with the *"lever,"* or formal awakening of the King when the courtiers, according to a scale of precedence, entered the royal bed-chamber. The most favoured were permitted to dress the king. A similar ceremony marked the retirement of the king in the evening. During the day, hunting, hawking, gaming and the search for royal favours filled the lives of these nobles. By graciously paying off their gaming debts, Louis was able to make them feel indebted to him.

Louis had more worthwhile aims in encouraging the arts and literary talents of his subjects. His reign coincided with, but did not produce, the masterpieces associated with writers like Molière, Racine, La Fontaine, Pascal, Bossuet and Mme de Sévigné. These writers had produced many of their masterpieces before Louis had assumed power, and Louis XIV's regimentation of the arts by imposing strict rules tended to stultify rather than release the native genius.

Determined to rule absolutely, Louis excluded from affairs of state his own relatives, the nobles and priests and relied upon men of middle-class origin to fill the important administrative offices of the state. One such man, Colbert, the most famous of all Louis's ministers, was not only the Controller-General from 1665-83 but also the Secretary of State for Marine and for the *Maison du Roi.*

Decisions on all important questions of government were taken by Louis XIV in the Council of State over which he presided, and which dealt with matters of diplomacy or war, or in the *Conseil des Dépêches* and the *Conseil des Finances* which dealt with internal affairs.

These decisions were implemented in the provinces of France by royal agents, the *Intendants*. Richelieu had first employed these officials, but it was during the reign of Louis XIV that the central government systematically established their authority over the various provincial assemblies. The *Intendants* were responsible for the administration of justice, the maintenance of law and order, the supervision of tax-collectors, the carrying out of public works such as road and bridge building, the regulation of trade and industry, the raising of the militia, the administration of poor relief and many other duties.

This centralized bureaucratic framework through which Louis governed, was laid over a political system that originated in medieval times. The older institutions were not destroyed until the French Revolution, but they were reduced to a shadow of their former power. The Estates General, the medieval body representing the three estates of nobles, clergy and third estate, was not summoned between 1614 and 1789. The Parlement of Paris after the *Fronde* did not challenge the royal authority until the period of the Orleans regency. Provincial assemblies or estates still existed in certain provinces, and these enjoyed the privilege of assessing and levying their own taxes. The amount was generally less in proportion to that paid by other provinces. Even this independence was undermined by Louis.

The People of France

France was by far and away the leading nation of western Europe in this period. Her population was between eighteen and nineteen million compared with the seven million of the Hapsburg Empire, the five million of Spain and England, or the three million of the United Provinces. Even the combined population of the German and Italian states did not exceed that of France.

It is convenient to classify French society into the three estates of nobles, clergy and the third estate, but the more realistic division is that of the privileged and the non-privileged classes.

The essential mark of the privileged classes was exemption from the payment of taxes either to the king or to a feudal overlord, and from the performance of certain feudal duties to an overlord. Although the spirit of feudalism had died out with the growth of the power of the monarchy, the framework of feudalism still survived.

The nobles, deprived of all political power after the *Fronde*, were encouraged by Louis to lead an idle life at court in order that he could watch over their activities. They were an extremely mixed class falling into two main sections. The *noblesse d'épée*, an impoverished class, was made up of the descendants of the old feudal families. They held either senior ranks in the army, or were dependent upon the King's favour for pensions and coveted posts in the royal household, such as the *Grand Maître*, a post held by Condé. By "domesticating" the nobles, Louis was able to prevent any challenge to

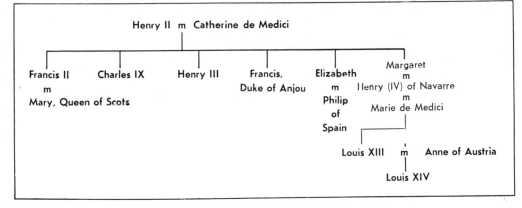

The family tree of Louis XIV, with the Bourbon coat of arms.

his authority. The other section of the nobility was the *noblesse de robe*, made up of people who had purchased all manner of official positions and titles, or who had intermarried with the older nobility. Rising from the bourgeois class, these nobles claimed equality with the more illustrious princes of the blood. Louis's policy of ennobling the wealthy undermined still further the position of the true nobility.

The clergy formed a very influential section of society which it mirrored, being marked by the extreme wealth of a tiny minority of bishops, and the extreme poverty of the majority of parish priests, whose standard of living was similar to that of the peasants. Louis XIV possessed the right of appointment to ecclesiastical positions. The great majority of the upper clergy were mere courtiers, and indeed were chosen from the younger sons of the nobility. Many were intent upon worldly pleasures rather than upon the spiritual aspect of their work. As a consequence the Church fell into disrespect in the seventeenth and eighteenth centuries.

The third estate was limited in practice to the wealthier middle-classes comprising the merchants, lawyers, tax farmers and financiers. Their wealth was amassed from trade, industry or in the collection of taxes, and was used to purchase those public offices which entitled the holder to tax exemption, or those estates which an impoverished nobleman sold to pay off his debts. Their wealth enabled them to buy exemption from the performance of feudal duties, and they strove to rise in the social scale by using their wealth to compensate for their lack of noble birth and breeding.

Set against these privileged orders were the unprivileged masses who, in an essentially agricultural country, were peasants or town artisans. Some peasants were more prosperous than others and approximately a fifth of the peasants owned land, while the peasantry as a class owned about a fifth of the total land, although they formed four-fifths of the population.

All peasants were in a degraded state, being regarded by the privileged classes as little better than beasts of burden. Their financial and other duties were heavy, demands being made upon them by the king, the feudal lords and the Church.

The Taxes

The *Taille* was the chief source of royal revenue, and its collection was the responsibility of the tax farmers, who were men who had purchased the right to collect the taxes of a particular district in order to take advantage of their office to amass a personal fortune. They cruelly extorted vast sums from the peasants and pocketed as much as half and even more for themselves.

The *Gabelle* or Salt Tax was another source of grievance: salt was vital to life, but the government, holding a monopoly over the salt mines, was able to extort a huge profit from its enforced sale. Besides these, the peasant had to pay his lord numerous feudal dues and *banalités*, which were payments made to the lord for the use of his mill, ovens, or wine press.

To the Church the peasants had to pay a *Tithe*, or tenth part, of their produce either as a money payment, or as a payment in kind.

These various payments had to be made out of the profits from a primitive type of farming. Output was low, most peasants growing just enough for themselves. The low prices which agricultural products fetched during the period further aggravated the position.

It is little wonder that even during the height of Louis XIV's reign revolts broke out amongst the peasantry. In 1662 the imposition of new taxes in the Boulogne area led to an armed revolt in which over six hundred rebels were killed, while the introduction in 1664 of the Salt Tax produced a long, drawn-out revolt in the Pyrenees. The revolts continued throughout Louis XIV's reign, and each revolt was brutally suppressed by the army. It is important therefore to remember when speaking of the glory of Louis XIV's reign, that it was a glory purchased at the expense of the peasantry.

The peasants also had to perform numerous duties to the king. It was during Louis XIV's reign that the *Intendants* were empowered to enforce the performance of the *Corvée*, or forced labour, needed to mend roads, bridges, or other public works. The peasants, of course, formed these gangs and resented the time spent away from the cultivation of their own lands. The peasants, too, could be recruited for service in the army or navy, while the privileged classes were excused. The demand for soldiers and sailors was particularly heavy during Louis XIV's reign, over half of which was spent in continuous war. A peasant, once enrolled, had no idea when he would next see his family, indeed whether he would ever see them again.

The nobles, too, made heavy demands exacting labour services to cultivate their estates. The right of hunting, enjoyed by the nobility, and forbidden to the peasantry, frequently resulted in the harming of the peasants' crops.

The majority of the peasants accepted the situation, knowing of no other existence. However, the trend towards the strengthening of the monarchy at the expense of the nobility in the seventeenth century cut at the very roots of feudalism. The encouragement given to the nobles to reside at Court away from their own estates deprived the peasants of any contact with their overlord, creating as a consequence much bitterness amongst the peasants as they paid dues, or performed services to their absentee lord. This bitterness was to increase steadily as more and more peasants came to own their own land.

Louis XIV made no attempt to alter in any fundamental way the society over which he ruled. Rather he perpetuated the deep divisions which existed, for it was in the interests of an absolute monarch to prevent the emergence of any social unity among the classes. By adopting the motto of "Divide and Rule," Louis hoped to show himself to be *Le Grand Monarch*.

Colbert and the Economy of France

If Louis was to succeed in his ambition of becoming "Le Grand Monarch," it was essential that the wealth and resources of his subjects should be mobilized to equip the armies through which he hoped to impose his will on Europe. For this task Louis looked to Jean Baptiste Colbert.

A draper's son from Rheims, Colbert had served Mazarin who had recommended him to Louis XIV. Conscientious, industrious and ruthless in his methods, Colbert, nicknamed "the North" after the cold wind, was a sombre person who, as he admitted, had no time for pleasure, but devoted his whole life to work. He first came into prominence in 1661 when he drew the king's attention to the unsatisfactory condition of the finances under the Superintendent of Finances, Fouquet, and it was on his instigation that Louis XIV had Fouquet tried and then imprisoned for financial corruption. Colbert succeeded him, becoming the Controller-General of Finance in 1665, and this office, together with the two secretaryships of state for the Marine and for the Maison du Roi, made him the most important of all Louis's ministers.

Financial Reform

Colbert found the financial state of France deplorable. In 1661 the revenues for the following two years had already been used up. The waste was the result of many factors, of which the most important were the high interest rates paid to the *rentiers*, or state creditors, the unfair system of taxing those least able to afford it, the extent to which the tax farmers pocketed such a vast proportion of the taxes for themselves, and a defective system of auditing.

To check embezzlement of the national finances, Colbert established a judicial tribunal in 1661 which exacted heavy fines from those found guilty. Those who had given information about the guilty were rewarded with a proportion of the fine. Colbert also reformed the government system of book-keeping, thus establishing an effective auditing of the accounts.

Though Colbert could not do away with tax exemptions, he tried to subject to much stricter scrutiny the claims to exemption made by the privileged orders. Tax farmers had to forgo a much greater proportion of the tax collected, and in this Colbert succeeded in doubling the effective part of the king's income. In 1667 the taxpayers paid 95 million livres, of which 63 million were paid into the Treasury; this was an improvement on the 83 million paid by the taxpayers in 1661 of which only 31 million reached the Treasury.

The *rentiers* or state creditors too suffered from Colbert's attention. He reduced their numbers and lowered the rate of interest on state loans.

These and other reforms made available large sums of money needed by Louis; yet so great was the king's demand for the conduct of his wars, and the support of his court, that the effects of many of Colbert's reforms were nullified.

Trade and Industry—Mercantilism

Colbert believed that the national revenue could best be improved by stimulating the economic activity of the people, and so a very important aspect of his work was that for the promotion of trade and industry.

He believed in and was guided by the generally accepted principles of the economy of his age that constitute the doctrine of mercantilism. The underlying basis was that precious metals constitute wealth, and since there was always a definite amount of bullion in circulation, it was in the interest of each country to acquire as much as possible of that fixed fund. Thus, it was believed, one country could only trade at the expense of another. Protective tariffs, acquisitions of overseas colonies as a source of raw materials for home industry, quantitative and qualitative regulations of manufacture, and the development of a national mercantile fleet were the practical implications of such an economic doctrine. It did not necessarily imply the abandonment of foreign trade but it justified an aggressive economic policy. The economic

French Huguenots fled when Louis revoked the Edict of Nantes.

motive was most important in the wars fought during the following two centuries, though in Louis XIV's mind his wars were fought for idealistic and dynastic motives. Colbert indeed was most impressed by the achievements of the small Dutch republic, which was one of the wealthiest nations, having a large overseas empire in the West and East Indies.

Determined to wrest this commercial supremacy from the Dutch, Colbert aimed to establish new industries in France, to exclude as far as possible foreign imports, to sell French exports abroad, to develop a mercantile fleet and to build up a colonial empire.

Some of the problems likely to hinder his schemes included the absence of any good communications system in France, the numerous internal custom barriers, and the addiction of the middle classes to the employment of their capital in the purchase of useless posts rather than industry.

New Manufactures

Yet Colbert did strive to increase the range and quality of industrial output. State subsidies, monopolies, and interest-free loans were offered to private individuals to found or revive industries like those concerned with cloth, silk, leather and tapestry. Skilled foreign workmen were encouraged to settle in France in order to introduce the latest techniques. Germans and Swedes came to build up the metal industries, and to work in the mines. The Dutch were employed in cloth-making and Italians helped in the silk industry at Lyons. Venetians helped to build up a glass industry in Paris and a lace industry elsewhere.

To ensure a high standard of craftsmanship, regulations were laid down, and inspectors appointed to enforce them. This interference irritated the manufacturers. To protect these infant industries from foreign competitors, Colbert imposed high tariffs on foreign imports. In 1667 prohibitive tariffs were drawn up designed to ruin the Dutch rivals. The Dutch retaliated and this contributed to the Franco-Dutch War of 1672. Yet Colbert did not wish to end all foreign trade as his attempt, which proved unsuccessful, to reach a trading agreement with England in 1669 showed.

To develop the trade of France, Colbert improved the long-neglected internal system of communications. River-ways were developed, canals were constructed and ports improved. He helped France to acquire merchant ships and escort vessels which challenged those of Holland and England and he created companies to develop overseas trade. In 1664 he founded the French East India Company. Yet these state-run companies failed to attract the financial support of the middle classes. Only the East India Company survived.

Much of Colbert's good work for industry was undone by Louis XIV's disastrous decision to repeal the Edict of Nantes in 1685, a mistake which led to the wholesale emigration of France's most hard-working and skilled section of the industrial community, the Huguenots. France's rivals benefited at the expense of France by the influx of these skilled Protestant refugees.

Louis and the Church

Louis XIV's objective was to identify God and His Church with the throne of France. His desire for mastery over the Church led to a conflict with the papacy over the age-old problem of the respective powers of the Church and state. Pope Innocent XI challenged the right of the French monarchy to possess the *régale*, the privilege of appointing priests in a diocese when there was no bishop, and of the enjoyment of the revenues of that see meanwhile. A quarrel similar to that of Henry VIII and the Pope broke out, but eventually in 1693 Louis XIV gained papal recognition of the *régale*.

Another religious problem facing Louis XIV was the position of the Jansenists, whom he regarded as heretics although they were a sect within the Roman Catholic Church. The Jansenists taught that Christians could be saved only by Divine Grace, which God alone would bestow. The best insurance for salvation was therefore to lead an upright godly life on this earth. Being men of severe morals, the "Puritans" of the Catholic Church, they naturally disapproved of and bitterly attacked the lax moral conduct of Louis XIV and his court. Louis XIV's confessors were however Jesuits, a rival group in the Catholic Church differing from the Jansenists in believing that all men, on their own free will, were capable of salvation. The Jesuits used their influence against their rivals, and secured a notable triumph when Louis and the Pope agreed to suppress Jansenism in 1710. In 1713 the Bull Unigenitus was promulgated, condemning Jansenist teaching, and this resulted in the persecution and imprisonment of its followers until the regent Orleans adopted a more tolerant policy in 1715.

The outstanding religious question of Louis XIV's reign, however, was the position of the French Huguenots. Permitted freedom of worship, and the right to hold public offices by Henry IV in the Edict of Nantes (1598), the Huguenots had been exemplary subjects by their loyalty and industry. There were about a million of them who lived in Normandy, Poitou and Languedoc.

Anxious to show that he was a good Catholic, and to remove a "state within a state," Louis XIV, influenced by a devout Catholic wife, determined on a policy of forcible conversion of these Protestants. Between 1680 and 1684 an outright offensive was conducted against them. They were forbidden to hold offices, to enter professions, to enter into mixed marriages, and their schools were closed. The king decided by 1685 that the Edict of Nantes was superfluous, and so, with the whole-hearted approval of his court, it was revoked in October, 1685.

The revocation resulted in the demolition of all Protestant places of worship, the banning of all Protestant services, the closing of all Protestant schools, and the baptism of all children into the Catholic faith. The greatest brutality was used to enforce the revocation. Both men and women were tortured and sent to the gallows.

Despite this, some two hundred thousand escaped abroad to England, Switzerland, the United Provinces, and Brandenburg. Those Protestants who remained in France were driven underground. While it is true that most rulers of western Europe attempted to stamp out dissent in their own countries, the persecution of the Huguenots was to have disastrous consequences for France, not merely in depriving French industry of skilled workmen, and capital, but also in rousing and rallying the Protestant countries to the menace of Louis XIV.

QUESTIONS

1. Discuss Colbert's contribution to France's strength under Louis XIV.
2. Describe and comment upon the religious policies of Louis XIV.

CHAPTER 16

LOUIS XIV AND EUROPE, 1661-1699

IN 1661 Louis XIV summed up the European situation in these words: "Spain was unable to recover so quickly from her great losses. . . . I had nothing to fear from the Emperor who was elected only because he was a member of the House of Austria. Sweden . . . had just lost a great king, all she could aspire to was to maintain her conquests during the infancy of her new king. Denmark was weakened by the preceding war with Sweden in which she had almost succumbed and thought only of peace and recovery. England could hardly breathe after her past ills, and only tried to strengthen the government under a newly re-established king who was well-inclined towards France. . . . The whole policy of the Dutch and of those governing Holland had only two aims—to sustain trade and to abuse the House of Orange; the least war would hinder them in the one as well as in the other aim, and their greatest support rested on my goodwill. . . ."

Supremacy of France

France was indeed the dominating power in Europe especially during the twenty years after Louis's assumption of power. Yet in the very menace of French domination lay the seeds of the decline in her power that set in after the formation of the anti-French League of Augsburg in 1686, a league of the rulers of Europe that successfully challenged the might of France.

The strength of France lay partly in her own resources, and partly in the weakness of the other powers. Because of her wealth and great population, France had the best army and diplomatic corps. Other rulers as well were dependent upon her wealth, especially Charles II of England. The gradual replacement of Latin by French was other evidence of France's pre-eminence. Identifying himself with the state, any glory that Louis acquired would reflect upon the honour of France. He frequently declared that *La belle gloire* was his goal. Glory was to be achieved by an aggressive foreign policy both by diplomacy and war.

Louis was attempting, by his policy of "magnificence," to tip the balance of power in favour of France. His efforts ultimately resulted in the other powers combining to correct it, but to begin with he succeeded brilliantly as a result of the weakness and preoccupation of his neighbours.

England

As the newly restored Charles II was dependent upon parliament for money, England's influence in Europe began to decline: parliament did not trust a Stuart king with an army, and the rule of soldiers in Cromwell's time had left the English with a hatred for standing armies.

In these circumstances Charles II turned for help to Louis, to whom any form of restriction on the sacred power of the monarch was intolerable. Louis endeavoured to release his cousin Charles from parliament's control by the secret Treaty of Dover (1670). By disbursing French gold, Louis secured Charles' promise to support French policies by English naval aid for the war against the Dutch, and the relaxation of the laws against Roman Catholics in England. But English public opinion was distrustful of the French alliance which implied support for the extension of French power, and the toleration of Roman Catholics. It veered round more and more to an alliance with the Dutch, England's old trade rivals, but co-religionists. The marriage in 1677 of Mary Stuart to William of Orange, the leader of the Dutch, brought this stout champion of the anti-French cause to the English throne in 1689, and from that time onwards England recovered the prestige and influence in European affairs that was so lacking during Charles II's reign.

United Provinces

The United Provinces were a confederation of the seven provinces in the north Netherlands, of which Holland since the achievement of independence from Spain was by far the most important.

Holland was dominated by the *regents*, the most powerful wealthy merchant families. Their fortunes had been made either in the East Indian trade, the sea-carrying trade of Europe, or by investments in government loans.

Although called the United Provinces, the seven provinces in fact were sovereign states each possessing its own "estates." These were all represented at the Hague in the States-General which conducted foreign affairs. A prince from the House of Orange was chosen as the *Stadholder*, or civil governor, by the individual states, and this latter office gave the House of Orange much influence in the formulation of federal policy.

Formation of a Merchant Republic, 1650-72

Throughout the first half of the seventeenth century there had been much tension between the estates of Holland and the stadholder over the policies to be adopted. The merchants of the estates wanted peace and the preservation of their own powers, while the House of Orange and its supporters wished for the continuance of the war against Spain. With the death in 1650 of William II of Orange, the estates took advantage of the fact that his son, the future William III of England, was only a fortnight old, by not appointing a stadholder, and by allowing the post of captain-general to lapse. Thus from 1650 until 1672 the "tyranny" of the House of Orange was ended and the United Provinces was in effect a merchant republic.

This republic, however, did not enjoy universal support. While the régime was supported by many wealthy merchants, and many religious dissenters it was opposed by the supporters of the House of Orange, the population in general, and was ultimately overthrown by the trade wars with England.

Anglo-Dutch War, 1652-54

Anglo-Dutch rivalry centred over trading rights between the respective East and West Indian Companies. Finally the English parliament passed a Navigation Act in 1651, forbidding import into or export of goods from English ports except in English ships or in ships from the country where the goods originated. The purpose of this act was to ruin the Dutch "carrying" trade. Over this issue the first Anglo-Dutch War (1652-54) broke out, in which neither side gained advantage.

John de Witt

It was the crisis of this war that brought to power John de Witt, a typical burgher-merchant, who in 1653 became the great pensionary of Holland and as such the unofficial prime minister to the Republic. An implacable opponent of the House of Orange, he possessed the statesmanship which enabled him to play a dominating role in the affairs of the Republic until his murder in 1672. His first task was to make peace with Cromwell, the Lord Protector of England. The peace completed, de Witt then took steps to strengthen his own position by appointing relatives and friends to posts in the administration. He reduced government loans to solve the Dutch financial problems, and during the Baltic Wars between Denmark and Sweden over the control of the Baltic Sea he succeeded in opening up a Dutch trade route through the Baltic Sound.

Second Anglo-Dutch War, 1665-67

With the restoration of the Stuarts in England in 1660 and the assumption to full power of Louis XIV in France in 1661, de Witt's régime was threatened. These monarchs naturally sympathized with the excluded House of Orange while the continuing economic rivalry with England and the growing trade rivalry with France as a result of Colbert's aggressive tariff policies were respectively to pave the way for the second Anglo-Dutch War 1665-67 and the first Franco-Dutch War 1672-79.

Temporarily de Witt staved off the French danger by negotiating an "unnatural alliance" with France (1662) at the time when Anglo-Dutch relations were becoming more and more strained, but when in late 1664 an

English fleet took possession of the Dutch colony of New Netherlands with its capital of New Amsterdam, soon to be recognized as New Jersey and New York, war broke out (1665).

During this naval war the most dramatic incident, described by Samuel Pepys, came in June 1667, when the Londoners, already visited by two scourges—the Plague, and the Fire—were amazed to learn of a strong Dutch fleet under de Ruyter sailing up the Thames. Sheerness was captured, the boom across the River Medway was broken, and the English flagship, the *Royal Charles* was carried off while the rest of the fleet was set on fire.

Peace was signed at Breda (1667) in which the English retained the New Netherlands, and the Dutch, Surinam. De Witt's most successful achievement was the modification of the Navigation Act in favour of the Dutch.

The War of Devolution, 1667-68

However the year 1667 was ominous in Franco-Dutch relations. Louis XIV decided to bring Spain and her possessions ultimately under his control by virtue of his Spanish-born wife, whose renunciation of the Spanish possessions in the Peace of the Pyrenees had been rendered invalid by the failure of the Spanish to pay Louis the marriage dowry. Asserting his Queen's claims under the ancient Law of Devolution, Louis in 1667 sent 50,000 men under Turenne, who marched into the Spanish Netherlands. The frontier towns fell and the Netherlands were overrun. At the same time French armies occupied Franche Comté.

The Triple Alliance, 1668

The prospect of a powerful French neighbour alarmed both the Dutch and English who rapidly made peace with each other. In 1668 England, the United Provinces and Sweden negotiated the Triple Alliance which was directed against the French expansion in the Netherlands by providing mutual protection in the event of a French attack.

Not anxious to have the Sea Powers and the Empire united against France, Louis decided on the prudent course of making peace with Spain, which he accomplished with the Treaty of Aix-la-Chapelle (1668).

Louis's aspirations had been checked by this alliance of Protestant countries, and for this affront to his royal dignity he could never forgive the Dutch. From this time onwards he planned to smash this nation of "cheesemongers." Pride, however, goes before a fall, and in his decision to destroy the Dutch were sown the seeds of his own downfall.

The Dutch War, 1672-79

In addition to the rebuff the Dutch had administered to him, and their extreme Protestantism, Louis hated the Dutch for their colonial supremacy.

French diplomacy was therefore directed in the period after the War of Devolution to the isolation of the Dutch by breaking up the Triple Alliance, and by neutralizing the Princes of the Empire. In this, Lionne, Louis's foreign minister, succeeded brilliantly, for not only did he detach England and Sweden from the United Provinces, but he gained their alliance. The English alliance was the mainspring of his schemes, for the English navy would be needed against the Dutch. Secret negotiations were conducted between Charles II of England and Colbert de Croissy representing Louis XIV. The French skilfully used as levers for the realization of their plans Charles II's desire to gain financial independence of parliament, which would enable him in turn to relax the penal laws against Catholic and Protestant dissenters.

In 1670 at a family gathering of the representatives of both monarchs at Dover, a secret treaty was signed. Charles agreed to provide a fleet and six thousand troops in the forthcoming war against the Dutch, and in return Louis not only paid him two million livres, but promised six thousand French troops to enable Charles to re-establish Roman Catholicism in England as soon as opportunity allowed.

Louis then turned to Sweden whose alliance was won by a similar lavish distribution of gold. The Great Elector of Brandenburg was the one notable exception among the German princes including the Emperor Leopold whose neutrality had not been bought by French gold.

At the same time that the French diplomats were isolating the United Provinces, Louvois and Vauban, were carrying out important reforms in the army. Fresh regiments, including a special corps of engineers, were raised; a new standard of discipline was being enforced by such officers as Colonel Martinet; the whole administration of the army was being over-hauled; and weapons were improved, particularly with the introduction of the flint lock, which simplified the system of firing. Artillery, needed for sieges, was improved; the conduct of sieges formed the essential character of seventeenth-century fighting tactics.

Colbert was performing a similar service to the French navy, so that Louis could count upon some two hundred ships. Naval gunnery and hydrography were established on a scientific basis. The blow fell in 1672 when Charles II declared war, while Louis, dispensing with the formality of a declaration of war, gave orders to his army to advance. William of Orange and his ill-equipped and ill-trained soldiers retreated into Holland, but by breaking the dykes and flooding the countryside, they checked the French advance. Nevertheless, the situation seemed hopeless and the States-General sued for peace.

Dutch Revolution, 1672

The power of de Witt and the merchant families, which had dominated

124

The Hague, Holland, where de Witt and his brother were murdered.

Holland for twenty years, was coming to an end. The young William of Orange symbolized the new spirit of defiance of the invader, replacing the old policy of appeasement and disarmament advocated by de Witt. William became *Stadholder*, and in effect, the leader of Holland.

The full cycle of the revolution was completed with the murder of de Witt, and his brother Cornelius by the infuriated mob in the Hague (August, 1672). Although William had nothing to do with the murder, he utilized the passions of popular vengeance to secure the replacement of de Witt's followers with those of his own in all the offices of State.

The Grand Alliance

For the remainder of his life, William was moved by one idea, that of defeating Louis XIV's ambition of dominating Europe. Assisted by the growing fears amongst the rulers of Europe of Louis's aggressive schemes, William was able to bring into being a Grand Alliance between 1672 and 1674 that not only saved the United Provinces from extinction but also warned Louis XIV of the consequences of aggression, a warning which he did not heed. The alliance included the Emperor Leopold of Austria and many German princes, including the elector of Brandenburg, Spain and Denmark.

By 1674 Louis found himself virtually isolated, for in that year all his allies with the exception of Sweden made peace with the Dutch. Charles II of England had been forced to summon parliament in his quest for money and only secured it by reversing the religious toleration he had granted to dissenters and accepting Parliament's Test Act against Roman Catholics. In 1674 England signed the Treaty of Westminster with the Dutch.

Despite Louis's serious diplomatic rebuffs, the military situation during the Dutch War was more favourable to the French, without the inevitable division of command which characterized the Allied armies. In the Netherlands the French had evacuated most of the Dutch territory and the campaigns consisted of besieging or defending key fortresses.

The year 1676 marked the opening of peace negotiations, though fighting was to continue for a further two years. The marriage of Mary, the niece of Charles II of England, with William of Orange strengthened the move towards peace. Louis was not anxious to see the growing union between the Sea Powers, and so in 1678 the Peace of Nymegen was signed.

The peace was composed of separate treaties between the opponents. The French restored Maastricht to the Dutch and conceded the right of reciprocal trading by lowering her tariff barriers against the Dutch merchants. Fortress towns in the Netherlands also were exchanged.

Lorraine continued to be occupied by the French after the Duke had rejected the French terms. Spain was the chief sufferer by her surrender of Franche Comté and the fortresses guarding her Netherlands, while the Dutch lost nothing. Yet apart from these territorial gains, Louis had succeeded in alienating the princes of the Empire, and arousing the permanent hostility of the Dutch.

Chambres de Réunion

In the years after the Peace of Nymegen, Louis utilized as an excuse for further aggression the very treaty which was supposed to guarantee the stability of Europe, namely the Treaty of Westphalia. This he did by interpreting some of the more vaguely worded clauses in order to justify the extension of French influence and territory. Just as Louis had tried to annex the Spanish Netherlands by getting his legal experts to discover an ancient but obsolete law, so in the period 1680-83 he set up courts of law known as the *"Chambres de Réunion"* in order to confirm the king's rights in Alsace, Franche Comté and Lorraine. Research into the ancient customs showed that at one time or another certain towns had been dependent upon these provinces. Thus in 1680 French sovereignty was proclaimed over the whole of Alsace, and to confirm this French troops occupied Strasbourg.

This *"Réunion"* aroused again the latent hostility of Europe, resulting in the formation of another anti-French alliance in 1681 composed of the United Provinces, Sweden, the Empire and Spain. Western Europe would have been plunged into war had not the Turks and Hungarians caused a diversion in the East with their advance on Vienna. Louis took advantage of the Allied preoccupation by besieging Luxembourg, which fell to Vauban in 1684. Spain and the Empire had to recognize Louis's annexations in the truce of Ratisbon. French diplomacy and arms everywhere were triumphant.

War of the League of Augsburg, 1688-97

Louis's inordinate greed for power however overreached itself. In 1686 Spain, the Empire, the United Provinces, Sweden and Bavaria formed the League of Augsburg. This came into existence as a result of Louis's fresh threat to seize the Palatinate on behalf of his sister-in-law, and when in 1688 Louis sent his armies into that province war once again broke out.

This unwarranted seizure was to prove a decisive blunder. By moving his armies away from the Netherlands to the Rhine, Louis enabled William of Orange to set sail for England. William had been invited by both Whig and Tory leaders, who saw in him the only alternative to James II, whose efforts to re-establish the Catholics in positions of authority by the exercise of the royal prerogative had revived just those issues which had produced the civil wars of the early years of the seventeenth century. James's flight to France cleared the way for William's acceptance in 1689 of the throne as a constitutional monarch with limited powers. As William III of England he was now in a position to fulfil the ambition which lay behind his acceptance of the English throne, namely that of aligning England with the military alliance against France. For the remainder of Louis's life, England with her wealth and her navy was to be the mainspring in the anti-French coalition.

The war was fought in many theatres. In Europe the war on land opened as we have seen with the French invasion of the Palatinate and then spread to the Low Countries, Ireland, northern Italy and Spain. At sea fighting broke out in the Channel, the Irish Sea, and the Mediterranean. Overseas, conflicts occurred in North America, the West Indies and India.

The war was essentially one of sieges rather than field campaigns, and in Vauban the French possessed the outstanding exponent of this type of fighting. In consequence the French were generally more successful.

In the Netherlands at Fleurus in 1690 any hope the Allies ever had of invading France faded with the Elector of Brandenburg's defeat. Namur fell to the French in 1692 but William three years later gained his one success by recapturing this important fortress.

In Ireland William enjoyed more success. To divert English resources from the Netherlands, Louis supplied men and equipment to help the deposed James II to stir up a rebellion in Ireland. There, the Irish Catholics, embittered by their sufferings at the hands of Protestant overlords and successive rulers from Elizabeth to Cromwell, rallied behind the Stuart cause. Their hopes for freedom, and Louis's hopes for an English diversion were dashed by William's great victory over James on the Boyne in 1690. Not merely did William's victory confirm the Protestant ascendancy in Ireland, but, at the same time,

George, Prince of Wales, at the Battle of the Boyne (July 1, 1690).

it enabled England to concentrate her resources for the war in the Netherlands.

Meanwhile at sea decisive engagements in the struggle for naval supremacy were taking place. At the outset of the war the French fleet was supreme, and allied merchant shipping suffered heavily at the hands of the French in all the waters round Europe. An invasion of England was planned, but Louis's plans were to be frustrated by Admiral Russell's great victory over the French in a six-day battle off Cape la Hogue, in which the French fleet was destroyed. Not only did this victory avenge the earlier Anglo-Dutch defeat at Beachy Head, but it gave the Allies that command of the seas which was to be the first English objective in the long series of French wars that followed. The battle was of similar importance to that of Trafalgar for the French never again put a battle fleet to sea. This change in the naval balance of power enabled the Allies to send a fleet into the Mediterranean with disastrous consequences for both French trade and French campaigns in Spain and Italy. Nevertheless, English and Dutch commerce continued to suffer from the attentions of French privateers.

French armies on the middle Rhine continued to achieve success, although the French devastations of the Palatinate aroused general indignation. In Spain Louis was stopped at Barcelona by the English, but he secured the neutralization of Italy in 1696.

By this time all the powers were ready for peace. Exhausted by the war, and anxious to have his hands free to deal with the approaching crisis of the Spanish succession, Louis was in a more conciliatory mood than previously when negotiations opened at Ryswick.

Peace of Ryswick and Peace of Carlowitz

By the arrangements finally agreed at Ryswick Louis recognized William III as King of England and by so abandoning his support for James II, he removed a major obstacle in the relations of England and France.

The Dutch were allowed to strengthen their defences by placing garrisons in some of the fortresses in the Spanish Netherlands, while their merchants benefited by Louis's relaxation of commercial regulations, including tariffs, hitherto directed against their trade.

With the exception of Strasbourg Louis agreed to restore all French conquests gained since 1678.

The peace of Ryswick settling quarrels among nations of western Europe was followed two years later by an equally important peace treaty between the Sultan and Emperor Leopold. The Emperor, who wished to be free to tackle the problem of the Spanish succession, dictated the Peace of Carlowitz (1699) in which the Turks surrendered to the Emperor Hungary and Transylvania; to Poland, Podolia; to Russia, Azov; and to Venice, the Morea.

Changing Balance of Power

Taken together the importance of the two peace treaties lay in the rise of the Hapsburg monarchy to a position similar to that held for so long by Louis XIV. In his capacity as Emperor of Germany, Leopold had successfully rallied the princes of the Empire to defend themselves against the French incursions, so forcing Louis at Ryswick to surrender many of his conquests. As the defender of eastern Europe from the Moslem Turks, Leopold not only won the gratitude of Christians everywhere, but also had freed himself from the Turkish menace. England, too, as a naval power had demonstrated her superiority over the French.

Thus with the question of the Spanish succession looming as the major unresolved problem of Europe, the emergence of the Emperor and England as powers capable of successfully challenging France both on land and sea was to be of profound importance.

QUESTIONS

1. Describe and criticize Louis XIV's foreign policy from the start of the War of Devolution to the Treaty of Nymegen.
2. Outline briefly the causes, events and effects of the Anglo-Dutch wars of 1652-54 and 1665-67.

CHAPTER 17

THE WAR OF THE SPANISH SUCCESSION, 1702-1713

THE clouds which darkened Europe after the Peace of Ryswick centred over Madrid. They had been gathering ever since Charles II ascended the throne of Spain and its vast Empire in 1665. Enfeebled in mind and body as a result of Hapsburg inbreeding, this unfortunate man, whose death was awaited from his birth onwards, had failed to produce an heir from his two marriages. His "Hapsburg jaw" was so developed he could neither chew nor talk. Who should succeed him was a problem all European rulers pondered.

Although Spain was in a decayed condition, exercising no positive influence in Europe, its potential resources of gold and silver (brought to Cadiz in the annual treasure fleet from the mines of Central and South America) as well as a considerable empire in Europe, made the throne a glittering prize for any ambitious prince. The acquisition of the wealth and the lands of this empire would alter decisively the balance of power in Europe and in an age when the leading ruling families were interconnected by marriage there were several claimants.

The Claimants

Louis XIV had a double legal claim. First, he was married to Charles II's elder half-sister, Maria Theresa, to whom the throne would normally pass after Charles II. Although she had conditionally renounced her claims to the Spanish inheritance when she married Louis XIV in 1660, the condition, namely the payment of the marriage dowry, had not been fulfilled. Thus Louis, and through him his son, the Dauphin, and his grandson Philip, Duke of Anjou, all had very sound cases. A further, rather weaker case could be made out on the grounds that Louis XIV's mother, Anne, was the eldest daughter of Philip III, and though she had also renounced her rights, there were doubts as to the legality of her renunciation.

Against these Bourbon claims were those of their rivals the Hapsburgs, Emperor Leopold and his heirs. Emperor Leopold's claim had a similar basis to that of Louis XIV. He, too, was a grandson of Philip III, being the child of Philip's youngest daughter Maria Anna, who, unlike Louis XIV's mother, had not renounced her rights to the throne. Again, Emperor Leopold was married to Margaret Theresa, the younger half-sister of Charles II. She too had made no renunciation of her rights.

A third claimant was the Electoral Prince of Bavaria, Joseph Ferdinand. His claim was based on the fact that his mother, Maria Antonia, was the daughter of the Margaret Theresa, who was Charles II's half-sister, and who was the first wife of the Emperor Leopold.

The situation was extremely complicated. Legal rights to the throne alone were insufficient to win the support of Europe as a whole. If either Louis XIV or the Emperor Leopold enforced their own claims, or those of their heirs to the whole of the Spanish inheritance, war would be inevitable between the Hapsburgs and Bourbons. Louis would never allow a Hapsburg Emperor of Germany to rule Spain and its empire, nor would Leopold allow a Bourbon to dominate both France and Spain. Equally, the maritime powers of England or Holland would not be prepared to see Louis tapping the resources of the Spanish empire unchallenged. A compromise was essential if peace was to be maintained, and considerable diplomatic effort to this end proceeded while Charles II still lived.

Partition Treaties

Louis XIV fully appreciated the need for a settlement, being a much wiser and more mature statesman in 1697 than twenty years previously when he had asserted his wife's claim to the Spanish Netherlands.

Accordingly, in October 1698 he agreed to the First Partition Treaty by which the young Electoral Prince of Bavaria, who had the advantage of being neither a Hapsburg nor a Bourbon, should inherit Spain, the Netherlands and the Indies, while the Bourbon prince, the Dauphin, should receive Naples, Sicily, Sardinia and the Tuscan ports, and the Hapsburg Archduke Charles should receive Milan. While this solution was unacceptable to the Emperor because it broke up his empire, it seemed to the other powers a reasonable compromise on a complex issue, but any chance of its being realized was lost with the death through smallpox of the Electoral Prince in 1699. Louis XIV was still prepared to negotiate, anxious to prevent any situation that might lead to war. In the renewed bargainings between Hapsburg and Bourbon, the influence of the sea powers under William of Orange was decisive, for the only acceptable candidate was Archduke Charles, the Emperor's younger son. In the Second Partition Treaty of 1699 he was to receive Spain, the Netherlands and the Indies, while the Dauphin was to increase his share by acquiring Naples, Sicily, the Tuscan ports and Lorraine. Although Louis and the maritime powers accepted this settlement, the Emperor refused his signature to a treaty which like its predecessor split up the Spanish Empire in Europe so radically.

Crisis of 1700
The Spaniards shared their rulers' resentment at the break up and absorption of their empire by the other powers. Realizing, however, that a foreign prince would inevitably come to the throne, the Spanish court and people increasingly favoured the French claimant on the grounds that as France was the strongest power, she would be in the best position to preserve the integrity of Spain and the Spanish empire. As the unfortunate king neared his end, two rival parties within the court battled for power. The pro-French party triumphed, and the pro-Austrian Queen of Charles II fled the country with her followers. Her flight was the opportunity for the French party to intimidate Charles II into signing a will in October, 1700, bequeathing Spain and its entire empire to Philip, Duke of Anjou, who was Louis XIV's grandson. He was chosen as the Bourbon candidate most likely to be acceptable to the sea powers. A fortnight later, Charles II died.

When Louis XIV heard of Charles's will, he was placed in a grave dilemma —whether to accept the Second Partition Treaty, or the will. To accept the Second Partition Treaty, to which he had subscribed, would mean the positive gains of Lorraine and southern Italy, but it could lead to war with Spain on the grounds that Spain did not wish to stand by and see her empire broken up, and possibly with the Emperor who coveted South Italy for himself, and who had refused to assent to the treaty. In such a war, France could hardly count upon the active support of the maritime powers.

To accept the will and so reject the treaty would undermine his reputation as an honourable man, for it would mean a breach of faith with the other signatories of the treaty. It would also mean war with the Hapsburgs, but war with them seemed inevitable whether he accepted the treaty or will. It was more questionable whether, on the Spanish issue alone, England and Holland would go to war with France. Undoubtedly the acceptance of the will would win the overwhelming support of the Spanish people, and considerable increase of power and wealth with his grandson as king of Spain.

The impossibility of enforcing the partition treaty against the determination of the Emperor and Spain finally decided Louis to accept the will. On 16 November, 1700, he brought his grandson Philip, Duke of Anjou, before the assembled court at Versailles, addressing them with these words:

"Gentlemen, here is the King of Spain. His birth has called him to the throne, the late King confirmed him in his rights . . . ; it is the command of Heaven; I have obeyed it with pleasure."

Louis then informed the rest of Europe. The Emperor immediately favoured war, but he found his potential allies, England and Holland, and some of the German princes, disinclined to fight. Without their help he was powerless.

Had Louis been content to restrain his ambition, it is more than likely that the rest of Europe would have quietly acquiesced in his breach of faith.

Louis's appetite for glory had however been whetted, and at the peak of his diplomatic success, he committed certain blunders that made war inevitable.

He announced in February, 1701, that he reserved the rights of Philip V, as his grandson was now known, and his descendants to succeed to the French throne. Such an announcement meant that the realization of the worst fear of the sea powers—a union of the French and Spanish thrones under one man—would become inevitable. The sea powers had already recognized Philip V on the understanding that he renounced the French throne. The subjection of Spain to France was soon demonstrated for Louis himself took the final decisions on all matters of Spanish policy.

Louis also went out of his way to arouse the enmity of the Dutch by sending French armies into the Spanish Netherlands to occupy the barrier fortresses, and he made commercial treaties with Spain such as that which gave France the exclusive right to supply slaves to the Spanish colonies. These treaties were to lead to the exclusion of the Dutch and English merchants from both the Indies and the Mediterranean.

In his dealings with England Louis made the gravest mistake of all inasmuch as he succeeded in uniting the whole English nation under William III against France. He recognized "James III" (the Old Pretender) as the rightful king of England when James II died. This was an insult to the English by nominating, as their future king, the Roman Catholic heir of a man whose own Catholicism had produced the wave of national indignation that had swept James II off the throne in 1688.

The Grand Alliance, 1701

As soon as Louis announced his decision to accept the will, William III began the negotiations which brought into being the Grand Alliance, in September, 1701, of the Emperor, England and Holland. In the Treaty of The Hague which set out the war aims of the alliance, they agreed to resist France's attempt to secure control of the Spanish possessions in the Netherlands and Italy, to use their forces to prevent a union of the crowns of France and Spain, to fight for the right of the Dutch to retain their garrisons in the barrier fortresses in the Netherlands and to wage a colonial and commercial war overseas. But as nothing was said about Spain and the Indies the inference was that the sea powers were not prepared to fight for Archduke Charles's rights to these areas, although the Emperor himself would not openly renounce his son's claims. In the following months other German powers joined the Grand Alliance. Against this combination stood France, backed by Spain, the Electors of Bavaria and Cologne, and two dubious allies, the Dukes of Savoy and Portugal.

Before the Grand Alliance officially declared war in May, 1702, its chief architect, William III, died in March. Though a chronic asthma patient, he had for thirty years devoted his energies against Louis XIV's ambitions and the savage criticisms of both his own countrymen, and of the untrustworthy politicians of Westminster. It must have been a grave disappointment to him that his last year of life had to be devoted to the rebuilding of the Grand Alliance.

Rise of John Churchill, Duke of Marlborough

It was fortunate that at this time of mounting crisis, the Grand Alliance did not fall asunder. That it remained in being was due in part to the overwhelming menace from Louis XIV and in part to the emergence of John Churchill, Duke of Marlborough, who was to assume its leadership. Marlborough's rise to fame is partly explained by his own qualities of leadership and partly by the great influence his wife Sarah exercised over Anne, the new Queen of England.

An experienced officer, Marlborough had first made his name when he crushed Monmouth's rebellion. He was to prove the outstanding military commander in the forthcoming war, both as a strategist in planning great campaigns, and as a tactician in carrying them out in battle. Like all great leaders he inspired confidence among the rank and file, showing an exceptional consideration for their well-being. Like Napoleon, Marlborough appreciated the point that the soldiers' best arms were their legs, and by rapid surprise movements Marlborough was both to outwit and destroy the French armies' reputation for invincibility, as well as to revolutionize the traditional methods of siege warfare which were so beloved by the commanders of the day.

The other outstanding Allied commander was Prince Eugene of Austria, who, like Marlborough, was a daring leader of men, ready to adopt the unorthodox and unexpected courses which enabled him with inferior numbers to inflict crushing defeats. His crossing of the Alps through "impassable" passes caught a numerically superior French army off its guard in northern Italy at the outset of the war, and the raid at Cremona was typical of a new type of warfare.

France had taken advantage of the lull following the Peace of Ryswick to strengthen her frontiers, which were guarded by fortresses so strongly held that she was virtually impregnable. Her immediate neighbours presented no threat, as she had treaties with Spain, Savoy and Bavaria.

The first two campaigning seasons of 1702 and 1703 produced no critical action on land or sea, but the year 1704 was a decisive one. Admiral Rooke's capture of Gibraltar in July, 1704, gave the Allies control over the entrance to the Mediterranean for the rest of the war and confirmed their ascendancy at sea. French and Spanish troops failed to remove the Union Jack from the Rock of Gibraltar.

On land Marlborough was to shatter the French reputation for invinci-

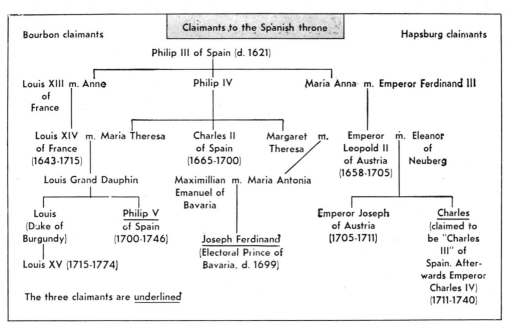

Rival claims that led to the War of the Spanish Succession.

bility. Vienna was threatened by the Franco-Bavarian army and its relief was vital if the Grand Alliance was to survive. This was easier said than done. Marlborough had to overcome the opposition of the Dutch States-General, which would never consent to any plan that involved denuding the Netherlands of troops in order to relieve Vienna, for to do so would invite a French invasion of the Netherlands. Marlborough had, accordingly, to plan his campaign with the utmost secrecy not merely to out-wit his enemies, but also his Dutch allies. When eventually he gave marching orders to move down the Rhine, not even his own officers knew their destination. Deliberately feinting to give the impression that he was about to invade France, he was able to pin down every French army from the Channel to Bavaria as he moved south with his 40,000 troops. Only when he joined up with Prince Eugene and Louis of Baden's forces near Ulm on the Danube was the great secret of his Bavarian destination revealed.

Blenheim

Meanwhile the Bavarians seized Donauworth and fortified the hill of Schellenberg which dominated the crossing of the Danube. Against this fortress Marlborough launched a savage attack in July, 1704, which resulted in heavy casualties on both sides, but which gave him the vital bridgehead for the invasion of Bavaria. He then devastated the country hoping to force the Elector and Marsin's army to give battle, but they refused, waiting for the

135

arrival of the French relief army. This joined them eventually and at Blenheim in August Marlborough and Eugene shattered the Franco-Bavarian army. This was a "famous victory" for its results were of great consequence. The French withdrew over the Rhine, and Germany was freed. For the remainder of the war the French were on the defensive, their military reputation seriously undermined. Vienna was saved, and with it the Grand Alliance. Marlborough was rewarded with the great estate of Woodstock and given the money to build the palace of Blenheim which became his family seat.

Ramillies

In contrast with the Blenheim campaign, that of the following year was relatively fruitless. An invasion of Spain was launched from Portugal but it succeeded only in uniting the Spaniards in fierce resistance against the Allies' attempt to overthrow Philip V.

This disappointing picture was altered in the following year when Louis prepared for an all-out offensive of his armies in the Netherlands, Germany, Italy and Spain. But before the planned offensive could be mounted, the French suffered once more a shattering defeat at the hands of Marlborough at Ramillies in May, 1706. This decided the fate of the Netherlands. At a critical moment in this battle, Marlborough, taking advantage of a fold in the ground, and carrying out feints on the left, switched his whole cavalry force and in a spectacular charge against the outnumbered French swept them from the field. The morale of the French army was destroyed and the entire Spanish Netherlands now fell into Marlborough's hands. As at Blenheim, the consequences were widespread. The French invasion of Germany was cancelled, while the French hold in Italy was decisively weakened.

The year 1707 was marred by Allied failures at Toulon and in Spain. The Allied attempt to seize Toulon by a combined Anglo-Dutch naval attack failed. Events in Spain too, took a turn for the worse in 1707. Quarrels between Archduke Charles and the British Commander Galway, the lack of adequate Allied reinforcements and the loyalty of the majority of Spaniards to Philip V combined to inflict the decisive defeat at Almanza that ruined the Archduke Charles's chances of the Spanish throne.

Oudenarde, Minorca, and Malplaquet

Whatever comfort Louis XIV might have drawn from these Allied reverses was soon to be dissipated in yet another disaster when, in an attempt to recover the Netherlands, a French army under the Duke of Vendôme was intercepted at Oudenarde in July, 1708. Once more Marlborough showed himself the master of manoeuvre. Almost encircled, the French only extricated themselves after 20,000 men were killed, wounded or captured. Marlborough followed up this success by taking the strongly-defended fortress of Lille which lay within the boundary of France, but this was only after immense losses.

The Allied failure at Toulon was also avenged when in 1708 the British fleet seized Minorca and so acquired yet another base which helped to consolidate its domination of the Mediterranean.

These disasters, the failure of crops resulting from an exceptionally severe winter of 1708-9 and the consequent hardships suffered by the French people, forced Louis to sue for peace. However, the peace negotiations of 1709 broke down over the Allies' demand that Louis should help to expel his own grandson from Spain. Willing to make large concessions, Louis was not prepared to submit to such a humiliation. Appealing to the loyalty of the French, Louis enrolled a new army under Villars, the most competent of all the French commanders. Moving into the wooded area near Malplaquet in an effort to relieve Mons, he was attacked by Marlborough and Eugene. Although driven from the field, the French retrieved their reputation in the bloodiest battle yet fought, in which the Allies lost 40,000 dead or wounded. Such casualties appalled the Allies and intensified the demand for peace. Serious fighting after 1710 was coming to an end in Europe.

The Tories and Peace

Political events in England were to play a decisive role in the years after 1710. The Whig ministry, representative of the powerful merchants who favoured the continuance of the war, was now becoming increasingly unpopular. Against it stood the Tory party which favoured peace, and which claimed that the war was being unnecessarily lengthened to serve the selfish interest of the Whigs and the ambitions of the Duke of Marlborough. Backed by the majority of the squires who bore the ever-increasing burden of land taxes, the Tory leaders induced Queen Anne to replace the Whig ministers by Tories in 1710. The return of an overwhelming Tory majority in the general election showed how strong the desire for peace was.

Henry St. John, a Tory leader, now entered into secret peace negotiations with Torcy, the French foreign minister. When the peace proposals were brought before parliament, Marlborough opposed them on the grounds that Britain had an obligation to her allies not to treat with France separately. This opposition was the opportunity the Tories wanted. After blackening his reputation, with malicious stories about his financial dishonesty and his greed for power, as well as belittling his military genius, the Tory Government dismissed Marlborough from his command in 1711.

The move towards peace was further strengthened with the death of the Emperor Joseph I in 1711, and the accession of his brother, Archduke Charles as Emperor Charles VI. Now that Charles had inherited the Imperial title and the vast Hapsburg lands in central Europe, the Allies obviously no longer had an interest in backing his claims to Spain and its empire. To do so would lead to the excessive concentration of power in the hands of one man, exactly the situation against which they had been fighting for so long. Nevertheless the Emperor Charles was still not prepared to forgo his title to Spain and the Grand Alliance was thus split and weakened.

In 1712 Britain deserted her allies when she made a truce with the French. This withdrawal of British regiments enabled the French army under Villars to recover some of the lost prestige and lost fortresses. While his allies were negotiating with the French at Utrecht the Emperor continued the struggle throughout 1713 but he had to acknowledge the inevitable and come to terms with France in the Treaty of Rastadt in 1714, in which he recognized the settlement as drawn up in the Peace of Utrecht of the previous year.

The Peace of Utrecht, 1713

The peace settlement negotiated by Henry St. John, Viscount Bolingbroke, was the subject of much controversy. Britain's allies considered it treasonable in that Bolingbroke had abandoned them in order to dictate as favourable a settlement for Britain as possible. There is some justice in this claim in as much as Britain made a separate truce with France in 1712, and had little love or respect for either the Dutch or the Emperor. Bolingbroke too was a man of few scruples. On the other hand, Bolingbroke and the Tories defended their action on the grounds that if peace was to be achieved Britain would have to take the lead since the Emperor's stubborn unwillingness to recognize the impracticability of acquiring the Spanish throne could prolong the war indefinitely.

The final agreement of 1713 was in effect composed of three themes which run throughout the otherwise complex story of international relations of the period. The first of these was the assumption that a balance of power existed between nations, and that it was the duty of statesmen to prevent it from being disturbed by any one nation becoming powerful enough to dominate the others.

The second theme was concerned with dynastic ambitions, for with them were bound up questions of prestige and power both of the ruling families and the country over which they exercised that power.

The third theme was concerned with commercial motives, for these were to play a prominent role in an age when considerations of commerce made vital the acquisition of trading rights and naval bases.

The Actual Settlement

Philip V was acknowledged as King of Spain and the Indies, thus realizing Louis's immediate object of placing a Bourbon on the Spanish throne.

But Philip V had to renounce his claim to the French throne in order to prevent the very real possibility of a union of France and Spain under one crown, for such a situation would have disturbed the balance of power. A series of deaths in the Bourbon family had left a sickly boy, the future Louis XV, as the heir to the throne, while Philip V was the next-in-line. Nor was the Emperor able to threaten the balance by acquiring all the Spanish empire in addition to his own Hapsburg dominions. He had to renounce his claim to the Spanish throne, and any chance that he might re-assert his claim was blocked by the provision that the Duke of Savoy should succeed to the throne in the event of Philip V dying without a direct heir. In compensation, however, the balance was redressed by the division of the Spanish empire in Europe between the Emperor and the Duke of Savoy.

The need to curb France's aggressive tendencies resulted in the renewal of the earlier Barrier Treaty negotiated between the Dutch and English. The Dutch who had suffered so much from French invasions were granted the right to garrison certain fortress towns in the Austrian Netherlands and their trade was protected from competition by the reaffirmation of the closure of the River Scheldt to foreign shipping. Antwerp was thus successfully barred from rivalling Amsterdam or London.

The defence of Britain's Mediterranean trade routes was assured with the confirmation of her rights over Gibraltar and Minorca seized during the war from Spain. In North America Britain acquired Acadia, Hudson Bay and Newfoundland, subject to certain fishing rights, as well as St. Kitts in the West Indies from France. Apart from these, Britain secured the prized "*Asiento*" from Spain that permitted her to send one shipload of merchandise a year and to supply slaves to the Spanish-American colonies. This concession was, in fact, to prove disappointing.

Britain also secured the French recognition of the claims of the Hanoverians to the English throne. Louis had to abandon the Stuart cause and the Stuarts left France to settle in Lorraine. The abandonment by France of their cause was to prove disastrous to the Stuarts. Lacking the support of most of the British public their only hope had lain in the support of a foreign power. The failure of the 1715 and 1745 risings can in part be ascribed to this.

In Germany the electors of Bavaria and Cologne recovered their former territories, while the King of Prussia had his title recognized by all the powers.

QUESTIONS

1. What part did the Duke of Marlborough play in the defeat of France in the War of the Spanish Succession?

2. Describe the chief provisions of the treaties of Utrecht and Rastadt. How did they affect the balance of power in Europe?

CHAPTER 18

EUROPE AT PEACE, 1713-1740

IN THE years after the Treaty of Utrecht, the story of Europe is one of comparative peace in contrast with the major wars from which Europe had just emerged, and those into which she was to be convulsed from 1740 onwards.

Although the settlement reached at Utrecht did not satisfy all nations, its preservation was the main objective of British and French diplomacy. Peace was vital for the consolidation of the new régimes that came to power in Britain and France. Accordingly these two nations, still the most powerful, co-operated in their efforts to settle the rivalries that disturbed Europe.

The last years of Louis XIV's reign were in marked contrast with those of the outset. The long wars with Europe had not merely ended in disaster to the nation's reputation for military invincibility, but also for national solvency. The national debt ran into two thousand million livres and was continually increasing and the expenditure, some 243 million livres, exceeded the revenue of 186 million livres. The interest rates on the national debt were high, and some third of it was due for immediate repayment. The deaths of countless numbers of peasants in the wars, and the disruption of the country's trade struck a serious blow at the true sources of national wealth. Despite the protests and suggestions of Racine, who brought to the King's notice the intense sufferings of the poor, and of Vauban who proposed a uniform tax to be borne by all classes, Louis refused to contemplate any drastic reform of the injustice of the tax system. Instead he banished Racine from court, and disgraced Vauban by the public burning of his book. Such was the reward for faithful service to Louis XIV.

The other great problem facing Louis XIV was that of the succession to the throne. The heir was his one great-grandson, a delicate boy of five in 1715, who was not expected to live. Accordingly Louis legitimized his children by Madame de Montespan, including the Duke of Maine, and placed them in line of succession. Nevertheless Louis had to make Philip, the Duke of Orleans, regent because he was the King's oldest legitimate male relative, but in his will Louis subjected Orleans' authority to a nominated council, while the Duke of Maine was appointed to the posts of the young King's guardian and commandant of the household troops.

Louis XIV, the sun king

magnificent palace of Versailles,
built by Louis XIV

ceremonious awakening
of Louis by his courtiers

LOUIS XIV OF FRANCE, THE GRAND MONARCH

French soldiers in India negotiating with
an Indian ruler

French traders and clergy
among North American Indians

THE FRENCH IN INDIA AND THE NEW WORLD

Eventually Louis XIV died in September, 1715, but relief rather than grief greeted the news. This relief took the form of a temporary reaction against everything for which he stood—absolutism, persecution, aggression and self-glorification.

Struggle for Power During Orleans' Regency

Philip, Duke of Orleans, was a shrewd and ambitious man whose character had decayed by 1715 through over-indulgence. His first action was to assume full control of the government unhampered by the Council of Regency and his detested rival, the Duke of Maine.

To broaden his political support, Orleans was forced to adopt, purely out of self-interest, a liberal policy. He revived the Parlement of Paris, which gave the middle-class an opportunity to voice opinions, and he elevated the nobility to positions of responsibility.

But as soon as he could, Orleans dispensed with both the Parlement and the help of the nobility. The latter's political inexperience made for inefficiency, and by 1720, with the exiling of the Parlement of Paris, Orleans returned to the absolute government of Louis XIV.

Orleans was now invulnerable. Before 1720 he could have been deposed, particularly by Philip V and the Duke of Maine, who were afraid that in the event of the death of Louis XV, Orleans would gain the crown of France, from which Philip was barred. A conspiracy between these two men was discovered in 1718, and Maine was imprisoned. Orleans now set about preserving the peace.

Orleans attempted to end the religious persecutions which marked Louis XIV's reign. He stopped the persecution of the Jansenists, releasing those who had been imprisoned and appointing a prominent Jansenist, Cardinal Noailles, to be head of the Church council. He initiated negotiations with the Pope to secure the withdrawal of the Papal Bull "*Unigenitus*," but these proved unsuccessful and by 1720 the persecutions of Jansenists were revived.

Similarly, Orleans wanted to end the persecution of the Huguenots but he met with even less success for, in the eyes of Frenchmen, they were not merely heretics but traitors, for they had revolted during the critical stages of the preceding war.

John Law and the Banque Royale

The chief problem, however, facing Orleans was that of the chaotic state of the national finances. So desperate was Orleans that he turned to the schemes proposed by John Law to overcome the mounting national debt.

John Law was the son of an Edinburgh jeweller. He had come to France with new ideas on wealth and currency in an age when banking was in its infancy. The key to his outlook was his belief that a large issue of paper currency would stimulate commerce from which true wealth was derived. He was anxious to substitute paper currency for coin in business transactions and hoped to provide it by a state-sponsored bank. Law first gained the Regent's confidence when he was permitted to establish a private bank, the "*Banque Générale*," which was allowed by the government to issue paper currency redeemable by gold. This bank prospered and in 1718 Law was allowed to make his bank a government institution, the "*Banque Royale*." Law was made the director-general and as such was virtually in control of the national finances. The notes of this bank were now accepted in the payment of taxes.

With the money which Law now had at his command, he formed the "Company of the West and of the Mississippi" in 1717, with the object of developing the vast and largely unknown basin of Louisiana. He bought the monopoly of the trade with Louisiana in return for a loan to the government and then between 1717 and 1719 he bought up the monopolies of the other trading companies, the French East India Company, the Africa Company and the China Company. Thus Law secured virtual control over French commerce.

In return for these monopoly rights, Law's company agreed to make a loan of 1,600 million livres to the state at 3 per cent to pay off the national debt. The government creditors were paid in shares of the company.

With such evidence of the strength of the company, the demand for shares rapidly increased, for people believed they were about to make their fortune. The value of shares increased in fact to forty times their original value. The royal bank recklessly issued more and more paper currency unbacked by bullion. This wave of speculation broke, however, when people began to redeem their notes, for it soon became apparent that the bank lacked the necessary gold to fulfil its obligations. The notes consequently depreciated in value by over 90 per cent by the end of 1720. People who had spent fortunes to purchase shares, or government creditors who had been paid back with shares, now found them valueless. Thousands were ruined. Only a fortunate few who had sold their shares before the collapse, made their fortunes.

Law fled, dying a pauper at Venice. His fundamental error lay in his failure to see that currency was not wealth but a medium of exchange and that public confidence in it was all-important.

The Hanoverians in Britain

In September, 1714, Queen Anne died. Her death created an anxious situation in Britain for there were two claimants to the throne, George, the Elector of Hanover, and James Stuart, the "Old Pretender" and son of James II, the king who had fled the country in 1688.

The possibility of Anne dying without a direct heir had been foreseen by Parliament since 1700 when Anne's last child, the young Duke of Gloucester, had died. To avert the possibility of James Stuart, Anne's half-brother, who had been brought up in exile at Louis XIV's court by his father as a Roman Catholic and as a firm believer in Divine Right, from claiming the throne as his by right, Parliament had passed an "Act of Settlement" in 1701. This had declared that in the event of Anne dying without an heir, the throne would pass to the Hanoverian line of the family.

Thus it was that in 1714 George, already the Elector of Hanover, became King of Britain. George was only acceptable to the nation because he was Protestant, and was prepared to accept the limitation imposed upon the monarch's powers by the Bill of Rights of 1689. In every other respect he was a most unattractive man. He never learned to speak English, and showed little interest in the affairs of Britain except insofar as they affected Hanover.

George I and the Whigs

George recognized that his chief support came from the Whig party whose support was vital since their opponents, the Tories, were too closely identified with the Stuart cause. He accordingly appointed Whig ministers Stanhope, Townshend and Walpole to the principal posts in the government, and his choice was confirmed by the Whig victory in the General Election of 1715 when the Tory majority in parliament, held since 1710, was shattered. For the next half-century the Whigs were to remain in power.

The election result confirmed the belief that the country above all wanted peace. A vote for the Tories was tantamount to one for the Stuarts. Had the Tories been returned, a Stuart restoration might well have been effected, in which case "James III" would certainly have tried to revert to his father's policies of restoring Roman Catholicism and Divine Right government. Such policies could only have resulted in another civil war. To avert this the country gave its support to the Whigs who saw in George I the best guarantee of the 1689 Revolutionary Settlement which had asserted Parliament's ultimate sovereignty over the King in the government of the country.

The Jacobite Rising, 1715

Despite the lessons that could be drawn from the election result the Jacobites still hoped to put James Stuart on the throne. Their leaders, the Earl of Mar in Scotland, Lord Derwentwater and the Duke of Ormonde in England, together with the exiled politicians in France, especially Bolingbroke, plotted throughout 1715.

In the autumn a rising broke out when the respective leaders proclaimed James Stuart as the rightful king. But the complete lack of support was all

The second Jacobite rising failed for lack of French support.

too apparent in Britain. Lord Derwentwater's small force was routed at Preston; Derwentwater and other leaders were executed.

Meanwhile in Scotland Mar proclaimed James at Perth, but when James landed in Scotland six weeks after the indecisive battle of Sheriffmuir, he failed to give the inspired leadership demanded by his disheartened supporters, and within a few weeks he and Mar returned to France.

Apart from the fundamental reason that the nation as a whole gave the Jacobites no support, other contributory factors in their failure were their weak and uninspired leadership and the government's counter-measures. Spies had kept the ministers informed of the conspiracy and they were able to take the necessary counter-measures by posting soldiers in the towns, and dispatching the navy to block any foreign assistance. The death of Louis XIV and the accession of the regent Orleans ended the Jacobites' hope of help from France. Lack of necessary help from Europe was also responsible for the failure of a second Jacobite rising thirty years later, in 1745.

Britain and Europe

Nevertheless, the Whig government was not going to take any chances and their policies both in Britain and in Europe were directed to the consolidation of the Hanoverian dynasty. They realized that peace was essential, especially in order to reduce the national debt, and it was this aim that governed the policies of the Secretaries of State, Townshend and Stanhope.

Peace, too, was necessary if Hanover was to be protected from foreign attack. With a king who was also the Elector of Hanover, it was inevitable

146

that Britain's links with the Continent would be close. The King himself had a keen understanding of European affairs while he was fortunate in having in Stanhope, the Secretary of State for the Southern Department, a man of outstanding ability and experience.

Such qualities were to be very much in demand, for on George's accession Britain was not merely isolated from her former allies because of her "betrayal" of them in the peace negotiations of 1713, but was on the verge of war with Sweden over George's claims to Bremen and Verden.

The Barrier Treaty, 1715

Anglo-Dutch relations were also strained. The Dutch were disappointed and felt betrayed by Britain over the settlement of the barrier fortresses in the Treaty of Utrecht. The great difficulty over these barrier fortresses was the quarrel between the Dutch and the Austrians. The Dutch insisted, as a precaution against any future French invasion, on garrisoning those fortress towns that lay within the Austrian Netherlands. The Austrians, however, felt this to be an infringement upon their sovereignty over the Netherlands.

The British managed to mediate between the Austrians and Dutch and in a new barrier treaty it was agreed that the Austrians would provide three-fifths and the Dutch two-fifths of the garrisons. Britain also made a treaty with the Emperor Charles VI, even though Charles and George were not on good terms. Under the conditions of this treaty, Britain recognized the Emperor's existing possessions.

The Triple Alliance, 1717

The best guarantee for the peace of Europe and the consolidation of the new régimes in Britain and France was, however, this revolutionary alliance, finally negotiated in January, 1717, between Britain, France and Holland. Its principal architects were Stanhope and the Abbé Dubois, the Regent Orleans' confidential adviser, who met secretly at the Hague and then in Hanover. Dubois was really trying to secure from Britain a guarantee for Orleans' succession rights to the French throne, but in the course of the negotiations, he had to pledge France to uphold the whole Utrecht settlement. By agreeing to confirm and maintain the provisions of the Peace of Utrecht, the leading naval and military powers showed their determination to preserve the peace of Europe. That Britain and France should draw together marked a complete break from their traditional opposition to one another. Although the two countries drifted apart during the 1730's and were to be involved in open war after 1744, for the immediate future they were to mediate between the conflicting schemes of Elizabeth Farnese, the ambitious Queen of Spain, and those of the Emperor. These conflicting schemes threatened the peace of the south of Europe. Britain and France mediated also between Charles XII of Sweden and his enemies in the Baltic, an antagonism which threatened the peace of Europe in the north.

The Trouble-Makers

Elizabeth Farnese was Philip V's second wife, whom he married in 1714, and she was to exercise a disturbing influence over Europe for the next thirty years. Cardinal Alberoni, Philip V's chief minister, was the real brain behind Spanish policy, but his schemes were admirably suited to the ideas of his ambitious mistress.

Alberoni was concerned with reviving Spain, which had declined gradually into a second-rate power by the eighteenth century. The expulsion of the Moors by the Inquisition had deprived the country of much of its economic vitality. The lack of any able ruler since the death of Philip II was an important factor in that the *Cortes*, or Parliament, no longer exercised any effective check on royal authority, while the complete hold of the Catholic Church over the lives of the people stifled any chance of reform. Alberoni planned to restore Spain's former greatness by a vigorous policy of internal reform and an aggressive foreign policy.

He attempted to improve agriculture, to found new industries and to reorganize the Treasury and the system of tax-collection, but little real progress was made. Alberoni did not give his reforms a chance to succeed because he was too impatient to revive, at the same time, Spain's influence in Europe.

In particular Alberoni wished to restore to Spain her lost empire in Italy. As an Italian he naturally wished to see the expulsion of the Austrians, and in this he was strongly supported by Elizabeth Farnese. She was determined to secure the succession rights to the duchies of Parma and Tuscany for her two sons, Don Carlos and Don Philip.

Alberoni's plans were bound to conflict with those of the Emperor Charles VI who claimed succession rights to the duchies by the Treaty of Utrecht. In order to further his own plans, therefore, Alberoni schemed to set his opponents at odds with each other. He induced the Turks to attack the Emperor in 1716 so that Austrian armies would have to be diverted to the Hungarian frontier. To hinder Britain, he played upon Charles XII's resentment of George I and managed to secure the Swedish king's promise to prepare an invasion of England in support of the Pretender. In France Alberoni plotted the French Regent's downfall in order to further Philip V's chances of the French throne in the event of Louis XV's death.

Austro-Spanish War, 1717-20

The opportunity to strike at Austria presented itself in August, 1717, when Alberoni took advantage of the arrest of the Spanish Grand Inquisitor by the Austrian authorities in Milan to declare war on the Emperor. A Spanish fleet was immediately dispatched against Sardinia, the Emperor's most vulnerable possession; and then in July, 1718, a second fleet followed up the Spanish success in Sardinia by seizing Sicily, which belonged to the Duke of Savoy. The Spanish troops soon overran the island where the inhabitants welcomed them as liberators, for many of the Sicilians had Spanish blood in their veins as a result of the former Spanish occupation.

This was the limit, however, of Alberoni's success. His plans far from distracting his enemies drew them closer together. Austria now joined the Triple Alliance, making it a quadruple one. The Turks made peace with the Emperor in 1718, thus releasing Austrian armies for the campaigns in the west. Charles XII's death in that year ended any chance of a Swedish-inspired Jacobite invasion of England, and the discovery of the plot to overthrow the Regent led to the expulsion of the Spanish ambassador in August, 1718.

Apart from diplomatic reverses, Spain suffered even more serious naval and military defeats at the hands of the Allies. In August, 1718, the British navy under Admiral Byng destroyed the Spanish fleet off Cape Passaro and so isolated the Spanish army in Sicily. British control of the Mediterranean paralysed any further efforts of Alberoni to conquer Italy, while a French army early in 1719 invaded Spain itself. With disaster imminent, Philip V was induced to dismiss Alberoni in 1719 and to accept Stanhope's scheme to modify the Utrecht settlement. The settlement finally reached in 1720 was a compromise between the conflicting ambitions of Philip V and Charles VI. The Emperor received Sicily in exchange for Sardinia, which went to the Duke of Savoy. The succession rights to Parma and Tuscany were guaranteed to Elizabeth Farnese's sons. Both Philip V and Charles VI mutually guaranteed each others' possessions and Philip again renounced the French throne. This settlement was a triumph for Stanhope's mediation on behalf of the cause of peace.

Settlement of the North, 1719-21

The settlement of the Baltic, which took place between 1719 and 1721, brought to a close the Great Northern War which had been waged since 1700 between Sweden under her ambitious warrior, King Charles XII, and the neighbouring Baltic countries—Russia under Peter the Great, Prussia, Poland, Hanover and Denmark.

The struggle was essentially one for the domination of the Baltic, and it was therefore bound to be the concern of all the Powers.

When Charles XII died in 1718, Sweden was ready for peace. Her resources were exhausted, and the danger existed that Russia would take advantage of this weakness to extinguish her once and for all. Therefore, agreements

149

were reached between Sweden and her enemies Hanover, Prussia, Poland and Denmark by a series of treaties between 1719 and 1720.

Freed from these enemies, Sweden was to remain isolated in face of Russia, for in 1720, Britain was paralysed by the South Sea financial crisis and the resulting death of Stanhope. Russia was able to invade Sweden and dictate the Peace of Nystadt of 1721. This treaty marked the transference of power in the Baltic from Sweden to Russia. Sweden was stripped of Livonia, Estonia, Ingria and Carelia, and only recovered Finland. From the great days of the seventeenth century under a succession of warrior kings, Sweden, in the eighteenth century, rapidly declined into a satellite state dominated by either France or Russia.

The Emperor's Plans

The statesmen of Britain, especially Stanhope, and of France, especially Dubois, can claim much credit for settling the outstanding trouble-spots of Europe in the years following the peace of Utrecht.

Unfortunately issues still existed which continued to threaten this peace after 1720. To settle these an international meeting was called for 1721, but the Congress of Cambrai, when it finally got down to serious discussion, made very little progress.

Among the outstanding issues were the ambitions of Emperor Charles VI. Charles VI was primarily concerned in securing from all rulers the recognition of his daughter, Maria Theresa's right to succeed to an undivided Hapsburg Empire. His only son having died in 1716, Charles published in 1724 a decree, the "Pragmatic Sanction," in which he asserted Maria Theresa's rights. He now sought the assent of all rulers, a task which occupied him until his death in 1740. So important was this assent to him that the other European rulers took advantage by extracting many concessions from him in return for their guarantees.

While most of the German princes readily agreed, some were unwilling. Charles Albert of Bavaria, the husband of the elder daughter of the previous Emperor Joseph I, and Frederick Augustus II, Elector of Saxony, husband

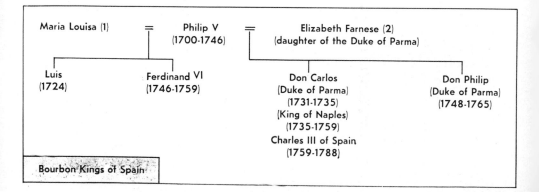

Maria Louisa (1) = Philip V = Elizabeth Farnese (2)
(1700-1746) (daughter of the Duke of Parma)

Luis (1724) — Ferdinand VI (1746-1759) — Don Carlos (Duke of Parma) (1731-1735) (King of Naples) (1735-1759) Charles III of Spain (1759-1788) — Don Philip (Duke of Parma) (1748-1765)

Bourbon Kings of Spain

Sir Robert Walpole (1676-1745).   *Cardinal Fleury (1653-1743).*

of Joseph I's younger daughter, both claimed they were the heirs to the Hapsburg lands through their wives.

Another of Charles VI's ambitions which caused trouble between the Emperor and the maritime powers of Britain and Holland was his attempt to revive the trade of the Austrian Netherlands. He established in 1722 an Ostend East India Trading Company to which he subscribed six million gulden in return for six per cent of the profits. The British and Dutch merchants vigorously protested, fearing the competition to their own trade.

Italy was still the bone of contention between Spain and the Empire. The Emperor resented ever having had to sign a treaty sacrificing his claims on Parma and Tuscany, and he now contrived to hamper Elizabeth Farnese in her efforts to put Don Carlos, her son, on the throne of Tuscany. This he sought to do by keeping out Spanish troops which alone could enforce Don Carlos' claims.

Ripperda's Proposals

By 1724 Elizabeth Farnese was impatient of reaching any satisfactory settlement at the abortive congress of Cambrai, and decided to enter into direct negotiations with the Emperor. Accordingly she chose as her special envoy Ripperda, a Dutchman, who has been described as a "projecting, speculating, enterprising, inconsiderate hot-headed fellow with great views rather than great parts." At Vienna he made certain daring, if impracticable proposals, such as the marriage of Elizabeth Farnese's two sons, Don Carlos and Don Philip, to the Emperor's two daughters, Maria Theresa and Maria Anna. Such marriages, had they ever come about, would have meant the

151

division of the Hapsburg possessions between Elizabeth Farnese's two sons.

The reconciliation of the Emperor and Elizabeth Farnese was made easier by an unexpected insult administered by France to Spain. In February, 1725, the Spanish Infanta, Philip V's young daughter, who had been betrothed to Louis XV, was returned to Spain by the regent, the Duke of Bourbon, because she was not yet of marriageable age. The Duke of Bourbon was anxious for the sixteen year old Louis XV to marry immediately in order to provide an heir as soon as possible. Should Louis XV die childless, the French throne would pass to the son of Bourbon's great rival, the late Duke of Orleans. To avert this, Bourbon secured the marriage of Louis XV to Marie Leczinska, the daughter of Stanislas the ex-king of Poland.

First Treaty of Vienna, 1725

The return of the Spanish Infanta was regarded as a deep affront by the outraged Elizabeth Farnese. The immediate effect was to hasten an agreement between the Emperor and Philip V, and in April, 1725, the First Treaty of Vienna was signed. The Emperor renounced all his claims on Philip's dominions, promised the succession of the Duchies to Don Carlos, and aid to Spain in the recovery of Gibraltar. In return Philip gave up his demand to garrison the Duchies with Spanish troops, confirmed the Emperor's rights to Naples and Sicily, supported the Ostend East India Company and guaranteed the Pragmatic Sanction. The Emperor also agreed to the proposed marriage of Don Carlos with Maria Theresa.

When news broke of this surprising alliance between two rival courts, the rest of Europe was alarmed. France feared that Austria and Spain were trying to "encircle" her, especially if the proposed marriage should take place. Britain and Holland were concerned about Spain's support of the Ostend East India Company, while Philip V's demand, made in 1725, for the return of Gibraltar threatened the key to Britain's control of the Mediterranean.

The League of Hanover, 1725

In order to meet the threat implied in the Austro-Spanish alliance, a counter-alliance was brought into being to maintain the settlement of Europe. The League of Hanover, created in September, 1725, was composed of Britain, France, Hanover, Prussia, Holland, Sweden and Denmark.

War seemed a very real possibility between the two hostile groups. In 1727 Spain actually declared war, but the Emperor was reluctant to fulfil his obligations to help Spain recover Gibraltar. War was averted by the leading ministers of France and Britain. In 1727 Cardinal Fleury succeeded the Duke of Bourbon in France, and the accession of George II provided Walpole with the opportunity of asserting his pacific policies in spite of the opposition of his more militant brother-in-law, Townshend. With Fleury and Walpole in control, the two leading powers of western Europe were able to save the peace.

Equally important in saving the peace were the incompatible aims of Charles VI and Philip V. The first Treaty of Vienna was to prove a short-lived marriage between two mutually irreconcilable and uncompromising partners. The Emperor was not prepared to give effective military support to the Spanish blockade of Gibraltar, nor was he prepared to fulfil his promise of allowing Maria Theresa to be betrothed to Don Carlos. Instead, he entered into some secret negotiations to secure the betrothal of his daughter to Duke Francis of Lorraine. When Elizabeth Farnese discovered this, she broke with the Emperor and turned back to Britain and France. The birth of the Dauphin in France in 1729 removed any further possibility of Philip acquiring the French throne, and so the way was cleared for the reconciliation between the two Bourbon powers. Britain, Spain and France settled their differences in the Treaty of Seville (1729), in which Spain agreed to restore the trading privileges of British merchants with the Spanish dominions, to end those she had granted to the Ostend East India Company and to raise the siege of Gibraltar. In return Britain and France supported Spain's claim to assert Don Carlos' succession rights to the Duchies.

Second Treaty of Vienna, 1731

This guarantee was put to the test two years later when the old Duke of Parma died. The Emperor sent in Austrian troops to occupy Parma. War seemed inevitable once again between Spain and the Emperor. Spain appealed to Britain and France for support according to the Treaty of Seville. Walpole once more was to save the situation by his master-stroke in diplomacy, the second Treaty of Vienna, between George II and the Emperor. George II, both as King of Britain and Elector of Hanover, agreed to guarantee the Pragmatic Sanction but in return for this coveted signature, the Emperor had to make an important concession. He agreed to allow Don Carlos, escorted by Spanish troops, to enter Parma and Tuscany. They were, in fact, transported to Italy by the British navy in December, 1731. The Emperor also suspended the Ostend East India Company.

War of the Polish Succession, 1733-38

France and Britain, working in close alliance, had saved the peace up to 1731, but from this date onwards a gradual rift between the two powers developed with disastrous consequences for Europe. Though Walpole and Fleury were still working for peace and internal prosperity, they were both subjected to the growing opposition of men seeking to revive the traditional policies that had convulsed Europe during Louis XIV's reign.

The immediate danger came from the war party in France led by Marshal Villars and Count Chauvelin. This was the party which clamoured for a return to the "glorious days" of Louis XIV. These men used their considerable influence to revive anti-Imperial alliances between the princes of the Empire and France in order to exploit a weakened Germany, and to strengthen the bonds between France and Spain in order to check the growing commercial and colonial power of their common rival, Britain.

The anti-Imperial and anti-British themes of the French and Spanish Bourbon policies were to dominate the story of European affairs for the rest of the century.

An essential part of France's traditional anti-Imperial policies lay in establishing French influence in the three weak states bordering on the Empire's north, east and south-eastern frontiers, namely Sweden, Poland and Turkey. The establishment of French influence in eastern Europe was bound to alarm not only the Emperor, but also Russia. In 1726 an alliance between Austria and Russia was concluded to rebuff French diplomacy, for in this alliance Austria and Russia agreed to act together in Poland to prevent it from falling under French influence.

Poland was, despite its territorial size, the weakest state in Europe. The elective nature of its monarchy produced a European crisis whenever a Polish king died, for the choice of his successor was a matter which vitally concerned the interests of the great powers. Such a crisis occurred when Augustus II died in February, 1733.

France supported the election of Stanislas, who was Louis XV's father-in-law. This was cause enough for Louis and his court to feel a desire to further Stanislas' candidature in order to secure French influence on the eastern frontier of the Empire.

Since Austria and Russia had their own candidate, Augustus III, son of the dead king, it soon became obvious that they would resist France. Fleury directed French diplomacy into building up an anti-Imperial alliance, for the conflict over Poland was to serve as a pretext for a greater struggle. In September, 1733, Fleury gained an alliance with the Duke of Savoy who was promised Milan in return for his support in the forthcoming struggle. Fleury also negotiated a treaty with Bavaria, and one with the Dutch guaranteeing French neutrality in the Netherlands so that neither Britain nor Holland should have cause to go to the Emperor's aid. Most important of all his diplomatic preparations was the First Family Compact which he negotiated in November, 1733, with Spain. By this compact France and Spain agreed to combine to expel the Austrians from Italy and to check the commercial policies of Britain.

While French diplomacy was seeking to strengthen France, Stanislas was smuggled across Europe to Warsaw where the Polish nobles, influenced by

Château at Fontainebleau, built during the reign of Louis XIV.

French bribes, elected him king in September, 1733. This was too much for the eastern Powers. Two weeks later Russian and Saxon armies invaded Poland to protect the "freedom of election," and with the aid of their bayonets the Polish Diet was induced to elect Augustus III who was already the Elector of Saxony. Stanislas fled from Warsaw to Danzig which Russian armies besieged. The following June, when the town surrendered, Stanislas fled to France disguised as a sailor. France had been unable to give him effective military aid, not only because of the difficulties involved in sending and supplying an army so far from her frontiers, but also because her armies were preoccupied in fighting the Austrians both on the Rhine and in northern Italy after war was declared on Austria by France, Spain and Savoy in October, 1733. The Polish issue was but one aspect of a much larger conflict that now developed between the Hapsburgs, supported by Russia and some German princes, and the Bourbons of France and Spain, supported by Savoy.

Britain's policy throughout was that of remaining free from any continental entanglements. It was Walpole's proud boast to Queen Caroline at the end of 1734 that although 50,000 men had been killed in one year, not one of them was British. Walpole refused to honour his obligation under the Second Treaty of Vienna to defend the Hapsburg lands, with the result that Britain lost both influence and prestige in European affairs.

Although the Polish issue had been speedily settled in the Emperor's favour, elsewhere his armies were beaten back and his lands invaded. On the Rhine, French armies captured Kehl and Philippsburg, two important towns, in 1734.

Meanwhile in northern Italy, the French, Sardinian and Spanish armies succeeded in overrunning the Milanese. This was the limit of their success for quarrels broke out between the Spanish and the Sardinians.

In southern Italy the Spanish forces of Count Montemar coming from Tuscany swept through Naples and Sicily, brushing aside the feeble Austrian opposition. This triumphant march came to a climax in July, 1735, when Don Carlos was crowned King of the Two Sicilies at Palermo, thus founding a Spanish Bourbon dynasty which was to last until Garibaldi and his "Thousand Redshirts" in a similar triumphant procession in 1860 swept it away.

Third Treaty of Vienna, 1738

For the following three years, each of the anti-Imperial powers entered into secret negotiations at Vienna, hoping to steal a march on their "allies." Eventually in November, 1738, the Third Treaty of Vienna was signed. Augustus III was recognized as King of Poland, but Stanislas renounced the throne "voluntarily and for the sake of peace," which implied that his election had been legal. As compensation for the loss of Poland, Stanislas was given Lorraine and Bar, which on his death were to go to his daughter, the Queen of Louis XV, and therefore in practice to France. This was a great triumph for Fleury's diplomacy since Lorraine was to be a valuable addition to France's eastern frontier.

The Powers recognized the transference of Naples and Sicily from the Emperor to Don Carlos, but this gain was counterbalanced by Don Carlos having to surrender Parma to the Emperor, and Tuscany to Francis the Duke of Lorraine as compensation for the loss of Lorraine to Stanislas. Francis was further compensated by his marriage to Maria Theresa, which made him the heir to the Hapsburg lands. Elizabeth Farnese particularly resented the loss of these two duchies, for she still wanted to provide for her younger son Don Philip.

To the Emperor perhaps the most important gain was that France acknowledged the Pragmatic Sanction, but this guarantee was soon to prove a dead letter, though during the treaty negotiations, Fleury had made good use of it as a bargaining counter in carrying off the prize of Lorraine in this masterstroke of French diplomacy.

QUESTIONS

1. Discuss the policy at home and abroad of the Duke of Orleans and his counsellors during the regency period.
2. What were the main threats to peace in the period 1713-31?

CHAPTER 19

RISE OF RUSSIA
AND DECLINE OF SWEDEN

THE true founder of modern Russia was Peter the Great. In the first quarter of the eighteenth century he transformed Russia, ending her isolation from European influence, and setting trends of a policy which, followed by his successors, made Russia a leading European power.

The Tsardom of Muscovy, as Russia was originally known, was centred on Moscow and the River Volga. It included Astrakhan and the middle Volga regions which had been conquered by the first Tsar, Ivan the Terrible, in the middle of the sixteenth century. During this and the following centuries an eastward expansion had led to the acquisition of the Urals and Siberia. The northern frontier stretched to the White Sea, and included Archangel. This port was the one direct outlet to western Europe, as the Swedes controlled the Baltic, but Archangel was frozen for six months of the year. The western frontier stretched to the fortress town of Smolensk, on the Dnieper, and the southern frontiers were vague.

Though huge in extent, the vast tracts of tundra, forest or steppe lands were thinly populated by some eight million people. Over them ruled the Tsar, whose power was absolute. Society was feudal, and birth and wealth were still the hallmarks of social classes. It was only in the frontier districts that people were freer.

Towns were small, and although the townsfolk were freemen they were hampered by regulations. Merchants and traders formed a very small, despised fraction of the total population, yet there were signs of a growth in their importance towards the end of the seventeenth century as trade and industry began to develop. The chief wealth of Russia lay in its hides, flax, furs and timber which found their way west through Archangel.

Contacts with the West were growing, although the great mass of people were still untouched by this new awareness of the civilizing influence of Europe. The Asiatic influence of the Tartars and the Greek Orthodox Church contributed to this isolation.

In the late seventeenth century the Greek Orthodox Church was split, following the condemnation of the "Old Believers" by the official Church.

157

The "Old Believers" were those who had refused to accept the liturgical reforms introduced in the seventeenth century by the Patriarch Nikon, and they set themselves against the growing westernizing tendencies of Russian leaders. They were persecuted by the ecclesiastical and secular authorities, which persecution in turn fanned the extremes of religious fanaticism. As many as twenty thousand "Old Believers" saved their souls by sacrificing themselves deliberately in the flames of funeral pyres. They opposed not only the Patriarch but the Tsar.

Thus, when Peter became Tsar, he found himself at the head of a country deeply divided on religious and cultural questions, but which was beginning to emerge from its long isolation from the rest of western Europe.

Peter the Great—Ancestry and Character

Peter, born in 1672, was the son of Tsar Alexis and his second wife. He had two half-brothers, Theodore and Ivan, and a half-sister Sophia. With the death of Alexis, Theodore succeeded to the throne, but died in 1682. Both Ivan and Peter were too young to assume power, and bitter rivalries existed between the two families of their respective mothers. The *Stryeltsky*, a privileged corps of musketeers, supported Ivan, but eventually the two boys were proclaimed joint Tsars, with their sister Sophia as Regent.

Peter, in contrast with the weak and ailing Ivan, was, in the words of a foreign envoy, "a youth of great expectancy, prudence and vigour. His stature is great and his mien is fine. He has such a strong preference for military pursuits that when he comes of age we may surely expect from him brave actions and heroic deeds." Tall, strong and restless, Peter possessed mental qualities to match these physical ones, being highly intelligent, inquisitive, determined and passionate. He was a born craftsman, keenly interested in military and technical matters. His interest in the sea originated from his boyhood love of sailing and boat building.

Before coming to the throne, Peter was busy developing his interests and experiences, travelling incessantly. On trips to Archangel he visited and worked in the shipyards, and sailed on the White Sea. He mixed with foreigners and men of all classes, and he played as hard as he worked. He loved to play the crudest kinds of practical jokes and spent days in orgies of riotous and drunken living.

Campaign Against Turkey

Peter's assumption of power in 1695, following the death of his half-brother, was marked by the outbreak of war against the Turkish Empire. At this time the Turkish Empire extended along the north coast of the Black Sea where the Crimean Tartars lived. These people had proved troublesome neighbours. Accordingly Peter organized a land expedition against the

Peter building a fleet

blockade of Azov by Russian galleys, 1696

Stryeltsky rising crushed by Peter in 1698

Peter visits London, 1697

Peter cutting the beards of his boyars

St. Petersburg, Russia's window on the west

EVENTS IN THE LIFE OF PETER THE GREAT

Russian rich

serfs being used as beasts of burden

Cossacks, fierce horsemen

Orthodox Church, an important part of Russian life

icon, or holy image

magnificent court reception given by Catherine the Great

SCENES FROM EIGHTEENTH-CENTURY RUSSIA

Turkish fortress of Azov, which was not successful at the first attempt, but the following year Peter attacked again by sea and the garrison surrendered.

The vital lesson of sea power was not lost upon Peter. Russia was still a landlocked power, and its people lacked the necessary maritime knowledge and naval skills. The immense task of building a navy might have daunted a lesser man, but to Peter, who was keenly interested, it represented a challenge. It was to the maritime nations of the West, notably Holland and England, that Peter looked for guidance.

The Great Embassy, 1697-98

In 1697 Peter and a party of Russians first visited western Europe travelling via Prussia and Denmark to Holland. At Amsterdam this party spent a profitable time in the shipyards. After five months they sailed to England and visited the naval dockyards at Chatham and Portsmouth. Peter then moved to Vienna where he concluded an alliance with the Emperor directed against the Turks. However this was to prove a failure, for the Emperor was anxious to conclude peace with the Turks as rapidly as possible in order to concentrate his attention upon the Spanish question, and in 1699 made the peace of Carlowitz. Peter's mission was abruptly ended by the news of the revolt of the *Stryeltsky* regiments.

The trip had been remarkable. It was the first time that a Russian Tsar had left his country. It confirmed Peter in his determination that Russians would have to be sent abroad for their education. The experience convinced him too of the superiority of the West in every aspect—army, navy, culture, trade, industry and administration. Even his coarse and awkward manners improved by his contact with the civilizing influences of the West.

On his return to Russia in October, 1698, Peter's immediate task was to crush the *Stryeltsky*, and this he did with his accustomed thoroughness. Resolved to avoid any future rising, he mercilessly avenged himself with a bloodbath of public executions, during the course of which some twelve hundred of his palace guard perished, while many others were sent to Siberia. He did not even spare his own wife Catherine and half-sister, Sophia, suspected of helping the conspirators, for they were shut away in a convent.

Reform

One of the first things Peter did on returning to Moscow was to launch an attack on the external symbols of Oriental life. He ordered nobles to shave off their beards and personally used shears on any reluctant peer. They had to adopt German or Hungarian style of dress in place of the long robes so characteristic of the East, and those who refused to adopt these new styles found they had to pay extra taxation. Peasants and clergy were exempt. These reforms aroused deep hostility amongst many, for the beard was of religious significance. He set aside the *Terem*, the custom by which women were secluded from public life. Smoking, hitherto banned, was encouraged partly because of the money it brought in for the government from the tobacco monopoly, partly because it was an outward sign of western habits.

Peter also attempted to reorganize local government, but the task that chiefly occupied him was that of ship-building. In this he employed his foreign shipwrights collected during his western travels. Keels of ships-of-the-line, frigates, galleys and transports were laid down and by 1699 he had fourteen warships. This number was to increase to fifty by the end of his reign. The army, too, was reformed.

The needs of the army and navy prompted the development of a whole range of dependent industries, and most of the reforms Peter introduced were designed to meet these defence needs, but being essentially practical, Peter introduced reforms when and where they were needed rather than to fulfil a prearranged programme. This was especially true of Peter's early years for he was, after 1700, to be preoccupied in a life and death struggle with Sweden. It is to this struggle that we now must turn.

Struggle for Baltic Supremacy

In dealing with Peter's struggle with Charles XII of Sweden it is first essential to set the conflict in its proper perspective. The dominant theme of the history of north eastern Europe between 1648 and 1721 is the struggle for the control of the Baltic. Besides Russia and Sweden, other powers namely Denmark, Brandenburg and Poland, were vitally interested. The two Great Northern Wars of 1655-60 and 1700-21 were the inevitable outcome of the rivalry that existed among the Baltic powers. The internal history of these countries was profoundly influenced by the result of these conflicts. Brandenburg was to take the place of Poland on the Prussian coast while Sweden, who had, as we have seen, by the middle of the seventeenth century wrested control of the Baltic from Denmark, was to surrender her predominance to Russia and Prussia (as Brandenburg became known after 1701) by 1721. The one thread of continuity in these rivalries is the rise and fall of Sweden under a line of remarkable warrior kings. By 1648 Sweden's imperialistic success had been so complete that she had aroused the enmity of all her Baltic rivals, but her own internal resources were too limited to permit her successfully to fight off the challenge to her supremacy represented by the Great Northern War.

Great Northern War, 1655-60

Charles X, who succeeded to the Swedish throne in 1654, used an imagined slight by the Polish King, John Casimir, as a pretext for invading Poland in 1655. This marked the opening of the first Great Northern War. His armies met with little military resistance, and swept through Poland.

Meanwhile, the Danes threatened to recover control of the Sound, so Charles withdrew his forces from Poland and in 1657 invaded Denmark. He overran the main part of the country, but the islands held out until they were captured following a remarkable winter campaign during which Charles made good his lack of a fleet by marching his troops over the frozen sea. After the resulting Peace of Roskilde, Charles renewed war with Denmark, determined to press home his advantage. But at this point Britain and Holland, who depended upon the Baltic for their naval stores, intervened. A Dutch fleet sent to assist the Danes, combined with the death of Charles X, made peace possible.

As the heir, Charles XI, was only four years old, it was left to the Regency to conclude the peace treaties of Oliva and Copenhagen. In the Treaty of Oliva, John Casimir renounced all claim to the Swedish throne and confirmed Swedish control of Livonia. He also confirmed Frederick William the Elector of Brandenburg's sovereign rights over East Prussia, a district previously held by the Elector as a fief of the Polish Crown. In the Treaty of Copenhagen, Denmark renounced Scania and Halland to Sweden but recovered the island of Bornholm.

Between 1660-1700 the Baltic countries were concerned with internal struggles between the monarchy and nobility, and there was comparative peace. Strong monarchies were to emerge in Denmark, Brandenburg, Poland and Sweden.

Denmark, Prussia and Poland

In 1661 the Danish monarchy became hereditary and absolute under Frederick III, a development thought necessary in order to strengthen the country to meet the growing threat to her security from troublesome nobles and from Sweden following the latter's victories over her. And we shall see, in a later chapter, how Frederick William, the Great Elector of Brandenburg, was laying the basis for his country's future greatness by establishing a strong centralized government.

Poland, too, was fortunate to have in John Sobieski a king who exercised more effective power than any of his predecessors or successors, yet he failed to reform the elective nature of the monarchy because of the refusal of the Polish nobles in the diet to sacrifice their powers. The nobles' retention of power ultimately led to the dismemberment of Poland in the following century.

Sweden

During Charles XI's minority the nobles had returned to power, and Sweden had fallen under French influence. The crushing defeat of Swedish troops at Fehrbellin (1675) by the Great Elector of Brandenburg, and the subsequent disastrous campaign in Pomerania, marked the beginning of Sweden's military decline.

These disasters were blamed upon the Regency and enabled Charles XI to assume complete power in 1682. He devoted the remainder of his reign, which lasted until 1697, to checking the power of the nobility by a policy of "reductions," by which the nobles had to restore estates taken from the Crown. He avoided rash military enterprises, and by reorganizing the treasury, the fleet and the army he made possible the military exploits of his more celebrated son, Charles XII, who was to squander the national resources of manpower and wealth in the pursuit of military glory. It was unfortunate for Sweden that Charles XII did not possess the same temperament as his father, for Sweden might well have remained a great power.

Great Northern War, 1700-21

Charles XII, only fifteen years old at the time of his accession in 1697, was the descendant of a line of kings who owed their fortunes to war. A violent and vigorous man of action, he enjoyed riding horses to death, and testing the sharpness of his sword on the throats of dogs and sheep. Tall, fierce-eyed and long-nosed, he had immense powers of endurance and self-control. Deeply religious yet fatalistic, he was a true warrior king, inspired by the exploits of Alexander the Great.

Meanwhile, an anti-Swedish coalition had been formed, composed of Saxony, Denmark, and Russia. The Empire and western powers were occupied with the Problem of the Spanish Succession. Augustus, Elector of Saxony and King of Poland, was the architect of this coalition and he was urged on by Patkul, a refugee noble from Livonia who had been declared a traitor by Charles XI. Denmark and Saxony both wished to acquire ports on the Baltic, and Peter wished to regain Russian territory lost to Sweden. Determined to avoid a war on two fronts, he waited until the day he signed a peace treaty with the Turks to declare war on Sweden. At this untimely moment, Denmark was being overrun by Swedish troops.

Narva and Poltava

While Charles XII's armies were overrunning Denmark, the Saxon and Russian armies were in Livonia where Augustus was besieging Riga. Peter, with another Russian army, was laying siege to Narva. Charles marched to the relief of this garrison, and though outnumbered five to one, he gained a resounding victory. This setback showed Peter the need for a well-trained army, and he began military reforms immediately. At the same time he gave Augustus sufficient assistance to keep the Swedes occupied in Poland, so that his reorganization would go on unhampered.

Charles entered Poland where he dethroned Augustus, and then he defeated Saxony. Patkul was handed over to the Swedes and broken on the wheel. In 1706 Charles, at the height of his power, was sought as an ally by France and other important western powers, but in the meantime Peter the Great had acquired Livonia, Estonia, Karelia and Ingria. So confident was Peter that he laid the foundations in 1703 of a new capital, St. Petersburg, which was to be his "window on the West."

When the Duke of Marlborough visited Charles' headquarters in Saxony to seek his support, he had noticed a large map of Russia which convinced him of the fruitlessness of his mission. He was soon proved right. Charles' eyes were turned not to the West but towards the East, and in the autumn of 1707 he embarked upon his disastrous Russian campaign, determined to overthrow Peter, his one unvanquished foe.

Charles' aim was to capture Moscow, but when he had reached Smolensk he realized that this was impracticable. Accordingly he turned south towards the Ukraine, where he had hope of the aid of the Cossack rebel Mazeppa. But during the severe winter of 1708-9, twenty thousand Swedes perished, and the remainder, tattered and sick, were demoralized. Mazeppa arrived with insufficient troops, and in May, 1709, Charles laid siege to the fortress town of Poltava in the hopes of relieving the desperate plight of his army.

During this siege, on his twenty-seventh birthday, Charles was wounded in the foot. Meanwhile, Peter had marched to the relief of the garrison, but although vastly superior in numbers and equipment he had such enormous respect for Charles that he hesitated to attack until he heard that Charles was wounded. This news emboldened Peter, and led to the battle of June 28. The Swedes fought heroically, but the odds were too great. Five thousand Swedish soldiers were killed, and the rest routed. Charles was taken to the Turkish fortress of Bender, where he was to remain an unwelcome guest, occupying most of his time in playing chess, for the next five years.

Poltava was one of the decisive battles of history, marking a turning point in the Great Northern War, which in turn resulted in Russia replacing Sweden as the leading Baltic power. Peter's work in reorganizing the army had been justified and his international reputation was enormously increased. He was now able to renew the anti-Swedish coalition with the additional support of Prussia and Hanover, while Augustus was reinstated as King of Poland.

The following year Peter also cleared the Swedes from Livonia, Estonia, and southern Finland.

Russo-Turkish War, 1711

Meanwhile Charles XII at Bender used his influence to persuade the Sultan, who hoped to recover Azov, to declare war on Russia. Threatened with this fresh danger Peter raised new armies. Proposing to sweep through the Turkish provinces of Moldavia and Wallachia, and posing as liberator of the Balkan Christians from their Moslem masters, Peter called upon them to revolt. Although he succeeded in gaining support from Moldavia, his army was outnumbered when he met the Turks at Stanileshte on the River Pruth. Without striking a blow Peter yielded, agreeing to surrender Azov and all his previous Turkish conquests and to allow the return of Charles XII to Sweden. Although a humiliating end to his southern project, Peter had saved his army from destruction.

Returning north, Peter campaigned in Poland and Pomerania, besieging Stettin, which fell in 1713. He then spent the next two years in Finland where his navy gained its first decisive victory over the Swedes and so contributed to the success of the military campaigns.

Last Years of Charles XII

Charles meanwhile had been proving a very awkward guest of the Turks. Refusing to leave although paid £10,000 to do so, Charles was only dislodged from his residence after an eight-hour siege by 10,000 Turks during the course of which they lost 200 men. Charles inspired so much respect that his life was spared. Finally in 1714 he returned to Stralsund, one of the few remnants of Sweden's empire, but even this fell to the combined armies of the reconstituted anti-Swedish alliance. Charles still refused to make peace and so ruined any possibility of retrieving some of his losses by playing upon the bitter jealousies that existed amongst his enemies, who had no desire to see Russia replace Sweden as the dominant power.

End of the Great Northern War

The death of Charles XII in December, 1718, when besieging a castle in Norway removed a major obstacle to peace. Ulrica Eleanora's accession was a signal for the return of the nobles to political power, and for an overwhelming demand for peace to allow the country to recover from the ruinous war which had overtaxed Sweden's strength. Sweden had lost almost a third of her male population, while her financial state was chaotic. Fortunately for Sweden her enemies were divided by their fear of Russia.

In the series of treaties that were signed between Sweden and Denmark, Prussia, Poland and Hanover, the British statesman, Carteret, played a major role, for Britain was equally concerned in keeping a right balance in the Baltic to safeguard her own sources of naval supplies. Sweden lost Bremen and Verden to Hanover, who paid her compensation. Prussia acquired Western Pomerania, including Stettin. Sweden lost Schleswig to Denmark and renounced her rights over the "Sound Dues."

Alone in the face of Russia, Sweden was forced to accept the Peace of

Death of Charles XII, marking the end of Sweden's greatness.

Nystadt in 1721, in which Peter's Baltic conquests were confirmed. Only Finland was restored to Sweden and Peter had secured his "window on the West."

Thus ended the struggle for the Baltic. Sweden henceforward rapidly declined to a satellite state dependent upon France or Russia who intrigued with one or other of the two groups of nobles, the "Hats" or "Caps," who held effective power. In contrast Russia under Peter, who now proclaimed himself "Emperor of all the Russias," had emerged as a great European power.

Peter the Great's Domestic Policy

In a very real sense Peter was the creator of Russia. He personally played a major role in drawing up reforms which affected the civil and religious administration as well as the lives of all his subjects.

In 1711, eleven years after he had dispensed with the old council of nobles, Peter created a Senate which, presided over by himself, was to become the principal organ of the central government. To relieve the Senate of excess work and to leave it free to decide on general policy, Peter later established nine Colleges each of which was responsible for the detailed work of a particular department of government.

Provincial administration was also reformed. To decentralize the country Peter had originally created ten provincial governments, but he later re-arranged the system and created fifty provinces, subdivided into districts, with each province ruled by a local, elected council. And, in an effort to develop a public-spirited middle-class, Peter reformed municipal government, with each town administered by members chosen from guilds which comprised all the townsfolk.

Originally, the needs of war inspired this new efficiency in government, but later Peter became anxious to promote justice and public-mindedness among his subjects. He made attempts to impose these essentially foreign concepts on the Russian way of life. His idea of an honest and efficient civil service was not recognized, because fear of punishment was Peter's only method of enforcing his will in a society which had not been educated to the ideal of public service.

Religious Reforms

Although he had broken loose from the traditional religious ceremonies surrounding the Tsars, Peter was a deeply religious man who appreciated that the Church had a vital role to play in the government of his subjects. He began to divert the surplus revenue of the enormously wealthy Church towards education and other charitable purposes.

Peter also overhauled the administration of the Church, placing it in the control of a Synod, whose president was under the control of the Tsar. As the Church was divided at this time between the official believers and the "Old Believers," Peter's task of reorganization was made easier. He also improved ecclesiastical discipline and behaviour among the clergy, and founded schools, hospitals, and almshouses. In addition, he was prepared to tolerate all shades of religious beliefs except Jews and Jesuits, provided the security of the state was not endangered. Besides the "Old Believers," Peter had Protestant and Catholic subjects, many of whom were foreigners working in the service of Russia.

Peter and the Landowners

Peter was to impose upon the landowners the duty of service to the State to an extent never previously attempted. Land-owning involved duties as well as rights and landowners were compelled to serve in either the army, navy or civil service. In 1722 he established a "table of ranks" which classified into fourteen grades all civil ranks with their military or naval equivalents.

Length of service and merit rather than birth or wealth were now the criteria for promotion. Peter abolished the old laws of inheritance whereby property was divided equally among the sons and substituted the law of primogeniture, whereby the estates passed down to the eldest son. By preventing the break-up of estates he aimed at maintaining a prosperous land-holding class, while the landless members of the nobility were encouraged to enter state service. This law however produced so much opposition that it was abandoned soon after Peter's death.

Nobles entering state service had to be efficient. Parties of young nobles were sent abroad to study western military, naval and administrative institutions. His efforts to compel landowners to send their sons to school in one of the many military or naval academies which were established, produced so much opposition that he was forced to abandon his ideal of compulsory elementary education.

Peter and the Peasants

Peter's attempts to form a nobility of service were broadly successful because he made no attempt to weaken their power over the peasants. Peter was, rather, to strengthen the landowners' authority over them, abolishing many of the peasants' legal rights and so reducing them all to the status of serfs. They had duties now both to their lords and to the State, and many were killed during their compulsory military service. A poll tax enforced by threat of death added to their financial burdens, which were three times as heavy at the end of Peter's reign as at the beginning. Not surprisingly, Peter's efforts to improve agriculture were not effective, for the peasants had other things to occupy their attention.

Financial and Industrial Reforms

Not tied to any economic doctrine Peter nevertheless realized that the power of the State rested on a healthy economy. His financial, commercial and industrial reforms were directed to this end. Many new taxes were imposed, such as those on salt, tobacco, beards and coffins. High import tariffs were introduced partly as a source of revenue and partly to protect the new industries which he founded. In some cases the needs of the war were responsible for this economic growth.

To stimulate trade Peter linked up the Black Sea with the Baltic by a canal system connecting the Volga and Neva rivers through Lake Ladoga. The founding of St. Petersburg and the acquisition of Vibourg, Reval and Riga provided far more suitable ports than Archangel which was frozen for some six months each year.

The Last Years

Peter's appetite was not satisfied by his gains at the expense of Sweden. After his victory in the Baltic, Peter looked south-east in particular towards the rich silk trade of the Persian-controlled Caspian provinces in order to forestall the Turks who had similar aims. In 1722 he declared war on the crumbling Persian Empire at the same moment as the Turks did so. Anxious to avoid a war with the Turks, Peter made an agreement with them whereby he retained control of the coastal strips of the Caspian that had been overrun, while the Turks retained their control over Georgia.

Peter spent his last year troubled by serious ill-health, suffering from epileptic fits which threw him into terrifying convulsions. He had already made preparations for the end, having had his wife Catherine proclaimed Empress. He had already hounded his son Alexis to death in 1718. Alexis, an idle, shiftless boy, had been so despised by his father that he had fled the country to seek refuge with the Emperor. Promised a pardon, he returned, only to be tortured as a result of Peter's suspicion that his son had plotted against him. Confessing, Alexis was imprisoned and there he died in 1718. Peter himself followed his son to the grave in 1725 after an acute fever brought on by a shipwreck in the icy waters off St. Petersburg.

Importance of the Career of Peter the Great

Peter had made his country a European power and had laid down policies towards Poland, Sweden and Turkey which his successors, and notably Catherine the Great, systematically developed. Taking advantage of and perpetuating the internal weaknesses of these powers, Russian influence was spread farther and farther west in the following centuries, involving her more and more closely in the tangled thread of European diplomacy. Peter made Russia a Baltic power at Sweden's expense, and by posing as the liberator of the Balkan Christians he had shown the way towards making Russia a Black Sea power.

His internal reforms laid the basis necessary for great power status. Peter provided his country with an effective administrative framework centred on his new capital at St. Petersburg, and strengthened the Czar's authority over the Church as well as over the State. He created an effective army and navy that gave reality to his power. Although the outward signs of his westernization policy produced a certain amount of opposition, he took care to retain the loyalty of the nobles by strengthening their control over the peasants, the class who had least cause to be grateful to Peter. For all his cruel and unpleasant characteristics it is impossible not to admire him. Essentially a man of action, he displayed, to a superlative degree, courage and determination in tackling the superhuman tasks which confronted him.

QUESTIONS

1. Give an account of the aims and achievements of Peter the Great both at home and abroad.
2. Give an account of the struggle between Peter the Great of Russia and Charles XII of Sweden.

CHAPTER 20

GROWTH OF BRANDENBURG-PRUSSIA

WHEN in 1640 Frederick William became the Elector of Brandenburg, one of the largest of the German principalities, he found his dominions widely scattered, lacking in any sense of unity, ravaged by war, thinly populated and poverty-stricken.

It was Frederick William who first tackled the problem of welding together these widely differing possessions into one state and of establishing his authority over that of the Estates. The foundations of the state's future greatness were a powerful and efficient army and a centralized administrative machine operating solely according to the ruler's will.

Frederick William's National Army

Conceiving it to be his duty to provide for the defence of his possessions in the dangerous and uncertain period of the mid-seventeenth century, Frederick William founded a national army. In 1653 this was made possible when the Brandenburg Assembly voted a tax, "the Contribution," to be levied from nobles and peasants alike. This was to become a permanent tax on all country districts of his dominions. The provincial Estates at first extracted concessions in return for this money, but during the War of the North (1655-60), in which he secured sovereign possession of East Prussia, the Great Elector set aside his promises to recognize the Estates' financial powers by raising even heavier taxes entirely on his own authority to finance his growing army. The Estates were powerless to resist since he could always rely upon his troops.

In 1667 the Great Elector took a further step in the destruction of the influence of the Brandenburg Estates, when he introduced the Urban Excise, which was a tax on a great variety of goods sold in towns. This tax was extended to all towns and made the Great Elector financially independent of the Estates.

With these two sources of income Frederick William built up his army, the size of which varied according to whether the country was at war or at peace. The army was a heavy burden for a small and poor country to bear. Modelled on that of Sweden, it distinguished itself during the wars. The nobles found in the army a better career than the Church for their younger sons, and the loyalty and obedience it bred to their commander-in-chief, the Elector himself, helped to consolidate his authority over a nobility which had lost its political privileges with the decline of the Estates.

Rise of the Civil Service

The problem of collecting the taxes and administering the army in its turn resulted in the development of a new bureaucracy, "the general war commissariat," which combined into one the duties of the War Office and the Treasury. Its officials were responsible directly to the Elector not only for the supervision of the collection of taxes, but also for the provision of the needs of the soldiers.

The general war commissariat controlled the activities of the provincial war commissariats which in turn were represented in the towns by a local commissary, and in the country by a rural commissioner. These officials' chief task was to collect the "excise" and "contribution," but their activities were gradually extended. Thus they inspected weights and measures, fixed food prices, granted licences, and enforced the government's trade and industrial policies. This extension of the activities of the general war commissariat was a gradual process continued by Frederick William's successors. It inevitably destroyed town self-government, and prevented the rise of a strong, independent middle class.

Frederick William believed that to make the country prosperous, it was the duty of the ruler to exercise a strict supervision over all economic activities. This was part of the theory known as "mercantilism."

By his active assistance to Huguenots and other Protestant refugees he encouraged some 20,000 immigrants to settle in his thinly-populated country, to the great benefit of the few varied textile industries which welcomed these skilled weavers from the persecutions of Louis XIV. Linen, silk, lace, candle, soap, paper, were but some of the many industries regulated by the State.

Trade was helped by the construction in the 1660s of a canal to link up the rivers Oder and Spree, thus diverting traffic from the Oder (the mouth of which was controlled by the Swedes) to Berlin. This town grew with the influx of trade from Poland and Silesia.

With the aid of Dutch financiers, Frederick William formed an African Company to found a trading post on the Gold Coast, and he bought the West Indian island of St. Thomas in order to participate in the slave trade. His ambitious schemes were to prove a failure, as the company went bankrupt and "Great Frederick's Burg" was sold. This failure was due to lack of capital, which in turn was the result of the absence of a strong middle class. Most people worked on the land as serfs of either the Elector or a nobleman. Their life was hard and unrewarding. Apart from the onerous labour services and other feudal obligations, they were borne down by the burden of taxes payable to either their lord or Elector. The poverty of the soil, and ignorance of efficient farming techniques kept the standard of living very low. In contrast, the nobles enjoyed exemption from taxation and other social and economic privileges as feudal overlords, despite the loss of their political power. Frederick William and his successors dared not interfere with the privileges of the nobility, for it was upon their services in the army or administration, that the security of the State rested. In comparison with their French counterparts, the nobility were poor, and were glad to be able to augment their income by service to the State.

The management of the royal estates, which embraced between one third and one quarter of all the land, was the responsibility of the "general finance directory" which had provincial chambers, the *Amtskammer*, which in turn supervised the activities of the Crown bailiffs. These officials collected the revenues and maintained law and order. With such a large proportion of the land under the direct control of the Elector, it is little wonder that Frederick William's outlook was still that of a feudal overlord. Despite his great contribution in welding together into one state, the scattered possessions he had inherited, Frederick William endangered this unity at his death by leaving a will in which he divided his lands between the sons of his first and second marriages.

King Frederick I, 1688-1713

Fortunately for the future of Prussia, the new Elector Frederick set aside his father's will. Lacking the vigour of the Great Elector he nevertheless continued his policies. In his love for pomp and ceremony, he modelled his court on that of Louis XIV. When the Emperor Leopold needed support for his claims to the Spanish throne, Frederick responded, in return for the imperial recognition of his coveted ambition, the royal title. On 18 January, 1701, Frederick was crowned, taking the title of King of Prussia to emphasize his independence of the Emperor since Prussia did not lie in the Holy Roman Empire. However, it was in Berlin that he had his magnificent palace built. His extravagant tastes were shown in his passion for jewellery and expensive presents, self-indulgences which were disastrous to the economy.

In contrast to his father and son, he was a patron of the Arts and Sciences. An Academy of Arts which fostered paintings and sculpture, an Academy for Science which promoted educational and agricultural projects, and the new University of Halle were founded under royal patronage.

Frederick William I, "The Drill Sergeant of Potsdam," 1713-40

It was during the reign of Frederick William I that Prussian despotism reached its height. He perfected the machinery of government created by his grandfather, the Great Elector, by building up a magnificent and efficient army and in asserting his authority in every sphere of the administration.

Frederick William ruled his country in a very real sense. Believing, like all the Hohenzollerns, that his power came from God, he considered a ruler's task was to rule and not to be occupied with "comedies, operas, ballet, masques, guzzling and boozing." He treated his ministers as servants, allowing them no initiative. The minutest details received his attention. He wrote his decisions on the margin of the reports presented to him, and threatened any official who dared question the royal command, or who showed any inefficiency.

This paternal but often harsh form of government is illustrated vividly in his treatment of the judges, whose decisions he did not hesitate to reverse if he considered them to be wrong. When his judges, having sentenced a Pomeranian grenadier to be hanged for the theft of 6,000 thalers, tried to justify their verdict, Frederick William, whose partiality for the Pomeranian grenadiers was well known, beat the judges with his stick, knocking out the teeth of one of them, and drove the others downstairs with bleeding heads. Nothing more was heard of the thief.

This bullying treatment of royal officials was typical. "They must dance to my tune, or the devil take me, I will have them hanged and roasted as the Tsar does and treat them as rebels." Naturally it did not win him the love of his subjects, but there was no sign of active opposition. The nobility remained loyal and the other classes were politically ineffective.

Frederick William unified the administration, combining the general war commissariat and the general finance directory when he created the "general directory." At the provincial level, the provincial war commissariat and the *Amtskammer* were also combined into the "provincial war and domains chambers." Although commoners were employed in the lower positions, the great majority of his senior officials came from the noble class, and especially from those who had served in the army. Unquestioning obedience was the chief virtue he sought and he felt it was most likely to be found among soldiers.

Frederick William's Army

Frederick William I was the "father of Prussian militarism," well deserving his title of the "Drill Sergeant of Potsdam." He personally drilled and trained his troops from the barrack-like court at Potsdam. The army was essential for a strong state and so Frederick William lavished 70 per cent of his total revenue upon it. He used every possible means to recruit soldiers both at home and abroad. Apart from the volunteers, he conscripted and even kidnapped the younger sons of peasants, and induced the nobles by special privileges to bring their peasants as army recruits even though this tended to aggravate the labour shortage in the countryside. In 1733 he introduced the cantonal system by which the country was divided into cantons of five thousand

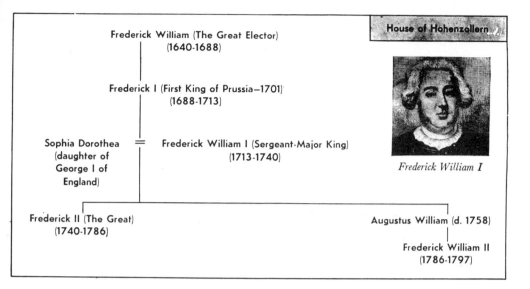

House of Hohenzollern

Frederick William (The Great Elector)
(1640-1688)

Frederick I (First King of Prussia—1701)
(1688-1713)

Sophia Dorothea = Frederick William I (Sergeant-Major King)
(daughter of (1713-1740)
George I of
England)

Frederick William I

Frederick II (The Great)
(1740-1786)

Augustus William (d. 1758)

Frederick William II
(1786-1797)

households. Each canton had to provide replacements for a particular regiment. The nobles provided the officers and were expected to send their sons to cadet colleges to serve as *Junkers*, or ensigns, in the army. His driving energy resulted in the size of his army increasing from 32,000 in 1713 to 80,000 in 1740. But the army's real efficiency in war was to be demonstrated by Frederick William's son.

His peaceful foreign policy, and his insistence on rigid economy at all levels, from the court downwards, enabled him to fill the Treasury which his father had depleted so that his son was to inherit a surplus of eight million thalers.

Frederick William I continued the lines of the policies of the Great Elector in encouraging immigrants. In 1732 he helped Protestant refugees who had been evicted from Salzburg to settle by giving them travelling expenses, cattle, equipment and other privileges. He curtailed the power of the guilds which hampered the development of industry and trade, while by making the journeymen produce identity papers he increased the extent of state supervision over industry. He also forbade the importation of foreign manufactured goods.

Crown Prince Frederick

Frederick William's single-mindedness in building up the essentials of a powerful state caused him to frown upon any activity which did not directly contribute to the strength of the State. The cultural activities sponsored by his father no longer received royal patronage. It was about this that he quarrelled violently with his son, the Crown Prince. The latter was a lover of French literature and music, surrounding himself with French wits, corresponding with Voltaire, writing verse or playing the violin. When his father

175

tried to stop these activities, Frederick tried to escape from Prussia with his great friend, Lieutenant Katte. The plan misfired and Katte was executed (1730) on the King's orders in the presence of Frederick, who would have suffered the same fate but for the intervention of the British ambassador.

With such a violent, unsympathetic man for his father, it is little wonder that Frederick developed those characteristics of an unhappy childhood, coldness towards his fellows, distrust of others, selfishness and self-sufficiency. Yet his inflexible determination was to prove the salvation of his country during the disasters of the Seven Years' War. Essentially a man of action, Frederick was to be reconciled to his father before the latter's death in 1740, by showing an understanding of the motives underlying his father's policy. Frederick's continuation of that policy made possible the emergence of Prussia as a major European power during his reign.

Frederick II, "The Great," 1740-86

Frederick's political ideas, which are revealed in various books he wrote, were based on the role of the King as the first servant of the State. "The prince is to the society that he governs what the head is to the body." The moral code was set aside in his notion that whatever action was committed in the interest of the State was right. His very first act, on becoming King, the invasion of Silesia, was morally unjustified, but politically advantageous.

Like all his predecessors he took an active part in the government of his country. Needing a mere six hours' sleep, he rose early, read through the dispatches before breakfast, and had answered them by his marginal comments by lunch. Undistracted by his family, he worked ceaselessly in his Potsdam palace. He treated his ministers, with whom he had little personal contact, as servants to be bullied and insulted. He soon showed dissatisfaction with the general directory, and although he retained it, he undermined the principle of collective responsibility when he created new and separate departments to take over specialized functions, which he considered were being inefficiently handled. Although these new departments, freed from royal interference on routine questions, were able to function more rapidly, nevertheless even a genius like Frederick was unable to co-ordinate policy because of the lack of real co-operation among the departments.

Law

In the field of legal reform, Frederick showed himself to be an enlightened ruler so long as the reforms were consistent with what he judged to be the safety of the State. Under his rule Prussia gained a single, centralized judicial system with a high court at Berlin, and a central court for each of the provinces, all presided over by judges of the highest integrity. A code of laws was drafted although it was not published until just after Frederick's death.

Prefaced by the idea that laws were to protect the rights of the individual, the code fell short of this ideal. Frederick was not prepared to sacrifice the support of the nobles in an attempt to gain for the serfs their natural rights. Yet Frederick was prepared to intervene, to dispute, and, if necessary, to reverse legal decisions, in order to secure what he considered was justice. In contrast with most European countries, justice was cheap and speedy. In civil courts, the sentences were comparatively lenient. A serious defect however was the judges' dependence on the King's goodwill.

Agriculture

Frederick's efforts to develop the economic well-being of the country was made in two phases, the first in the period between the wars, 1746-56, the second in the period after the Seven Years' War 1763-86.

His greatest single achievement was the draining, reclaiming and colonizing of the marshy land along the lower Oder. Some three hundred new villages were created in these wastes and over 300,000 immigrants settled in Prussia altogether. After the devastations of the Seven Years' War, forty million thalers were granted to the peasants for rebuilding and restocking their farms with seed and livestock. Improvement schemes were undertaken to clear forests, drain swamps, build canals such as the Bromberg Canal linking West Prussia to the Oder. The introduction of new crops like potatoes, turnips and sugar beet, selective livestock breeding, and scientific rotation of crops helped to create an agricultural revolution similar to, if not as extensive as the one in England.

For serfs working on the Crown estates, Frederick limited feudal labour services, and gave many of these workers hereditary possession of their holdings, but he was unable to help those on the estates of nobles. In certain respects the lot of the peasants deteriorated as a result of the improved methods and large-scale farming necessary to feed the large army, since the noble landowners forced many peasant proprietors out of their holdings.

Trade and Industry

Frederick's seizure of Silesia, a province noted for its textiles and such raw materials as iron, coal and lead, showed his concern for enriching his country.

As a mercantilist, Frederick considered it to be the State's duty to stimulate and regulate industry though he favoured individual rather than state-run enterprises. Skilled spinners and weavers from abroad were encouraged to settle, and rural schools in which spinners and weavers could be trained, were established. Government monopolies were granted to woollen and silk manufacturers. Government bounties were paid to silk growers and planters of mulberry trees, and warehouses were built to store either the raw silk, which the government sold to the manufacturers, or the finished product. While silk

177

and woollen goods were the largest items of Prussian exports, many other industries developed through government help which took the form either of loans from the state bank or of protective tariffs. The Silesian iron ore mines were developed, a porcelain industry was founded at Berlin as were many other industries. When Frederick died in 1786, Prussia had become a European producer, even though the expansion cannot be compared with that of the nineteenth century.

Internal trade kept pace with this industrial progress by the abolition of internal tolls and the building of canals to link the North and Baltic seas. Foreign trade however lagged behind and tended to decline as a result of Frederick's protectionist tariff policy which prohibited the import of more than 490 articles.

General Criticisms

Although Frederick was admired by his contemporaries, as well as by posterity, as an outstanding example of a benevolent despot, the excessive concentration of power into the hands of the King meant that the character and ability of the ruler was all-important. Under the control of a lesser man like his successor Frederick William II, Prussia declined; hence her humiliation at the hands of Napoleon on the battlefield of Jena.

The most serious criticisms of the system founded by the Great Elector and continued by his successors were the stifling of initiative at all levels and the excessive worship of the army. The lack of initiative prevented the growth of parliamentary institutions and established a tradition of blind obedience to authority that was perpetuated by Bismarck in the nineteenth century and helped to make possible the rise of Hitler's dictatorship in the twentieth century, while the dominance of the army contributed to much human suffering in Europe.

Despite this, the rise of Brandenburg-Prussia, under her remarkable rulers, is one of the marvels of German history, and it is against the background of the times in which they lived that their actions must be judged. In contrast with most other rulers, the Hohenzollerns dutifully performed their task of defending, unifying and administering their scattered possessions and in this respect they were exemplary.

QUESTIONS

1. Give an account of the services rendered by the Great Elector to Brandenburg-Prussia.
2. Compare the domestic policies of Frederick William I and Frederick II, "The Great."

CHAPTER 21

THE HAPSBURG MONARCHY

THE period 1648 to 1789 is notable for the virtual disappearance of the medieval Holy Roman Empire, and for the emergence of a strong Hapsburg Empire.

Although the form of the medieval empire still existed up to 1806 with an emperor elected by certain leading German princes, and an Imperial Diet representing member states, in fact the Treaty of Westphalia marked its replacement by the emergence of 343 sovereign states. The Empire was "neither Holy, nor Roman, nor an Empire." In the conditions of the seventeenth century, the emperor could no longer exercise effective power over the German princes. Nor was there any true sense of national unity among ordinary Germans, whose outlook was parochial. This contrasted with Britain and France where the people felt a deep sense of loyalty to their native country. The most politically advanced states in central Europe were, in the north the kingdom of Prussia under the Hohenzollerns, and in the south-east the Hapsburg empire.

The Hapsburg rulers dominated central Europe throughout the period. Without exception the rulers of the Hapsburg lands, from Ferdinand III to Joseph II, took their duties seriously, convinced that God had entrusted them with the task of ruling His people. Devout upholders of the Roman Catholic faith, their sense of duty was enhanced by the Imperial title which was, in fact, a hereditary possession of this dignified royal family. As emperors of the Holy Roman Empire, they felt themselves particularly responsible for defending Germany from the intrusions of the Turks and the French.

To speak of the Hapsburg lands as a political unit at this time would be misleading. They formed a diverse empire, and even a common allegiance to the Hapsburg ruler did little towards its unity as he was referred to by different titles in the various provinces.

Emperor Ferdinand III was the Duke of the Austrian lands, and these were predominantly German and Catholic. Bohemia, Moravia and Silesia, which included Czechs and Germans and in which there were many Protestants, made up the Kingdom of the Crown of St. Wenceslas, a title which was the hereditary possession of the Hapsburgs. Hungary, Transylvania, Croatia, Slavonia and Dalmatia formed the Crown of St. Stephen, a title to which successive Hapsburgs were elected by the Hungarian Diet. In 1648 Ferdinand's rule over these last-named areas was nominal. In Hungary the Magyars were the dominant race, Slavs of one kind or another forming the backbone of the peasantry. The Greek Orthodox and Protestant Churches were rivals of the Roman Catholic Church.

Effects of the Thirty Years' War

The Hapsburg lands had been devastated by the conflicts of the Thirty Years' War, especially in Bohemia. The population of Bohemia dropped from 1,700,000 to 900,000 during the war as a result of violent death or Protestant emigration. There was a similar, if less serious, decline in the other Hapsburg lands.

The resulting labour shortage came at a time when the landowners were seeking to use their estates as a source for the production of corn and other commodities which were to be sold to the Imperial armies or townsfolk. Accordingly landowners exploited labour services and other feudal obligations to the full. Serfs, with their own holdings, had to work at least three days a week on the lord's demesne, while over a quarter of the peasantry worked every day. Serfs had to provide horses, carts, ploughs and had to buy corn, wine, fish, salt and other products from their lord besides endure the burden of taxation from which the lord was exempt.

Towns, too, had suffered severely. Their trade and industry had come to a standstill suffering from the competition of the landowners and from the religious persecutions which had driven the industrious Protestant classes abroad.

The Roman Catholic Church had by 1664 successfully prevented the open preaching of Protestantism in Bohemian and Austrian lands, as a result of widespread expulsion, execution or conversion of Protestants. A leading role in this development was taken by the Jesuits. Protestant sects still survived in secret, however. Similar persecutions occurred in Hungary.

After his eldest son's death in 1654, Ferdinand devoted his last three years to helping his younger son Leopold acquire the titles and crowns of the Hapsburgs. Crowned king of Hungary in 1655 and of Bohemia in 1657, Leopold had to wait until after his father's death in 1657 before being crowned Emperor at Frankfurt in 1658.

Leopold I, 1657-1705

Leopold inherited a dangerous situation. Charles X, the Protestant king of Sweden, had in 1655 invaded Poland, driving out its King John Casimir. Charles X then put forward claims to both the crowns of Poland and Bohemia and so threatened to renew the religious controversies.

In order to resist this threat to the Catholic Church in central Europe,

Leopold completed an alliance with John Casimir, but the anti-Catholic combination broke up when the Danes attacked Charles X. This enabled Leopold to help John Casimir to recover Poland.

The revival of the Turkish power was an even more serious threat, for the fate of Christianity itself, and not merely Catholicism, was soon to be at stake. The menace became apparent when Transylvania was over-run in 1662. The Turks then launched an attack on royal Hungary and Austria, marching up the Danube on to Pressburg and Vienna.

The Emperor appealed to the crusading spirit of the various rulers to resist this threat to Christianity. Support came from Louis XIV of France, Philip IV of Spain, the Great Elector of Brandenburg and Pope Alexander VII besides the force of 20,000 men voted by the Imperial Diet. This Christian army caught the Turks as they tried to cross the river Raab, and shattered their force in this battle at St. Gotthard, 1664. The Turks concluded the Peace of Vasvar which provided for a twenty years' truce, but which permitted the Turks to retain the vital fortresses on the Danube.

Criticized bitterly by many, especially the Hungarians, for not following up this victory to rid Hungary of the Turks once and for all, Leopold was probably induced to make peace partly by military caution in not wishing to jeopardize his gains, and partly by ambitions to secure his claims to the Spanish throne.

Leopold's preoccupation with the Spanish issue alienated the Magyars of Hungary, who felt betrayed by Leopold when he made peace with the Turks. Some now conspired to overthrow him. This plot was crushed brutally in 1670, and was followed by a wave of religious persecution that swept many Protestants out of Hungary. It was among some of these Protestant exiles that a further conspiracy was hatched in 1678 by Count Teleki, himself a Calvinist, that had as its objects the restitution of political and religious freedom.

The fresh rising provided the opportunity for the Turks to renew their attack. So menacing did the Turks become that in 1681 in order to win the loyalty of the Hungarians, Leopold restored political and religious freedom. Teleki and his supporters, fearing such concessions might undermine the success of their rebellion, intrigued with the Turks and joined their armies in over-running Hungary, burning villages, executing and enslaving their inhabitants. The Hapsburg army under Charles of Lorraine withdrew from Hungary, and Vienna came under siege. Its garrison withstood the onslaughts from July to September, 1683, with great courage. As in 1664, so in 1683 a new Christian League once more came into being, and it was the turn of the Polish armies to bring relief to Austria. Their armies swept down from the heights overlooking Vienna, and catching the Turks off-guard cleared them from the field. Vienna and Europe were saved from Moslem conquest.

For the next sixteen years Leopold's armies were engaged in the task of expelling the Turks bag and baggage from Hungary. As Hungary more and more came under Leopold's control, so did his prestige and authority increase. By 1687 he was once more able to induce the Diet to recognize the Hapsburgs' hereditary claim to the Crown of St. Stephen, and to confirm this, he had his son, Joseph, crowned as king of Hungary in 1687. Although the political independence of the Hungarian nobility was curtailed, Leopold made no attempt to interfere with their social or economic privileges.

The liberation of Hungary was completed by 1699 when the Turks yielded the whole of Hungary (except the Banat) and Transylvania to Leopold in the peace of Carlowitz.

Despite the subjection of Hungary to the Hapsburgs, the Magyars were still to prove troublesome in the early years of the eighteenth century.

Meanwhile in Bohemia there was much discontent caused by the continued exploitation of labour services by the landowners. This discontent reached its peak in 1680 when some peasants, taking advantage of the sufferings caused by a plague which had swept through the Hapsburg lands killing thousands, appealed to Leopold for help. Leopold responded to the petition with the result that it encouraged others to make similar appeals. These the landlords arrested, and when Leopold forbade further direct appeals, the serfs revolted. They refused to perform their feudal services, and armed themselves with scythes, flails and sickles against the soldiers dispatched to put down the rising. A cruel, bloody revenge was taken against the peasants, many of whom were executed or imprisoned.

Joseph I (1705-11) and Charles VI (1711-40)

Joseph succeeded to the Hapsburg dominions and Imperial Crown on his father's death in 1705. Apart from the continuing troubles in Hungary, Joseph was primarily engaged in enforcing the Hapsburgs' claims to the Spanish throne, but by the time of his death through smallpox, in 1711, it was apparent he had failed in this task.

Archduke Charles who succeeded his brother as emperor had been the Hapsburg claimant to the Spanish throne. In the peace settlement of Utrecht, the Emperor was compensated for the loss of the Spanish throne by the acquisition of the Netherlands, part of the Milanese territory, Naples and Sardinia, which made Austria the dominant power in Italy. Even these new territories failed to satisfy Charles, and the peace of Europe was to be further troubled by the continuing rivalry between the Austrian Hapsburgs and the Spanish Bourbons over Italy.

The central problem facing Charles was that of the succession, for with it was tied up the whole question of the unity of the Empire, since the one bond of common loyalty was the Hapsburg ruler. His brother's death had left

Charles the sole male heir. Although the female succession was recognizable in Austrian and Bohemian lands, in Hungary a male succession alone was recognizable. The certainty of a female succession was assured with the death of Charles' infant son in 1716 and the birth of his two daughters Maria Theresa in 1717 and Maria Anna in 1718. Charles had already promulgated in 1713 the famous document, the Pragmatic Sanction, in which he had declared that on his death all the hereditary possessions of the Hapsburgs should pass, failing a male heir, to his daughter. With Maria Theresa's birth it became his over-riding ambition to secure the recognition of her claims by the various diets of his dominions, and by the great powers. The great sacrifice Charles made in extracting what proved to be empty promises of recognition from the great powers is a tragic story of misplaced trust.

In contrast with the dismal story of international treachery, the reign of Charles VI was one of splendour centred around a magnificent Imperial Court at Vienna which rivalled Versailles in attracting the nobility from all parts. Many built their fine palaces around it. It was an age of elegance and culture with the Emperor as the chief patron of the arts.

But the attraction of Vienna resulted in the impoverishment of town and country, for the nobles neglected the management of their estates and were interested in them only for the revenues, which they squandered and gambled away in the social life at Vienna.

Another consequence of this movement towards Vienna was the decline of local independence. The central administration was increasingly able to assert its authority over the provincial estates and town corporations, for the great nobles who traditionally championed local liberties were competing in increasing numbers for high offices at Vienna.

To expand the imperial revenue, Charles attempted to develop the trade with the East Indies and the eastern Mediterranean. He declared Trieste and Fiume free ports and ended the monopoly of the Adriatic trade so long enjoyed by the merchants of Venice. The textile and porcelain industry of Silesia, too, benefited from Charles' encouragement.

The new spirit of bureaucracy can be seen in Charles' treatment of the Hungarian "liberties" which he had sworn to cherish but which he treated with scant respect. Hapsburg policy was to limit Magyar independence, and Charles followed the traditional policy of playing off one race against another.

Yet Charles' lands still bore the marks of a medieval state despite the trends towards centralized bureaucracy. The Church dominated the life of his subjects. The Jesuits, especially, still continued their repressive persecutions of Protestants, who were expelled from Salzburg and many other towns. The Emperor assisted by dispatching soldiers to enforce these expulsions for the sake of religious uniformity despite the great blow to trade and industry entailed by the loss to the Empire of these hard-working subjects.

Maria Theresa, 1740-80

Charles VI's death in 1740 put his life-long work to the test. Would the great powers respect his daughter's claims to the Hapsburg lands, and her husband Francis of Lorraine's claim to the Imperial throne?

The young heiress was not left in doubt for long. Frederick the Great, the new Prussian king, taking advantage of Austria's military weakness, seized Silesia, the most valuable of all Maria Theresa's provinces, without the slightest justification. This was the signal for Charles Albert of Bavaria to claim the Imperial throne. Maria Theresa's difficulties presented a splendid opportunity for her enemies, France, Spain, Saxony and Savoy, to form an anti-Hapsburg alliance to pursue their own individual ambitions, while giving nominal support to the claims of the Bavarian elector who was crowned Emperor in 1742. With Britain and Holland remaining faithful allies of Maria Theresa, Europe was plunged into a war, fought not only in Europe but overseas for the next twenty years. The details of the War of the Austrian Succession, 1740-48, and the Seven Years' War, 1756-63, are dealt with later.

For the Hapsburg dominions the consequence of Frederick's successful seizure of Silesia, as recognized in the Treaty of Aix-la-Chapelle, 1748, was profound. Determined to recover Silesia, Maria Theresa took full advantage of the truce between 1748 and 1756 to embark upon a programme of reform designed to remedy the fundamental weaknesses that had allowed her lands to be violated by her greedy neighbour.

The basic weakness was the obsolete administrative system which prevented the Empress from tapping and organizing the vast financial and military resources of her possessions. The reason for this lay in the power of the Estates to grant or withhold supplies. These grants had been inadequate. Maria Theresa and her advisers, Haugwitz and Kaunitz, believed that only by creating a more powerful, unified administration could revenues be collected in sufficient quantity for the survival of the Empire.

The task of reorganization was entrusted to Count Haugwitz, a great admirer of the Prussian civil service. He developed the plan of reorganizing the entire Austrian administrative system, divorced from local and feudal influences.

The hub of the new machinery of government was the Council of State, a body of expert advisers on both internal and foreign questions whose recommendations were binding on the administrative bodies. It can be compared with the British Cabinet which is made up of ministers who are heads of different departments of government. In the same way Kaunitz and Haugwitz, the outstanding members of the Council of State, were respectively head of the State Chancellery and the newly-created Ministry of the Interior. The Chancellery, reorganized in 1753, was responsible for foreign affairs, and the Ministry of the Interior for developing the financial resources of the

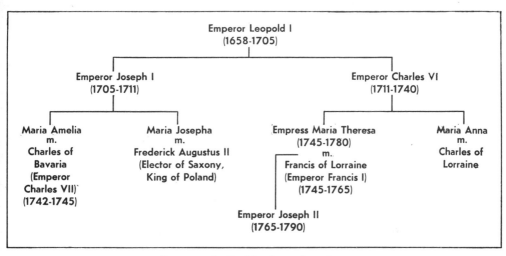

Emperors in the Hapsburg dynasty.

monarchy as well as exercising supreme control over internal administration. Other ministries reorganized included the War Office, while two new departments of administration were created. The Directory of Commerce was set up to develop trade and industry. A Supreme Court was established at Vienna as the highest legal body. This step separated for the first time the judicial and administrative functions of government.

The local government reforms of this period after 1748 were part of this process of unifying and centralizing the administration. The Bohemian and Austrian lands were subdivided into ten provinces controlled by two governing bodies, one for Bohemia and another for Austria. These bodies were directly responsible to the Ministry of the Interior. Each of the provinces was subdivided into "circles," which were placed under a royal official, the *Kreishauptmann*, whose chief aim was to enforce royal policy at the expense of the feudal privileges of the nobles, and to whom the peasants looked for protection in disputes with their feudal overlords.

Although Maria Theresa made no direct attempt to extend the bureaucracy into Hungary, she adopted a policy of cautiously undermining the Hungarian liberties, which she had guaranteed in her coronation oath. The powerful Magyar nobles were encouraged to enter the Imperial service. Thus she continued her father's policy of weaning the nobles away from their local ties.

The key problem in making the central government's authority effective was the control of finance, for upon this depended the success of the army reforms. Maria Theresa succeeded in persuading the Estates of Bohemia and Austria to vote taxes for ten years in advance. These "ten year recesses" as they became known, transferred the financial control to the monarchy in effect, and made possible the other reforms necessary to improve the technical efficiency. A military academy for training officers was founded, regular camps and annual manoeuvres were instituted and improved conditions of service resulted in higher morale and discipline. The effectiveness of these reforms was to be tested in the Seven Years' War when the army fought with much greater discipline.

Other financial resources developed by Maria Theresa to make her independent of the estates were the imposition of direct taxes upon the nobles and clergy, the introduction of a poll tax and the careful collection of revenues from mines, custom duties and government monopolies on salt.

Co-regency of Maria Theresa and Joseph, 1765-80

Maria Theresa continued to exercise a close hold over policy even after her husband's death in 1765. Her son, Joseph, was elected Emperor, and for the next fifteen years, mother and son, advised by Kaunitz, ruled the Hapsburg lands. Differences were, however, to arise between the Empress, with her conservative ideas, and the Emperor with his radical ones.

Although Maria Theresa had laid the foundations of a strong, unified state dominated by the new bureaucracy, she had little sympathy for the new ideas originating in the writings of the French philosophers. She was no believer in the doctrines of the "Age of Reason" which stressed man's reason and rights and bitterly attacked the Church's teachings and influence. Although the feudal power of the nobles and Church had been checked, Maria Theresa was still a devout supporter of the Catholic Church, for she considered it an essential influence in setting and maintaining the moral standards of her subjects.

Yet the new ideas affected the views of officials upon whom she and Joseph had to depend. Joseph himself, although brought up in a court steeped in the influence of Catholicism, was to become a great admirer of the philosophers and to enter into correspondence with Voltaire, the outstanding opponent of the Roman Catholic Church. Keenly interested in ruling his empire, and aware of his responsibilities, Joseph was the most well-intentioned of all the "Enlightened Despots." Genuinely concerned for the well-being of his subjects, he tried with limited success to put into practice many advanced ideas which he outlined in a memorandum he drew up on coming to power in 1765. He proposed sweeping administrative reforms to remedy the inefficiency, expense, delays and corruptions that were characteristic of the royal bureaucracy. His anti-clerical views were seen in his educational schemes which aimed at lessening the influence of the Catholic Church over the youth of the country, and in his proposals to dissolve those monasteries which he considered served no useful purpose. He was anxious to foster commerce by state action, and to safeguard the rights of the individuals. In fact he did not quite achieve what he had hoped for.

Such ideas were heresy for Maria Theresa, but a permanent breach between mother and son was averted by the deep love which existed between them and which was strengthened by domestic tragedies, and by the soothing influence of Kaunitz.

Religious questions particularly revealed the gulf between Joseph and his mother. In the 1760s the Jesuits had been expelled from France, Spain, Portugal and Naples. Of all the Catholic sovereigns, Maria Theresa alone was their stout defender. When in 1773 Pope Clement XIV suppressed the order, the contrast between the sorrow of Maria Theresa and the pleasure of Joseph was marked. When thousands of Moravians switched from the Catholic to the Protestant faith in 1777, Maria Theresa was horrified and issued decrees persecuting them by forbidding meetings and exiling their leaders. Joseph, a fervent champion of toleration, protested even to the point of resignation in his efforts to minimize the effects of this persecution.

Hungary was another cause of friction. Maria Theresa's policy of bringing Hungary under the control of the central government by taking Magyars into service, was too slow for the ambitious Joseph. He wanted an outright incorporation of Hungary. But it was not until his mother's death that he was free to try to put this scheme along with many others into practice with disastrous consequences.

Joseph as Sole Ruler, 1780-90

The new spirit which guided the Hapsburg dominions following Maria Theresa's death was embodied in the "Patent of Toleration" of 1781, in which Joseph permitted freedom of private worship to all his subjects even though Catholics alone were to enjoy the right of public worship. Protestants or Orthodox Christians had to worship in buildings bearing no outward resemblance to churches. Such dissenters were granted full civil rights to enable them to enter any trade.

The Emperor continued the policy of restricting the influence of the Catholic Church, by forbidding bishops to appeal to Rome or to publish any Papal Bulls without the Emperor's consent, and even the visit of Pope Pius VI to Vienna in 1782 failed to move Joseph.

This attack on the Church was accompanied by a large-scale dissolution of the monasteries and confiscation of Church property. Seven hundred out of two thousand monasteries, especially those of the contemplative orders, had disappeared by 1790, and those which survived had to justify their existence either by caring for the sick, or by providing education. The revenues of the dissolved monasteries were diverted to charitable, medical, educational or industrial purposes. To provide future priests with an education freed from the restrictive influences of the ecclesiastical training colleges Joseph established five new state-run colleges widely dispersed throughout his empire.

It is little wonder that the far-reaching reforms outlined aroused the deep resentment of the Catholic Church. The ordinary folk found Joseph's religious reforms distasteful. In the Netherlands for instance Joseph had decreed that there should be a uniform observance of a religious festival, the *Kermesse*, which had been the occasion for a holiday and feasting. Hitherto it had been celebrated at different times in different towns, and the citizens of one town had been able to take advantage of the neighbouring town's festivals.

Reform and Revolt

Joseph's legal reforms were his most admirable achievement, lasting until the collapse of the Austrian Empire in 1918. He continued the work begun by his mother of reorganizing the administration of justice by the creation of a complete hierarchy of courts from the high court at Vienna downwards. These courts were presided over by judges chosen for their integrity. A new criminal code was compiled in 1787 which was in accord with the more humane views of the time. Terror and savage vengeance as the principles of punishment were replaced by penalties just sufficiently severe to deter. A new civil code, too, was begun, and although not completed until 1811 contained modern ideas on the laws of marriage and of inheritance.

The desire for uniformity which had led Joseph to extend his legal reforms to all districts aroused much opposition from the vested interests adversely affected. Especially in the Netherlands and Hungary magistrates displaced by the new courts without compensation were bitter critics.

At the same time as he introduced his legal reforms Joseph extended to the Netherlands and Hungary the administrative reorganization begun by Maria Theresa. These were the very areas which she had excluded for fear of the opposition which would be aroused. In his passion for uniformity Joseph ignored such qualms. By the decree of 1787, a single council was established for the Netherlands which was subdivided into three circles under the charge of Intendants. Hungary, too, was similarly reorganized; German replaced Latin as the official language; and the Diet was abolished. It was this reorganization cutting at the roots of the local independence that sparked off the revolts in the Netherlands and in Hungary.

In the Netherlands the Estates of Brabant refused to vote taxes until the legal and administrative reforms were revoked. The clergy joined the lawyers and politicians in their opposition by refusing to implement the religious reforms. Joseph accordingly abolished the Estates of Brabant in 1789 and this in turn provoked the Belgians into driving out the Austrian garrisons and declaring the United Provinces of Belgium independent (1790).

In Hungary a similar rebellion of conservative subjects against a reforming emperor took place. In addition to the widespread resentment caused by his religious and administrative reforms, Joseph's attempts to abolish serfdom and the nobles' right of tax exemption aroused the bitter hatred of the Magyar nobility, and at the same time raised the hopes of the peasantry.

Maria Theresa and Joseph II, co-rulers of the Hapsburg Empire (1765-80).

Joseph was genuinely appalled at the degradation of the serfs who formed the overwhelming majority of his subjects. During the co-regency he had initiated schemes of land reform to enable peasants to purchase their own holdings, and to end peasant labour services. Despite a peasant rising of 1774-75 which resulted from frustrated hopes of the peasantry, the patent of 1775 marked the end of the limitless exploitation of peasants by landlords.

As sole ruler Joseph continued his policy of helping the serfs by a series of decrees that gave them freedom of movement, marriage and property ownership. While there was substantial resistance in Austria and Bohemia from the nobility, Joseph was able to withstand it. In Hungary, however, Joseph's attack on Magyar privileges produced a serious peasant rising against the Magyars who tried to frustrate the reforms. This rising coincided with the renewal of the war against the Turks, so when the estates of Transylvania refused to authorize men or money for the war until Joseph had restored the Hungarian Diet, Joseph was forced to give way and in 1790 withdrew most of the administrative reforms. Even though the decrees abolishing serfdom were retained, they were never put into effect until 1848.

It was in this atmosphere of failure in the Netherlands· and in Hungary that Joseph died in 1790. Just before he died, he suggested his epitaph, "Here lies Joseph who failed in everything he undertook." Although many of his ambitious schemes were premature and aroused the implacable hostility of the Church, the nobility and the corporations, his reign was a memorable one in the transformation of the Hapsburg Empire to a modern state.

QUESTIONS

1. Describe the Turkish threat to Europe during the latter half of the seventeenth century, and say how it was met by the Emperor Leopold I.
2. Write an account of the reforms of Emperor Joseph II between the years 1780 and 1790. Explain why some of his measures failed and others had more permanent results.

CHAPTER 22

HAPSBURG-BOURBON RIVALRY
IN EUROPE, 1740-1748

IN THIS and the following chapter we shall be tracing the story of the struggle for control not only of central Europe but also for predominance in world trade and colonial enterprise. Both in Europe and overseas the settlement reached at Utrecht was, in the course of this conflict, shattered. Whereas the clash between the Hapsburgs of Austria and the Hohenzollerns of Prussia for possession of Silesia was dynastic and continental, the clash between the Hanoverians of Britain and the Bourbons of France and Spain was for commercial and colonial supremacy. These two currents of a continental and an overseas struggle flowed from the same source—the essential struggle for power.

This bid for power was marked by three main wars fought between 1739 and 1763—the Anglo-Spanish War (1739-48), which soon merged into the much more important War of the Austrian Succession (1740-8) and the Seven Years' War (1756-63). While the principal contestants remained in the opposite camps, in the War of the Austrian Succession the Hanoverians fought as allies of the Hapsburgs against the Bourbons and Hohenzollerns, but in the Seven Years' War they joined with the Hohenzollerns at the same time as the Bourbons switched to the Hapsburg side.

The outcome of these struggles was a significant shift in the balance of power as settled at Utrecht between the great powers both in Europe and overseas. By successfully challenging Hapsburg power in Germany, Frederick made Prussia a major power to be reckoned with, and dealt a serious blow to the influence of the Hapsburgs as emperors of Germany. In the overseas struggle, Britain dealt a similar blow to both France and Spain by establishing herself as the leading colonial, commercial and naval power. The consequences of these changes were of the profoundest significance for the future history of Europe.

Anglo-Spanish War

The war which began in 1739 is sometimes referred to as the War of Jenkins' Ear because of the part played by the ear of that unfortunate captain of the *Rebecca* in arousing national passions against the Spanish for their ill-treatment of British sailors on the Spanish Main.

The crisis of 1739 really arose out of the deep trade rivalry between Britain and Spain. British merchants were trying to open up their trade with Spanish America, while the Spanish government was seeking to keep out all foreign competitors by a system of obsolete trade laws which she could no longer enforce. The Spanish colonists might have tolerated the restrictions on their trade with foreign countries, had their mother country, Spain, provided them, at competitive prices, with the manufactures and other products of Europe.

The British had succeeded in driving a wedge into this closed market when in the Asiento Treaty of 1713 the British South Sea Company was granted by the Spanish government the right to provide the Spanish colonies with Negro slaves from West Africa and to send each year one shipload of merchandize to the great fairs at Vera Cruz and Cartagena.

Their appetite whetted, the British merchants were anxious to push open the door still more into these markets, and the Spanish colonists themselves were equally eager for British goods which undercut those of the Spanish merchants. Thus a vast contraband trade grew up in which unlicensed British traders took part. The Spanish authorities entrusted the enforcement of their trade laws to the "guarda costas," who waged unofficial war against any merchant engaged in this illegal trade.

Unofficial "Incidents"

The outrages committed by the guarda costas resulted in such incidents as befell Captain Jenkins. The guarda costas were little better than pirates who grossly abused their "right of search" in confiscating cargoes they claimed to be illegal. Between 1713 and 1731 some 180 British ships were illegally pillaged. The British merchants also complained of the delays and small returns in the legitimate trade. Between 1717 and 1733 only eight of the annual ships reached the fairs. The Spaniards in their turn complained of the British abuse of the privilege of supplying goods in the annual ships and the general disregard for their trade laws.

It was the Jenkins case which the parliamentary opposition to Walpole eagerly used to force him into demanding redress from Spain. These opposition members championed the claims of the British merchants who considered that their trade, threatened by the growing French competition, would expand only as a result of war with Spain. Negotiations were opened with the Spanish Government at El Pardo and a partial agreement was reached. Walpole, anxious though he was to avoid a war, could not ignore the pressure not only from opposition politicians, but also from merchants and the general public. All alike condemned the agreement. The feelings of the British public were expressed by Pitt and Carteret who thundered against the Spanish claim to search vessels. The public were spoiling for a fight and Walpole reluctantly had to give way. In October, 1739, Britain declared war.

Naval Expeditions Against Spanish American Colonies

The chief British objective was to paralyse Spanish colonial trade by the destruction of the principal ports. It was hoped that this would prevent the sailing of the annual treasure fleet upon which the Spanish government was completely dependent for its finance. A famous incident of this period was Commodore Anson's attack on the Spanish ports at Paita, on the west coast of South America. His marines held the customs port for three days, seized the treasure, and only abandoned the town after setting fire to it. Anson also seized the Manila treasure galleon in the Philippines. But the eventual cost in lives and hardships suffered by the British, when weighed against the damage done to the Spanish empire, hardly made the exploits worth while. The strictly limited naval war marking the outbreak of hostilities in Europe was quickly to be engulfed in the greater struggle which opened with Frederick's seizure of Silesia.

The War of the Austrian Succession

In April, 1740, Crown Prince Frederick succeeded his father Frederick William I to the throne of Prussia as Frederick II. This young man of twenty-eight was intensely ambitious not only to make a name for himself

The Anglo-Spanish War consisted mainly of sea battles such as this one between the "Centurion" and the "Covadonga."

but also to strengthen his state even to the point of disturbing the peace of Europe. He was governed by self-interest rather than principles in serving the state to which he was devoted: "If there is anything to be gained by being honest, let us be honest," he wrote. "If it is necessary to deceive, let us deceive." It is therefore hardly surprising that as ruler of a very poor kingdom, he should cast his covetous eye on Silesia, one of the most valuable provinces adjoining Prussia but belonging to his Hapsburg neighbours.

It was the news in October, 1740, of the death of the Emperor Charles VI and the accession of the twenty-three-year-old Princess Maria Theresa to the Hapsburg Empire that inspired Frederick to seize Silesia. The decision was that of an impetuous and ambitious young adventurer but it was never regretted by Frederick even though it was to dominate the remainder of his reign. Always ready to seize any opportunity which served his interests he realized that Maria Theresa's position was weak while his own was strong. He had inherited from his father not only a magnificent army but also a full treasury. The Emperor Charles VI had laboured to secure worthless signatures from the rulers of Europe to the Pragmatic Sanction when he would have been better occupied in strengthening the administration and the army of his empire. Little had been done to unify the various parts of the empire into a compact dominion. Lacking any common political, economic or military system it was extremely vulnerable. The army and the civil service, unpaid for two years in 1740, were demoralized in the extreme. Maria Theresa herself lacked any political experience, while her mediocre husband Francis was extremely unpopular. Her strength lay in her courage and charm. Through these characteristics she won the loyalty of her restless subjects who rallied to the defence of her lands. Deeply influenced by Christian principles, she regarded the struggle with Frederick as one between right and wrong.

Frederick's Success

The death of Empress Anne of Russia in 1740 removed Frederick's fear of an immediate Russian attack on his eastern frontier, so in December of that year he marched into Silesia. In return for this province he told Maria Theresa he would vote for her husband as the next emperor. Maria Theresa refused, but her armies were defeated at Mollwitz by Frederick's soldiers. This Prussian victory influenced other claimants to Hapsburg lands to come forward.

Up to this point Fleury had exercised a decisive influence over French policy. His main concern was to keep France free from any continental commitments in order to concentrate her efforts in the struggle which he saw looming up with Britain for world trade and colonies. Anxious to avoid war with Austria, Fleury had recognized the Pragmatic Sanction in 1738, but this policy, although it was in France's best interest, did not win the support of

Schoenbrunn Palace at Vienna (eighteenth-century), home of the Hapsburgs.

many ministers. Like Walpole in Britain, Fleury's last years in power were marked by growing opposition to his peace policies. Outstanding among his opponents was the Comte de Belleisle who, more than anyone else, was responsible for reviving the traditional anti-Hapsburg feeling. He was anxious to re-establish the policies of Louis XIV which had been to promote disunity in Germany in order to establish French influence.

Belleisle, a master of intrigue, secured from Louis XV support for the idea of a French-inspired anti-Hapsburg alliance to further the claims of Charles Albert of Bavaria to the Empire. Charles Albert had been the one German ruler who had resolutely refused to recognize the Pragmatic Sanction, advancing his own claim to the Imperial title through his wife. Powerless to enforce his claims unaided Charles Albert eagerly welcomed the backing of France.

Anti-Hapsburg Alliance

It was Frederick's victory at Mollwitz which enabled Belleisle to put his ideas into practice. Shortly after the battle, Belleisle set out on a diplomatic tour of Germany in order to bring into being an alliance of all those princes who wished to extend their own power at the expense of the Hapsburgs. In the summer of 1741 a treaty aimed at the break-up of the Hapsburg empire was signed. France agreed to support by military aid Charles' claims to the Imperial throne. Prussia, Saxony and other German Electors agreed to support by their votes Charles' election in return for the mutual recognition of their own claims—Prussia laid claim to Silesia, and Saxony laid claim to Moravia. Spain and Sardinia joined the alliance intent on spreading their influence in northern and central Italy.

France had thus committed herself to a continental struggle in the hope that she would profit from the destruction of her traditional enemy. She was ultimately to discover what a gigantic blunder she had committed for she was to waste resources and manpower which could have been far more profitably expended upon the commercial and colonial struggle with Britain.

Maria Theresa's Critical Position

For the moment this blunder was not apparent. The position of Maria Theresa seemed desperate. In the autumn of 1741 six states were ranged against her, their promises regarding the Pragmatic Sanction having been conveniently forgotten. From her three potential allies, Britain, Holland and Russia, little could be expected. George II's policy was governed by two conflicting considerations—support for Maria Theresa, and fear of an attack on Hanover. Britain, treaty-bound to protect Maria Theresa, traditionally supported the Hapsburgs against the Bourbons. Parliament accordingly voted £300,000 subsidy for Maria Theresa. The fear, however, that his beloved Hanover would be attacked by either Prussian or French armies, led George as a German Prince Elector into purchasing the neutrality of Hanover by agreement to vote for Charles as Emperor.

The United Provinces were too weak and divided to give any effective aid and had no desire to threaten their commercial prosperity by being involved in war. Russia, too, was paralysed by a disputed succession, and a threat of war from Sweden.

Charles Albert's Franco-Bavarian forces were within three days of Vienna when Maria Theresa made her courageous appeal to her Magyar subjects. By recognizing their independent position in the Empire and appealing to their chivalrous desire to defend their innocent and outraged queen, Maria Theresa won their support.

What really saved Maria Theresa, however, was a lack of common purpose among her enemies. A secret treaty she made with Frederick, granting him Silesia, made Frederick appear untrustworthy to his allies. Charles Albert invaded Bohemia instead of occupying Vienna, and was crowned Emperor Charles VII at Prague.

His election marked the first break for three hundred years in the tradition that a Hapsburg should be Emperor and was the high-water mark of the anti-Hapsburg success. Henceforth the tide changed. On the very day that Charles VII was crowned at Frankfurt, his own capital of Munich was stormed (February, 1742) by the Hungarians. Bavaria was overrun and devastated. In this same month, Walpole was forced to resign by his opponents for his weak handling of the war. His successor, Lord Carteret, was to give much more effective support to Maria Theresa, for her survival was vital if Britain's real enemy, France, was to be destroyed and her influence checked.

British statesmen were divided as to the basic strategy to be followed in the conduct of the war against the Bourbons. One set led by Pitt favoured a naval war overseas, and criticized entanglements in Europe as a waste of money. The other set, including Carteret and the Duke of Newcastle, favoured a continental policy of reviving the "Grand Alliance" against the Bourbons. Although ultimately these two policies were reconciled during the Seven Years' War, in the War of the Austrian Succession Carteret's plan of a revived "Grand Alliance" was followed.

Break-up of the Anti-Hapsburg Alliance

The first result of his influence was seen in July, 1742, when Maria Theresa was persuaded once more to sacrifice Silesia in the Treaty of Berlin which she signed with Prussia. Since the truce of Klein-Schnellendorf (1741) Frederick had renewed the war, following the revival of Maria Theresa's fortunes. He had invaded Moravia. When an Austrian army had marched to the relief of Brunn which Frederick was besieging, he repulsed it at Chotusitz. This action encouraged Carteret in his mediatory efforts to restore peace in Germany. The Treaty of Berlin destroyed Belleisle's dream. Frederick's desertion meant the break-up of the anti-Hapsburg alliance. Saxony too made peace and French armies in Bohemia were now threatened. Maria Theresa, now free from Prussia, and determined to annex Bavaria as compensation for the loss of Silesia, invaded the electorate in 1743, driving the Emperor Charles VII into exile in Frankfurt.

Meanwhile Carteret had secured from parliament an additional £5 million for the conduct of the war. With this money he hired mercenaries to bring the strength of the "pragmatic army" up to 30,000. Under the command of George II, who lacked all military qualities except that of courage, this army marched south to link up with the Austrian army in Bavaria. It stumbled into a trap set for it by the opposing French army under Marshal Noailles at Dettingen on the River Main, but owing to the incompetence of a French subordinate commander, and the bad behaviour of the French infantry, the battle of Dettingen ended in a French defeat and withdrawal from Germany.

Hapsburg v. Bourbon in Italy

In 1741 the Spanish Bourbons and the Hapsburgs renewed war with each other in Italy. The kingdom of Charles Emmanuel, Duke of Savoy, commanded the Alpine passes into Italy, and as the British navy controlled the Mediterranean, all army supplies for both sides had to go overland through these passes. The Hapsburgs and the Bourbons sought to upset the balance of power which existed between them by gaining the support of Charles Emmanuel. The bait used was Charles' interest in the Austrian Milanese adjoining his kingdom. His frequent change of alliances gave rise to the story then current, that each morning the King's aide-de-camp asked his Majesty on which side he intended to fight that day.

The Treaty of Worms

At first Charles Emmanuel fought against Austria but he changed sides when it became clear that the expulsion of the Austrians would only result in their replacement by the Spaniards. In any case, while Austria could offer immediate territorial concession in the Milanese, the Spaniards, who first had to conquer them, could only hold out a hope which depended upon military victory. It was because Maria Theresa knew that her bargaining power was stronger than that of Elizabeth Farnese that she held out against the cunning old fox in his Alpine lair. However when in 1743 he was threatening to switch back to the Bourbons, Carteret forced Maria Theresa to agree to the Treaty of Worms (1743). Austria surrendered part of the Milanese in return for a Sardinian army of 45,000 men, while Britain agreed to furnish Charles Emmanuel with subsidies of £200,000 and to keep a British navy in the Mediterranean to forestall any seaborne invasion of Italy from Spain.

Designed to expel the Bourbons from Italy, the Treaty of Worms was Carteret's greatest blunder. The Austrians particularly resented the way in which their ally had forced them to surrender a substantial part of the Milanese, but more important, the treaty provoked France into renewing her Family Compact with Spain. In the Treaty of Fontainebleau (October, 1743) France agreed to help Spain to win an Italian principality for Don Philip and to recover Minorca and Gibraltar. This resulted in France officially declaring war on Britain and Austria in March, 1744, although of course since 1741 French armies under Bavarian colours had been fighting the Hapsburgs. Britain was drawn further into the Continental struggle since the Netherlands now became the battleground.

From May, 1744, onwards the French armies swept all before them in the Netherlands. An Austrian army under Charles of Lorraine finally forced Louis XV to move half his army from the Netherlands to Alsace.

Frederick the Great Re-enters the War

It was at this stage that Frederick renewed the war. His fears were revived by the Treaty of Worms in which the signatories guaranteed to fight for the defence of Maria Theresa's empire without excepting Silesia. Afraid that a revitalized Austria might try to recover her lost province, and taking advantage of Austria's pre-occupation with the war against France in the west, he struck at Austria once more. Prussian armies marched into Bohemia (August, 1744). Prague fell, but then Frederick made a serious mistake by advancing on Austria through the Bohemian mountains. His supply lines were endangered by the Hungarians. Faced by Austrian and Hungarian forces, in a difficult country Frederick retreated into Silesia by the end of 1744.

Frederick's position was made worse in 1745 when the Emperor Charles VII died in January. His son Maximilian Joseph, the new Elector of Bavaria, made peace with Maria Theresa and promised to vote for Maria Theresa's husband Francis as the next emperor in return for his electorate. Saxony was also won over to the Austrian camp as a result of jealousy of Prussia and under the persuasion of British subsidies, while the Saxons agreed to enter the war against Prussia.

Frederick invaded Saxony and took Dresden. Owing to the exhaustion of his finances he was prepared to be moderate in his demands in the Treaty of Dresden. Once again Maria Theresa recognized the loss of Silesia, but Frederick agreed to vote for her husband as the next emperor.

End of the War—Peace of Aix-la-Chapelle

For the remainder of the war in Europe, fighting was limited to the Netherlands and Italy. In the Netherlands the French continued their successful advance from 1745 onwards, defeating the British at Fontenoy. This French victory encouraged Charles Edward to land in Scotland to raise the Jacobite standard once more on behalf of his father. Although the details of the "Forty-Five" do not concern us here, the successful march through the Highlands, and the entry into England by "Bonnie Prince Charlie" so alarmed George II that he recalled his son, Cumberland, and his forces from the Netherlands to crush the rising. While Cumberland was busy pursuing the Jacobites all the way back to the north of Scotland, and earning his reputation of "butcher" by his savage reprisals, in the Netherlands Marshal de Saxe took full advantage of the situation to press home his victories. Even Cumberland's return to the Netherlands could not prevent the French from overrunning Brussels and Antwerp and threatening the United Provinces by the end of 1747. This threat was removed by the signing of the Peace of Aix-la-Chapelle in 1748.

While the advantage in the Netherlands lay with the Bourbons, in Italy it lay with the Hapsburgs. After Maria Theresa had made peace with Frederick, Austrian troops from Germany joined those of Sardinia to prosecute a vigorous campaign from 1746 onwards. The French and Spanish armies were expelled and the way for peace was prepared when the influence of Elizabeth Farnese ended with the death of her husband Philip V in 1746.

War-weariness of all the powers now made peace possible. In the conference which met at Aix-la-Chapelle in the spring of 1748, the important terms were arranged between Britain and France, and these were only subsequently accepted by the Austrians. The guiding principle was the return to the balance of power as established at Utrecht. Austria confirmed the cession to Sardinia of part of the Milanese, to Don Philip, Parma-Piacenza, and to

Frederick, Silesia. In return Austria recovered the Netherlands from France while the Dutch recovered their right to garrison the barrier fortresses. Francis was recognized as emperor.

So far as the European struggle was concerned the Treaty was inconclusive and unsatisfactory to all parties, except Frederick who was not even a signatory to it. The Powers' recognition of his control over Silesia was only reluctantly accepted by Maria Theresa, who felt her allies, notably Britain, had let her down. From 1748 Maria Theresa sought ways to avenge herself on her arch-enemy, the King of Prussia.

France's ambitions too had been frustrated. The object of preventing the election of a Hapsburg emperor had failed, while the chances of France establishing her influence in Germany were frustrated by the rise of Prussia.

Britain's status in the eyes of her allies was diminished. She had by her "desertion" of Austria lost the goodwill her subsidies had created.

The Dutch, too, had emerged with little real credit. Their weak, wavering policy throughout, and the lack of national spirit when their frontiers were threatened demonstrated that Holland had sunk to a second-rate power.

Among the clauses of the Treaty were some dealing with the colonial and commercial rivalries between Britain and Spain and France. In those dealing with Anglo-Spanish rivalries, it was agreed that the Asiento Treaty should be renewed for a further four years. The original cause of the struggle over the right of the guarda costas to search British ships was not mentioned. A similar unsatisfactory truce was called to the Anglo-French rivalry when both powers returned their mutual conquests. In America the British returned Louisburg much to the dismay of the American colonists who appreciated the stranglehold Louisburg exercised over the mouth of the St. Lawrence, and in turn over their Canadian possessions. In India, on the other hand, the French restored Madras.

In order to understand why this peace did not settle Anglo-French rivalries, we must turn to the great colonial struggles which had begun during the course of the war in Europe. These struggles had been subordinated by the respective governments to the continental contest. No substantial military aid had been sent to the North American colonists, and the British navy had been mainly occupied in European waters. More far-sighted were the local commanders and governors representing the rival governments.

QUESTIONS

1. "The War of Jenkins' Ear": why is this an inadequate description of the reasons why Britain declared war on Spain in 1739?
2. Which European powers took part in the War of the Austrian Succession? What were their motives for taking part?

CHAPTER 23

ANGLO-FRENCH COLONIAL STRUGGLE, 1744-1757

BETWEEN the colonization of Virginia in 1607 and Georgia in 1732 thirteen colonies had come into existence along the eastern coast of North America. Apart from a common loyalty to the British sovereign who was represented in each colony by the Governor, and a common ancestry in most cases, there was no real unity among the colonists. To all intents and purposes each colony was self-governing through locally-elected colonial assemblies.

By not interfering, the British government's policy of "salutary neglect" enabled the colonies to develop as expanding agricultural, commercial and industrial communities. Tobacco, cotton, rum, shipbuilding, farming were, among others, the occupations of these vigorous people who numbered one and a half million by the middle of the eighteenth century. As their numbers increased so did their desire to expand west through the Allegheny mountain barrier and settlers from Pennsylvania and Virginia were beginning to find passes through the mountains into the Ohio Valley. Settlers from the New England colonies and New York were also moving towards the St. Lawrence and Lake Ontario.

It was this expansionist movement west and north-west coming into head-long conflict with the French claims for dominion in these areas that lay at the root of the rivalry. It was essentially a struggle for land deemed vital by both sides for their existence.

The French Colonies

The French colonies presented a complete contrast to those of Britain. The effective French settlements in the north were confined to the St. Lawrence around Quebec. In addition the French had created a network of trading forts along the Great Lakes. The French *habitant*, or colonist, was principally employed in the fur trade, trapping and exporting furs to Europe. Few in number, about 54,000, the French had been largely responsible for the exploration of the interior. In contrast with their British counterparts, these French settlements were strictly controlled by the French government represented at Quebec by a governor and a large number of administrators.

Besides the St. Lawrence, the other area of French influence was around the mouth of the Mississippi, where the French had built New Orleans. Along the Ohio and Illinois the French had begun to build forts with the object of linking up their possessions around Quebec with those around New Orleans, and to assert their claim to the large surrounding area which they called Louisiana.

The struggle which broke out after 1744 turned upon the control of forts situated at strategic places, in particular those guarding the rivers, which in the absence of roads were necessarily the chief lines of communication. Governor William Shirley of Massachusetts organized an expedition from Boston in 1745 against Louisburg, the French fort on Cape Breton island guarding the mouth of the St. Lawrence. This expedition assisted by a British naval squadron succeeded in capturing the port after a short siege in June, 1745.

By controlling Louisburg the British gained a stranglehold over French Canada for not only were they in a position to prevent the arrival from Europe of French soldiers, but they could ruin French trade. It was, as we have noted, with great consternation that the British colonists learnt of the return of Louisburg to the French in the Peace of Aix-la-Chapelle. To counteract this the British built Halifax in Nova Scotia.

Incidents, 1748-56

While the siege of Louisburg was the outstanding incident during the war, the peace following 1748 was marked by growing tensions which resulted in unofficial fighting before the Seven Years' War was officially declared in 1756. Acadia was one area of conflict. Acquired by Britain at the Treaty of Utrecht, it had been renamed Nova Scotia. The boundaries between the British and French territories were a matter of constant dispute. The French had established new forts there and paid the Indians bounties for British scalps. In their turn the British had expelled some five thousand French settlers.

The chief bone of contention was the Ohio, for this river was the vital link between the Mississippi and St. Lawrence settlements. To forestall the French, an "Ohio Company" was formed in Virginia to develop the Ohio Valley. A group of Virginians started to build a fort at the junction of the Monongahela and Ohio rivers in 1754 but were driven off by the French who completed it, naming it after their governor, Duquesne. When Colonel Washington and a group of Virginia militiamen attempted to recapture it, they were forced to accept defeat.

Taking advantage of the tension in North America, the "War Party" in Britain persuaded Newcastle's government to dispatch an expeditionary force of two regiments under General Braddock to America. This force which landed in 1755 marched against Fort Duquesne in July straight into an ambush prepared by the French with their American Indian allies. Braddock and many of his men were killed.

Meanwhile the French government in their turn sent reinforcements to Canada. It was with ill-defined orders to intercept that Admiral Boscawen was dispatched with a naval squadron by Newcastle to Newfoundland. Off its foggy shores in April, 1755, Boscawen lay in wait for the French fleet, but succeeded in capturing only two vessels, while the main fleet with the reinforcements slipped safely past. Boscawen's action resulted in France actively preparing to attack Britain and Hanover. The startled reaction of the British government sparked off the chain of events that created a new alignment of the powers in preparation for the war. Before dealing with this "Diplomatic Revolution" let us turn to two other spheres of conflict.

Rival East India Companies

The products of India, notably spices, cottons and calicoes had been in much demand in Europe since the Middle Ages. After the voyage of Vasco da Gama had opened a sea-route to the East, merchants from Portugal, Holland, France and England eagerly sought their fortunes in the spice trade. East India Companies came into existence with monopoly rights, and these companies secured permission from native rulers to erect "factories" along the coast of India. While in the sixteenth century the Portuguese and in the seventeenth century the Dutch, had been the leading trading powers, by the eighteenth century supremacy had passed to the British and the French. The chief British factories were Madras, Calcutta, Bombay and Surat, while those of the French were Pondicherry and Chandernagore.

When these factories had first been established in the 17th century, India had been effectively governed by the Moghul emperors through their provincial governors or *nabobs*, but after the death of Emperor Aurangzeb in 1707 a decline set in. Later emperors lacked any effective authority. Provincial governors became virtually independent princes and civil wars between rival claimants occurred whenever these native princes died. By the middle of the eighteenth century India was in a state of absolute confusion. It was in these troubled waters of Indian politics that the French and British fished for trading privileges to outdo each other.

Dupleix—the Conflict of 1744-50

It was Dupleix, the brilliant Governor of Pondicherry between 1741 and 1754, who first saw the opportunities of interfering in native politics to further French interests. He built up "sepoy forces" composed of Indians trained and led by European officers. These were to assist native princes in their struggles for power who in return were to reward the company with territorial and commercial privileges. France would thereby gain a foothold in India.

Before Dupleix could put his plan into operation war broke out with Britain in 1744 during the course of which the French captured Madras (1746) while the British besieged Pondicherry (1748). In the peace settlement Madras was restored to the British.

The real chance for Dupleix to carry out his ambitious plans came in the following two years when succession wars were being waged in the Deccan and the Carnatic. Dupleix sent his brilliant lieutenant Bussy and a sepoy force to support the claims of Mozaffar Jang in the Deccan and in 1750 succeeded in placing him on the throne. In return this pro-French *nabob* made Dupleix his deputy over the provinces of southern India.

Similar success at first attended Dupleix in the Carnatic where he championed the claims of Chunda Sahib. The British East India Company, to combat their rivals, championed Mohammed Ali whom the pro-French *nabob* besieged at Trichinopoly. If this town, Mohammed Ali's capital, were to fall, the British would lose control in the south-east. Their prestige in the eyes of the Indians was as low as that of the French was high. The situation was black.

Robert Clive—the Conflict of 1750-6

It was the intervention of Robert Clive in this critical situation that not merely saved Britain's influence in the south-east of India, but laid the basis for the establishment of British rule in India. Clive had been originally sent out in 1744 by his parents as a clerk in the East India Company's factory at Madras. This high-spirited young man of eighteen had found life dull, and subject to fits of depression he had twice attempted to take his own life, but the pistol misfired.

Soon after his arrival in India Madras was captured. Disguised as an Indian he escaped and joined the East India Company's army as an ensign. He soon displayed exceptional qualities of leadership, judgement and courage. These were to be demonstrated in 1751 when he was allowed to put into practice his bold plan to save Trichinopoly. With a small force of five hundred he attacked and captured Arcot, the capital of the pro-French *nabob* whose forces were in Trichinopoly. This surprise blow had the desired effect. The enraged *nabob*, with a force of ten thousand men, laid siege to his own capital. Clive's small force successfully withstood a fifty-day siege before being relieved.

In the following year Clive defeated the pro-French *nabob* and his rival Mohammed Ali was restored to the throne of the Carnatic. The situation was thus completely reversed. The Indians looked more and more to the British. Dupleix, his plans shattered, was recalled and ended his days in disgrace. Clive, in contrast, on his return to England in 1753 was rewarded with a pension and great honours by a grateful nation. For the moment a truce was called in India, but this was soon to be broken with the renewal of war in 1756. It was in June of that year that Clive returned to India as the Governor of Fort St. David, which lay south of Pondicherry.

The West Indies

In many respects the commercial rivalry between the British and the French was most acute in the West Indies. Despite the Spanish claim to exclusive influence, British, French and Dutch merchants had, over the course of time, acquired these valuable tropical islands. The French controlled St. Dominique, Martinique and Guadeloupe, the British held Jamaica, Barbados and the Leeward Isles. These islands were valued both for the sugar exported to Europe and for the slave market they afforded to merchants involved in the "Triangular Trade." The Atlantic ports like Bristol, Liverpool, Nantes and La Rochelle owed their growth to these merchants. Their ships sailed to West Africa where their cargoes of Indian cottons were exchanged for Negro slaves supplied by Arab slave dealers. These unfortunate people were crowded into the ships for the dreadful "middle passage" as the voyage from the West African coast to the West Indies was known. Those that survived were sold to the sugar planters of the West Indies, for only Negroes were capable of working in the tropical heat on the plantations.

This slave trade was regarded as the most profitable of all enterprises by British merchants who enjoyed a greater measure of it than their French rivals. On the other hand the French sugar-planters were undercutting their British rivals by some 25 per cent. Although strictly regulated by trade laws preventing colonies from trading with any foreign country, and although the British West India planters tried to keep up the price of sugar by the Molasses Act of 1733, illicit trading between the French planters and the New England rum manufacturers was increasing.

Their trade threatened, it is little wonder that the "West India Interest" in Parliament favoured war, and when actual hostilities broke out they followed the best tradition of the Spanish Main. Essentially a naval conflict, the fortunes of the war swung in favour of the British with their mastery of the seas. When peace was signed in 1748 the British returned their conquests.

The Diplomatic Revolution

During the period between the War of the Austrian Succession and the Seven Years' War, a change in the alliances of the major powers took place which was regarded as so dramatic that it is always referred to as the "Diplomatic Revolution." The reconciliation between the Hapsburgs and the Bourbons, together with the break-up of the alliance of Austria, Britain and Holland, was indeed revolutionary.

The new alignment was first conceived by Kaunitz, the shrewd adviser of

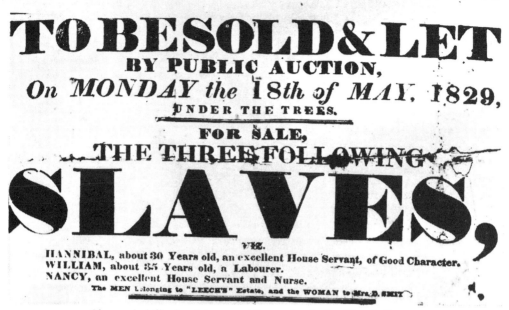

Slave sale bill advertising a public auction in the West Indies.

Maria Theresa. The overriding objective of Austrian policy after 1748 was the recovery of Silesia. Kaunitz was convinced that Britain would not help Austria because of increasing overseas commitments, and the fear that Hanover would be attacked by Prussia. Kaunitz drew this conclusion from British policy during the War of the Austrian Succession. Although Britain had fought for Austria, relations had been far from cordial. Austria had felt let down, for British statesmen in their efforts to isolate France, had forced Maria Theresa to make concessions to Frederick. Although the British government was not prepared to break with Austria in favour of an alliance with Prussia, Kaunitz had no such sentimental attachments to Britain. As a substitute for the British alliance, Kaunitz looked to Austria's age-old rival, France, whose military strength, if won over, would be of far greater value than British subsidies. He was prepared to bribe her with the Netherlands.

His first attempts to detach France from her alliance with Prussia failed because France was too preoccupied in internal troubles and was anxious to remain at peace. She was not prepared in any case to ally with Austria so long as the latter was in alliance with her own chief enemy Britain, even though their relations were growing very cool.

British Approach to Prussia

The situation was altered by the growing Anglo-French tension overseas, especially in North America. Alarmed lest France and even Prussia might attack Hanover and the Netherlands, the British government appealed in vain to Austria. Accordingly Newcastle, the prime minister, opened negotiations with Prussia and Russia. In September, 1755, his ambassador at Moscow, Hanbury-Williams, made a subsidy treaty with Russia whereby Russia agreed to maintain on her frontiers adjoining Prussia large forces in return for British gold. These forces were to serve as a guarantee against Prussia seizing Hanover, for Tsarina Elizabeth was only too eager to have an excuse for overrunning Frederick's lands.

Convention of Westminster

The news of this Anglo-Russian alliance startled Frederick, whose chief interest lay in remaining at peace. Both Austria and Russia had adopted threatening attitudes while his so-called ally France was too preoccupied to render him effective aid. Necessity made strange bed fellows and even though Frederick and his uncle George II were not on good terms, they both desired the neutrality of Germany. Accordingly Britain and Prussia concluded the Convention of Westminster in January, 1756. Both powers agreed to use their influence to maintain the peace in Germany in order to protect Hanover and Silesia from attack.

Both Newcastle and Frederick miscalculated the consequences of this agreement on the rest of Europe for it was to bring into being a rival alliance that made war possible. Newcastle misjudged the Russian reaction. Tsarina Elizabeth deeply resented Britain's alliance with her enemy Prussia, because it frustrated her intended attack upon East Prussia. Frederick miscalculated France's reaction. France feared isolation. Her arch-enemy Britain was not merely an ally of Prussia, but on good terms with Spain. The opportunity had thus arisen for Kaunitz to put into effect his proposed Austro-French alliance. Despite difficulties over Austria's refusal to commit herself to a war against Britain, negotiations were concluded. In May, 1756, the First Treaty of Versailles was signed.

First Treaty of Versailles

This was a defensive alliance between Austria and France for mutual assistance if either were attacked by a third power. As Austria made the provision that she would not fight against Britain, and as Britain was the only power liable to attack France, the agreement was one-sided, but although limited in extent, it was a diplomatic revolution. The Austrians regarded it as a prelude to an even closer union, while the French hoped that it would secure peace in Europe and leave them free to concentrate on the overseas struggle.

The outbreak of war in April, 1756, was not unexpected. Preparations for the renewal of war which unofficially had been waging in North America and India since the Peace of Aix-la-Chapelle were speeded up in western Europe during the spring of 1756. The French were not only threatening to invade England, but they seized the important British naval base of Minorca in the western Mediterranean, defeating Admiral Byng in so doing.

The loss of Minorca was the climax of a series of disasters for Newcastle's government. Fort Oswego in northern America had also fallen to the French. In order to find a scapegoat for these disasters the British ministers court-martialled Admiral Byng, who was later shot despite the court's plea for clemency, "in order to encourage the others" as the French writer, Voltaire, explained.

Four months after the outbreak of the Anglo-French struggle, Europe was startled by the news that Frederick the Great had launched an attack on Saxony. This attack precipitated a great European war. Why did Frederick risk losing his hard-won Silesia by violating the peace? The explanation lies in Frederick's determination to destroy, by a bold stroke, a coalition which he believed had already come into being to break up Prussia. Surrounded by three hostile countries, Russia, Austria and Saxony, Frederick decided to attack Austria before she attacked him. He also wished to discourage France from entering, on Austria's behalf, a war in which she had nothing to gain and everything to lose. He also hoped that his new ally, Britain, would restrain Russia, but this hope was not realized.

Frederick's ill-advised plan simply hastened the anti-Prussian coalition. By the First Treaty of Versailles, Austria called on French aid, and Russia and Sweden joined them as partners in the treaty. The Imperial Diet of German princes also declared war, and in 1757 Austria's Second Treaty of Versailles with the French completed the Diplomatic Revolution.

Second Treaty of Versailles

By the terms of this, France agreed to supply men and money each year to Austria until the anti-Prussian alliance had achieved the destruction of Prussia, in return for which France would acquire a few north-eastern border fortresses. This treaty was the most sacrificial blunder that French statesmen have ever committed, and an extraordinary triumph for Kaunitz's diplomacy. France had no fundamental conflict with Prussia, and should have kept clear of Continental entanglements to reserve her resources for the overseas struggle.

QUESTIONS

1. Write an account of Anglo-French rivalry in the period 1744-56 in North America and India.
2. What was the Diplomatic Revolution? Trace the stages by which it came about.

CHAPTER 24

CONTINENTAL AND COLONIAL CONFLICT: THE SEVEN YEARS' WAR

THE prospects for Prussia in 1757 were bleak. With a small population of four million and slender resources, she found herself surrounded by the three greatest powers whose combined populations and resources were ten times as great. Frederick's only hope lay in preventing the juncture of his enemies' forces and dealing with them separately. Prussia's chief asset was the genius of her King as a military commander. He was to show himself the master of both defensive and offensive strategy while his dauntless courage in the face of apparently hopeless odds was to be the main inspiration of his soldiers. Added to this was the unity of command, the discipline of his army and the short supply lines on which his forces operated.

Throughout the war, Frederick treated Saxony as a Prussian province. He used it as a springboard for his campaigns into Austria through Bohemia. Routed at Kolin he raised the siege of Prague and was driven out of Bohemia (1757). The Austrians re-occupied Silesia.

The news from the other fronts was also bad. In the east, the Russian army defeated the Prussians at Gross Jägersdorf (August, 1757). In the north the Swedes invaded Pomerania, while Prussia's western flank was exposed by the French victory over the Duke of Cumberland's "Army of Observation," which had been formed for the defence of Hanover. The French occupied Hanover, a base from which to launch an invasion of Prussia. The outlook was grim.

Frederick's survival was mainly due to his own genius. In the last two months of 1757 Frederick gained two of his greatest victories. In November he out-manoeuvred and overwhelmed a Franco-German army at Rossbach in Saxony as it tried to envelop his left flank. This victory was rapturously received in Britain, where Frederick was acclaimed the "Protestant hero."

Switching his armies from Saxony to Silesia he engaged the Austrians at Leuthen. By a skilful manoeuvre he concentrated the main attack against the Austrian left flank, his columns advancing obliquely to the enemy. Before the Austrians had time to reform their columns, Frederick had shattered their flank. This method of the "oblique attack" which Frederick adopted with

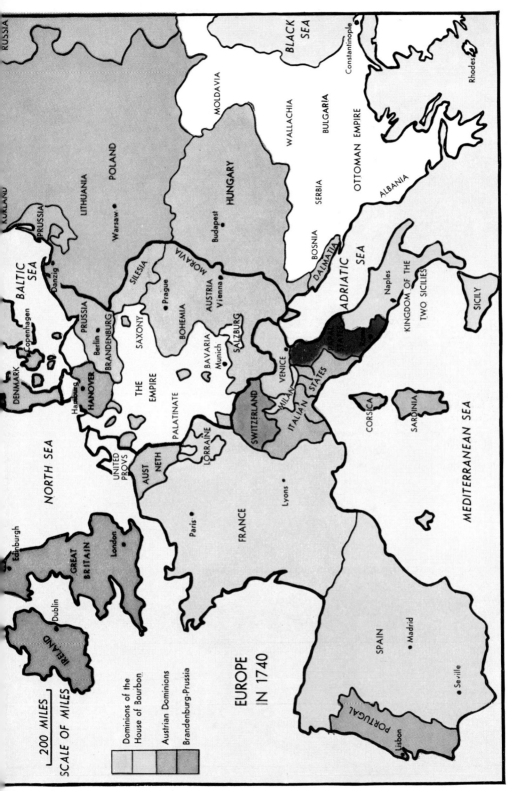

EUROPE
IN 1740

SCALE OF MILES

200 MILES

Dominions of the
House of Bourbon

Austrian Dominions

Brandenburg-Prussia

RUSSIA

BLACK SEA

Constantinople

Rhodes

MOLDAVIA

WALLACHIA

BULGARIA

OTTOMAN EMPIRE

SERBIA

ALBANIA

POLAND

LITHUANIA

Warsaw

HUNGARY

Budapest

BOSNIA

DALMATIA

ADRIATIC SEA

PRUSSIA

Danzig

SILESIA

MORAVIA

AUSTRIA

Vienna

SALZBURG

Naples

SICILY

BALTIC SEA

Copenhagen

PRUSSIA

Berlin

BRANDENBURG

SAXONY

Prague

BOHEMIA

BAVARIA

Munich

VENICE

MILAN

ITALIAN STATES

KINGDOM OF THE
TWO SICILIES

DENMARK

Hamburg

HANOVER

THE EMPIRE

PALATINATE

SWITZERLAND

CORSICA

SARDINIA

MEDITERRANEAN SEA

NORTH SEA

UNITED
PROVS

AUST
NETH

LORRAINE

Lyons

Edinburgh

GREAT
BRITAIN

London

FRANCE

Paris

IRELAND

Dublin

SPAIN

Madrid

Seville

PORTUGAL

Lisbon

CL/HIST 2—O

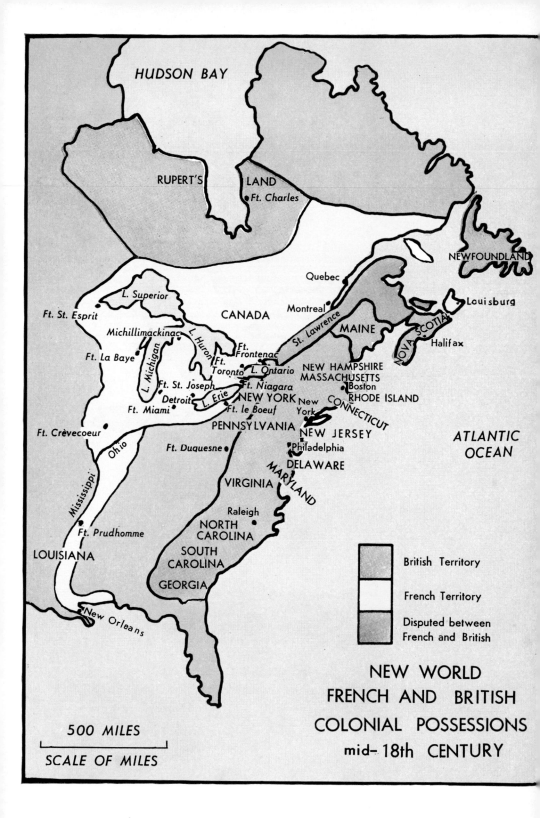

HUDSON BAY

RUPERT'S LAND
• Ft. Charles

NEWFOUNDLAND

Quebec
Montreal
CANADA
Ft. St. Esprit
L. Superior
Michillimackinac
Ft. La Baye
L. Michigan
L. Huron
Ft. Frontenac
Ft. Toronto
L. Ontario
Ft. St. Joseph
Ft. Niagara
Detroit
L. Erie
Ft. Miami
Ft. Crèvecoeur
Ohio
Ft. le Boeuf
Ft. Duquesne
Louisburg
St. Lawrence
MAINE
NOVA SCOTIA
Halifax
NEW HAMPSHIRE
MASSACHUSETTS
Boston
RHODE ISLAND
NEW YORK
New York
CONNECTICUT
PENNSYLVANIA
NEW JERSEY
Philadelphia
DELAWARE
MARYLAND
VIRGINIA

ATLANTIC
OCEAN

Mississippi
Ft. Prudhomme
Raleigh
NORTH CAROLINA
SOUTH CAROLINA
GEORGIA

LOUISIANA
New Orleans

British Territory

French Territory

Disputed between
French and British

NEW WORLD
FRENCH AND BRITISH
COLONIAL POSSESSIONS
mid-18th CENTURY

500 MILES

SCALE OF MILES

considerable success enabled his army to use their inferior numbers to gain local superiority on the enemy's flanks. Prussia was saved and Frederick's reputation enhanced.

Pitt's War Plans

These two great victories at Rossbach and Leuthen were to have a decisive effect upon the help received from his ally Britain. Britain's fortunes were finally in the capable hands of William Pitt, whose rise to power in June, 1757, had been delayed by the opposition of George II and the Whig magnates. Pitt had long been opposed to Britain becoming involved in Continenta struggles but Prussia's struggle for existence, and her heroic victories had finally convinced him of his earlier mistake. The defence of Hanover and financial aid to Prussia now became vital, if subordinate, parts of his overall plan to destroy French colonial and commercial threats overseas. Parliament voted £1,200,000 to be used to reform the Hanoverian army. This army safeguarded Prussia's western frontiers while at the same time keeping large French armies tied down in Europe. British subsidies to Frederick too were increased. Without these Frederick could not have kept an army in the field.

The key to the whole of Pitt's policy was the navy's control of the sea. French ports were blockaded to prevent her sending reinforcements overseas, while "commando" raids on the French coast were organized. These helped to distract still further the French armies in Europe.

The 1758 Campaigns in the East and West

The hopes that Frederick may have had of making peace with Maria Theresa were not fulfilled, for she was to reveal qualities of resolution in adversity comparable to those of Frederick himself. Frederick's sole object in the later campaigns was to keep his enemies at bay and in this he succeeded, although at an enormous cost in human and material resources. The 1758 campaign opened disastrously for him when he invaded Moravia and his supply lines were cut. He was forced to retreat into Bohemia. Learning of a Russian invasion of Brandenburg, Frederick switched his forces to repel this attack. In one of the bloodiest encounters at Zorndorf he forced the Russian general Fermor to withdraw into Poland, and so prevented a union of Russian and Austrian forces. Meanwhile two Austrian armies had attacked Silesia and Saxony. Frederick moved first to the relief of Dresden and then to the relief of Neisse in Silesia. Austrian forces barred the way and here Frederick suffered a defeat, but the Austrians failed to follow up their victory and Frederick was able to slip past and relieve Neisse. The campaign ended with no permanent advantage gained on either side.

In the west the French fought with little enthusiasm, for they knew they were fighting primarily for Austrian interests.

211

Choiseul and the 1759 Campaign in the West

The Duke of Choiseul became the resourceful new French Foreign Minister in December, 1758. This "Gallic Pitt" was to infuse a new vigour into the conduct of the war, but this renewed energy was to be directed against Britain in an attempt to stem the growing tide of success which British armies under Pitt's inspired direction were achieving wherever they were in conflict with the French.

Choiseul's policy meant less aid to Austria. In the third Treaty of Versailles he cut French financial aid to Austria by half, limited France's military support to 100,000 men, and refused to guarantee recovery of Silesia. In a desperate effort to reverse French defeats, Choiseul determined on a renewed thrust against Hanover, and an invasion of Britain, but both these plans failed. The Hanoverian army stopped the French at Minden, and the French invasion fleets destined for Britain were destroyed by Boscawen at Lagos Bay, near Gibraltar, and by Hawke at Quiberon Bay in Brittany.

Kunersdorf and the "Miracle of the House of Hohenzollern"

Despite his ally's successes, the 1759 campaign was disastrous for Frederick. The Russians and Austrians attacked Brandenburg, and at the battle of Kunersdorf Frederick lost over 25,000 men. During the course of the rout Frederick tried to check the disaster shouting, "My children, will you desert your father? Dogs, would you live for ever? Will no cursed bullet hit me?"

Yet Prussia was again to be saved. The quarrels between Austrians and Russians resulted in the Russians withdrawing into Poland, while the Austrians refused to engage with the remnants of Frederick's forces. He was thus able to recover most of Saxony which Imperial forces had overrun earlier in the year. British subsidies and other revenues enabled Frederick to continue paying for the war. Most important of all, Frederick's survival, "The Miracle of the House of Hohenzollern," was due to his own indomitable will, which inspired all whom he led to make the supreme effort and which filled his enemies with the greatest fear and respect.

In 1760 the Austrians, joined by the Russians, re-invaded Silesia and Frederick was unable to expel them. More success greeted his efforts in Saxony, where after their defeat at Torgau the Austrians retreated.

The 1761 campaign confirmed the stalemate that existed. Prussia remained unconquered, but vulnerable. Pitt resigned in October, 1761, and George III and Bute, his new chief minister, favoured peace. British subsidies to Prussia were stopped and peace negotiations were opened with France. To Frederick this was an act of treachery which he deeply resented for the rest of his life. Yet fortune once more smiled on him. A cessation of hostilities was unexpectedly to occur.

In January, 1762, the death of Tsarina Elizabeth removed Frederick's most implacable foe. Her successor, Tsar Peter III, had an unbounded admiration for Frederick and his army, and an extreme loathing of the Austrians. Russian armies were immediately evacuated from East Prussia and eastern Pomerania, and in a peace treaty Peter agreed to allow Russian troops to be used against their former ally, the Austrians. Before this could be effected, Peter III, whose policies had aroused great hostility in Russia, was murdered by a group of courtiers including Gregory Orlov, who loved Peter's wife, the remarkable Catherine. She now had herself proclaimed Empress. Although she repudiated the agreement in which Peter had promised Frederick military aid, she refused to renew the war against him. As Sweden soon followed Russia's example in making peace, Austria had to do the same, for alone she was unable to recover Silesia.

By the Peace of Hubertsburg in February, 1763, between Austria and Prussia, Frederick was recognized as master of Silesia after seven long campaigns. Prussia was elevated to the status of a major power, while the prestige of the Hapsburgs continued the decline which was to end in 1806 with Napoleon's declaration of the end of the Holy Roman Empire.

Anglo-French Conflict in North America

The news of French victories in North America during the Seven Years' War and the consequent threat to British possessions there, brought William Pitt to power. He was soon to justify his claim: "I know that I can save this country and that no one else can." To Pitt the conquest of Canada was the primary task, while the operations in Europe, India and the West Indies played a subordinate, though important role. The key to success in Canada lay in the blockade of the French ports, for by preventing the French from sending reinforcements, and destroying French trade, Pitt realized that not only would he be able to supply and support his troops at will, but that Britain's overseas trade, so vital for the economic life of the country, would be protected. Since the success of his plans ultimately rested upon sound leadership and public support, Pitt paid very careful attention to these matters when planning the large expedition of twenty thousand men for Canada. Abercrombie, supported by Amherst, Howe and Wolfe, was appointed to command the armies, while Boscawen was in charge of the naval forces.

British forces landed in North America in 1758 and the campaign opened with a three-pronged attack on the French positions. Wolfe and Amherst, supported by Boscawen, lay siege to Louisburg, the French naval base guarding the approaches of the St. Lawrence. After five weeks it surrendered in July, 1758. Less successful was Abercrombie's thrust against Fort Ticonderoga where his forces were repulsed with heavy losses. This delayed the expedition's progress until the following year. Meanwhile the dying veteran, Forbes, with an expedition from Virginia, made an epic march through mountains and forests against Fort Duquesne. Hearing of his approach, the French retired after burning the fort down. It was rebuilt and renamed Pittsburg because, in the words of Forbes, "the spirit of Pitt inspired the enterprise." By the end of 1758 the British had seized the key points. The vital struggle for the Ohio had been decided, and the forces were poised for an attack on Quebec. Even before this citadel was captured the war in Canada was really decided. Outnumbered and cut off from the source of their supplies, it was only a question of time before the French had to admit defeat.

Capture of Quebec

In 1759 Wolfe and Admiral Saunders sailed down the St. Lawrence with a force of ten thousand troops and twenty ships-of-the-line against the virtually impregnable position of Quebec. Guarded on one flank by cliffs 400 feet high (the "Heights of Abraham") and by Montcalm's forces on the other, Quebec stood on a peninsula in the St. Lawrence. Wolfe first attempted to carry the landward defences. This approach met with disaster. Anxious to seize the town before winter set in and froze the St. Lawrence, Wolfe staked his fortunes on the only other alternative, the scaling of the treacherous cliffs. On the night of 12 September, the ships' boats, filled with soldiers and propelled by muffled oars, landed opposite a small, almost perpendicular goat-track leading up the cliffs. Heroically this force scaled these cliffs, and by early morning it was assembled on the plains. Montcalm, taken by surprise, hurriedly mustered his soldiers to meet the danger. In the ensuing battle the British in a bayonet charge drove the French from the field. Both Wolfe and Montcalm were killed but Wolfe died happy in the knowledge that the French were running and his mission accomplished. Meanwhile Amherst captured both Fort Ticonderoga and Crown Point on Lake Champlain, and Montreal, the last French stronghold, fell a year after Wolfe's victory. The fighting was over, and Britain had gained a new empire.

Anglo-French Conflict in India

In India, too, fortune finally smiled on the British, mainly through the efforts of Robert Clive. On the day he returned to India, 20 June, 1756, there was committed in the dungeons of Fort St. William at Calcutta the notorious atrocity which led to Clive's interference in Bengal. The new native ruler Siraj-ud-Daula, who preferred the French to the British, led a vast Indian force against the small British garrison. The governor fled with the women and children leaving the men to defend the fort. Assured that their lives would be spared the 146 defenders surrendered only to suffer a fate even worse than death in battle. They were all imprisoned on a hot sultry night in the "Black Hole of Calcutta," a prison eighteen feet square with only two small windows

214

for ventilation. Their sufferings were later described by Holwell, the deputy governor, one of the twenty-three survivors who were released on the following morning. Water passed to the inmates through the bars in skins merely aggravated rather than assuaged their thirst, driving them into a delirium. In their efforts to reach and remain at the open windows men fought and trampled on each other like animals, and all but the strongest succumbed. When orders were given to release them, twenty minutes elapsed before these orders could be executed, the survivors being almost too weak to move the great numbers of dead bodies piled up against the inward-opening doors.

Conquest of Bengal

When Clive heard of this atrocity he immediately organized a force to secure redress from the ruler. Apart from the brutality of the incident, to have ignored such an attack on the company's headquarters in Bengal would have meant an end to British influence in this province. Accordingly in October, 1756, Clive embarked with his force of 900 Europeans and 1,500 sepoys aboard Admiral Watson's fleet. The vital importance of British control of the seas was now demonstrated, for this force was able to sail unmolested to Bengal. By January, 1757, Clive had recaptured Calcutta and forced Siraj-ud-Daula to pay compensation to the company. Clive then

Clive at Plassey. This battle established British rule in Bengal.

captured the French fort at Chandernagore, a vital store house of the French East India Company. Learning that Siraj-ud-Daula was plotting with the French to expel the British, Clive entered into secret negotiations with Mir Jaffar, one of Siraj-ud-Daula's generals, with the intention of placing him on the throne. In return Mir Jaffar agreed to desert the French cause. Clive then marched on the Nabob's capital at Murshidabad.

Battle of Plassey

It was during the course of this march that Clive demonstrated his outstanding courage, determination and judgement in the face of apparently hopeless odds. As he moved north he had to make a most difficult decision—whether or not to cross the river Hugli separating him from the enemy. Once crossed there would be no return since the monsoons which were about to break would swell the river into a raging torrent. Facing his small force of three thousand was that of the Nabob, whose fifty thousand troops were reinforced by two hundred Frenchmen. While all his officers were against the crossing, Clive decided that he could not let the opportunity slip. Having crossed the river they took up positions in a mango grove at Plassey where the battle which decided the fate of India was fought on 23 June, 1757. An artillery bombardment followed by a charge threw the Nabob's ill-disciplined forces into confusion. They fled leaving five hundred dead while Clive's total losses were a mere twenty-two. It was only after the battle that Mir Jaffar came forward. He had waited to see how the battle would turn out. He was then proclaimed Nabob of Bengal, while Siraj-ud-Daula, who had fled, was soon murdered.

With a friendly nabob on the throne, British influence in Bengal was firmly established. That Mir Jaffar was dependent upon the support of the British forces was shown by the enormous sums of money and the privileges he bestowed upon Clive and the company.

Just after these dramatic events had taken place in Bengal, the French made a renewed effort to dislodge the British from the Carnatic. To counter this, Pitt dispatched Sir Eyre Coote in charge of three regiments. The French made desperate efforts and by the end of 1758 had seized Fort St. David and Arcot and were threatening Madras, but a British fleet soon asserted its supremacy over the rival French naval squadron, which then withdrew.

In the meanwhile the withdrawal of French troops from the Northern Circars enabled Clive to seize this province. The loss of this, the abandonment of the Deccan and the raising of the siege of Madras marked the beginning of the end for the French. The end came with the British victory at the battle of Wandewash in 1760 enabling them to clear the French from the Carnatic, and with the capture of Pondicherry in 1761.

Similar success attended British efforts in the West Indies where in the spring of 1759 the British conquered the French sugar island of Guadeloupe. In February, 1762, a powerful squadron seized Martinique and all the other islands fell without a struggle.

In 1758 the British also gained control of French slave trading stations on the west coast of Africa. These conquests were of great value to the British sugar and slave merchants, with corresponding disastrous results for the French.

Pitt's Resignation

When George III succeeded his grandfather in October, 1760, Pitt was at the height of his power. Yet within a year of George III's accession, Pitt, the idol of the people and the architect of victory, was driven from power and replaced by the Earl of Bute.

Disliking what he regarded as the "corruption" of "party" politics and believing that Britain had now accomplished her purposes in the Seven Years' War, George III exercised his powers of ministerial appointment to bring into office men who, he hoped, shared his point of view and would help him to give effect to it. Bute was appointed to the Cabinet as Secretary of State in March, 1761, but conflicts soon arose between ministers old and new over the conduct of the war. George III and Bute were anxious to end "this bloody and expensive war," as the King described it. Peace negotiations were opened in 1761 with France. Pitt and Choiseul failed to agree on the proposals partly because Pitt was demanding too much, and partly because Choiseul was seeking to draw Spain into the war and was therefore playing for time.

With the death of Ferdinand in 1759 and the accession of Charles III a revolution occurred in Spanish foreign policy. Charles III had inherited from his mother, Elizabeth Farnese, all her ardent dislike of the British. Choiseul accordingly cultivated the Spanish alliance and in August, 1761, on the day that Pitt broke off the peace negotiations with France, France signed the Family Compact with Spain. Spain agreed to enter the war if peace had not been reached by May, 1762.

Pitt knew of the existence of this Franco-Spanish alliance, and being convinced that Britain would eventually have to fight with Spain began to prepare for war with her. When, however, he advocated an immediate declaration of war on Spain on the grounds that the treasure fleet upon which the Spanish government relied, had not sailed, he came into violent conflict with Bute and his colleagues in the Cabinet, who were backed by George III. Pitt accordingly resigned in October, 1761.

Pitt was soon proved right. With the arrival of the treasure fleet at Cadiz, the Spanish government broke off relations and in January, 1762, Britain and Spain once more went to war.

British forces were sent to the West Indies where they seized Havana in

Cuba, while Manila in the Philippines was also captured the same year.

These further successes convinced the French and Spanish of the need for a settlement. Peace negotiations were re-opened and resulted in the Peace of Paris signed in April, 1763, between Britain, France and Spain. This peace was ratified by Parliament.

Britain's conquests of Canada, St. Vincent, Tobago, Dominica and Senegal were confirmed. Britain recovered Minorca in exchange for Belle Isle which was returned to France. France recovered her fishing rights in Newfoundland, and the West Indian islands of Guadeloupe, Martinique, St. Lucia and Marie Galante, as well as Gorée in Africa. In India she recovered her original trading factories but was forbidden to fortify them.

Spain ceded Florida to Britain in exchange for Havana, recovered Manila and secured Louisiana from France.

Importance of the Peace of Paris

The treaty was of outstanding importance despite the vehement criticism with which Pitt attacked it. Pitt's charges were that full advantage had not been taken of France's plight to ruin her once and for all. By returning her West Indian islands, and her fishing rights in Newfoundland Pitt maintained that France could recover her former naval power. Nevertheless Britain had emerged as the undisputed colonial, commercial and naval power. The establishment of Britain's supremacy in Canada, India and on the world's oceans at the expense of her nearest rival, France, was of profound significance for a country entering an industrial revolution. Overseas possessions both as sources of raw materials and markets for manufactured goods were to become more and more vital to the economic well-being of the country.

In contrast the struggle contributed to the overthrow of the French monarchy. The war contributed substantially to France's enormous financial difficulties, while the loss of overseas possessions and the ruin of her trade was disastrous to the recovery of her economy.

This peace together with that signed between Prussia and Austria at Hubertsburg brought an end to these long-protracted struggles of Hapsburgs and Bourbons. Until the outbreak of the Revolutionary Wars in 1792, comparative peace reigned in Europe even though in North America and India the French, during the War of American Independence, were to try unsuccessfully to retrieve their losses.

QUESTIONS

1. Explain why Frederick the Great was eventually successful in the Seven Years' War.
2. Outline the Anglo-French conflict in North America and account for France's defeat in 1763.

CHAPTER 25

CATHERINE THE GREAT

PRINCESS SOPHIA, as Catherine was first known, was the daughter of Christian, Prince of the small German duchy of Anhalt-Zerbst, and his wife, the vivacious Princess Johanna. Born in 1729 and brought up against the dull background of a rigid and strictly Lutheran court, Princess Sophia's first step into the European limelight was taken when, almost fifteen, in January, 1744, she set out with her parents to answer the summons of the Empress Elizabeth of Russia to reside at her Imperial court. The purpose of this invitation was to arrange the marriage between Princess Sophia and the heir to the Russian throne, Peter of Holstein. The prospect of being the mother-in-law to a future ruler of Russia filled Princess Johanna with joy for she was an ambitious woman, and she accompanied her daughter on her journey to St. Petersburg and then to Moscow. Sleighs sped the royal party on their way across the winter wastes of Russia. Their reception was impressive, with costly gifts showered upon them. The climax came with a magnificent entry and reception in the older capital of Moscow with its oriental domes of churches and monasteries. In the Imperial palace of the Kremlin, Sophia first met her future husband Peter, the Grand Duke.

Peter of Holstein was the Empress Elizabeth's nephew. Without any children of her own, Elizabeth looked to Peter, the grandson of Tsar Peter the Great, to carry on the Romanov dynasty. Since the death in 1725 of Peter the Great, Russia had been troubled by disputed successions. No less than five rulers had ascended the Imperial throne—the Empress Catherine I (1725-27), Tsar Peter II (1727-30), Empress Anne (1730-40), Tsar Ivan VI (1740-41) and finally Empress Elizabeth. One can imagine how disturbing these changes were.

Had love been the sole consideration, Catherine would never have married Peter. He was a frail, pock-marked youth, whose unhappy unbringing after his parents' death had made him cowardly, cruel and capricious. His one passion was an inordinate fondness for his toy soldiers. As Catherine wrote after they were married, "Peter took no notice of me but was always occupied with his valets, playing at soldiers, exercising them in his room, changing his uniform twenty times a day." He insisted on her playing cards with him, and when he lost he would sulk for days. He had no manners and put out his

219

tongue at people like a naughty child. He kept hunting dogs in a room so close to her bedroom that she was annoyed by their barking and smell.

In complete contrast with her betrothed, Catherine herself was a high-spirited, intelligent and ambitious girl. Dark, with rich brown hair, slender in build, her deep forehead and firm mouth and chin were the main physical indications of her exceptional abilities and determination. Her charm and vitality amply compensated for her lack of beauty.

Unattracted by Peter, she was prepared to go through with the marriage to further her ambitions of becoming the ruler of Russia. "I did not care about Peter but I did about the Crown." Accordingly Catherine began to prepare for her future role by submitting to instruction in the Greek Orthodox faith into which she was admitted in 1745 when she took the name of Catherine in place of Sophia. After this ceremony she married Peter and thus became the Grand Duchess.

The Grand Duchess

The next seventeen years were to prove wretched ones for Catherine. Despite the externally magnificent life which she and Peter led in one or other of the splendid palaces at their disposal, they lived in a gilded cage with excessively strict regulations governing their activities, regulations which were the responsibility of Besthuzhev, the Empress Elizabeth's Minister. He was strongly pro-Austrian and feared that the court of the Grand Duke Peter and Grand Duchess Catherine might become the centre of opposition to his policies. Peter was known to have an intense admiration for the Prussian king, Frederick the Great. The Empress Elizabeth, too, made life intolerable for the couple. Jealousy and disappointment that they had produced no heir underlay the petty persecution which troubled Catherine. Their lives might have proved tolerable had they loved each other, but in fact it was a loveless match. Their characters were incompatible.

Lonely and frustrated in her marriage, humiliated by the Empress and bored by the interminable court functions, Catherine was forced to seek compensating distraction. Happily she had the reserve of strength needed to overcome her misery and turned more and more to dancing, riding and reading as outlets for her mental and physical energies, with the consequent development of her intellect and character. She was deeply impressed by the French classics and especially formative upon her outlook was the biography of the great French king, Henry of Navarre, whose life gave Catherine an ideal which she always kept before her.

Just as her mental energy found an outlet in reading the works of the leaders of the "Enlightenment," so too did she find relief from the unhappiness of her married life in love affairs with other men. Yet she never allowed her feelings to cloud her cool, calculating reason. The first affair was with the

Court Chamberlain, Sergei Saltykov who it was widely believed was the father of her son Paul born in 1754. Since she was never allowed by the Empress Elizabeth to care for her baby, his arrival brought no happiness to Catherine and in later years the gulf between mother and son became very marked. Of a different nature was Catherine's attachment to the British ambassador, Hanbury-Williams, who had been sent to Russia in 1755 to negotiate an Anglo-Russian treaty. This treaty was virtually undone when Britain signed the "Convention of Westminster" with Prussia, for Frederick the Great and Elizabeth were on the worst of terms. Elizabeth regarded Britain's action as a gross betrayal. In order to restore British influence, Hanbury-Williams looked to Catherine as the future ruler of Russia. With this object in mind he corresponded with her and his letters reveal his love for her. Between 1757 and 1762 Russia was fighting in the Seven Years' War as an ally of Austria against their common enemy Prussia whose sole ally was Britain. By working through Catherine, both the British and Prussian governments hoped to influence Russian policy. It was known too, that the Grand Duke Peter was a great admirer of Frederick the Great and that on coming to power he would completely reverse Elizabeth's policy of hostility towards Prussia. That Peter and Catherine might soon come to power was considered

Winter Palace at St. Petersburg at the time of Catherine the Great.

a distinct possibility since the Empress's health was declining rapidly.

As her end drew near so did the Russian dread of Peter's accession increase since Peter made no secret of his intention to reverse Russian policies and to side with Prussia against her former ally Austria. Catherine, too, was deeply alarmed for she knew that Peter might get rid of her.

Elizabeth finally died in December, 1761. Despite her faults her death was widely lamented. She was a lovable woman who had been a generous and sympathetic patron of the arts, and her reign had been one of splendour and noted for operas, ballet, drama, paintings and architecture.

The Empress-Consort

With Elizabeth's death Peter was proclaimed Emperor Peter III. While Catherine won the hearts of Russians by her grief and devoted vigil at the lying-in-state of Elizabeth, Peter lost all their respect. His drunken orgies at the period of court mourning and his deliberate disruption of the funeral procession angered all Russians, as did also his talk of divorcing Catherine. Apart from his personal behaviour, Peter's total disregard for Russian prestige, interests and traditions antagonized all classes. He concluded peace with his hero Frederick of Prussia and proposed to allow a Russian army to fight against Austria. This succeeded in turning the Russian army against him. At the same time Peter further alienated the ordinary Russians by his open contempt for the "Orthodox faith" which was the basis of their lives. His attempt to remove the icons from churches and to force priests to shave off their beards brought much distress.

A conspiracy came into existence led by the Orlov brothers, who had great influence over the Guards who were vital to their success. The Orlov brothers wished to replace Peter by enthroning Catherine as Empress in her own right to secure their own power. The conspiracy came to a head in June, 1762, when popular anger and discontent with Peter reached fever point. When Peter had one of the Guards officers arrested the effect was to detonate the explosion. The Orlov brothers acted swiftly and had Catherine proclaimed Empress at St. Petersburg. Her enthusiastic reception by the army as she made a triumphant entry into her capital on 28 June, 1762, was equalled by that of the citizens. The news rapidly spread and was welcomed with similar joy in other cities. The navy at Kronstadt, too, declared for Catherine. So spontaneous was the warmth of Catherine's reception that when Peter heard about it he was too dumbfounded and cowardly to act. Meekly accepting the inevitable he allowed himself to be seized and stripped of his decorations.

The Empress

Although crowned Empress, Catherine's position in the first years was far from strong. Two dethroned emperors were still alive, her husband Peter III, and Ivan VI, whom Elizabeth had displaced in 1741. Although both were lodged in prison, and were weak characters, they still could serve as figure-heads to rally the oppressed peasants by any ill-disposed person. Catherine had come to the throne by revolution with no legal or divine right to it.

The immediate danger from Peter was removed by his death a few days after Catherine's accession. While she probably knew nothing of a plot to kill him, the Orlov brothers most certainly had him murdered, for not only was Peter's existence a threat to Catherine, but so long as Peter lived Grigori Orlov's ambition to marry her was frustrated. Catherine condoned the murder by taking no action to bring the murderers to justice.

The danger from Ivan VI was likewise soon removed. A pitiful young man, he had for many years been imprisoned on an island fortress. Ill-treated by his bored gaolers, deprived of light and fresh air in his dungeon home and lacking the warmth and love of parents, this miserable wretch was the figure-head of a wild and ill-planned conspiracy against Catherine in 1764. As the rebels made a bid to rescue Ivan in order to place him at the head of their plot, his gaolers whose instructions were to kill their prisoner rather than allow him to escape, stabbed the unfortunate man to death. This news brought Catherine great relief despite the vileness of the crime.

To strengthen her position still further, Catherine curried favour with her subjects by bestowing decorations and position, and dispensing money and estates to the leading people. Her coronation ceremony in the ancient capital of Moscow with the dazzling balls, carnivals and other festivities won her the loyalty and love of the Muscovites. Her charm, generosity and personal kindness captivated her admirers. Though German-born, Catherine had ever since her arrival in Russia gone out of the way to identify herself with her adopted land.

Catherine and the Enlightenment

While foreign policy occupied much of Catherine's time after her accession, especially her dealings with Poland, she found time to devote her attention to domestic affairs. Her overriding passion was self-glorification. Anxious to establish herself as the greatest woman in history, she aimed at making her reign one of splendour and at focusing the attention of contemporaries and of posterity upon her achievements. Posing as the most enlightened ruler of the time, she drafted her decrees with a view to creating a popular image of herself as the wise and humane mother of her people.

With this in mind she entered into lengthy correspondence with the leading philosophers of the day, notably with the Encyclopaedists and with Voltaire. Her letters to the latter began in 1763 and continued until the philosopher's death in 1778. To the Encyclopaedists, Diderot and d'Alembert, she showed considerable generosity, providing the former with an extensive library.

The Nakaz

In accordance with the enlightened views she professed, Catherine informed Voltaire of her intention to reform the whole legal system of Russia. This was chaotic in the extreme with a mass of contradictory laws. The need for order and for a legal revision to check arbitrary rule necessitated an entirely new code. To draw this up she planned to summon a grand legislative commission comprised of delegates from all social classes. For their guidance Catherine compiled a set of instructions known as the *Nakaz*. This famous document took her two years to complete (1765-67) and is the chief title to Catherine's claim to enlighten-

Catherine the Great (reigned 1762-96).

ment. It contained the new philosophical ideas current in the West, many of which were not suitable for adaptation to Russian society. The *Nakaz* was a remarkable revelation of Catherine's political sense. Underlying her philosophy is that of the absolutism of the sovereign, who is the sole source of all civil and political power, but whose primary job is to serve the people. Many of the articles, which were eliminated in the final form of the *Nakaz* because of their revolutionary implications, dealt with the most pressing of all the internal problems facing Catherine, namely that of serfdom. To Catherine serfdom was an affront to the individual. The burdens of the peasants far from decreasing had grown heavier throughout the century, while the nobility enjoyed more and more privileges with fewer obligations. Catherine realized however that to abolish serfdom would alienate the nobility upon whom she relied. Serfdom was at the basis of the social and economic foundations of the State. Accordingly whatever sympathy Catherine had for the mass of her subjects, she was unwilling to risk the upheavals which would occur if she put her enlightened views into practice.

The deputies of the legislative commission, some 565 in all, assembled in Moscow in June, 1767, from all parts of the Empire in response to the Imperial manifesto. They set to work debating the reports which they had brought with them setting out the needs of the class they represented. Soon, however, insoluble problems arose with the conflicting claims of the different classes. There seemed no bridge between those who said that serfdom must continue, either out of self-interest, or in the interests of agriculture, and those who said it must go because of the miseries it entailed for human beings. The merchants' deputies demanded privileges similar to those of the nobility while the nobles demanded greater powers in provincial administration. By the end of 1768 after prolonged debates, the commission dispersed, never to be summoned again. It achieved absolutely nothing except to strengthen Catherine's position on the throne by this gesture to reform, and by the acclaim she won from the civilized world. It is however doubtful whether she wished it to achieve any practical results. The outbreak of war against Turkey in 1768 gave Catherine a ready excuse not to re-summon the commission.

Pugachev

In May, 1773, the Don Cossack, Pugachev, raised the standard of revolt against Catherine. Proclaiming that he was the Emperor Peter III who had miraculously escaped murder by Catherine's henchmen, he promised to liberate the serfs from their feudal bondage by killing off the nobility and redistributing the land among the peasants. Believed by the simple peasants, Pugachev quickly rallied supporters from the cossacks who sought freedom not merely from their feudal burdens, but from religious persecution at the hands of the Orthodox Church. With most of her forces fighting against the Turks, Catherine found difficulty in preventing this peasant revolt from spreading swiftly like a steppe fire towards Moscow. All landowners who fell into Pugachev's hands were brutally murdered, and many in panic took refuge in the towns. Early successes encouraged more and more peasants to join his ranks so that in the winter of 1773-74 Pugachev was advancing on Moscow at the head of some fifteen thousand men. The turning point came only after Catherine had ended her war with Turkey in July, 1774, when she directed the troops returning from the Turkish front against the rebels. Faced by these veterans many of Pugachev's supporters deserted, while the rest were defeated at Chernoyarsk. Pugachev was finally betrayed and brought in an iron cage to Moscow where he was publicly beheaded. Apart from the ringleaders, Catherine treated most of the rebels humanely, although the landowners failed to exercise the same restraint.

The origins of the revolt lay in the depressed state of the peasants whose hopes had been raised only to be dashed by the failure of Catherine to give practical effect to her professed desire to end the degrading state of serfdom. The Russian peasants had no cause to be grateful to Catherine, for after the revolt she sanctioned an increase in the powers and privileges of the landowners, for whom Catherine's reign was a golden one.

In 1774 Catherine took as her last true love one of the most extraordinary men in history, Grigori Alexandrovich Potemkin, who until his death in 1791 was to exercise a decisive influence over her and over the fortunes of Russia. Born in 1739 of an old but undistinguished family, Potemkin entered the army and was soon attracted by the glamour of the court at St. Petersburg, where he first met Catherine and with whom he fell in love on sight. Tall, ambitious, brilliant and amusing he easily attracted Catherine's attention. A deep love developed between the two and Catherine came to rely upon Potemkin in matters of State and he showed great ability as a soldier, diplomat and administrator. Realizing that his stormy love affair with Catherine might lead to his dismissal from court with consequent loss of power, Potemkin and Catherine agreed to end their association while he was to retain his power over matters of State.

An Age of Elegance

It was after Potemkin had become her confidant that Catherine's reign became one of exceptional splendour. Foreigners were astounded by the richness and scale of the entertainments of the Empress. She gave frequent banquets and receptions to mark anniversaries and victories, and on such occasions appeared dressed in magnificent, jewel-bedecked gowns. A similar luxurious standard of living was maintained by the nobles either on their own estates or in Moscow but it was only made possible by the toils of the serfs whose labour services were increased to pay for the extravagance.

Catherine showed herself a keen patron of the arts. Calling upon the services of many distinguished foreign as well as Russian architects, Catherine spent vast sums on buildings especially to beautify St. Petersburg. Painters and sculptors, too, benefited under Imperial patronage. Catherine spared no expense in building up collections of famous paintings, while creative artists were encouraged by the Academy of Fine Arts at St. Petersburg. In the world of literature and drama, progress was made by the establishment of a translator's commission which made readily available translations of major works of foreign literature, especially those of France, while the establishment of a Russian academy boosted interest in native literature. It was, however, the theatre which particularly flourished. Operas, ballets, plays and concerts were performed although in this field as in literature the foreign influence was strong.

Catherine was admired by contemporaries for her encouragement of learning, and in this activity, as in so many others, she was following the example set by Peter the Great.

Catherine, like Peter, had ambitions to establish a system of education and went to the extent of setting up two commissions to examine foreign schools. On the basis of their reports she issued a decree in 1786 establishing a national system of schools, but in practice her proposals came to little. Apathy, prejudice and the ignorance of the masses were the rocks upon which her

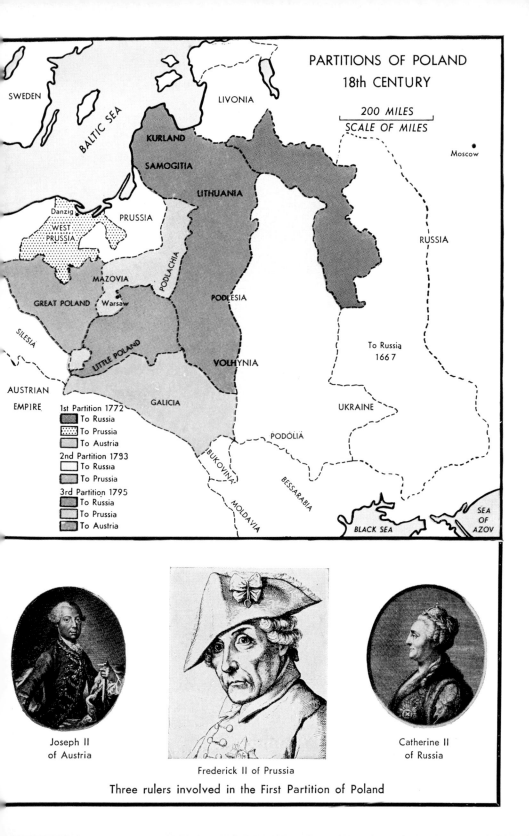

PARTITIONS OF POLAND
18th CENTURY

200 MILES
SCALE OF MILES

SWEDEN

BALTIC SEA

LIVONIA

KURLAND

SAMOGITIA

LITHUANIA

Danzig
PRUSSIA
WEST
PRUSSIA

MAZOVIA

GREAT POLAND   Warsaw

PODLACHIA

PODLESIA

SILESIA

LITTLE POLAND

VOLHYNIA

AUSTRIAN
EMPIRE

GALICIA

1st Partition 1772
  To Russia
  To Prussia
  To Austria
2nd Partition 1793
  To Russia
  To Prussia
3rd Partition 1795
  To Russia
  To Prussia
  To Austria

BUKOVINA

PODOLIA

MOLDAVIA

BESSARABIA

Moscow

RUSSIA

To Russia
1667

UKRAINE

BLACK SEA

SEA
OF
AZOV

Joseph II
of Austria

Frederick II of Prussia

Catherine II
of Russia

Three rulers involved in the First Partition of Poland

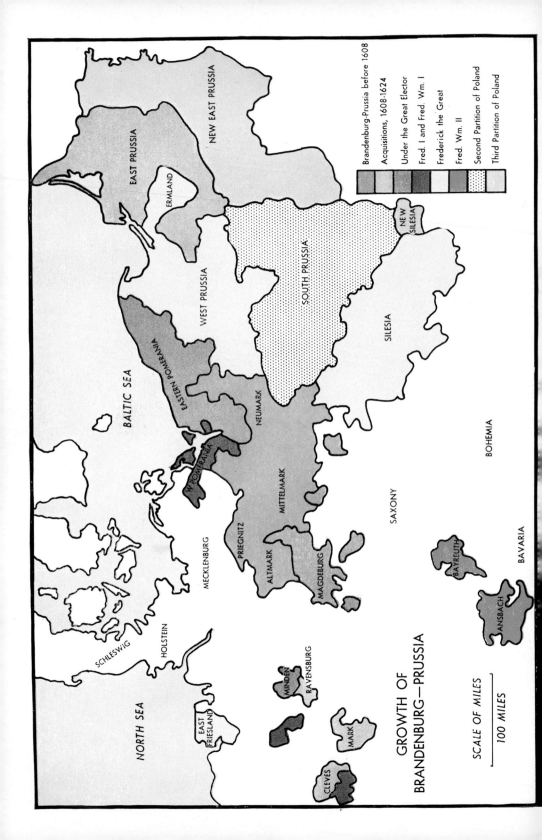

GROWTH OF
BRANDENBURG—PRUSSIA

SCALE OF MILES

100 MILES

Brandenburg-Prussia before 1608
Acquisitions, 1608-1624
Under the Great Elector
Fred. I and Fred. Wm. I
Frederick the Great
Fred. Wm. II
Second Partition of Poland
Third Partition of Poland

NORTH SEA

BALTIC SEA

SCHLESWIG

HOLSTEIN

EAST
FRIESLAND

MECKLENBURG

MINDEN

RAVENSBURG

MARK

CLEVES

PRIEGNITZ

ALTMARK

MITTELMARK

MAGDEBURG

W. POMERANIA

EASTERN POMERANIA

NEUMARK

WEST PRUSSIA

ERMLAND

EAST PRUSSIA

NEW EAST PRUSSIA

SOUTH PRUSSIA

NEW
SILESIA

SILESIA

SAXONY

BOHEMIA

BAVARIA

BAYREUTH

ANSBACH

Academy of Fine Arts, St. Petersburg (now Leningrad), founded by Catherine.

schemes foundered, although among the nobility there was no longer the rooted opposition which had caused the collapse of Peter's schemes.

The cost of maintaining this splendour led Catherine, solvent at the beginning of her reign, into serious financial troubles. The costly wars with Turkey also added to the national debt. To counter the deficit she issued paper money recklessly, with the result that the peasant had to work even harder to overcome the reduced value of the currency.

It is significant that although figures reveal a constant expansion both of the import and export trade, the overwhelming percentage of the import trade was concerned with luxury goods from the West. These were paid for by the exports of iron, flax, linen and timber, which were sent to Britain and other countries.

Catherine profited from the lesson of the Pugachev uprising, and strengthened the provincial governments, of which there were fifty in the whole country. A governor was appointed who controlled the hierarchy of officials.

Official posts in judicial and financial administrations were filled by members of the nobility, whose powers increased as a consequence. No strong middle-class came into being to counter-balance this.

QUESTIONS

1. How did Catherine become Empress of Russia? What dangers threatened her position and how did she overcome them?
2. What is meant by the phrase "enlightened despotism"? Illustrate your answer by reference to the work of Catherine the Great.

CHAPTER 26

THE TRAGEDY OF POLAND

THE last thirty years of the eighteenth century witnessed the trial and execution of the Polish nation in the course of a tragic drama of three acts. These coincided with the three partitions of 1772, 1793 and 1795, which resulted in the complete disappearance of Poland from the map of Europe and the absorption of her peoples into one or other of the neighbouring countries of Russia, Austria or Prussia. It has always been, and still is, Poland's sad fate to be sandwiched between Germany and Russia, each alike unwilling to permit the emergence of a truly independent Poland. Apart from ambitious and aggressive neighbours, Poland's decline throughout the eighteenth century must be ascribed to internal conditions to which we now turn.

Despite its physical extent, Poland was "a geographical expression." There was no real bond of unity among its people. Strong, resolute government, which alone could have forged a sense of national consciousness and responsibility among the Poles, was both absent and impossible under the existing political conditions. To explain the political defects is to explain to a large extent the anarchy that prevailed.

Defects of the Constitution

Poland, in theory an elective monarchy, was in fact an aristocratic republic. The few wealthy landowners who held the power were irresponsible and selfish, and jealous of each other's rights. They levied all taxes and exercised justice, and were able by the "right of confederacy" to form an association with other nobles for the achievement of their aims by force if necessary. Such action legalized civil war.

The smaller landowners, or *szlachta*, and the great landowners held a representative diet twice a year. The nobles had full control and elected the king. This election was always disputed, and the king himself, elected by bribery, simply served the private interests of the nobles.

The effective authority of the diet was paralysed by the *liberum veto*, which allowed a single nobleman to veto a measure to prevent it from becoming law. Anarchy resulted, as the nobles could never agree.

In an essentially feudal society, there was no common interest. The mass of the nation was composed of eight million serfs, whose feudal obligations to their overlords were always increasing. War and disease had reduced the peasant population by a third, with a corresponding reduction of the land under cultivation. Those peasants remaining were forced to work harder.

Warsaw was Poland's only large city, and its craftsmen were exploited by the nobility. The nobles refused to engage in trade or industry, and this added to the poverty of the small middle-class. In such an unproductive and isolated society, cultural and scholastic movements were unknown.

There was not even religious harmony to compensate for the lack of political unity. The majority of the population was Roman Catholic, but in the east there were some 600,000 Greek Orthodox Christians, and in the north, some 200,000 German Protestants. These minorities were persecuted by the Catholics, and in 1736 the Diet passed a law depriving Protestants of civil liberties.

Geographical factors contributed largely to Poland's weakness, for there were few natural barriers to guard her extensive frontiers except the Carpathian Mountains in the south. The plain of Poland was a standing invitation to the aggressive tendencies of her powerful neighbours, especially when she lacked not only the armies, but also the will to defend herself.

Russo-Prussian Opposition to Polish Reform

Both Frederick the Great and Catherine had a common interest in maintaining Poland in her weakened condition. Moreover, Catherine had no desire to continue a burdensome war against Prussia. Abandoning the traditional alliance with Austria Catherine looked to Prussia to uphold the rights of Protestant and Orthodox minorities in Poland and to preserve the "Polish liberties," that is the Polish Constitution, as the best way to maintain the state of anarchy, and thereby to make easier the fulfilment of the territorial designs on Poland which both she and Frederick entertained.

Frederick the Great's main objective was the acquisition of the Polish district known as "West Prussia," which separated his province of "East Prussia" from that of Brandenburg, but he was nevertheless very concerned after 1763 to avoid war in order to allow his weakened resources to recover from the ravages of the two mid-century wars. For the realization of his objective of West Prussia, he was content to rely on an alliance with Russia.

Catherine felt that success in foreign affairs would distract popular disappointment from her failure to introduce internal reforms, and would also win for herself and her country the respect of Europe. The objective of Russian foreign policy was expansion, north-west, west and south-west. This brought her into conflict with Sweden, Poland and the Turkish empire. Catherine's dream of the partition of the Turkish empire between Russia and Austria, with Russia acquiring the Black Sea, the Dardanelles and

Constantinople, was known as "the Greek project," and gave rise to the "Eastern Question" which troubled the following century.

To further her territorial ambitions in Poland and Turkey, Catherine posed as the champion of the persecuted Greek Orthodox subjects against Polish Roman Catholics, or Turkish Moslems. The interconnection bêtween the Polish and Turkish problems is an essential feature of the period. It is, however, to the affairs in Poland that we must first turn.

The chain of events which led directly to the partition of Poland began with the death of Augustus III in 1763. Frederick the Great and Catherine immediately showed their common interest in Poland by an alliance they negotiated in March, 1764. They agreed to secure the election of Stanislas Poniatowski, who was in love with Catherine. Besides keeping out candidates of other foreign powers, it was widely believed that Catherine supported his candidature in order to marry him and acquire Poland, while Stanislas, whose love for Catherine was very real, was only too glad to be elected if this increased his prospects of a marriage with the Empress. Coming from a powerful Polish family that looked to Russia, Stanislas had hopes that with Russian aid, he and his family would be able to restore law and order in Poland. Elected king by the Polish Diet assisted by the presence of Russian troops in September, 1764, his prospects with the Empress were soon to vanish for Catherine had no intention of marrying him. However, Catherine herself was to be disillusioned, for Stanislas had no intention of being a mere Russian puppet.

Polish Reform Movement

Stanislas Poniatowski belonged to a group of patriotic nobles, foremost among whom was his own Czartoryski family. This group was determined to effect a programme of constitutional reform in order to end once and for all the attempts of foreign neighbours to exploit Poland's weaknesses. Prominent among their reforms was the abolition of the "liberum veto." Such a programme to strengthen the State at the expense of the privileges of Polish nobles pleased neither Russia nor certain of the less patriotic nobility. Accordingly Catherine ordered her ambassador at Warsaw, Repnin, to stir up trouble in Poland by championing the civil rights of the religious minorities, and by deporting to Russia those Roman Catholic bishops who objected. By organizing a "confederation" at Radom (November, 1767) of those Polish nobles who were opposed to the constitutional reforms, Catherine took a further step to stamp out the reform movement. Backed by this Confederation, as well as by the Russian army, Catherine forced in 1768 a specially unrepresentative diet to grant full civil rights to the minorities, and to ratify an agreement making Poland a pure puppet state of Russia.

Catherine's action in persecuting the Roman Catholics and enforcing civil rights for other religious groups provoked the fiercest patriotic resistance. In 1768 a group of Roman Catholic nobles in Podolia formed an armed "confederation" at Bar with the objectives of keeping their country free from a dictated religious toleration at the hands of Russia, and ending the programme of political reform by dethroning Stanislas. This confederation gained much general support and similar confederations were formed elsewhere in the country. Poland was thus engulfed in a civil war which ravaged the countryside. Non-Catholic peasants were slaughtered by Polish patriots in the name of the Roman Catholic faith and national independence. This struggle was not, however, confined to Poland for it was soon to involve the other great powers.

The "Confederates," as the Roman Catholics were known, looked to the Catholic powers, Austria and France, both of which provided material and diplomatic aid. The persecuted on the other hand looked to Russia whose armies, in the name of toleration, overran Poland in an effort to crush the Confederates. Frederick of Prussia was annoyed with Catherine for provoking the trouble, fearing lest the peace of Europe might be endangered by the conflicting aims of the great powers.

Frederick's fears were soon justified. In order to divert Russian armies from Poland and thereby to help the Catholics, France's foreign minister, Choiseul, was to stir up trouble between Russia and her traditional enemy, Turkey.

Russo-Turkish War, 1768-74

Vergennes, the French ambassador at Constantinople, played upon the Sultan's grievances against his traditional enemy, Russia. When in October, 1768, a contingent of Russian troops pursuing some Polish nobles violated the Turkish frontier and destroyed a Turkish town, the Sultan declared war.

Taken by surprise Catherine hurriedly mobilized her armies. In the spring of 1769 the main Russian army captured the important fortress town of Khotin. Meanwhile Catherine sent her Baltic fleet into the Mediterranean under the command of Count Orlov, who was assisted by three British admirals. This fleet was to support a rising among the Greek Christians, but the Turks were able to crush it. When, however, a large Turkish fleet appeared to challenge the Russians, it was driven into Chesme Bay, where it was destroyed by fireships (1770). The Russians failed to follow up this success as they might have done by forcing the Straits and attacking Constantinople. On land they continued their successful advance conquering the Black Sea coast, including the Crimea, while in the provinces of Moldavia and Wallachia their armies penetrated as far as the Hapsburg frontier.

These Russian victories alarmed both Prussia and Austria, neither of whom wanted to see Russia in a position to dictate a settlement of the

Satirical print: The rulers of Europe divide Poland among themselves.

Balkans or Poland. In two meetings which Frederick the Great had with the Emperor Joseph, the Prussian king came away convinced of the danger of a clash between Austria and Russia. Joseph, he believed, would fight to keep Russia permanently away from the Danube and the Hapsburg frontier. The possibility of a European war in which Austria was aiding Turkey against Russia caused Frederick grave concern, for Prussia was treaty-bound to Russia. He did not wish to be dragged into any war to further Russian ambitions.

Partition Arranged, 1772

It was with the objective of preserving European peace and of forwarding Prussia's territorial ambitions that Frederick suggested the partition of Poland. By enabling Catherine to find "compensation" in Poland, she would be prepared to sacrifice her Danubian claims, Moldavia and Wallachia, from Turkey, while Frederick saw his own chance of acquiring "West Prussia" without having to fight for it. Moral scruples set aside, Frederick's suggestion was readily agreed to by Catherine and both rulers signed an agreement to this effect. Austria's attitude, however, reflected a distinct gulf between that of the Emperor Joseph, backed by Kaunitz, and that of the Empress Maria Theresa. "I cannot look on quietly," she declared, "at the aggrandisement of these two powers, but still less do I wish to join them." Maria Theresa's moral scruples were overruled by her son who saw the chance of acquiring Galicia (a district in southern Poland) not only as compensation for the loss of Silesia, but also as a means of preserving the balance of power. "In the event of a total destruction of Poland," Joseph wrote, "we must get a good morsel." Austria's policy had completely changed from supporting the Poles against the Russians, to co-operating with Catherine in the dismemberment of their country.

It was in August, 1772, at St. Petersburg that Catherine, Frederick and Joseph signed the first Partition Treaty. Adding yet another national group to her empire, Austria acquired eastern Galicia, a district containing some three million Poles and noted for its valuable salt mines. Prussia seized West Prussia with the exception of Danzig and Thorn, a district containing just under a million inhabitants most of whom, being German, were easily incorporated into Prussia. Russia acquired Polish Livonia and White Russia, a district bordering on the Upper Dvina and Dnieper rivers and containing over one and a half million inhabitants who, being Russian and of the

Stanislas Poniatowski.

Orthodox Faith, were easily assimilated. The Polish Diet, powerless to resist, had to accept this Partition Treaty in 1773, and thus was forced to sanction the loss of a third of its territory and population.

This act of international robbery had no moral justification, being based on the principle of "might is right." Such were the low standards of international morality of this period. While the peace and balance of power among the Eastern powers was preserved, the destruction of Poland was not really in their long-term interest. Particularly was this true of Austria, whose gain of Galicia at the sacrifice of honour was a dubious asset. Indeed the partition of Poland had the opposite effect from that which the great powers intended, for not only did it prove to be the salvation of Sweden and Turkey from a similar fate but it gave a great impetus to the rebirth of Polish nationalism. In short, partition of Poland created more problems than it solved.

QUESTIONS

1. Explain and comment upon the weaknesses of Poland in the period before its first partition.
2. Trace the various stages leading to the first partition of Poland, commenting upon them.

235

CHAPTER 27

THE EASTERN QUESTION AND
THE LATER PARTITIONS OF POLAND

SINCE Charles XII's death in 1718, the monarchy in Sweden had been powerless, dominated as it was by two rival parties, the privileged land-owning aristocracy otherwise known as the "Hats," and the well-to-do peasant proprietors, the "Caps." Sweden, like Poland had been a "football of international politics" booted first by France who exerted her influence through the "Hats," and then by Russia who looked to the "Caps." Both France and Russia were interested in Sweden in their quest for mastery of the Baltic.

When the ambitious Gustavus III ascended the Swedish throne in 1771 he was determined to use force both to save his country from Russia, and to restore the power of the Crown. Educated in Paris, and an ardent admirer of France and her "Philosophers," Gustavus secured French financial aid to effect a military *coup d'état* in August, 1772. This coup overthrew the power of the Swedish nobles and re-established that of the monarchy. In the new constitution of 1772 the old tyrannical and ineffective republic was replaced by a limited monarchy. Gustavus did not destroy the constitutional authority of the Diet which still enjoyed the rights of making laws and voting taxes.

Although both Russia and Prussia had in their 1764 alliance pledged themselves to maintaining the Swedish constitution they were so pre-occupied in Poland that they were powerless to intervene. The accession of a strong monarchy in Sweden was the best guarantee for her from suffering Poland's fate at the hands of Russia.

Gustavus III, Enlightened Despot

Once the revolution was achieved, Gustavus then carried out major reforms which both strengthened Sweden and won for him the title of an enlightened despot. He stimulated the trade and economy of his country by abolishing internal tariffs, relaxing the onerous gild regulations, and estab-lishing free ports and free market towns. Financial stability was established by the new system of coinage based on silver in place of the debased paper currency. Religious toleration was granted to non-Lutheran Christians and

236

Jews were given permission to practise their religion and to engage in trade. Important legal reforms were effected and a free press established. Such reforms brought Gustavus great popularity especially in the first ten years of his rule, but this was to disappear later as a result of his prodigal spending on public buildings, the Court and the army.

In his efforts to exact more money from his subjects he aroused much discontent. He came into conflict with Parliament and from 1786 to 1789 dispensed with it altogether. His enlightened despotism had degenerated into a personal absolutism resting upon military force. It was little wonder that the nobility retaliated finally by assassinating him in 1792. While enlightened despotism was to be a temporary phase in Swedish history, it occurred at a time when Sweden was so weak that she could well have suffered Poland's fate.

Treaty of Kutchuk Kainardji, 1774

The Polish partition proved to be the temporary salvation of Turkey. After Russian armies had overrun the Danubian principalities of Moldavia and Wallachia, and her fleet had destroyed that of the Turks, the way lay open for an advance to Constantinople. Catherine, however, hesitated, being unwilling to risk war with Austria whose objections to having Russia as a neighbour in place of Turkey we have already noted. The partition of Poland opened the way for a settlement. Russia could give up these Turkish conquests but secure compensation in Poland. Other circumstances which impelled Catherine to make peace with the Turks included the serious peasant rising among the Don Cossacks led by Pugachev which broke out in 1773.

Accordingly in 1774 the Empress and the Sultan agreed to peace, drawn up in the treaty of Kutchuk Kainardji. The provisions of this treaty included Turkish tolerance of Greek Orthodox Christians in Turkey, with the right of Russia to interfere on their behalf, recognition of Crimean independence, and the right of Russia to navigate freely in Turkish waters. Russia thus acquired, by the use of the Black Sea and the Straits, a passage to the Mediterranean. Turkey's Greek Orthodox subjects were to provide Russia in future with an excellent excuse to meddle in Turkish affairs. This, however, was to bring her into conflict with Austria, Britain and France, none of whom wanted to see Russia take the place of Turkey.

Catherine's Later Triumphs

While the Treaty of Kutchuk Kainardji was a great triumph for Catherine's diplomacy, it was in the years after 1774 that she attained fresh peaks of success in the fields both of war and diplomacy. For these later triumphs she was indebted to Potemkin who both advised and inspired her. Russian influence in the affairs of western Europe was becoming increasingly greater as the century drew to a close.

Catherine's prestige in the capitals of Europe was particularly enhanced by her mediation over the problem of Bavaria—a problem which almost brought Austria and Prussia to blows in the half-hearted "Potato War" of 1778 to 1779. Emperor Joseph had long coveted the Electorate of Bavaria in order to consolidate his Empire and to compensate him for the loss of Silesia. Frederick the Great, however, was not prepared to stand by and see his old rival extend his power in Germany. Both Austria and Prussia mobilized their forces and in July, 1778, Frederick invaded Bohemia. Both rulers were anxious to avoid hostilities though unwilling to lose prestige. Apart from minor skirmishes both armies stood facing each other, and soon went into winter quarters. The efforts of the Prussians to secure their food supplies gave the name of the "Potato War" to this bloodless campaign.

The clash between Frederick and Joseph was really settled by the firm attitude which Catherine took in backing her ally, Frederick, for she made it clear that if Joseph did not renounce Bavaria, she would intervene on behalf of Frederick. Joseph gave way and Catherine dictated the final settlement at the Peace of Teschen (May, 1779). While Frederick had checked Joseph's ambitions and schemes, the real significance of the affair lay in the emergence of Russia's influence in the affairs of central Europe. With France embroiled with Britain in the War of American Independence, Catherine had matters all her own way.

Emergence of the "Eastern Question"

Catherine's gaze in these years after 1774 was really directed towards the Turkish Empire rather than Europe. The Treaty of Kutchuk Kainardji whetted rather than satisfied the insatiable appetite of the Russian bear for Turkey. The next bite came in 1783 with the annexation of the Crimea, a provocative action which Turkey nevertheless formally recognized in the Treaty of Constantinople in the following year. This new acquisition enabled Russia to become a Black Sea naval power for it led to the construction of a naval base at Sebastopol in the Crimea.

These successes prompted Catherine and Potemkin to realize their ultimate ambition, the "Greek Project." This scheme involved the partition of the Turkish Empire into two parts, both of which would be dominated by Russia.

For the realization of this dream, she turned to Joseph, whose objections to these Russian schemes of expansion were bought off by the promise of Balkan territory. Although the plans of an Austro-Russian deal were first drawn up in 1782, it was not until her impressive tour of the Crimea in 1787, during the course of which she met Joseph, that their alliance was confirmed.

By this time the former Russo-Prussian alliance was dead, following the death of Frederick the Great in 1786. The climax of Catherine's Crimean tour was her review of the large Russian fleet at Sebastopol. This, together with the Austro-Russian alliance and the mobilization of Russian soldiers was too much for the Sultan, and he declared war on Catherine (August, 1787). Joseph then entered the war with his attack on Belgrade but the Turks pressed his armies back across the Danube. The first decisive Russian success came with the capture of Ochakov after one of the bloodiest sieges ever. The fall of this fortress enabled Catherine once more to overrun Moldavia and Wallachia. Austrian forces captured Belgrade. It seemed that the end of the Turkish Empire was near and the Greek project was about to be realized.

The death of Joseph in 1790 led to Austria dropping out of the war and in the following year Catherine made peace with the Turks. The Peace of Jassy confirmed Russia's gains under the Treaty of Kutchuk Kainardji, and her acquisition of the Crimea, while the Sultan further conceded the coastal region between the rivers Bug and Dniester. This peace relieved Russia once and for all from the threat of Turkish power, and confirmed her control of the Black Sea coast, but it did not accomplish Catherine's greatest ambition, that of the Greek project. From the end of this war in 1791 to her death in 1796, Catherine was preoccupied with Poland once more.

Poland after the Partition of 1772

Whilst the partition of 1772 was the first step towards the removal of the Polish state from the map of Europe, its effect upon the Polish people was exactly the opposite, for in the last quarter of the eighteenth century there was, in the words of a Polish historian, "one of the most magnificent examples of national regeneration that any people have ever realized." Inspired partly by the new ideas which emanated from French and English writers and partly by the work of native writers, the Polish reformers, led by their enlightened king, Stanislas Poniatowski, endeavoured to carry through the necessary constitutional reforms to strengthen what remained of the kingdom after the first partition. Their work was made the more possible by the break-up of the Russo-Prussian alliance following the death of Frederick the Great in 1786 and the involvement a year later of Russia and Austria in the Turkish war. They came nearest to success when in 1791 Stanislas persuaded the Diet to agree that the Polish crown should become hereditary in the family of the Elector of Saxony; that while the king should control the army and head the government, legislation should be the province of the Diet; that the *liberum veto* and the right of confederacy should be abolished; and finally, that though Roman Catholicism should be the official state religion, all other beliefs should be tolerated within the borders of Poland.

Such a constitution offered Poland a new lease of life and every likelihood of an independent future. Unfortunately it came too late. Only Austria among Poland's neighbours, welcomed the possibility of a strong Roman Catholic state likely to be able to check the ambitions of Russia and Prussia; these two neighbours were already contemplating further encroachments at Poland's expense.

Extinction of Poland

Until 1792, Poland's neighbours were not in a position to pursue their designs against her. Prussia feared lest she might yet be involved in war with Russia; Russia was held back by the knowledge that Austria and Prussia had, for the time being at least, agreed to guarantee Poland's integrity; and in any case, Russia was still at war with Turkey.

In 1792 the situation changed to Poland's disadvantage. Her defender Leopold II of Austria died; his successor became involved in the war against the French Revolution and had to rely on Prussia for support. The Austrian defeat by France in the Netherlands in 1793 lowered her international prestige so that Russia and Prussia felt free to ignore her in their anti-Polish plans. Prussia, free from Austrian pressure and the fear of war with Russia on other issues, no longer felt compelled to disguise her real policy of hostility towards the reformed Poland. When therefore the pro-Russian party in Poland invited Russia to intervene and restore the old constitution, the reform party to its disgust found Prussia unwilling to honour the pledges of protection she had given in 1791. Not only so, but when Russian armies defeated the Polish patriot Poniatowski at Zielence in 1792, Prussian armies also invaded Poland so as to be in at the kill and the division of the spoils.

Terms of the Second Partition, 1793

With Austria a non-participant, Prussia and Russia alone determined the nature and extent of the second partition of Poland in 1793. Russia took eastern Poland—the lion's share—Prussia had to be content with Danzig, Thorn and Posen; and an angry but pre-occupied and therefore powerless Austria was left out in the cold.

No one was really satisfied by this arrangement. Austro-Prussian relations became strained; Prussia resented the fact that her gains were little more than a quarter of those of Russia and there were Polish patriots not yet reconciled to the liquidation of their nation's independence.

It was these latter whose well-meant but fatally unsupported activities provoked the final dismemberment of their country. A Russian decision in 1794 to disarm all Polish troops led to a national revolt so sudden and surprising that the Russians were expelled first from Cracow and then from Warsaw and Vilna. Prussian intervention failed to dislodge the patriots, led

Gustavus III of Sweden.

Tadeusz Andrzej Kosciusko.

by Kosciusko, from Warsaw, but severely taxed the resources of the defenders. Hence when Russia recovered from her surprise, and resumed the offensive while Austria marched into south Poland, Kosciusko was defeated and captured and Warsaw compelled to surrender.

Since it had thus been left in the last resort to Russian troops to suppress the Polish rising, it was Russia who determined the nature of the third and final partition, having first isolated Prussia by an agreement reached with Austria.

Terms of the Third Partition, 1795

By the third partition, Russia took all Polish territory lying between Galicia and the lower Dvina; Prussia acquired Warsaw and the land between the Bug and the Dnieper; while Austria, having this time asserted her interest, secured Cracow and the rest of Galicia. Thus did the three predatory neighbours implement their determination to "abolish everything which might recall the memory of the existence of the Kingdom of Poland." History is not, however, so easily undone. As we shall see later, Poland was re-created in the nineteenth century and the assaults on her existence in the twentieth century first by Hitler and again by Russia did not remove her permanently from the map of Europe.

QUESTIONS

1. Why and how was Poland partitioned in the period 1772-95?
2. Describe Catherine's relations with Turkey from the Treaty of Kutchuk Kainardji (1774) to that of Jassy (1791).

CHAPTER 28

AGE OF ENLIGHTENMENT

THE seventeenth and eighteenth centuries are noted for the intellectual activity which developed among the peoples of western Europe. Throughout the Middle Ages men's minds had been chained to the teachings of the Church and this powerful institution had claimed a monopoly over every branch of knowledge from the nature of the universe to the nature of God. What it believed and taught in these matters was based either upon an unquestioning acceptance of the theories of classical writers, especially those of ancient Greece, or upon an equally uncritical reading of the Bible. The theories of Greeks like Aristotle that the speed of falling objects varied according to their weight, or like Ptolemy that the sun moved round the earth, or the Biblical explanation of creation, were alike accepted as fundamental and indisputable facts. To doubt them was to be guilty of heresy.

The Church's authority over the government of states was likewise considerable. The close alliance which existed in all countries between the Church and the State was due to the mutual need each had of the other. The Church wanted the full support of the ruler to enable it to preserve its control over the lives of the people as well as its own privileged position, while the ruler looked to the Church to provide the cement which held society together and to afford a justification for the exercise of absolute authority.

This exaggerated respect for authority in matters of the mind had been weakened in the fifteenth century by that renewed study of classical antiquity which we call the Renaissance, and in the sixteenth century by the appeal to private judgement which was the essence of the Reformation. It is true that Luther and Calvin, while claiming the right to think for themselves, would have denied this right to others who did likewise but came to different conclusions; but having rejected authority they were unable to establish their own views as a new universal orthodoxy; they found it impossible to halt the appeal they had made to reason. This appeal was powerfully reinforced in the seventeenth and eighteenth centuries by the work of many philosophers and men of letters and it is to this aspect of the history of these centuries that we give the name of "The Enlightenment." Not all the thinkers who contributed to it necessarily held the same detailed convictions; but all alike were convinced that the universe was a rational system which would only yield its secrets to investigation based on reason and unfettered by limitations imposed by an unquestioning acceptance of religious dogma.

The Scientific Revolution

In the seventeenth century the successful challenge presented by men like Galileo, Newton, Leibnitz and other scientists to the Church's teachings on the nature of the universe revolutionized not merely man's knowledge of the physical world, but also the methods by which this knowledge was acquired. Whereas the Church taught that certain fundamental truths revealed in the Bible were to remain unquestioned, the new theories which Galileo, Newton and others put forward were arrived at by analytical observation leading to the formation of general laws. Such an analytical approach can be illustrated by reference to the discoveries of these men. Galileo unearthed some of the great truths of the universe by observation through his telescope, including the fact that the Milky Way was composed of an infinite number of stars and not meteors. His theory of the ebb and flow of tides was based on the Copernican theory of the earth's rotation. Though Galileo's teachings were condemned by a Vatican council in 1632, he had undermined Aristotle's pre-eminent position. Isaac Newton (1642-1727), Professor of Mathematics at Cambridge, was the author of a famous book, *Philosophiae Naturalis Principia Mathematica*, which had a profound bearing upon the study of natural law. Outstanding among his theories was that of gravitation, but the chief importance of the *Principia* was that it presented the universe as being governed by a coherent system of laws which could be discovered by the workings of the human reason on the observed facts.

As the century progressed so did the spirit of scientific inquiry advance in most countries of western Europe. In England the Royal Society was founded under the patronage of the newly restored Charles II in 1660 with Robert Boyle as one of its founders. Such a society encouraged the spread of scientific research not only in England but overseas. In Tuscany, for instance, the Archduke patronized the work of Viviani, a follower of Galileo in conducting experiments in the density of liquids. To systematize research one academy was founded at Cimento, and a similar one at Naples. Leibnitz (1646-1716) was a great seventeenth-century German philosopher, whose contributions to the fields of science, mathematics, theology, history and law were great. Among these were the differential and integral calculus.

The work of these scientists in formulating fundamental laws of astronomy, physics and mathematics resulted in men accepting the idea of a body of natural laws governing every branch of knowledge, which could be understood through the application of reason. The study of medicine developed with men like Haller and Willis, who studied the physiology of the human

243

body; Harvey, who discovered the circulation of the blood; and Locke, who provided the scientific basis for the study of psychology by his theory that all knowledge, opinions and behaviour were derived from the senses, and not from the presence of innate ideas. At the same time Linnaeus, the son of a Swedish clergyman, began the work of classification of plants and animals which is still used.

Descartes and the Theory of Knowledge

This scientific revolution was partly the reason for, and partly the result of a fundamental change in methods of thinking. Under the dead hand of the Church the acquisition of knowledge had been frustrated by the teachings of certain indisputable facts; but the disproving of so many of these by the methods of observation, analysis and deduction led philosophers to adopt new approaches in their contemplation of the more abstract questions of life. Prominent, and in many ways the founder of the new philosophy, was René Descartes (1596-1650), a Frenchman, who lived much of his life in Holland. He consciously divested his mind of every human prejudice, founding his philosophy on the basic assumption that the only thing of which he was certain was his ability to think. From his observed ability to think, he deduced that he existed. This was the significance of his well-known statement, "Cogito ergo sum" ("I think therefore I am"). By his use of this process of logical deduction Descartes had a deep influence on the minds of all later philosophers, for he taught that reason alone was the method of arriving at the truth.

The Social Sciences

Compared with the remarkable advances in natural science made in the seventeenth century, the social sciences (dealing with the life of man in society) were backward. As in the natural sciences, so in the social sciences, England paved the way in the seventeenth century, though in the following century France was to take over the lead. In Thomas Hobbes (1588-1679) and John Locke (1632-1704) England produced two of the leading political philosophers of the time, both of whom adopted the "contract theory" to justify, in the case of Hobbes, the exercise of absolute power, and in the case of Locke, the exercise of constitutional power by rulers. By adopting the "contract theory" both writers provided an alternative to that of "Divine Right," which was the basis of nearly all European monarchies.

Hobbes published his book, *Leviathan*, in 1651 just at the end of the civil wars when most people were crying out for a return to law and order. His basic ideas were that every government, be it a monarchy or an assembly, must possess absolute and undisputed power. This was the Leviathan, the all-powerful ruler. He went on to claim that this Leviathan came into existence when men, finding their lives "solitary, poor, nasty, brutish and short," entered into an eternally binding contract with each other to establish this sovereign ruler. Once established there was no power to take away sovereignty from the Leviathan.

John Locke modified Hobbes's theories in the second *Treatise on Civil Government*. Writing in a way which was later taken to justify the "Glorious Revolution" of 1688, Locke accepted Hobbes's idea of a voluntary contract between the governed and the ruler, but unlike Hobbes regarded rulers as parties to the contract and bound by the restrictions it applied to them. Whenever a ruler, as James II, tried to exercise more power than his contract authorized, Locke believed the contract was automatically dissolved and the subjects were entitled to rise up in revolt: this is what had happened in 1688. James II was succeeded by William III, whose powers were strictly limited by Parliament in the "Bill of Rights." The Divine Right theory had received its mortal blow in England. Constitutional monarchy had been established.

At the same time that Englishmen struck for freedom from political tyranny, so too did they secure partial religious freedom by an act of 1689. Englishmen had tired of the long wars of the seventeenth century brought about in part by theological controversies, and though still deeply suspicious of Roman Catholicism, which was so associated with their arch-enemy France, Englishmen were prepared to be far more tolerant and broadminded towards non-Anglican Protestants.

With a king whose powers were strictly limited, and with large numbers of non-conformists permitted to worship God freely, it is little wonder that seventeenth-century England provided the inspiration for much of the writings of the eighteenth century, although by this time the greatest intellectual influence came from France.

France and the Enlightenment

The explanation for this lies in the fact that French literature of Louis XIV's reign was so superb that France was universally recognized as the leading cultural country. French language, manners and ideas came to be adopted by the educated classes throughout Europe irrespective of national barriers. A further contribution to France's pre-eminence was made by the *Salons* which flourished in Paris and which were centres for the exchange of the ideas of the best brains. Outstanding amongst the many literary giants were Voltaire, Diderot, Montesquieu, d'Alembert, Quesnay and Rousseau. With the exception of Montesquieu, these men came from the middle class.

The growth of trade and industry in eighteenth-century France had led to a rapid development in the power and wealth of the middle classes. As in Britain, so in France this new middle class became conscious of its power, and the more conscious it became, so proportionately did it contribute to the undermining not only of the feudal organization of society, and in particular of the position of the Church, but also of the basis of the Leviathan state that had come into existence in France. Aware of their growing economic strength, it was not unnatural that the middle classes should begin to demand political power, for trade and industry were profoundly affected by government regulations.

A further contribution to the decay of the *Ancien Régime* was provided by the bitter internal conflicts which occurred between the Jesuits and Jansenists, and between the King and his Parlements.

The religious struggles rendered absurd the idea of a single, absolute and exclusive religious truth and by openly dividing and weakening the Roman Catholic Church helped to lay it open to attack from the pens of deists, atheists and sceptics, all of whom appealed to human reason in their search for truth rather than to divine revelation. As in religion so in the political conflicts between the Parlements and the King did constitutional questions arise concerning the basis of royal power.

It is with this background of a decaying feudal order of society, brought about partly by the development of a powerful and self-conscious middle class, and partly by the internal religious and constitutional conflicts, that the works of the philosophers must be studied. It was these men who were to subject the institutions of their country to a strict scrutiny and to find them wanting. This task was not without its dangers for most of the philosophers were to find themselves at odds with the forces of the establishment by having their writings burned, suffering imprisonment in the Bastille or being exiled. A consequence of this persecution was that much of their literary work took the more devastating form of satire and ridicule. The outstanding master and deadliest critic of all was Voltaire.

Voltaire, 1694-1778

Voltaire was the pen-name of François Marie Arouet. The son of a lawyer, he attracted the attention of Regency society by his wit and writing, and it was during this period that he endured a spell of imprisonment in the Bastille following a quarrel with a nobleman. He then came to England in 1726 and during the three years he spent here he became a great admirer of English laws and literature. In his *Lettres sur les Anglais* in 1734 written after his return, he contrasted the spirit of freedom which pervaded English life with the tyranny that existed in France, using ridicule and satire with devastating effect. The book was publicly burned and Voltaire had to flee once again. He spent much of the following twenty years in exile at the court of Frederick the Great. In 1753, after quarrelling with his host, he returned to France settling on his estate at Ferney for the remainder of his life.

François Marie Arouet, usually known as Voltaire.

Voltaire's achievements were recognized during his life-time. The volume of work that flowed from his pen was enormous. His books, dealing with every branch of knowledge that affected the human race—science, philosophy, politics, literature, history—included *Oedipus*, 1718, *Henriade*, 1725; *Lettres sur les Anglais*, 1729; *Siècle de Louis XIV*, 1751; *Essai sur les moeurs*, 1753; *Candide*, 1759. Besides these, he published many plays, poems, pamphlets and corresponded with all the principal rulers of his day—Frederick II, Catherine II, Joseph II.

Voltaire's Outlook

Because of his vital interest in all human conduct, the range and influence of his ideas was enormous. A fervent believer in the human reason, he attacked anything which restricted it. The advocate of freedom of speech and thought, he particularly directed his shafts against the Church's power over men's minds. He primarily aimed at overthrowing the whole system of Catholic theology because it claimed to speak with authority in every realm of knowledge. To Voltaire religious dogmas and beliefs were a tissue of errors.

Not content merely to attack the Church generally, Voltaire showed humanity in championing the cases of individuals who were victims of religious prejudice and tyranny. One such case concerned Jean Calas, who was alleged to have murdered his son to prevent him from turning Roman Catholic. Although Calas was executed, broken on the wheel, Voltaire took up the unfortunate man's case and after three years secured a reversal of the verdict. It was shown that Calas' son had, in fact, committed suicide. This celebrated case was a milestone in the history of religious toleration as well as a victory for justice over prejudice. But though Voltaire was no Christian he was no atheist. He recognized that the creation implied the existence of a creator, a Supreme Being, but apart from this he was far more concerned with the problems of life on this earth.

The Encyclopaedists

While Voltaire did not completely deny God, Diderot, the founder of the Encyclopaedist movement, did. Diderot (1713-84) was a firm believer in the generally accepted idea of man's progress and perfectability: this would be achieved by the acquisition of knowledge through reason. With this in mind, in 1751 he undertook the immense task of editing an Encyclopaedia designed to cover every branch of knowledge. Apart from the acquisition of knowledge, Diderot was concerned with revolutionizing the process by which knowledge was gained, and to this end encouraged the adoption of scientific methods of analysis.

This Encyclopaedia was the most important literary enterprise of the time, and it was not until 1772 that it was completed. Apart from Diderot many of the other philosophers contributed articles to it including D'Alembert, Marmontel, Rousseau, Voltaire, Buffon, Quesnay and Holbach. These men took the opportunity of reviewing the institutions of the *Ancien Régime* in the light of reason, and it was inevitable that the Encyclopaedia became a platform from which they launched a massive and devastating onslaught against the tyranny, prejudice and superstition that characterized so many of these institutions. Diderot was a warm-hearted man who hated the system of privilege that was the hall-mark of contemporary society. Anxious to sweep it away, Diderot, like Voltaire, distrusted the masses and believed reforms would only come from an enlightened ruler. He was no democrat although he was more liberal than Voltaire. The basic idea underlying his philosophy was that man's political power should be proportionate to his property.

Montesquieu, 1689-1755

Unlike most of the other philosophers, Montesquieu was an aristocrat, but despite this he had a violent hatred of despotism, clericalism and slavery. He had first made his mark in 1721 with his *Lettres Persanes*, which was a satire on French manners and institutions. It was, however, for his *L'Esprit des lois* that he was best known. Published in 1748 it was the fruit of years of travel, observation and thought on the political institutions of countries he had visited, and like so many other writers, he was a particular admirer of the British constitution. He hoped to see established a monarchy whose powers would be limited by a "corps intermédiaires" and by fundamental laws. He showed in his book that the structure of constitutional types of government is influenced profoundly by many factors including social evolution, climate, religion, soil, trade and industry. He taught that a country's constitution and legal system depended upon and varied according to the relationship that existed among these factors. No two countries could have exactly the same kind of constitution, for the combination of these factors would never be the same. He believed that constitutional types of governments were suitable for people living in the temperate zones.

In his admiration for the British constitution he wrongly assumed that the legislature, executive and judiciary were separate, and in their separation lay the best guarantee for liberty. In fact Parliament which is the legislature contains not only legislators but also ministers and judges. Despite his misinterpretation, Montesquieu was the advocate of a system of limited monarchy to counter the despotism of that of France, and his book and ideas were to have a wide appeal not merely to European intellectuals, but also to the makers of the American constitution. This, as finally drawn up, embodied his theory of a separation of powers.

The Physiocrats

The physiocrats were a school of French economists which was founded by François Quesnay, who began his brilliant career as a biologist and who then became the physician to Mme de Pompadour and Louis XV. Turning to the study of economics, in 1756 he published his first essays on this subject in the Encyclopaedia and then followed them up in 1758 by his *Tableau Économique*. The two essential ideas of the physiocrats were the prime importance of agriculture, and the existence of natural economic laws. Interested in the source of true wealth as vital to the prosperity of society, and concerned to ensure that the greatest number of people participated in the wealth they produced, Quesnay and his followers considered the existing economic policies embodied in the mercantilist system not only restrictive but also damaging to the production of wealth. The mercantilists believed it was the government's duty to protect and if possible enlarge the national share of wealth, of which there was a fixed amount, by a system of protective regulations not only upon international and colonial trade but upon industry. The physiocrats believed that these protective regulations by establishing prohibitive tariffs and preventing colonies from trading direct with foreign countries created economic rivalries among nations that resulted in war. Industrialists and merchants favoured by the mercantilist system acquired, so the physiocrats believed, an undeserved and privileged position. Compared with the agricultural classes they only produced a fraction of the national wealth. Since agriculture was the true source of wealth it was the landowners who should enjoy absolute security of their property. Provided the agricultural interests were safeguarded, then the physiocrats favoured a system in which the individual alone was free to produce what he would and dispose of it how he could, free from all state regulations. Self-interest would ensure that each individual in such free competition would strive for his own wealth and happiness. Their motto of *"Laissez faire, laissez passer"* was coined by Gourlay, a royal *Intendant* of commerce.

The teachings of this economic school were to have a profound effect not only upon a future great French statesman, Turgot, but also upon the Scottish economist, Adam Smith, who in 1776 published his *Wealth of Nations*. This book developed the arguments of the physiocrats and laid the basis of the freer trade policies which Pitt and later British statesmen were to adopt and thus enable Britain to lead the world in trade and industry.

In practice this doctrine of free enterprise undoubtedly brought great wealth to the industrialists and merchants, but also much suffering to the industrial workers, who were left to the mercies of the individual employers. Influenced by *laissez faire*, the statesmen no longer believed it to be their duty to regulate conditions in industry, with the result that the first effective factory act came years after the beginning of the Industrial Revolution.

Rousseau

Jean Jaoques Rousseau stands in a class all by himself among the French philosophers. He was the one true radical amongst them. The son of a watchmaker, he came to Paris from his native Geneva in 1742, entering into the circle of the philosophers and becoming a close friend of Diderot to whose Encyclopaedia he contributed. However, while he shared their profound opposition to the tyranny of the Church and State, Rousseau revolted against the entire philosophy of the Enlightenment. It seemed to him that in its reliance upon reason, it took no account of man's primitive, powerful and irrational emotions. Disillusioned and ill at ease in the sophisticated, corrupt Parisian society, he sought refuge and solitude in 1756 in the Hermitage, a country house on the edge of the forest of Montmorency near Paris. Here during the next six years he produced his three greatest works, *Julie, ou la Nouvelle Éloise, Émile, ou l' Education* and *Le Contrat Social.* These works were to exercise, and still do, a profound influence upon those seeking a solution to the problem of the relationship of freedom and authority, but there is no final agreement as to his meanings. To some Rousseau is the champion of the modern individual, standing for unlimited freedom, while to others Rousseau appears as the founder of a disciplined state socialism depriving the individual of all freedom of action.

Rousseau's experiences in Parisian society had convinced him that there was a need for a complete moral regeneration. In a prize essay, *Discourse on the Arts and Sciences*, written in 1750, Rousseau condemned the vices of contemporary society, believing that civilization had resulted in the habits of hypocrisy, artificiality, deceit, insincerity, and made a plea for a return to a "state of nature" in which alone man would recover his innocence and goodness. *Le Contrat Social* which he wrote in 1762 was a new code for society. The state which he portrayed, far from guaranteeing individuals their freedom, in fact subjected them all equally to the power of the "general will" which alone was sovereign. The "general will" alone knew what was to be done for the best interests of the State, and laws were its expression. The individual's true freedom lay in voluntary obedience to these laws, and only by entering into such an association would the individual find moral renewal. The question which has caused much controversy, and to which Rousseau failed to give a clear answer is what he meant in practice by the general will. Some understood Rousseau as an advocate of democracy in which all people would directly share in the management of affairs. Others regard Rousseau as an advocate of the doctrine of the all-powerful state, for he clearly distinguished between the general will and the will of the majority. Whereas the general will would never be wrong in legislating for the best interests of the State, the will of the majority could frequently be so.

Whatever the interpretation, Rousseau's influence cannot be ignored, especially upon the great Jacobin leader, Robespierre, who, during the French Revolution, tried to put Rousseau's teachings into practice by identifying his own will with that of the "general will" during his dictatorship of 1793-94.

Other revolutionary leaders equated the "general will" with the "sovereignty of the people" and tried to put into practice the fundamental lesson they drew from this doctrine of the idea of popular consent in all matters of government. There was no doubt about Rousseau's doctrine of individual equality before the law for he denounced the degrading dependence of certain classes on others. His famous opening sentence was "Man is born free, but everywhere he is in chains." In destroying the feudal organization of society the revolutionaries of 1789 were again merely trying to put into

251

practice Rousseau's new and profound teachings of equality before the law.

Education, too, owed a great deal to Rousseau. In his *Emile* Rousseau again showed his concern for the individual. The prime purpose of education was not to make the personality of one individual dependent upon that of another, but rather to safeguard it from this and to allow it to develop freely. In an age when "spare the rod and spoil the child" was the accepted rule, Rousseau's ideas were revolutionary, but equally influential upon the development of educational thought. Rousseau did not mean that pupils should be undisciplined, but rather that they should obey school rules, just as citizens should obey the general will, voluntarily and knowing that it was in their best interests to do so.

Romantic and Religious Revival

Rousseau was in accord with, and helped to foster, a new emotional spirit that was challenging the dominion of reason. From the middle of the century a new appeal to the human heart was being made by writers, preachers and artists everywhere. This "romantic" feeling was reflected in the popular enthusiasm for the beauties of the natural world, and the simple purity of the "noble savage." There was a growing taste for the countryside, and the natural charms of an English- or Chinese-style garden in preference to the formal and geometric lay-out of French gardens. Fashions, too, reflected a desire for greater simplicity, and a new interest developed for the simple life of peasant folks. The growing emphasis on simplicity, tenderness and feeling was a reaction against the disciplines and formality of the "salons," and against the tyranny of the intellect over the emotions.

Rousseau's first great book *Julie* was in fact a simple love story that helped to create a taste for romance and for the simple beauties of the woodland scene, a book in which the heart triumphs over the mind. Rousseau, however, was not the first in this field, for England was already producing poets and novelists who were making a similar appeal. James Thomson's *Seasons*, 1744; Edward Young's *Night Thoughts*, 1745; Gray's *Elegy*, 1750, marked this romantic revival in poetry. At the same time was born the modern English novel with the publication of Smollett's *Roderick Random*, 1748; Fielding's *Tom Jones*, 1749, and Sterne's *Tristram Shandy*, 1760.

In John Wesley and Count Von Zinzendorf, England and Germany produced the two greatest leaders of a spiritual awakening that was so important as to constitute a second Reformation. The Methodist revival in England and the Pietist movement in Germany both aimed at making religion a personal matter, a "religion of the heart."

Unlike the Methodists, the Pietists founded no new Church. They abhorred dogmas and creeds, and were tolerant of all shades of opinion within the

Engraving by Hogarth of White's Chocolate House in London (1720).

Christian Church, believing that a personal religion was what counted. The personal struggle for salvation was all-important, and it was immaterial whether one was a Protestant or a Roman Catholic as long as one sincerely believed in Christianity. The Pietists denounced the widespread acceptance of Deism, which was a religion based upon the belief that God reveals himself through the harmony and order of nature, but which denied the essential doctrines of Christianity. Pietism provided the warmth and emotion needed in any true religion.

While Pietism spread throughout Germany, the Methodist revival was winning new souls to Christ in Britain. John Wesley, following his "conversion" in 1738, journeyed and preached throughout the length and breadth of the British Isles bringing joy and the hope of salvation to each individual. A gifted preacher and a born organizer, his revivalist meetings attracted thousands who otherwise might have been neglected by the established Church. Although the bishops and priests obstructed Wesley, banning him from using the local pulpits, Wesley overcame all opposition, building chapels, printing hymns many of which his brother, Charles, composed, and publishing religious tracts to spread his message. It was the Methodists who turned despair into hope for many who were condemned to live out their lives in the miserable conditions of the new industrial towns and who felt unwanted. What might have become gin drinking revels turned into religious revivals, for the new Methodist chapel provided the necessary social and religious centre of fellowship. No single Englishman of the eighteenth century influenced the minds of so many with such beneficial results.

The two religious revivals described owed nothing to reason, and everything to emotion. A total and complete acceptance of Christ's message of salvation was what was demanded and was the complete opposite of the

253

rationalists' approach to religion. Yet in their concern for the individual the revivalists were at one with the rationalists.

The Arts

As literature and religion had been influenced by this new "romantic" movement, so, too, did art reflect these trends even though the "classical" style was still dominant. In this field France predominated, and apart from Hogarth most of the great artists were French, including Boucher, Chardin and Fragonard. Boucher's work still portrayed the brilliant, charming but dissolute society of Louis XV. His graceful, pastoral scenes and numerous "Venuses" reflected contemporary taste. Chardin's *La Bénédicité* was an example of the growing taste for the unaffected and natural, for it portrayed a peasant woman and her two children saying grace before a meal. The outstanding English painter of this period was William Hogarth. His pictures, *Gin Lane*, *Idle Apprentice*, *The Rake's Progress* and many others, while they exaggerated, yet captured and satirized some of the contemporary social vices of the period. To be independent of the patronage of the wealthy classes, unlike so many of his contemporaries, Hogarth used his paintings as the originals for numerous engravings which he sold to make a living.

The sum total of these new ideas amounted to a revolt against the very foundations of contemporary European society over which the authority of the Church and State had so long predominated, and in which the individual counted for so little. Believing that reason could unearth the knowledge vital to human progress, these philosophers criticized any restraints placed upon it. Destructive in their criticisms of so many contemporary institutions, the philosophers were, in fact, only clearing the ground in preparation for rebuilding the ideal human society. They varied naturally in their views of an ideal human society, but they all had one thing in common, namely a great respect for the individual and his right to liberty of thought, speech and worship. Just as all great events in the history of mankind are the product of men's ideas, so too, was the French Revolution, which broke out in 1789, the product of this "Age of Enlightenment."

QUESTIONS

1. What was the "Scientific Revolution"? Write briefly about the achievements of some of the leading scientists in the seventeenth century.
2. Write an account of the work and importance of the following writers of the eighteenth century:
   (*a*) Voltaire, (*b*) Montesquieu, (*c*) Diderot, (*d*) Quesnay, (*e*) Rousseau.

CHAPTER 29

LOUIS XV AND THE DECLINE
OF THE BOURBON MONARCHY

A S A sickly youth of five years old Louis XV came to the throne of France on the death of his great-grandfather, Louis XIV, in 1715. Not expected to live, in fact he was to survive until 1772 with disastrous consequences, for he was to bequeath to his successor, Louis XVI, the legacy of revolution and death on the guillotine. While it is true that many of the financial, constitutional and religious problems which beset France in the eighteenth century had originated during the reign of Louis XIV, Louis XV, by his reckless and irresponsible policies, not merely failed to remedy them but succeeded rather in aggravating them to such an extent that the well-intentioned but ineffective Louis XVI was powerless to do anything to check the forces threatening to destroy the *Ancien Régime*.

From the accession of Louis XV to his assumption of real power, the reins of government had been held by three men, the regent Orleans, 1715-23; the Duke of Bourbon, 1723-26; and the Abbé Fleury, 1726-43. Fleury had undisputed authority, enjoying the complete trust of his royal master. A very able man, he rose above the court factions. His chief claim to greatness lay in his outstandingly successful conduct of foreign affairs in which the emphasis was on preserving the peace by maintaining the alliance with Britain, a policy initiated by the regent Orleans. Like Walpole in Britain, Fleury's influence began to decline as rival war parties came to power and France was already at war unofficially when he died in 1743.

Louis decided to assume personal responsibility for the government. Henceforward he personally presided over his royal council, but he was soon to show a deficiency in those qualities needed for one exercising this supreme responsibility.

Character of Louis XV

Louis was not without intelligence, for he possessed a remarkable memory as well as a discerning judgment. He had the necessary ceremonial dignity of bearing and at the outset of his reign enjoyed the affection of his subjects. But he lacked the necessary interest and industry to perform the duties of his office, as well as the force of character to assert his authority. Suffering from a sense of his own inadequacy, he found difficulty in making firm decisions and thus paralysed the whole machinery of government after his assumption of personal responsibility.

Bored with his role of king, Louis became idle, seeking distraction in hunting and in love affairs with ladies of the court, of whom Mme de Pompadour and Mme du Barry were but two outstanding examples. Yet his pleasures did not satisfy him and he developed a morbid obsession with death.

The Monarchy in the generation preceding the Revolution was far less absolute than liberal historians have in the past implied. The King was subjected to many restrictions and the grandeur that surrounded him had tarnished. There were many cracks in the magnificent centralized system that had reached its perfection during the reign of Louis XIV. There was much confusion and overlapping of authority. Political administration was entangled with the administration of justice to the detriment of both.

Opposition of the Parlements and Court Factions

The most effective check upon the King was the powerfully organized aristocracy of lawyers, in particular those magistrates who were members of the thirteen Parlements, or high courts of appeal, especially that of the Parlement of Paris, which enforced its right to register or reject royal edicts.

This right was generally recognized by the Monarchy though in the last resort the King could enforce his decrees by holding a *lit de justice* or by exiling the parlement. The record of opposition of the Parlements was impressive and was made possible by the solidarity of the provincial Parlements with that of Paris.

Even in the administration of the provinces, the thirty *Intendants* upon whom the King relied were far from being the tyrants they have been depicted. Trained civil servants, they were the most enlightened and enterprising of public servants, being responsible for law and order, tax collection and administration. Since they were representative of the central government their authority was frequently challenged by the provincial Parlements.

Louis' government was discredited by rival court factions seeking influence over him. One such faction was that led by Mme de Pompadour, who came into prominence after 1745. Her influence was both real and important, for even when the King ceased to love her she continued to act as his principal adviser. A charming, vivacious woman, she was a friend of the philosophers, and consequently an enemy of the Church. She had close connections with important Parisian financiers who exerted strong pressure through her on the King. With such a weak-willed King who allowed himself to be dictated to by one or other faction, there was no consistency or direction

256

in government policies. Ministers came and went. Louis gave his confidence to no one, not even his chosen ministers for they found him constantly intriguing behind their backs. It is against this background of court intrigue that the constant changes of French foreign and domestic policies must be viewed.

Ineffectual Foreign Policy

During the next eleven years until Choiseul took over it is impossible to say who was in charge. France was induced into signing the ruinous treaties of Versailles, which committed her to a European war as an ally of Austria against Prussia, while receiving no aid against Britain in return. As a result, she fell behind in the colonial struggle with Britain and by the time Choiseul revised France's policies it was too late. The failure to see where his country's true interest lay is the indictment with which Louis should be charged.

Weaknesses of the French Church

This same disunity and lack of leadership can be seen in the internal government of France. Domestic policy even more than foreign policy is subject to powerful pressures for the interests of more people are affected. During Louis XV's reign the monarchy was steadily being undermined by the combined attacks upon its religious and financial foundations. Interconnected, these attacks are here dealt with separately for clarity.

A monarchy by Divine Right implied a general acceptance of the religious basis of society, but in the eighteenth century the Church was subjected to the attacks of the philosophers for its power over men's minds, and of the Jansenists for doctrinal and moral reasons. Had the Church been united it might have repelled these attacks, but it was divided between the upper and lower clergy. The upper clergy—the bishops and abbots—monopolized the greater part of the land and wealth of the nation and were drawn from the highest ranks of society. The bishops were all too frequently men who had little calling to the ministry, being courtiers dressed up in the rich episcopal vestments and bearing the ring and crozier of office. Plurality, too, was rife for a man frequently held several ecclesiastical offices from which he drew princely sums. In striking contrast with the wealth of the higher clergy was the poverty of the humble curés, or parish priests, whose lot in life was little better than that of the feudal serfs for whose spiritual welfare they were responsible and who had little respect or love for their ecclesiastical masters.

Decline of the Church's Popularity

Voltaire was among the severest critics of the upper clergy. He made people aware of much that was wrong, yet the Church still pervaded the life of the ordinary man, who was baptised, married and buried by it.

Jansenist Controversy

Such religious enthusiasm as existed in the eighteenth century French Church came from the Jansenists, who differed from the Jesuits over the problem of acquiring God's grace. The Jansenists had attacked the Jesuit acceptance of outward conformity, believing that religion was much more a question of personal conviction. They were tolerated for a time by the Regent Orleans, and their support came from the Parlements, many of the lower clergy, the general public and anybody who opposed privilege. The Church repeatedly tried to stamp out Jansenism and in 1750 made a fresh attempt. The Archbishop of Paris ordered the clergy to refuse the sacraments to any person who was unable to produce a *billet de confession* signed by a priest who had accepted the Bull *"Unigenitus"* and thereby had shown his disapproval of Jansenism. This brought the Parlement of Paris into the conflict, for they championed the Jansenists and issued a Grand Remonstrance in 1753 asserting their claim to be defenders of the fundamental laws of the kingdom. Louis exiled the Parlement from Paris, but subsequent riots forced him to give way. The *billet de confession* was abandoned. Yet, popular as it was for its challenge to royal authority in these matters of religion, the Parlement was not "democratic." It was a partisan corporation, jealous of the privileges of the lawyers who were its sole members. It subsequently opposed reforms which threatened its members' privilege of tax exemption as firmly as it had opposed the Crown's religious policy.

At the same time, Machault, Louis XV's Controller-General, was attempting to introduce new taxes from which no one was exempt. This measure was opposed by the Parlement and all privileged orders. Louis dismissed Machault, choosing to support the Church in its struggle with the Parlement over the Jansenists, and thus threw away an opportunity to lessen the national debt by spreading the burden of taxation.

Downfall of the Jesuits in Europe

After the middle of the eighteenth century the persecution of the Jansenists and the Huguenots began to die down with the spread of the more tolerant ideas of the Enlightenment. It was the turn instead of the Jesuits to come under attack, for they had for so long inspired much of the religious persecution in France. The campaign against the Jesuits was not, however, confined to France but involved all the leading Catholic countries of Europe— Portugal, Spain and the Hapsburg empire.

The first blow fell in Portugal where since the middle of the century King Joseph's enlightened prime minister, the Marquis de Pombal, had been engaged in efforts to strengthen royal authority and to introduce sweeping reforms. His activities brought him into conflict with the Jesuits who were already

St. Ignazio sanctuary in Spain, a modern Jesuit monastery.

engaged with considerable success in commercial and political enterprises as well as missionary ones. Taking as a pretext an attempted assassination of the King, Pombal charged the Jesuits with complicity in the plot and outlawed the Society in 1760. Its property was confiscated and its members were expelled from the country.

As in Portugal so in France it was the Jesuits' secular interests that brought about their downfall. In France their enemies were many—the philosophers, the Parlements, the Jansenists, the ordinary people and not least those closest to the King—Mme de Pompadour and, after his rise to power in 1758, the Duc de Choiseul. A bankrupt Jesuit sugar enterprise in Martinique provided the stimulus to anti-Jesuit proceedings. The question at stake was whether the Jesuit society collectively or the individual director of the company was responsible for the company's debts. The courts found the society responsible, and the Parlement of Paris upheld this decision and declared the society to be incompatible with loyalty to the crown. Thus in April, 1762, the King outlawed the French branch of the Jesuits.

The downfall of the Jesuits in France foreshadowed a similar fate in Spain. When Charles III left Naples to become King of Spain in 1759, he brought with him two Italians as his confidential ministers. One of these, Squillacci, gave much offence to the Spaniards by his reforms. These provoked a riot

259

in Madrid in 1766. Charles III was forced to dismiss his unpopular minister, replacing him by a nobleman, the Count d'Aranda, who found that the Jesuits had been at the root of the disturbances; so Charles III, although a devout Catholic, determined to expel them for their interference in the running of the country. In 1767 the Jesuits were arrested and exiled to Rome.

Ferdinand, King of Naples, the Duke of Parma and Joseph and his mother Maria Theresa, co-regents of the Hapsburg lands, took the same action against the order despite the protests of Pope Clement XIII (1758-69).

At length Spain and Naples put pressure on Pope Clement XIV (1769-74) and he issued a famous Bull, *Dominus ac Redemptor*, which declared an end to the Order. The Society refused to submit to the Papal Bull and many of its members took refuge in Prussia, Poland and Russia.

Renewal of Anglo-French Competition, 1763-83

The year 1763 was one of bitter humiliation for France and her ally Spain, in contrast with the crowning triumph for their common foe, Britain, whose seizure of their overseas empires in North America, the West Indies and India was recognized in the Treaty of Paris. Yet within twenty years the situation was almost reversed for it was Britain who in the Treaty of Versailles of 1783 signed away an important part of her empire when she recognized the independence of her thirteen American colonies. While in no sense did France or Spain fully recover their lost empires, they had their revenge in having aided the Americans to win their freedom.

Choiseul, Louis XV's Foreign Minister (1758-70), compassed the ruin of Britain's overseas trade and empire by both diplomatic and military means. The essential keys to French diplomacy after 1763 were the Bourbon-Hapsburg alliance and the Family Compact with Spain. In continuing the alliance with the Hapsburgs which France had concluded in 1756, Choiseul, Louis XV's minister, believed he could bolster French influence in northern and eastern Europe, while the close alliance with Charles III of Spain would enable both powers to counter British designs in the Mediterranean and the Caribbean. He therefore arranged several Hapsburg-Bourbon marriages. The Emperor Joseph II married the Bourbon Infanta, and Joseph's youngest sister, Marie Antoinette, was to become the wife of the future Louis XVI.

Choiseul was also responsible for reorganizing France's military and naval forces in preparation for a future conflict with Britain. Important reforms too, were carried out in the French army and navy. Incompetent officers were dismissed and improvements were made both in recruitment and training.

Among the actual successes of Choiseul's policy of reviving France's power and influence was the acquisition of Lorraine in 1765. Fleury had established that, with the death of the Polish king Stanislas, Lorraine should pass to

France, and Choiseul made certain that the treaty was carried out despite Hapsburg objection.

While the acquisition of Lorraine was not directly engineered by Choiseul, he was solely responsible for the acquisition of Corsica in 1769. This island was an important naval base in the western Mediterranean for operations against the British bases of Gibraltar and Minorca. The Corsicans originally were under the rule of the Genoese Republic but they did not prove amenable subjects. On two occasions Genoa called upon France to aid her suppress revolts. It was on the occasion of the second revolt that Choiseul's offer to purchase the island was accepted and Corsica came under French control in the very year that its most famous son, Napoleon Bonaparte, was born at Ajaccio, the capital.

Downfall of Choiseul

This was Choiseul's last major success. Within a year Louis had dismissed his most outstanding minister since Fleury. After the death of his ally, Mme de Pompadour, in 1764, Choiseul's position had been steadily undermined by the *Devotees*. This was a hostile court faction which included Mme du Barry, and their objection to Choiseul stemmed from the part he had played in expelling the Jesuits.

The crisis came to a head when the Jesuit peer D'Aiguillon had his privileges suspended by the Parlement. Choiseul supported the Parlement, and D'Aiguillon, together with Mme du Barry, demanded his dismissal. In December, 1770, Choiseul was banished to his estates.

Last Years of Louis XV

Choiseul's dismissal was really a blow directed against Parlements, and in 1771 Louis struck again, abolishing them altogether. Had he acted as decisively earlier in his reign, the opposition to royal power might not have become so organized and vocal, with results that would have altered the history of France. As it was, Louis had acted too late. While foreseeing clearly the clouds of discontent rapidly darkening the twilight of his years, he was not unduly concerned to alter his ways for he knew that it would not be he but his unfortunate successor who would suffer when these clouds burst. "*Après moi, le déluge*" has been attributed to him, and the underlying idea was soon shown to be correct. Louis XV died in May, 1774, after a long reign of fifty-nine years. He had outlived his son, so it was to his grandson, Louis XVI, that the throne passed.

QUESTIONS

1. Why did the Bourbon monarchy decline during the reign of Louis XV?

2. Explain why the Jesuit order was dissolved in Europe.

CHAPTER 30

ROAD TO REVOLUTION IN FRANCE

NO NATION desires to overturn an established system of government unless there is something radically wrong with the existing order; and before we attempt to trace the history of the early years of the reign of Louis XVI we may perhaps pause at this point to examine the many sources of discontent which were already at work in France by 1774.

Political Causes of the Revolution

In France in the eighteenth century, absolute monarchy existed in perhaps its most extreme form. This absolute system of government has been described in the chapter, "The Glory of France." It is sufficient to note here that there were few limits to the King's power, and his advisory council (*le Conseil du Roi*) could only make suggestions that Louis was not bound to accept, while his provincial officials were merely executants of the policy laid down in minute detail in Paris.

The entire system of absolute monarchy depends upon the character of the monarch himself. Under a competent ruler like Louis XIV absolute monarchy had been practicable. But under Louis XVI all the flaws inherent in this system of government were only too apparent. Louis XVI was a weak, well-meaning person whose intentions were far better than his abilities. His fluctuating government policies, designed to please everyone, succeeded in pleasing no one.

Social Factors

In spite of the conflicting social division of the nation there was scarcely any section of the community without its grievances against the existing régime. The nobility had been deprived of all political power in the course of the seventeenth century; their former role in the political life of their country had been taken over by professional royal officials, recruited from the ranks of the middle class. The monarchy had sought to distract the attention of the aristocracy from this loss of influence by encouraging attendance at court. This turned the nobility into absentee landlords, intent only on extracting as much money from their estates as possible in order to hold their own in

262

the extravagant life of Paris. Thus were the interests of feudal landowner and feudal peasant divorced and irreconcilable hostility between the two created. The nobility could never, even if they had wished, challenge the power of the crown with the support of the peasantry. Yet not all the aristocracy succumbed to the planned distraction and, while they cherished their feudal social privileges, there were those among them who resented their political impotence.

The middle-classes (the *bourgeoisie*) other than the minority serving as royal officials had resentments of their own. Engaged largely in trade and commerce they found the government's interference an irritating restriction on their activities, and the internal customs duties between province and province an intolerable burden upon their enterprise and profits. Above all, intelligent and educated as they were, they chafed against a social structure which, based on birth, afforded them no opportunity for social and political advancement.

The bourgeoisie shared with the peasantry and serfs the whole weight of taxation, nobility and clergy being exempt therefrom, although the bourgeoisie were able to buy public office which exempted them from taxation. It was perhaps the peasantry who were the most deeply wronged section of the nation. Although by the late eighteenth century from 30 per cent to 40 per cent of the land was owned by the peasants, their livelihood was far from secure. Living in wretched and impoverished conditions they resented intensely having to surrender a great part of their meagre income in taxes either to the State (the *taille*, the *gabelle*, *capitation*), the Church (tithe), and their feudal overlords (rents, *banalités*, or payments for their compulsory use of the lord's oven, mill and wine-press). Obligations which took them away from the cultivation of their own land rankled bitterly. The weekly labour services on the estates of an all-too-frequently-absent landlord, the *corvée*, by right of which the *Intendant* was empowered to raise labour gangs to build roads, and the liability to service in the army created more and more discontent, especially towards the end of the century when most of the peasants were personally free.

Their anger was further increased by the attempts of many lords to revive obsolete feudal claims and to bring up to date the records of feudal obligations. The reason for this development was in part the desire of the older and impoverished nobility to increase their income and in part the efforts of the newer nobility to place the management of their estates on a business-like footing. The peasants had little chance of appealing successfully to the local Parlement.

Feudal grievances apart, the peasants resented all efforts made by the government or other reformers to improve the traditional type of subsistence agriculture. Efforts were made by the physiocrats to introduce scientific methods of farming similar to those which had led to the agricultural revolution in Britain a decade or two earlier. The idea which prompted these attempted reforms was the belief that the recurrent famines to which France was subject could only be avoided by the development of large-scale agriculture. These reforms involved the enclosure of the large numbers of small peasant holdings, as well as the village common land, in order to form large and therefore efficient farm units. To all this the peasants were bitterly opposed. They resisted any attempt to dislodge them from their land or to end their age-old right to the common upon which they grazed their cattle. It is little wonder therefore that the efforts of the physiocrats to establish agricultural societies, internal free trade in corn, and to end the state regulation of corn prices, received a hostile reception from the peasantry. In this respect the peasants were their own worst enemies for until such reforms could be effected there was no hope of raising their low standards of living.

Financial Factors

To these political and social discontents must be added the effect of an inefficient and over-strained financial system. The wars of the previous hundred years had exhausted French monetary resources and recourse had been had on a large scale to borrowing. Heavy national debt had led to ever increasing rates of taxation, direct and indirect, and the method of tax collection made a bad situation infinitely worse. The government sold the right to collect taxes to individuals wealthy enough to advance to the government immediately the money it sought to raise. These tax farmers sold part of their rights to yet other men and all these intermediaries saw to it that the sums finally collected from the taxpayer included a handsome margin of profit for themselves. Often enough when the taxpayer had met all his obligations he found himself with hardly ten per cent of his income left for his own needs. This was the cost the Third Estate had to bear for the tax-free privilege of the other two social orders.

Literary and Intellectual Factors

Yet these conditions, political, social and financial, could be paralleled in countries other than France; nowhere else, however, was there quite the same ferment of ideas as in France. There for some years, and often with the patronage of the Crown who failed to take seriously the writing on the wall, men had been disseminating ideas which directly or indirectly were critical of the régime. The work of the French intellectuals of the period has been referred to in a previous chapter on the Enlightenment. It was from the writings of such men that the dangerous ideas of liberty, equality and fraternity, which were to be the slogans of revolution, spread among the literate sections of the Third Estate; and it was from this section of the nation that the leaders of the revolution in its early stages were drawn.

Immediate Causes of the Revolution

It was the misfortune of Louis XVI to pursue policies, both at home and abroad, which served to bring all these many rivulets of discontent into a swollen river which swept him and the privileged classes to their death.

In view of the precarious financial situation which he inherited, it should have been Louis' prime object to abstain from foreign adventure but one of his first actions was to appoint as Secretary for Foreign Affairs Vergennes, who favoured an aggressive foreign policy directed against Britain and designed to destroy her trade with her American colonies. In the dispute between Britain and her colonies which by 1775 had resulted in open hostilities Vergennes saw his golden opportunity. Louis XVI, as an absolute ruler, was not anxious to support rebellious subjects against their king. His conscience, however, was eased on this point when the Americans issued their Declaration of Independence; he could now persuade himself that in helping the Americans he was helping an independent sovereign power rather than rebels. Moreover, Vergennes ultimately convinced Louis that a policy of neutrality on the part of France might well endanger France's own possessions in the West Indies. Finally the British forces in America met with a resounding defeat at Saratoga Springs in 1777 and the American diplomat then in Paris, Benjamin Franklin, made the most of this situation. By suggesting that this colonial success provided a suitable opportunity for a negotiated peace between America and Britain, he persuaded Vergennes and Louis to enter into a military and commercial alliance with his country against Britain. Within a few months Britain and France were officially at war and a French army and navy were despatched to America.

Foreign intervention on the American side proved decisive. The Peace of Versailles in 1783 recognized American Independence and rewarded France

Marie Antoinette and Louis XVI, ill-fated monarchs of France.

by the cession of Tobago in the West Indies and permission to establish trading posts in India and Senegal. In the short term this looked like a resounding triumph for the policies of Vergennes but in the long run these gains proved dearly bought. Far more important was the impact of the American war on the outlook of Frenchmen and the state of the nation's finances.

French soldiers who had been sent to help the American colonies win independence from Britain returned home convinced that "No taxation without representation" was a principle worth fighting for. Frenchmen who had helped Americans to secure freedom from the "tyranny" of George III saw no reason why they should continue to endure the greater tyrannies and injustices of their own king and government. It was no accident that the Marquis de Lafayette, who had fought for the Americans, became the commander of the revolutionary national guard in 1789.

Failure of Financial Reform

Between 1774 and 1776, Louis XVI had summoned Turgot to take the financial problem in hand. As a result a policy of rigorous economy had been outlined. Turgot abolished many useless offices, established central control over all departments of state, checked the corruption of farmers-general and tried to reduce the extravagance of the court. To help the peasants, he established internal free trade in corn by removing customs barriers restricting freedom of distribution. These barriers had caused severe shortages in some areas while there had been abundance in others. He also abolished the *corvée*; in its place he substituted a tax payable by all classes including those who had hitherto enjoyed tax exemption. This aroused the bitter opposition of the privileged orders and a faction at court persuaded Louis XVI to dismiss the minister whose policies, had they been fully implemented, might have saved France from revolution.

Turgot was succeeded by a Swiss banker, Necker, who had to deal with the financial consequences of the intervention in America, an intervention which cost France some two thousand million *livres*. Necker's policy for financing the war was that of raising loans. He maintained that the limit of the taxable capacity of the nation had already been reached. To attract loans he was compelled to offer high rates of interest, as much as 10 per cent and in 1781 he misrepresented the true state of French finances when he published his celebrated *Compte rendu au roi sur les finances de la nation*. In this document he announced a surplus of revenue over expenditure when in fact there was a deficit of some forty-six million livres. This statement was accepted by the general public so the true seriousness of the financial situation was not realized, and in these misleading circumstances Necker became exceedingly popular. His ministerial colleagues were less easily deceived.

The return of the King and royal family to Paris from Varennes, where they had fled in 1791 during the Revolution.

Sceptical about the truth of his *Compte Rendu* they were also jealous of the popularity it brought him. Thus by 1781 they had secured his dismissal from power.

The next notable financial minister was Calonne, who was controller-general between 1783 and 1787. At first he tried to carry on Necker's policy of raising loans and in order not to discourage potential investors made no attempt to cut down court and other expenses. This reckless financial policy only increased the national indebtedness, and it became obvious even to Calonne that only by expanding revenue from taxation could the rising deficit be checked. With this in mind Calonne proposed certain radical reforms of the whole system of taxation, foremost amongst which was the imposition of a direct tax on all landowners and a stamp tax from which nobody, including the privileged orders, was to be exempt. In order to secure approval of his proposals Calonne induced the King to summon an "Assembly of Notables" composed of men nominated by Louis and charged to discuss the suggested reforms.

When this Assembly met in 1787 it was seen to be a body pledged to defend the privileges of the aristocracy, clergy and bureaucracy. Calonne's proposals, especially the land and stamp taxes, were bitterly attacked. Louis XVI was persuaded to dismiss the reformer and appoint in his place the Cardinal de Brienne. The Assembly's only advice to the King was that he should summon the Estates-general.

Before taking this advice Louis and Brienne tried a further gambit.

Rebuffed by the Assembly, Brienne sought the approval of the Parlement of Paris for his schemes. Since many members of the Parlement were themselves exempt from taxation they were as unsympathetic as the Assembly had been and refused to register the necessary edicts. On this the King intervened, exercising his royal authority to enforce registration and as a mark of his displeasure exiled the Parlement to Troyes. Subsequently he weakened, agreed to Parlement's return to Paris and withdrew his insistence on the new taxes. A renewed quarrel with the Parlement in 1788 led the King to stiffen his attitude again and this time Parlement was suppressed entirely.

Such anger was aroused among the legal classes of France over Louis' suppression of the Parlement that Louis dismissed Brienne, restored the Parlement, and recalled Necker. Necker advised him to recall the Estates-general, which he did. Each member of each Estate brought with him a list of the grievances of the various constituencies (*Cahiers des doléances*). Louis allowed the Third Estate as many members as the two privileged orders combined, but he made no alteration in the traditional voting procedure which allowed the privileged classes to outvote the Third Estate. This made a clash between the two inevitable and is another instance of Louis' lack of foresight.

Famine and Unemployment, 1788-89

The winter of 1788-89 was not the happiest time for an election of a representative body. The year 1788 had been a year of famine and its effects were desperately evident in the winter. To make matters worse there was wide unemployment following the influx of and competition from British manufactures which were permitted into the country as a result of the Anglo-French free trade treaty of 1786. As 1788 gave way to 1789 the discomfort of freezing cold was added to hunger and unemployment; even the great rivers turned to solid ice.

Miseries such as these brought to Paris hordes of half-starving unemployed artisans. In search of food, work and warmth these men and their women-folk were to swell the ranks of the mobs which were soon to exercise a decisive influence upon the nation's destiny.

QUESTIONS

1. Why was there a revolution in France in 1789?
2. What attempts were made during Louis XVI's reign to solve France's financial problems, and why were they unsuccessful?

REVISION SUMMARY

THE GLORY OF FRANCE, 1643-1715

CHAPTER 31

THE FRENCH REVOLUTION, 1789-1795

IT WOULD be difficult to imagine a man more unfitted to guide the destiny of France in 1789 than the king, Louis XVI. A man conscientiously concerned for the welfare of his people, his good intentions were offset by his ill-trained mind, irresolute judgement and limited intelligence. Easily influenced as he was by the opinions of others, his policies lacked consistency, swinging to and fro between the reforming tendencies of a Turgot or a Necker and the reactionary urgings of the queen, Marie Antoinette. The discontents which lay at the root of the revolution were not of the king's making, but his ineptitude contributed largely to the course which it took.

It was unfortunate that Louis was such a devoted husband for in his queen he had a wife who was far more likely to aggravate than to correct the defects of his character. Ignorant, like the king, of the reality of national conditions, she laboured under the additional handicap of unpopularity because of her foreign Austrian extraction. Being unreasonable, impulsive, prejudiced, determined and extravagant, her influence, when she gained the king's ear, was highly disastrous. It was Marie Antoinette who shipwrecked the schemes for financial reform in the years 1770-89 and it was she who later counselled the flight to Varennes and the appeal for foreign aid. If France was unfortunate in her king, both France and the king were doubly unfortunate in their queen.

Formation of the National Assembly

When the Estates-general met in May, 1789, it expected to take decisions as customary by noting the collective opinion of each estate. Since this would enable the two privileged estates to overrule the one unprivileged estate, the latter formed itself into a separate body, calling itself the "National Assembly."

This action was taken on 17 June, 1789, and three days later the National Assembly found itself locked out from its usual meeting place. Adjourning to a neighbouring tennis court the new body took an oath not to disband until it had given France a new constitution. At first, this Oath of the Tennis Court seemed likely to be still-born since the king refused to recognize the self-constituted National Assembly and ordered it to deliberate as part of the Estates-general. It was in this crisis that the Third Estate found its real leader.

This was the Comte de Mirabeau who, though a nobleman, had because of his realization of the necessity for reform, successfully offered himself for election by the people of Aix-en-Provence as their representative in the Estates-general. In the deliberations of that body Mirabeau soon revealed himself as probably the only man with a policy which, had it been accepted and consistently followed, might have saved the French monarchy from destruction and the country from the worst excesses of the revolutionary turmoil.

Briefly, Mirabeau's policy was to establish a strong though limited monarchy. He opposed the extremist elements in the Estates-general and National Assembly while at the same time urging the king to put forward a plan of reasonable reform. Mirabeau's position as a nobleman representing the Third Estate seemed to fit him admirably for the task of reconciling Court and people. Actually it proved to be his undoing. His connection with the people gave the Court reactionaries an excuse to describe him to the king as a traitor to his order, while his access to and contact with the Court enabled the more extreme revolutionaries to denounce him as one who, under the guise of a friend, was seeking to betray the cause of reform.

Although the Court refused to take his advice and ultimately ruined his plans, Mirabeau was not entirely unsuccessful. He forced the king and privileged orders to recognize the National Assembly. His death in 1791 removed the only statesmanlike figure in the early stages of the revolution.

Influence of Paris

The significance of Mirabeau's success was lost on the Parisian mob. It seemed to these starving, destitute people that their representatives at Versailles were allowing the Court to draw red herrings across the path of reform. When early in July, 1789, it was learned that the king had again dismissed the reforming Necker, the Parisians took matters into their own hands. Organizing a military force of their own they seized the Bastille, a prison for political offenders.

Almost devoid of prisoners and only lightly garrisoned, the Bastille was hardly a formidable objective. But the old fortress represented in the eyes of its destructors all the hated régime of privilege for the few and injustice for the many and its fall was to them like the collapse of this system. It was a symbolic rather than a substantial victory they had won: it was not without practical results. Within three days of the fall of the Bastille, Necker was recalled to office, the king re-opened negotiations with the National Assembly and himself saluted the tricolour, the flag of the Revolution. The Parisian mob had now tasted power and its example was imitated throughout the provinces where the local population made attacks on the chateaux of the nobility.

At the same time, a Parisian mob, spurred on by the lack of food in the capital, marched on Versailles and obtained a promise that the Court would remove to Paris.

The king took up residence in the Tuileries, the National Assembly followed the Court to Paris and the influence of the Paris mob was henceforth a determining factor in the course of the revolution.

Work of the National Assembly, 1789-91

On 4 August, 1789, the National Assembly did away with the last remnants of feudalism by abolishing the privileges of the nobility and clergy, by dissolving the industrial gilds and by condemning the sale of political offices. By the end of the same month they drew up the Declaration of the Rights of Man, which asserted the equality of all men irrespective of birth, denied state control of religion, and advocated rule by the will of the people.

Some of these ideals failed partly because they were too lofty for the times, and partly because the assembly had to work increasingly under the eye of the Parisian mob. In any case it daily became obvious that the task of constructing a new system of government and way of life was infinitely harder than that of destroying the old one.

From discussion of abstract principles the Assembly turned to the practical task of reform of local government. All the old provinces were abolished along with their special rights and royally-appointed officials. They were replaced by eighty-three departments all roughly equal in size and administered by committees elected by "active citizens." Somewhat disappointingly an active citizen was defined as one who paid the equivalent of three days' wages in direct taxes, a qualified franchise which was hardly an expression of the doctrine of the equality of all men.

Next, judicial administration was taken in hand. Each department was to have its court of justice and the principle of trial by jury was introduced for criminal cases. The judges were, however, to be elected locally, an unhappy arrangement which opened the door to grave abuses. To make a judge's position dependent upon his popularity with those who might come before him was not the way to secure a strict application of the law.

Meanwhile the problem of national finance still awaited solution and the wealth of the Church seemed to the Assembly a heaven-sent solution to a difficult situation. Eventually the property of the Church was confiscated, a rough calculation of its value was made, and paper money issued to the total of the computed sum. Acceptance of this money was compulsory.

To this dispersal of their property the clergy naturally objected, but their opposition only brought worse disaster upon their heads. The Civil Constitution of the Clergy in 1790 abolished the old ecclesiastical divisions of France, made every new department a bishopric and reduced the clergy to the status of salaried servants of the State. All clergy refusing to accept this decree lost their livings. Since however many of the dispossessed were priests whose ministry had been acceptable to their parishioners, the revolution now had to cope with a division of the unprivileged classes into revolutionaries and anti-revolutionaries. The attack on the Church therefore ultimately led to civil war.

Finally in 1791 the National Assembly fulfilled its tennis court oath by giving to France a new constitution which set very definite limits to the king's power and made provision for the regular meeting of a national representative body. The king accepted the new constitution, though unwillingly, and popular elections were held at the end of 1791. As a result there met a new representative body, known as the Legislative Assembly.

New Personalities and Political Groupings, 1791-95

The most statesmanlike of the new personalities to appear after the death of Mirabeau was Danton. Although his early career was marred by the September Massacres, which occurred when he was Minister of Justice, at a later period he did his best to stop such excesses and thereby lost his own life. A strong man in times of crisis, Danton's weakness was a lack of interest in the dull but necessary daily routine of government administration. His was the dominating figure of the Convention and his death was almost as great a blow to the interests of France as was that of Mirabeau.

At first intimately associated with Danton was Robespierre, a man of utter sincerity but dangerous fanaticism. The title of statesman can hardly be applied to Robespierre; he was too fond of theories which, however logical, were not always expedient or practical. His sincerity itself was a danger; it prevented him from realizing that those who could not accept his theories were nevertheless often enough no less sincere than he was himself.

Believing that only force would secure the permanent success of the revolutionary cause, Robespierre was the guiding spirit of the Reign of Terror. When Danton urged the abandonment of such a ferocious policy, Robespierre interpreted this attitude as treachery and sent his erstwhile colleague to the guillotine. Though Robespierre was not responsible for the decision to outlaw Christianity in revolutionary France, he did apparently think that the worship of the Supreme Being would be an adequate substitute. Only a man whose mind had been closed by the logic of reason to the force of tradition would have imagined that the devout peasant whose grievances were against the Church rather than the Christian faith would find in a vague Being, however supreme, anything so life-like and appealing as the Christ he had worshipped so long. By his cloudy theorizing and untimely logic Robespierre eventually aroused such strong opposition that he became a victim of the instrument

Left to right: Danton, Robespierre and Marat conferring.

the use of which against others he had so ardently advocated. He was guillotined in July, 1794.

The third outstanding figure of the second phase of the revolution was Marat, a doctor by profession and a demagogue by nature. Violently anti-monarchical he owed his influence to his talent as a mob orator. The crude appeal which he made to the worst passions of the worst elements of the Parisian population he followed up in his vitriolic writings in a journal which he edited known as *"L'Ami du Peuple."* Marat and his journal were the instruments which roused the Paris mob to the perpetration of the September Massacres of 1792. Fittingly enough, his own death was a violent one. Charlotte Corday, a young provincial noblewoman, gained admittance to him under the guise of a friend of the Revolution and stabbed him to death. Though she was executed for her crime, it is by no means certain that she had not done France a great service.

These three men based their power upon two political clubs to which they belonged. Robespierre was the outstanding member of the Jacobin Club, so-called because a group of Breton representatives to the National Assembly had been accustomed to meet nightly in an old Jacobin convent to discuss the political business of the next day. The general public were ultimately allowed to attend their discussions and these Parisian Jacobins encouraged the formation of affiliated societies in the provinces, so managing to spread their ideas very widely.

Danton and Marat were members of the Cordeliers Club, a body whose views were originally more extreme than those of the Jacobins. It was a purely Parisian organization and its influence was in consequence mainly confined to the capital.

Though they did not actually constitute a political club another group deserves notice, namely the Girondins. They owe their name to the fact that several of their leaders represented the Gironde district. Eager revolutionaries, they were at first allies of the Jacobins and succeeded in 1792 in gaining ascendancy in the legislative chamber. When later it became clear that the Girondins supported a policy of war against those foreign powers who were opposed to the Revolution, the Jacobins turned against their former friends and the struggle between these two groups had no small effect on the character of the Revolution. What that effect was we shall see better as we follow the progress of events in France after 1791.

The king's acceptance of the constitution was suspect from the first. The extreme revolutionaries felt that he had accepted it only because his flight from France had been intercepted at Varennes. They also objected to his continued protection of the nobility and the Church. The Jacobins had now gained enough power to obtain their own way in the Legislative Assembly over more moderate groups, and the king, by inviting Austria and Prussia to declare war on the Revolution, put the seal of doom on the monarchy. The republican cause now became the national cause.

By playing upon the popular fear of foreign invasion engendered by this last event the Jacobins and Cordeliers roused the mob to a state of frenzy. The power of the king was suspended, and royalists were thrown into prison where they were ultimately murdered out of hand one night in September, 1792, by a hysterical mob. Unable to control the situation, the Legislative Assembly dissolved itself and ordered new elections.

The new representative body called itself the Convention, and the struggle between the Jacobins and the Girondins to gain control of it determined the fate of the king. The Jacobins triumphed; Louis was tried and executed in 1793 on a charge of intriguing with foreign powers against the Revolution; the Girondin leaders were arrested, and Robespierre reigned supreme.

February, 1793, was beyond doubt a period of severe crisis. La Vendée, one of the southern provinces not greatly affected by some of the evils of the Ancien Régime, revolted against a decree which made service in the revolutionary armies compulsory. This was the signal for revolt in some of the other great provincial towns which had grown resentful of the extent to which Paris was dictating the course of national events. Added to this was the fact that Austrian and Prussian armies were already on French soil.

The Reign of Terror

To meet this occasion Robespierre instituted a Reign of Terror to suppress reaction in parts of France and to arouse courage in the nation at large.

He set up a revolutionary tribunal to hunt down suspected traitors, and a committee of public safety to organize effective national defence. In the provinces, deputies on mission arrested as alleged traitors those who, if they had not opposed the Revolution had at best done nothing actively to further it. Throughout the nation large numbers of nobles, priests and wealthy middle-class citizens were thrust into prison and condemned on suspicion and without trial. Among them was the queen who was guillotined in October, 1793. At the same time the provincial revolts in La Vendée and elsewhere were suppressed with ruthless brutality. A new calendar was drawn up, numbering the years from the beginning of the revolution and renaming the months, the decimal system of weights and measures was adopted, Christianity was condemned and the worship of the goddess of reason established. And with it all the tide of foreign invasion was first stemmed and finally repulsed.

Danton now urged that the Terror had accomplished its aims; on the other hand a group of extreme Jacobins under the leadership of Hébart pressed for the continuance and indeed intensification of the Terror. Robespierre first allied with Danton and destroyed the Hébartists, then shifted his ground and destroyed Danton. For a while the Terror continued with many of Danton's supporters being sent to execution. Yet Robespierre's own end was fast approaching. With Danton's party destroyed and Robespierre's party divided, the balance of power in the Convention tipped in favour of a moderate centre party whose members reflected the changing mood of the nation. France, even Paris, had become bored by executions and satiated with blood. Robespierre's opponents organized themselves secretly, then openly jeered at him in the Legislature and found the public on their side. Thus encouraged they arrested him and at last executed him along with those of his supporters who remained faithful to him. The Terror at last was ended (July, 1794).

The Convention

The task of the Convention now was to construct a constitution to replace that of 1791, which had included many reform measures. The remains of mob rule were liquidated and the revolutionary tribunal and the committee of public safety were both made subordinate to the Legislature. The Jacobin Club was dissolved. There was a reaction against the early revolutionary passion for government by elected committees; the Directory was created. This was to consist of five men who were to hold office for five years, one of their number retiring each year. Legislation was to be the function of two councils elected by the people. By the Law of Two-Thirds, however, this proportion of the new councils were to have been members who had served in the Convention. A popular rising against this stipulation was easily suppressed and the Directory governed France from 1795 to 1799. Its accession to power marks the end of the active stage of the revolution.

Results of the Revolution

What had France gained from six stormy, turbulent, cruel years? First, the old political, social, financial and judicial inequalities had vanished. The feudal privileges of the nobility were never revived and the wealth and power of the Church never restored. Taxation had been placed on a fairer basis and every man could be sure of something more approaching impartial justice than he could have obtained before 1789.

Second, the absolute power of the monarch, indeed monarchy itself, had given place to the assertion of the principle of the right of the people to a voice and share in the determination of government. It is true that Napoleon later became an autocratic emperor and that the old royal family were for a time restored in the nineteenth century; but Napoleon's régime was a temporary interregnum and the later Bourbons never recovered all the powers which had been enjoyed by Louis XVI and his predecessors. In any case, the ultimate future of France lay in republicanism, not in monarchy.

Third, the foundation of a more efficient system of administration had been laid and the principle of local self-government in such matters had been so effectively asserted that even Napoleon's reversal of it did not permanently destroy it.

Fourth, France had at last been welded into a real national unity and though local loyalties remained, feudal provincialism and separatism were never strong enough to be a likely cause of political disintegration.

Abroad, the immediate result of the French Revolution was to intensify repressive absolute government. That however was only a temporary defensive reaction on the part of established governments. The ultimate and permanent effect was to stimulate the growth of representative government. The rule of the people by the people, one of the marked features of the history of the nineteenth century, and its rapid development in that age rather than earlier or later, may be directly traced to the example set by the people of France in the years 1789-95.

QUESTIONS

1. Describe the reforms carried out by: (*a*) the National Assembly of 1789-91; (*b*) the Convention of 1792-5.
2. Account for the failure of attempts to establish a limited monarchy in France between 1791 and 1793.

CHAPTER 32

THE FRENCH REVOLUTIONARY WARS, 1793-1801

WHEN revolution began in France, the European states were not at first unduly alarmed. France's continental neighbours hoped that pre-occupation with affairs at home would make her less aggressive abroad. In Britain many people and politicians felt that they could hardly blame Frenchmen for imposing upon the Monarchy restraints similar to those which the British people had imposed upon their king in 1689. Yet four years later no less than six states were in arms against France and her revolution.

Fundamental Causes

The attitude of Europe changed when it was seen that the movement in France might threaten the whole fabric of European life.

Absolute monarchy was a form of government common almost everywhere in Europe; even in Britain, in spite of the revolution of 1688, the king remained the active head of the executive body. The kings of Europe feared that this self-assertion on the part of the people of France might encourage peoples of other countries to act in a similar fashion. In self-defence, therefore, the European monarchies felt bound to come to the rescue of Louis XVI and the cause of kingship in France.

Furthermore, it was feared that the oppressed classes in other countries might follow the example of the French Third Estate. In addition, the power of the Catholic Church, and, ultimately, Christianity, was threatened by events in France.

These fears were not mere possibilities. The leaders of the Revolution in November, 1793, issued their famous Edict of Fraternity in which they invited oppressed peoples in every state to rise against their rulers and promised such rebels the armed assistance of France.

Moreover, those nobles, the emigrés, who had already fled from France lost no opportunity of playing upon the fears of the governments of the countries in which they had sought refuge. Add to this the fact that many of the princes of the Empire who held estates in France had suffered financial loss and the changed attitude of the European powers towards the French Revolution after 1793 becomes understandable.

Immediate Causes

The failure of Austria and Prussia during their campaign against the Revolution in 1791-2 was one reason why matters came to a head in 1793. Both countries were halted unexpectedly by revolutionary armies in France. European politicians sensed danger to themselves when two major powers had failed to repress the Revolution. In addition, French troops advanced into Holland, thus violating her neutrality and threatening England. Lastly, the execution of Louis XVI frightened the crowned heads of Europe. Hence in 1793 the alliance of Austria, Prussia, Holland, Spain, Sardinia and Britain was organized by the younger Pitt under the title of the first coalition.

War of the First Coalition, 1793-96

The War of the First Coalition began with a series of victories for the Allies. The Austrians invaded Holland and the French commander, Dumouriez, defeated at Neerwinden, 1793, surrendered to his enemies. Austrian and British troops together completed the conquest of the Netherlands and laid siege to Dunkirk. Meanwhile Spanish troops successfully invaded France itself and Prussia threatened another invasion from the east. These French disasters led the royalists of La Vendée, as we have seen, to think that the time was opportune for a royalist protest.

In this crisis in the affairs of the Revolution, Robespierre set up the Reign of Terror. Conscription was introduced and fresh armies put into the field. This remedy was drastic but effective.

First, the new armies compelled the Allies to raise the siege of Dunkirk, 1793. On the eastern front, the Austro-Prussian invasion was repulsed. Spanish troops were expelled from southern France in 1794 and at home the revolt in La Vendée was crushed. Then the French armies again invaded and conquered Holland in 1795. By the middle of that year Spain and Prussia admitted failure and signed the Treaty of Basle. A year later Spain went further and became a French ally. The first coalition was no more.

In 1793 the British navy had been driven from Toulon. In 1794 the British fleet had at the Battle of the First of June engaged the French fleet in an attempt to prevent a corn convoy reaching port. The French fleet had been defeated but the cornships had got through.

It was in attacks on the colonies of the French and her allies that Britain scored her greatest successes. In 1795 a Dutch alliance with France laid the Dutch colony of the Cape of Good Hope open to attack and conquest. Similarly the French sugar islands of the West Indies were captured. Thus did the navy preserve Britain from invasion and extend the British empire.

By 1796 only three of the great powers who had formed the coalition of 1793 remained unsubdued—Austria, Sardinia and Britain. The revolutionaries resolved to concentrate first on the land powers. The main attack was to be made by an invasion of Austria across the Rhine, but there was to be a diversionary expedition against Austrian possessions in Italy. This minor effort was entrusted to a young Brigadier-General, once a corporal, Napoleon Bonaparte.

Napoleon's First Italian Campaign, 1796-97

Invading Italy in 1796, Napoleon first drove a wedge between the forces of Austria and Sardinia and then dealt with each in turn. Sardinia was the first to succumb with the result that Savoy and Nice, first captured by the French in 1792, remained in French possession.

Austria in Italy offered stern resistance, yet in three stages her resistance was overcome. First Lombardy, then Milan and finally Mantua fell into Napoleon's hands, and the defeat of the Austrian Archduke Charles at the Battle of Tagliamento in 1797 destroyed all hopes of an immediate recovery.

Meanwhile, Napoleon had frustrated the efforts of the Pope to come to the rescue of Catholic Austria. Two invasions of the Papal States had induced the Pope to make peace and even to concede territory.

In 1797 Austria signed the Peace of Campo Formio. By this treaty Lombardy and the Austrian Netherlands passed into French possession, Austria gaining in return Venetia. Lombardy was afterwards incorporated by the French with Modena and part of the Papal States as the Cisalpine Republic.

The year 1797 found Britain facing alone an alliance of France, Spain and Holland and these powers now made a determined effort to destroy British command of the sea and thus make possible a successful invasion of Britain. But by dealing with their opponents one at a time, Jervis and Nelson subdued

Napoleon's troops defeat the Mamelukes at the Battle of the Pyramids.

the Spanish and Dutch navies so that by the end of 1797 the danger of invasion had receded.

Napoleon's Egyptian Expedition

At this juncture Napoleon received permission to lead an expedition to Egypt to menace British power in India. He conquered Malta *en route*, and in Egypt he defeated the native defenders at the Battle of the Pyramids. His naval transport, however, was attacked by Nelson at the Battle of the Nile, and Turkey (of whose empire Egypt was a part) declared war on France. Prevented by the British from advancing into Syria against Turkey, Napoleon decided to leave his troops and return to France.

The War of the Second Coalition, 1799-1801

The Second Coalition was formed by Russia, who wanted Malta; Turkey, who wished to recover Egypt; Austria, who wished to establish power in Italy; and Britain.

Like its predecessor, the Second Coalition got off to a good beginning. Joint Austrian and Russian forces swept the French out of Italy with the exception of Genoa. Good progress was also made in the task of destroying French power in Switzerland, recently re-organized as the Helvetian Republic.

By September, 1799, allied unity had begun to dissolve; most of them were more intent on furthering their own interests than in defeating the French. At the end of the year Austria alone of the continental nations remained at war with France.

A second Italian campaign by Napoleon was as brilliant in its execution and results as the first. The Austrians at Marengo in June, 1800, were decisively beaten. They retired to Venetia and Napoleon took possession of Genoa, Milan and Piedmont. Thus was the Cisalpine Republic re-established.

·Defeat in Italy was not Austria's only misfortune. Another French force, advancing through Germany, had at Hohenlinden, 1800, been as successful as was Napoleon in Italy. With the way thus open to Vienna, Austria decided the time had come to make peace. The resulting Treaty of Lunéville, 1801, re-affirmed the Peace of Campo Formio and Britain was again left as the sole resister of French ambition in Europe but this was not her only problem.

Britain versus France

Neutral powers had for long disliked the extent to which Britain pressed her right to prevent trade with France. France now induced Russia, Sweden, Denmark and Prussia to join the League of Armed Neutrality to resist British interference with cargoes heading for French or French-controlled ports.

Of the members of this League, Denmark was perhaps the most important;

TIDDY-DOLL the great French Gingerbread-Baker, drawing out a new Batch of Kings. — his Man, Hopping Talley, mixing up the Dough.

Cartoon by Gillray: Napoleon and Talleyrand make new kings by the dozen.

hence Britain concentrated on the Danes. Nelson sailed for Copenhagen, bombarded the town and captured or destroyed the navy.

The back of the League was thus broken and when shortly afterwards the Tsar Alexander I succeeded Paul and made an agreement with Britain, the threat from the armed neutrality had lost its sting.

In 1802, the position being one of stalemate with France supreme on land and Britain undefeated on the seas, the Treaty of Amiens was arranged. Britain undertook to restore the French West Indies and the Cape of Good Hope while Malta was to be given back to the Knights of St. John. Britain kept only Ceylon and Trinidad. France for her part undertook to withdraw from the Papal States and Naples.

Such a treaty was little more than a sham. France was left still controlling the puppet republics she had established in Holland (Batavian Republic), Switzerland (Helvetic Republic), Genoa (Ligurian Republic), and northern Italy (Cisalpine Republic). The British navy retained command of the seas but Britain had surrendered most of what this supremacy had won for her. Yet for the moment both France and Britain were too exhausted to continue the struggle.

QUESTION

1. Explain why the French revolutionaries became involved in war with other European countries in 1792 and 1793.

CHAPTER 33

NAPOLEON AND THE NAPOLEONIC WARS, 1803-1815

NAPOLEON first drew attention to himself when he suppressed the reaction against the Revolution in La Vendée in 1793. He became a national hero when, in 1796, he turned a minor diversion against Austria into a major campaign of the highest importance. This success induced the Directory to entrust him with the Egyptian campaign. Though that campaign was a failure, the inability of the Directory to deal effectively at that time with the Second Coalition placed them in no position to criticize Napoleon.

Returned from Egypt, Napoleon, realizing the unpopularity of the government, conspired with politicians Siéyès, Ducos and Lucien Bonaparte to overthrow the Directory. In November (Brumaire, according to the new calendar), 1799, the legislative assemblies were induced to move from Paris to St. Cloud, whither also troops were dispatched. Failing to persuade the Assembly to dissolve, Lucien Bonaparte, Napoleon's brother, announced to the troops that a plot was afoot in the Assembly to overthrow the Republic. The army was thus deceived into an invasion of the Assembly and the legislators fled in alarm. Later, a few returned and voted that a provisional government be set up consisting of Siéyès, Ducos and Napoleon Bonaparte.

Siéyès now produced a new constitution headed by three consuls of whom Napoleon was to be the chief, so unworkable that Napoleon accepted it, realizing that it would afford him the opportunity of gathering all power into his own hands.

In 1802, by popular vote, Napoleon became First Consul for life. Then in 1804 a plot against his life was discovered, and during the resulting tension the legislative chambers asked him to take the title of Emperor. Very willingly Napoleon agreed. But in addition to France he wanted Europe.

Causes of Renewal of Hostilities

The truce of 1802 had been long enough to enable Europe to realize the danger which threatened from France under Napoleon. The Emperor had used the interval for extending French influence wherever possible. In Germany he had built up a pro-French connection among the smaller states as a counter weight to the predominance of Austria and Prussia. In Italy he had secured his own election as President of the Cisalpine Republic and annexed Piedmont. In Switzerland he had increased that country's dependence upon France.

To the distrust these Continental developments created in Britain must be added the anger of British manufacturers who found that the Peace of Amiens had not led to the re-opening of the French market to British goods. Napoleon for his part accused Britain of bad faith in as much as she had not handed back Malta to the Knights of St. John as she had undertaken to do. Moreover he held the British government responsible for the way in which he had been criticized and ridiculed in the British press. In 1803, rather than wait for Napoleon to renew hostilities at a time most convenient to himself, Britain declared war on France.

Failure of Invasion Plans

Napoleon decided that the only way to defeat Britain was by conquest following invasion. His plan was that the French and Spanish fleets should draw the British fleet from the Channel, double back to Europe and hold the Straits for the few hours necessary for the transport of the French troops waiting in Boulogne.

In its execution the plan went wrong from the beginning. Only the French fleet managed to put to sea and though it drew Nelson off after it to the West Indies and duly doubled back Nelson had realized what the enemy tactics were and warned the Admiralty. The result was an action off Cape Finisterre after which the enemy could do no more than limp back to harbour. A few months later the French and Spanish ships ventured forth to sea again but were decisively beaten by Nelson at Trafalgar in 1805. Napoleon's scheme for the invasion of Britain was dead.

The Third Coalition, 1805-07

By this time Britain with Austria, Prussia and Russia had formed the Third Coalition. It was not a success. Napoleon inflicted a serious defeat upon Austria at Ulm in 1805. Next, he met the combined forces of Austria and Prussia at Austerlitz and his victory there was so overwhelming that Austria signed the Treaty of Pressburg. Before delivering a last blow at Prussia, Napoleon formed sixteen of the German states into the Confederation of the Rhine. They agreed to provide him with an army and to withdraw from the old Holy Roman Empire.

Napoleon now inflicted on Prussia a crushing defeat at Jena (1806) and marched on into Berlin. Russian opposition was destroyed at the Battle of Friedland in 1807.

Napoleon now made peace with his defeated enemies. By the Treaty of Tilsit of 1807 Prussia lost territory west of the Elbe and in Poland. Russia was forced to enter into an alliance with France and to close her ports to British goods. This treaty marks the high tide of Napoleon's power in Europe. This then is a convenient point at which to leave for the time being the story of Napoleon's military career and examine his work in France.

Napoleon's Government and Administration of France

Under Napoleon, codes were drawn up covering commercial, civil and criminal law. All careers were now open to men of talent, irrespective of birth. Corporate property was vested in the State, and private property was divided equally among the heirs of the owner. A jury system was instituted. The Church became further subjugated to the State, and civil marriage and divorce became part of French life, although Catholicism remained the state religion.

Paradoxically, amidst the reforms, Napoleon's position as Emperor was a re-creation of the monarchy. The new Council of State was composed of members nominated by Napoleon, and the Senate, which was the chief law-making body, was also under the control of the Emperor.

Napoleon's government, too, like that of the Ancien Régime was centralized. The paid officials of local government resembled those of pre-revolutionary times. Finance and education were both under central government control. Aristocracy reappeared as a result of the returning émigrés and because of the titles bestowed by Napoleon upon family and friends. Most important, Napoleon's aggression in Europe was a continuation of late eighteenth-century French foreign policy.

Economic Warfare, 1806-07

It was to the destruction of British trade that Napoleon looked after 1807 in order to defeat his outstanding enemy. His object was not to "starve Britain into surrender" but to make it impossible for her to continue the war through lack of supplies and finance. The Berlin decrees which initiated this policy were issued in 1806. They declared the British Isles to be in a state of blockade. All European ports controlled by France or her allies were closed to British goods and any merchandise falling into French hands was to be confiscated. The British government replied with a series of Orders in Council, 1806-7, which endeavoured in similar fashion to establish a blockade of France and her allies and forbade neutrals to enter such ports on pain of being diverted to Britain if caught trying to do so.

In the long run Britain showed herself better able to dispense with continental trade than the continent showed itself able to dispense with British trade. This was largely because the British blockade was more successful than that of Napoleon owing to her more effective sea power. Yet both sides suffered. Damage was inflicted on British trade by the loss of the continental market and merchant shipping was undermined by the activities of privateers. Rigorous scrutiny of neutral shipping led Britain also into war first with Denmark and later (1812) with America.

The consequences to Napoleon and France were even more disastrous. Great hardship was inflicted upon the peoples of the Continent through their inability to obtain British goods, so that licences were ultimately issued for the import of selected British manufactures.

More important was the reaction produced by the system on Napoleon's allies. Hitherto it had been the governments of Europe who had been so anxious to crush the French tyrant; now, the peoples of Europe, realizing that the ruin of their trade and their growing personal privations had come upon them simply to satisfy the interests and ambitions of a Frenchman, became as eager as their rulers to see France and Napoleon overthrown. In short the spirit of nationalism was awakened and this was ultimately the root of Napoleon's undoing.

The Peninsular War

In 1808, Portugal finally refused to maintain a ban on British goods, and consequently suffered total defeat under Napoleon. Advancing from Portugal into Spain, Napoleon bullied Charles IV into renouncing Bourbon rights to the Spanish throne and replaced him with his own brother, Joseph Bonaparte. In reply to this, Britain despatched Wellesley (later the Duke of Wellington) with an army to Portugal, but the French were still able to make favourable

A French caricaturist mocks the fashions of Napoleon's time.

terms by the Convention of Cintra. Shortly afterwards, Wellesley was able to threaten French lines of communication in Spain, and after scoring a victory at Talavera in 1809 he returned to winter in Portugal.

In 1809 Napoleon left the Peninsular War because Austria had declared war on France. He occupied Vienna the same year and defeated the enemy at Wagram. By the Treaty of Vienna Austria ceded her Illyrian provinces to France and Galacia to the Grand Duchy of Warsaw (a Napoleonic re-creation out of old Poland). Napoleon also took the Emperor's daughter as his second wife because his first wife had failed to provide him with an heir.

Meanwhile, Wellesley, backed by the enormous sea power of Britain, was gaining victories in the Peninsular War. In 1812 he captured the chief military towns of Spain, defeating the French near Madrid at Salamanca; and the following year, having defeated Joseph Bonaparte at Vittoria, he was ready for an advance into France itself.

Moscow Campaign, 1812

By 1812 Russia, too, refused any longer to enforce the continental system. In reply to this defiance, Napoleon in 1812 advanced from eastern Germany into Russia. At once he was in difficulties. His supplies ran short, his troops deserted, and sickness reduced the numbers of those who loyally tried to follow him. He could win no decisive victory for the Russians deliberately avoided a pitched battle, retreated as the French came on and laid waste the territory they abandoned so that the invaders were unable to live off the country.

Still the invader pressed on, thinking that an entry into Moscow would win the campaign for him. Reaching his objective, however, he found Moscow deserted and in flames. He could now do nothing save open negotiations for peace. These the Russians deliberately protracted until the beginning of winter and then allowed them to collapse. Napoleon, outwitted, had to turn back to France.

The severity of the Russian winter took heavy toll of the retreating French troops. The Russians pursued, constantly attacking the enemy's rearguard. Eventually, Napoleon seeing the hopelessness of the situation and fearful of its effect on his position in France, left the army and pushed on ahead himself, to be followed some time later by a mere remnant of the host with which he had set out. Europe now knew that Napoleon could be beaten even on land.

The War of Liberation

The year following the Moscow fiasco saw the development of a further threat, this time from Prussia. The Prussia of 1813 was vastly different from that which Napoleon had humiliated in 1806.

A series of reforms, particularly in the army, had regenerated Prussia to the point where she was able to declare war on France. Britain, Russia and Austria joined Prussia, forming the Fourth Coalition. At first the Allies suffered setbacks, but at Leipzig they inflicted such reverses on Napoleon that he retired in disorder to France.

By now Wellesley was Duke of Wellington. His victories, combined with the revolt of Holland and the approach of the Allies almost to the gates of Paris, led France to turn upon her ruler. Napoleon, forced to abdicate by his subjects, was permitted by his victors to retire to Elba. Louis XVIII ascended the French throne.

The Hundred Days

Terms of peace were now embodied between France and the Allies in the First Treaty of Paris. France retained the boundaries she had had in January, 1792, and some of the colonies taken from her in the course of the war were restored. A conference of powers was next called to settle the affairs of Europe generally.

Its deliberations were rudely interrupted in 1815 by the news that Napoleon had escaped from exile, had been welcomed in Paris and that Louis XVIII had fled. Recourse was had again to arms. British and Prussian troops began to march on France from the north-east and Austrians and Russians from the east. Napoleon marched into the Netherlands, hoping to crush British and Prussians separately before they had chance and time to combine in a united front.

Falling first on the Prussians, he succeeded in driving them, as he thought, far enough to the north-east to prevent them from joining the British. He next turned on Wellington at Quatre Bras. After standing his ground during the first day's attack Wellington retired north under cover of night. The next day Napoleon made contact with him again and until about four o'clock in the afternoon the British forces had to bear the French attack unaided, but at that hour the Prussians at last joined Wellington. Together Wellington and the Prussian general Blücher at Waterloo made a final and supreme effort. The French, overwhelmed by superior numbers, fled from the field.

Napoleon returned to Paris, thence to the coast and surrendered to the British navy. The Allies, this time refusing to treat him as an emperor, banished the fallen conqueror to the island of St. Helena, where he died in 1821.

France, for supporting Napoleon in this last bid for power, now had to pay a price. By the Second Treaty of Paris her boundaries shrank to those of 1790; she was called upon to pay an indemnity of £28 million and to support an army of occupation for five years.

Napoleon's eclipse was as complete as his noonday splendour had been dazzling. What were the reasons for his ultimate failure?

Causes of Napoleon's Fall

One reason is to be found in his fatal adoption of the continental system. Its effect upon the developing nationalism among the peoples of Europe has already been noted. It made a vast difference to the morale of the soldiers sent against Napoleon in the final campaigns to feel that they were fighting for the life and liberty of themselves and their families. Thus Napoleon was defeated not so much by kings and governments as by the peoples of Europe.

Next, the Russian and Peninsular campaigns must be regarded as further factors in Napoleon's fall. The Peninsular campaign undermined his military strength and rendered him too weak to fight the powers of central Europe. The Moscow campaign was the signal for the outbreak of the War of Liberation and the formation of the Fourth Coalition.

The British navy played no small part in the overthrow of Napoleon. By preserving Britain from invasion the navy foiled Napoleon's only effective means of crushing his most determined enemy and did much to make the Peninsular War an allied success.

External factors were not the only circumstances behind Napoleon's failure; there was also discontent at home. French Catholic opinion was alienated when Napoleon annexed Church possessions in Italy and arrested and imprisoned the Pope. In addition, French discontent grew as taxation mounted and liberty dwindled. Finally, failure abroad removed the only reason for continuing to tolerate Napoleon's sovereignty.

Napoleon's fall was in part due to his own character. By 1815 it is possible that his energies were becoming exhausted and his genius beginning to decline. Success had made him over-confident of his own invincibility and unduly contemptuous of his subordinates' failures. This attitude bred resentment in the victims of his scathing criticism which flamed up when defeat stared the conqueror in the face.

Results of Napoleon's Career on Europe

Though Napoleon fell in 1815 France and Europe still bear some impress of his career. It was he who first introduced the practice of permanent compulsory military service which even liberty-loving Britain has been compelled from time to time to adopt. Allied to such "conscription" is the militaristic outlook which dominated Europe at least until 1950.

Yet we owe more than additional arts of war to Napoleon. The principles of the civil code of law which he drew up for France have been widely adopted elsewhere; so that the Code Napoleon, together with elements of Roman law, is at the root of many modern legal systems. Further, wherever Napoleon went, he took with him a government and administration of an efficiency often unknown before. Though it was disliked as the imposition of a foreigner, the countries which experienced it appreciated it enough to

Gillray depicts Napoleon menaced by Russia, Britain and Spain.

emulate it when they recovered their independence. In this respect two countries above all others owe a special debt to Napoleon.

First, Italy. Napoleon's rule there gave to the people a practical demonstration of the fact that Austrian rule was neither essential nor inevitable, and revealed to the Italians the benefits to be derived from unity and good government. Thus Napoleon aroused that spirit of Italian national patriotism which ultimately led to the achievement of unification under Sardinia.

Second, Germany. Here again, Napoleon proved that Austria was not the only leader of the country; indeed he inadvertently pointed to Prussia as the natural heir to Austrian predominance. By his organization of the Confederation of the Rhine he set the example for the future constitution of Germany. His destruction of the Holy Roman Empire and many petty princedoms removed obstacles from the path of unification, while the spirit of nationalism invoked in Prussia in opposition to his rule, created the moral force through which such unification was to be ultimately realized.

QUESTION

1. Describe and account for the decline in Napoleon's power after the Treaty of Tilsit (1807-14).

CHAPTER 34

REACTION, 1815-1825

SINCE 1793 Europe had been fighting, first against revolution and then against military despotism. Hence by 1815 warfare had become hateful and revolution discredited. The Congress of Vienna, resuming its labours after the battle of Waterloo, gave full expression to the reactionary mood of the hour.

The Congress of Vienna

The work of the Congress, effected mainly by Metternich of Austria, Alexander I of Russia, Castlereagh of Britain and very soon Talleyrand of France, was based on two principles, those of legitimacy and the balance of power. The first of these two meant the recognition of the rights of those former sovereign princes who had been deprived of their power and territory by Napoleon; the second meant a distribution of territory and population among the European states such that no one of them would be in a position to overawe the rest.

On the basis of these principles the Congress adopted four aims. The first was to establish a ring of strong states round France so as to prevent the possibility of any further aggressive French conquests. The second was to restore as far as possible the political map of Europe as it had existed in 1793. The third was a determination to secure the peace of Europe and the last was to reward those powers which had been members of the final coalition against Napoleon.

Thus Holland was united with Belgium and those German states not incorporated with Prussia were associated in the German Confederation under Austria. The Swiss Confederation was extended to include Valois, Geneva and Neuf-Chatel, and Genoa was given to Sardinia.

The principle of legitimacy was invoked in the attempt to re-create pre-revolutionary Europe. The Emperor of Austria recovered Lombardy and Venetia, the King of Sardinia was restored in Piedmont, Nice and Savoy; Bourbon rulers returned to Naples, Sicily and Spain. The temporal power of the Papacy was re-established by the re-creation of the Papal States in mid-Italy, while Parma, Modena and Tuscany received back their Hapsburg rulers.

Prussia, in addition to her gains along the Rhine, received also part of

Saxony and the former Swedish Pomerania. Warsaw and the surrounding district went to Russia, as did Finland. Norway was added to Sweden and Britain extended her empire to include Heligoland, Malta, the Cape of Good Hope, Ceylon and Trinidad.

It was the Tsar Alexander I who showed greatest keenness in devising means to avoid all future war. To this end he proposed the formation of a Holy Alliance, the member states of which would undertake to settle their differences "in accordance with the principles of the Christian religion." Britain declined to join because Castlereagh saw in such an alliance nothing save "sublime mysticism and nonsense." A more practical scheme developed as a result of British criticism. This was the Quadruple Alliance of Russia, Prussia, Austria and Britain, formed to preserve the settlement of 1815 and to solve international problems without recourse to war. Congresses of the member states were to be called whenever such problems arose.

Criticism of the Congress

Being wise after the event, it is easy to see the mistakes of the diplomats of 1815. It was a mistake to disregard the spirit of nationalism which had done so much to accomplish the defeat of Napoleon. The union of Catholic and Latin Belgium with Protestant and Germanic Holland, the redivision of Italy among princes of non-Italian blood, the partition of Poland between Russia and Prussia, the incorporation of Norway with Sweden and the restoration of Austrian supremacy in Germany were all contradictions of the desire of the peoples of Europe to be ruled by members of their own national group.

It was equally a mistake to pay so much attention to the interests of ruling houses and families and to ignore by so doing the wishes of the people. This conflicted with another growing principle, that of popular or democratic government.

Apart from mistakes of principle there were errors of detail. The Diet of the Germanic Confederation at Frankfort in which all the German states were represented, had to be unanimous in its decisions before such decisions could become operative. Hence a state like Austria, which was not an exclusively German power, could and did veto developments desirable from a German point of view because they conflicted with her own non-German interests. Austrian presidency of the Diet offended Prussia and so fanned the rivalry between these two powers that fifty years later it had to be settled by war.

It is important to note also that the work of the Congress took no account of those ideals of liberty and equality which had been born of the French Revolution.

Finally it must be admitted that almost all the arrangements made by the Congress of Vienna were subsequently undone. Italy was ultimately united under Sardinia, as was Germany under Prussia. Holland lost Belgium in 1839 and in the early twentieth century Sweden and Norway agreed to separate. Nice and Savoy passed into French possession in 1860 and even Heligoland changed hands after negotiations between Britain and Prussia in 1890.

In spite of these weaknesses the work of the Congress had its commendable features. If Sardinia's power had not been extended in 1815 the unification of Italy might have been delayed longer even than it was; and though Austria was president of the Germanic Confederation, at least the Holy Roman Empire was not revived.

Also, the intentions which inspired the Congress were worthy ones, designed to preserve the peace, and if its settlements were not ideal they at least gave Europe forty years of tranquillity.

Finally it was at the Congress of Vienna that one important piece of humanitarian reform was at least begun. At Castlereagh's suggestion the slave trade was examined and condemned and this was a move towards its ultimate abolition.

The Concert of Europe

The Quadruple Alliance became known as the Concert of Europe. At its first meeting at Aix-la-Chapelle in 1818, Alexander I proposed that regular meetings should review both special difficulties in Europe which might arise and the general trend of European affairs. Castlereagh opposed this last suggestion, which involved possible interference in the domestic affairs of neighbour states. France was also admitted to the Congress in 1818, making the Alliance a quintuple association.

Two years later, in Austria at Troppau, a Congress met again to discuss revolts in Naples. The reactionary Austrian chancellor Metternich induced the liberal Alexander I to issue a protocol declaring that the Alliance would take action to suppress revolution wherever it threatened the interests of the allied powers.

After a two months' adjournment the Congress of Troppau reassembled at Laibach and authorized Austria to suppress the revolt in Naples, an authorization upon which Austria proceeded to act energetically.

Verona in 1822 proved to be the scene of the last of the congresses of the Concert of Europe and the occasion of its meeting was the outbreak of revolutions in Spain, in the Spanish colonies and in Greece. Britain objected to interference by the concerted powers in any of these matters and succeeded in blocking action in the colonial and Greek issues. France, however, was permitted to suppress the revolution in Spain itself, whereupon the British representative withdrew from the Congress, Britain ceased to be a member of the alliance and the Concert of Europe was at an end.

This attempt to outlaw war in Europe failed for three main reasons.

First, the Concert of Europe had as its primary intention the maintenance of the arrangements of 1815. Yet these arrangements were too imperfect, as we have seen, to endure unchanged indefinitely.

Second, the failure was in large measure due to British opposition to Metternich's insistence on the principle of collective action against revolution. Castlereagh and after him Canning, speaking in the Concert for Britain, maintained that every nation should be free to determine its own form of government without external pressure.

Third, weight must be attached to the action of America, a power outside the Concert, who made it clear in the Monroe Doctrine that any European state which intervened unasked in the affairs of any South American republic would have to reckon with the hostility of the United States. This, as we shall see later, was an important factor in 1822.

Metternich and his Policy

The dominant figure in European diplomacy after 1815 was the Austrian chancellor Metternich. In much of his outlook Metternich belonged to the eighteenth rather than to the nineteenth century. No European monarch was more convinced than he of the divinity of kingship and hereditary right. Not even his emperor was more determined than Metternich to hold together on this basis the ramshackle Austrian empire.

As Austrian foreign minister, Metternich aimed at strengthening the internal stability of the empire he served, raising its international status and checking its rivals, Russia and Prussia.

As a European statesman he sought to suppress revolution wherever it occurred and maintain monarchy wherever it existed. His European and Austrian aims marched well together, for the Austrian empire was a strange collection of peoples of many different nationalities desiring either national or liberal self-government. The growth of these forces of liberalism and nationalism must therefore be checked outside Austria as the best guarantee that they would not take root within Austria.

For the institution of a reactionary régime in Austria Metternich had a free hand. He established a vigorous press censorship, state control of education and strict exclusion of all foreigners of known or suspected revolutionary convictions.

In 1819 he found an opportunity for introducing a similar régime into the Germanic Confederation, when a reactionary politician, Kotzebue, was murdered by a liberal-minded student. Metternich, playing upon the fears of the German rulers, induced them in the confederal Diet to sanction the Carlsbad Decrees (1819). These decrees placed all teachers under strict political supervision and forbade them to express to their pupils approval of liberalism or nationalism. Student organizations in the universities were prohibited except where formed with government permission. The press was censored and a spy system set up to ferret out the existence of any secret revolutionary societies.

Considering that he was fighting against the spirit of his age, Metternich was amazingly successful. He imposed his views on the Congress of Vienna and the Concert of Europe while it lasted and it was thus due to his influence that national and liberal aspirations were so markedly frustrated in Europe generally between 1815 and 1846. Only a very skilful diplomat could have enhanced the prestige of Austria as Metternich did without provoking the hostility of his rivals Russia and Prussia.

The reasons for Metternich's ultimate fall in 1848 are as plain to see as his achievements are remarkable. He underestimated the forces against which he was fighting. In the later stages of his career, moreover, he met his match as a diplomatist when Palmerston, as British Foreign Minister, threw his weight on the side of liberalism and nationalism.

Reaction in Spain and Italy, 1815-25

The supremacy of reaction between 1815 and 1825 is shown by events in Italy and Spain. In 1820 the king of Spain, under threat of revolt, attempted to restore the mildly liberal constitution he had withdrawn. The Congress of Verona authorized French intervention on behalf of the Spanish monarchy, and the liberal cause in Spain collapsed. Indeed, had it not been for the Monroe Doctrine announced by James Monroe, President of the United States of America, which stated that America would regard foreign interven-

Alexander I of Russia.   *Count Metternich of Austria.*

tion in the affairs of North and South America as "the manifestation of an unfriendly disposition towards the United States," the Congress would also have intervened in the revolt of the Spanish American colonies.

In Italy, too, the Congress authorized Austria to support the king of Naples against a revolt which was attempting to establish a national liberal government for the whole of the country.

France, 1814-25

In France in the first ten years after the Congress of Vienna reactionary influences were originally by no means supreme but as time passed they grew in intensity as it became obvious that the restored Bourbons had "learned nothing and forgotten nothing."

When Louis XVIII returned to France "in the baggage of the allies" he brought with him a charter which seemed to promise a not unreasonable division of power between king and people, especially since it provided for the control of finance by the representative legislative chambers, as well as decreeing the continuance of trial by jury, the freedom of the press and religious toleration. It is true that the right to vote was restricted by a property qualification and that the charter itself was granted as a privilege rather than conceded as a right. Nevertheless it was far from being a return to the absolutism of the Ancien Régime or to the tyranny of Napoleon.

Though Louis XVIII up to 1820 loyally tried to abide by the charter, it roused the opposition of three political groups. The ex-émigrés nobility headed by the heir-presumptive, the Duke of Artois, desired the abolition of the charter and a return to the system of government which the revolution of 1789 had swept away. At the other extreme were republicans who longed for a return to the constitution of 1792. Finally there were the Bonapartists, sincere admirers of the Napoleonic régime, who wished to see France ruled once again by a member of the family of the Corsican adventurer and the country following a vigorous, even an aggressive, foreign policy. On the whole the first of these three parties was the most dangerous.

When in 1820 the Duke of Berry, a nephew of the king, was murdered, the ultra-royalists forced the government to adopt a reactionary policy including press censorship and church-controlled education. When Louis XVIII died in 1824 and was succeeded by his brother, the Count of Artois, who became Charles X, France moved steadily towards a severe crisis.

QUESTIONS

1. What were the main ideas that the delegates at the Congress of Vienna tried to embody in the peace settlement?
2. Explain (*a*) the aims and (*b*) the influence of Metternich in European politics during the years 1815-30.

CHAPTER 35

THE REVOLUTIONS OF 1830

THOUGH the spirit of reaction was so triumphant in the first fifteen years after the Congress of Vienna, the forces to which it was opposed were not totally destroyed. They were merely driven underground. The result was an outburst of revolution in 1830 which, though not entirely successful, yet loosened the fabric of Metternich's Europe and prepared the way for its final collapse.

Reign of Charles X, 1824-30

The revolutionary movement in 1830, as in 1789, began in France. The government of Charles X grew increasingly reactionary. It reinstated the old aristocracy and increased the power of the Church. Finally, in 1829, Charles dismissed the moderately liberal cabinet he had been forced to accept and called on the reactionary leader Polignac to form a new administration. At the same time the king moved to St. Cloud from Paris, annulled the election of 1830 (with its anti-royalist candidates elected by the people), imposed a new restricted franchise, and suspended all anti-Polignac newspapers from publication.

France was angered by these Ordinances of St. Cloud. Journalists, workers and deputies rioted in Paris, barricades were erected and street fighting broke out. The king was disconcerted to find the army in sympathy with the rioters and he had to withdraw the troops from the capital.

But the movement had now spread to the country generally. The king made concessions but even the revocation of the Ordinances failed to save him; the revolutionaries turned to a member of the royal family known to be of more liberal views than Charles X. This was Louis Philippe, a descendant of the younger brother of the famous Louis XIV. Louis Philippe accepted from the revolutionaries the office of Lieutenant-General of the Kingdom while promising the King to safeguard the position of the heir to the throne, Charles X's son, Louis, Duc d'Angoulême. On the strength of this promise Charles abdicated—and on the strength of the abdication Louis Philippe felt free to ignore his promise. At the invitation of the Legislature he took the title of King of the French. One by one the European governments, thankful that a republic had not been set up, recognized the new ruler.

Charles, by his conservative, reactionary policy had alienated the majority

312

French political cartoon of the 1840's. Entitled "the forbidden fruit," it shows Louis Philippe turning into a pear.

of the nation. His only supporters were those who like himself thought it possible to ignore all that had happened in France since 1789 and discovered too late how wrong they were.

The revolution of 1830 did much more than replace a reactionary king by a liberal one; an elected king had replaced one born to the position. Divine Right was now as dead in France as it had been in England for a hundred and forty years. Moreover the attempt to revive Bourbon absolutism had failed and the ultra-royalists were discredited.

Slight constitutional changes of detail followed. The July Ordinances of St. Cloud were condemned and the king's right to legislate by such means limited. The franchise qualification was widened to include a greater proportion of the middle classes and the king's ministers were made responsible for policy to the legislative chambers.

So far as Europe at large was concerned, the revolution had made a breach in the settlement of 1815 and in consequence the outbreak in France was the signal for similar movements elsewhere which we may now examine.

The Belgian Revolution, 1830-39

The union of Belgium and Holland decreed in 1815 had never been a happy one, partly because of temperamental differences and partly because of the unwise conduct of the dominant partner, Holland.

Belgium and Holland differed in language, in group origin, in religion, in historical tradition and in density of population. The Belgians spoke French, while Dutch was a language of Germanic origin. Catholicism was the religion of Belgium but Holland was Protestant. Holland had enjoyed two hundred years of independence, but Belgium had remained a part of the Hapsburg Empire. Belgians greatly outnumbered the Dutch.

Only a tactful government could have overcome these difficulties, and Dutch administration was anything but tactful. It showed no consideration for Belgian national pride. Dutch was made the official language, and Belgians were excluded from administrative posts. Although Belgium's national debt was smaller than Holland's, taxation of the people of both countries was equal. The crowning folly of the Dutch was to attempt to determine the lines on which the education of the Roman Catholic priesthood in Belgium should be conducted.

By 1830 the Belgians had come to regard themselves as an oppressed majority. When the news of the July revolt in Paris reached Brussels, the audience at the opera house that evening, after listening to a patriotic work, ran into the streets crying "Let us imitate France." Rioting and street fighting against Dutch troops which tried to restore order in Brussels spread throughout the country. Anti-Dutch activity became the order of the day.

A national congress called by the rebels declared Belgium an independent sovereign power. The king of Holland sent his son to negotiate with the congress but when he had had time to mobilize an army, the king broke off the negotiations. He sent ten thousand men into Belgium and at the same time appealed for foreign aid.

The chances of collective European action against Belgium were thin. The Concert of Europe was no more. The Austrian government was fully occupied by its fears of subversive movements in Italy. Louis Philippe of France, owing his throne to a revolution, could hardly support Holland. Britain, glad to see the establishment of a buffer state between herself and the greater Continental powers, was not unwilling to see the Belgian cause succeed. Prussia feared the outbreak of liberal activity within her own borders and wished to be free to deal with it if the necessity arose. As for Russia, she was busy checking nationalism in Poland.

Consequently at the Congress of London in 1830 called to consider the situation, the European powers agreed to recognize the independence of Belgium, and after Britain had successfully opposed the candidature of the second son of Louis Philippe for the new throne, a suitable candidate was

314

found in Leopold of Saxe-Coburg who, by a strange coincidence doubtless, was a relative of the future Queen Victoria.

Holland refused to accept these London arrangements and re-invaded Belgium. Only military action by France and naval action by Britain saved the situation for Leopold. Even so, it was not until 1839 that Holland finally admitted defeat. Belgian independence was finally recognized and her neutrality guaranteed by all the European powers in the Treaty of London of 1839.

Revolution in Poland, 1830

Poland, revived by Napoleon as the Grand Duchy of Warsaw, had been given to Russia in 1815. Alexander I, in his more liberal days, had tried to establish a liberal constitution, but the Russian grand dukes in Poland who represented the Tsar were incapable of being loyal to this sort of government. Moreover, Poland longed for her independence and for the return of her stolen territory.

The July Revolution in France affected Poland much as it affected Belgium. It was, however, the army rather than the citizens who raised the standard of revolt by an attack on the palace of the Grand Duke. The Duke fled and prospects of success for the revolutionaries seemed bright for it would take time for Russia to get her soldiers into Poland.

Unfortunately, quarrels broke out among the moderate and extremist elements of the revolution, and by the time the argument was resolved Warsaw was under siege. When Warsaw collapsed, so did the revolt. Eighty thousand rebels were sent to Siberia.

From the course the struggle took it is clear that its lack of success is explained by the divergence of aim among the leaders and by the numerical superiority of the Russian forces brought against it.

To these factors a third can be added. The Poles had expected foreign aid and no aid came. France was satisfied to use the possibility of her intervention as a means of extorting from the Tsar the recognition of the monarchy of Louis Philippe. Once the Tsar had conceded this point France was no longer interested. Britain was sympathetic to Polish liberalism but not prepared to wage a campaign in so distant a quarter of the Continent. Austria and Prussia had troubles enough of their own. Polish patriots had to wait for thirty years before attempting again to achieve their aims.

QUESTIONS

1. What were the reasons for the lack of European opposition to the Belgian and Polish revolutions of 1830?
2. Explain the causes of the revolutions of 1830 in Europe.

CHAPTER 36

THE REVOLUTIONS OF 1848

AFTER the tumults of 1830 had died away there followed some seventeen years of uneasy quietude until, in 1848, discontent found open expression again, and again most successfully of all in France.

France, 1830-48

The revolution of 1830 had extended political power to the wealthier middle class. Louis Philippe sought to identify himself closely with this newly enfranchised group. He walked in the streets of Paris unguarded, he sent his children to middle-class schools, he was industrious and well-intentioned. He shared the unwillingness of the middle classes to admit to political power humbler social groups, and not being a forceful personality he was singularly unsuccessful in raising his country's international position. Thus his virtues were also his limitations and discontent steadily grew during his reign. Between 1830 and 1848 the French people were becoming increasingly aware of what the revolution of 1789 had failed to achieve.

This discontent gave rise to writers who put forward theories for the relief of social ills. Pre-eminent among these new prophets was Louis Blanc, who laid the foundations of French socialism by arguing that all workshops should be owned by the State and that all workers should share in the profits produced by their own labour.

Side by side with social discontent went political unrest. While socialists looked to an ideal future, republicans looked to an idealized past. Political power entrusted to a government of the people seemed to be a cure for economic inequality. Ultimately, the socialists with their economic solutions and the republicans with their political ones would clash, but in 1848 they united temporarily to overthrow a government they both hated.

A third discontented group was the Bonapartist faction. Centred round Louis Napoleon Bonaparte, a nephew of Napoleon I, this group, dreaming of a Continent again dominated by French influence, was contemptuous of Louis Philippe's weak foreign policy. The Bonapartists made the most of the contrast thus presented between France under Louis Philippe and France in the days of Napoleon I. They argued that only a Bonaparte would restore France to her former status as a great European power. To those Frenchmen who pointed out that Napoleonic glory had been accompanied by the loss of

316

domestic liberty, the Bonapartists replied that such loss had been merely intended as temporary and that Napoleon, had he not been deposed, would in his own good time have restored much of the liberty he had destroyed. Thus there was cultivated the "Napoleonic legend"—the theory that Napoleon had been a tyrant through force of circumstances rather than choice and that only under a descendant of his could France hope to recover her former prestige.

By 1840 the government of Louis Philippe realized that the possible combination of socialism, republicanism and Bonapartism might produce a serious crisis. Yet, instead of adopting a policy of positive reform, the government resorted purely to repression. All political or industrial associations were prohibited unless their formation had government approval and that was not readily forthcoming. The Press was censored and journalists who persisted in criticizing the government were prosecuted. Support for the government in the chamber of deputies was secured by corruption of its members and finally the franchise was curtailed.

Revolution of 1848 in France

Discontent came to a head in 1848. Street fighting, supported by the army, broke out in Paris. In an attempt to save the situation, Louis Philippe abdicated in favour of his grandson, but the people, refusing to accept this, established their own assembly and declared France a republic.

The socialists now declared for a new economic deal, and the republicans for a new permanent government only, with no economic changes. National workshops promising well-paid work for all were opened by the socialists, but because of the enormous number of applicants these workshops were forced to close.

This closure was highly unpopular in Paris and four days of stern fighting between socialists and republicans occurred before the latter made themselves masters of the capital. They established universal suffrage and provided for a president of the republic with a fixed term of office of four years.

With socialism discredited and republicans unpopular with socialists, France turned to the Bonapartists and Louis Napoleon Bonaparte was elected the first President of the Second French Republic.

There are interesting parallels between the revolutions of 1830 and 1848 in France.

In 1830 the revolution had been mainly a political affair; in 1848 an economic factor—the rise of socialism—played an influential part; but in both cases the immediate crisis was provoked by the reactionary policy of the government in power. In 1830 it was the middle classes who had asserted their right to share political power; in 1848 the lower classes demanded further extension of political power which would include the unpropertied workers.

These differences of origin produced differences of result. In 1830 a Divine Right king had been replaced by one whose claim rested on popular choice; in 1848 a movement more radical in origin swept monarchy away in favour of republicanism. Hence far more radical changes were involved, universal suffrage replacing a suffrage based upon property qualification. Finally, the revolution of 1848, unlike that of 1830, had produced an economic experiment —the national workshops—which, though it failed, constituted only a temporary setback for the socialism which inspired it. This new economic theory, as we shall see later, produced great changes in the attitude of the state towards the social and industrial life of the country.

Revolution in Austria-Hungary, 1848

The Austro-Hungarian empire in 1848 was fertile soil for the growth of liberalism and nationalism. Its wide geographical boundaries embraced a medley of different racial groups. Austria itself was German in population and tradition but the rest of the empire included some four other groups divided into six sub-groups.

In the provinces of Bohemia, Moravia and Galicia dwelt the Poles and Czechs, Slavonic in origin. Slavs too were the Serbians and the Croatians who lived in that part of the empire bounded by the Danube, Drave and the eastern coast of the Adriatic. Separating these two branches of the Slav group were the Magyars of Hungary and the Rumans of Transylvania. Finally, in the extreme south-west, Lombardy and Venetia were of course Italian.

Only a firm central government could have held together this "mouldering edifice," but the Emperor Ferdinand I was a feeble ruler who did not enforce Metternich's reactionary policies. Revolutionary ideas grew unchecked within the empire.

Louis Kossuth

Hungary produced the first crisis. The nationalists and the liberals, under the leadership of Louis Kossuth, sank their differences temporarily in order to unite in opposition to the imperial government.

Kossuth's programme of reform aimed at the separation of Hungary from Austria, the establishment of a Hungarian republic, the abolition of all remnants of feudalism and the annexation by Hungary of the Slav province of Transylvania. Though not all the revolutionary elements in Hungary were in favour of the whole of this programme, they were prepared to line up behind Kossuth in casting off the Austrian yoke. When, therefore, the news of the revolution of 1848 in France reached Hungary, Kossuth had little difficulty in inducing the Diet to demand Hungary's freedom and the establishment of a liberal constitution for the Austro-Hungarian empire as a

Giuseppi Mazzini. *Louis Kossuth.*

whole. This latter request won the approval of the population of Vienna, an approval which expressed itself in riots. Alarmed, the central government gave way. Hungary set up her own ministries of war, finance and foreign affairs and the Diet moved to Pest.

From Hungary revolution spread to Bohemia, where the Czechs endeavoured to win for themselves the independence which had been achieved by the Magyars. Unfortunately there was in Bohemia a large German minority who would have preferred to see the province become part of a vast German state and the two factions, German minority and Czech majority, indulged in civil war, a luxury they could not afford. This folly provided the Austrian commander, Windischgratz, with the opportunity to open a stern and effective bombardment of Prague and the city was firmly reduced to order.

Complications arose in Hungary. The Slav minority demanded independence from the Magyars, and to gain this they allied themselves once more with Austria. Ferdinand abdicated in favour of the energetic Francis Joseph, and a campaign against the Magyars began.

At first the Magyars met with success. The Slavs, realizing they were being exploited by Austria, withdrew from the fight. But when Louis Kossuth proclaimed an independent Hungarian republic, the moderates, who did not want complete separation from Austria, turned against him. Russia too, fearing that a republican Hungary would encourage the establishment of a republican Poland, came to the support of Austria. Kossuth had no alternative but to flee the country. Left without a leader, the Magyars submitted to the creation of an administration which, entrusted as it was entirely to the hands of German officials, left them nationally in a worse position than before the revolution.

By 1849 the revolution in the Austrian empire had failed. The causes of that failure are not hard to see.

First, the revolutionaries were too divided in their aims. Liberalism did not always agree with nationalism and even the ranks of the liberals were split between constitutional monarchists and republicans, at least in Hungary.

319

Second, the failure was in part due to the lack of consistency among the leaders of the nationalist majorities. Logic should have shown the Magyars that they could not deny to the Slavs in their midst the independence they themselves had extracted from Austria; and the Czechs and Germans of Bohemia should have realized that in some form of compromise lay their only hope of permanent success.

Third, Austria made full use of the opportunity presented to her by skilful exploitation of the disunity of her opponents.

The short-sightedness of the Slavs must rank as a fourth factor. They failed to perceive in time that there was no more hope of obtaining independence by the generosity of Austria than there was of obtaining independence at the hands of the Magyars.

To these particular reasons for the failure of the revolutions of 1848 in Austro-Hungary there must be added one or two more general considerations. The Austrian government succeeded in securing foreign help; the revolutionaries failed to do so. Francis Joseph looked upon the separate movements in Bohemia, Hungary and Vienna as essentially one; whereas the revolutionaries in each province were too self-absorbed to make common cause when the central government recovered from its initial surprise.

Revolution in the German Confederation

If liberalism and nationalism walked separate ways in Austria-Hungary, they went hand in hand in the Germanic Confederation.

The news of the revolution of 1848 in France immensely stimulated reformers in Germany and an assembly of liberals and nationalists unofficially representative of almost every state in the Confederation met at Heidelberg in March, 1848. There they drew up a scheme for the creation of a national parliament which, elected by universal suffrage, would control the affairs of all German states, including the German-speaking provinces of the Austrian empire. Since Austria was at the time preoccupied with Hungary, she was unable to offer any resistance to the schemers at Heidelberg and the smaller German states were too afraid to do so. The Vor-Parliament, as this self-appointed assembly of reformers was called, turned therefore an alert eye towards Prussia.

Prussia was ruled by Frederick William IV who, though a strong believer in monarchy, was not unwilling to experiment with representative institutions within narrow limits. He consented to a meeting of the Prussian *Landtag*, and when popular celebrations of his decision led to an accidental skirmish with his troops he promised that his ministers should become responsible to that body instead of to the Crown alone.

Thus encouraged the National Assembly met at Frankfort. It avoided the thorny difficulty of the inclusion or exclusion of the German provinces of the Austrian empire by long discussion of the "fundamental rights of the German people." Meanwhile Austria resolved her internal revolts and was free to deal with German affairs. To secure the aid of his army against possible Austrian intervention, Frankfort hastily offered the crown of a united Germany to Frederick William IV.

They were too late. The recovery of the Austrian government had induced the Prussian ruler to change his policy. The concessions made to liberalism in Prussia were withdrawn and he refused the shadowy crown offered to him. He feared to face war with Austria and had no wish to support liberalism by fighting a monarchy as divine as his own. Moreover he was too much of an autocrat to accept a democratic crown. Finally, he was influenced by Otto von Bismarck who urged that German unity would only be achieved by Prussian supremacy and under absolute monarchy.

With this change in Prussian policy the hopes of uniting Germany in 1848 collapsed. The members of the Frankfort parliament dispersed and the Germanic Confederation was left unchanged with Austrian domination intact.

Revolution in Italy

We have earlier seen that the Congress of Vienna fastened upon Italy the shackles of alien and reactionary government—shackles which the spasmodic efforts of 1820 failed to break. Further risings in Parma and Modena against the political power of the Pope were equally unsuccessful due to Austrian action.

From 1831 to 1847 the ideal of a free and united Italy was kept alive largely by Giuseppi Mazzini in spite of the fact that, after a period of political imprisonment, he was for many years an exile in Britain. From this refuge he kept up a constant stream of propaganda which was disseminated throughout Italy by the Young Italy Party, concentrating public attention both in Italy and outside it on the idea of freedom from Austrian domination and self-government in a liberal republic. Though he recognized that force would be essential to the realization of his dreams, Mazzini insisted that the minds and will of the people must be thoroughly prepared if eventual success was to be achieved.

Thus, Mazzini was the prophet of Italian unity rather than its creator, but the practical work of the men who followed him would have been almost impossible had not the prophet preached so persistently and persuasively. Mazzini's great achievement was to teach his fellow countrymen and women to think of themselves as Italians rather than primarily Milanese or Neapolitans. He replaced local by national patriotism.

It was a new pope who, in all innocence, set the match to the inflammable material Mazzini had scattered about Italy by 1848. Elected pope in 1846,

French Revolutionaries in the Tuileries Palace, 1848.

Pius IX decided to pursue a liberal policy in the Papal States. One of his first steps was to release all prisoners in his domains suffering for their political opinions. He also allowed a civil guard to be established in Rome. These measures produced results he had never imagined. In Tuscany and Piedmont they were taken as signals for nationalist demonstrations. Sicily shook off Neapolitan control, the Hapsburg ruler of Naples itself was compelled to establish constitutional government and the bewildered Pius IX had to follow this example.

The news of the revolution in Paris and of the initial collapse of Metternich's ministry in Vienna led to a successful attack on Austrian power in Venice and Milan. The rulers of Tuscany, Parma and Modena took fright and fled or capitulated voluntarily to the nationalist and liberal elements within their dominions. Two questions were now in every Italian mind: could Austria be expelled from Lombardy and would Sardinia, who alone had the military resources remotely capable of attempting the task, undertake such an enterprise? It was an attempt worth making but who would see the cause through?

Thus the Pope was alarmed to discover that he, universal head of the Catholic Church, had provoked a war on Catholic Austria. It is hardly surprising that he quickly repented of the liberalism he had formerly professed

Now that Pius IX was no longer the champion of unity, attention switched to Charles Albert of Sardinia caught in an agony of indecision as to whether or not to lead Italy against Austria. He agonized too long. By the time he had come to a decision Austria had had time to prepare her defences and the Milanese had already invaded Lombardy. They regarded Charles Albert's belated stand against Austria as an attempt to reap the fruits of their own labours. They gave him no co-operation. Hence the Sardinian troops faced Austria alone at the vital battle of Custozza in 1848 and were decisively beaten. Meanwhile Pius IX had denounced the attack on Austria, and the Hapsburgs having recovered their position in Naples, the Pope fled to them for protection. Mazzini and the extreme democrats not yet willing to admit final defeat took advantage of the Pope's flight to declare Rome a republic.

The tide, however, was running against the revolutionaries. In March, 1849, Charles Albert risked another engagement with Austria at Novara and was again defeated. He was forced to abdicate in favour of his son Victor Emmanuel. Austria crushed piece-meal the revolutionary governments in Tuscany and Lombardy and then concentrated her efforts on the republic of Rome. A stern siege followed, the heroes of the defence being Garibaldi and his irregular "red shirts." The combined weight of Austria, France and Naples proved more than the irregulars could match. The Roman republic fell. The new king of Sardinia made the best terms he could with Austria, and Mazzini and Garibaldi fled abroad.

The revolution of 1848 in Italy had failed but it had not been wholly in vain. Henceforth Sardinia was clearly marked as the potential leader. Charles Albert had not covered himself with glory, but his sins could not be laid on the shoulders of his young successor who, moreover, soon showed himself a man of greater wisdom and courage than his father.

Henceforth too, the movement for unity was anti-clerical. This was the fault of Pius IX for he did not abdicate. His abrupt change of policy was held not only against him but against the Church he headed. This Church was now regarded by the nationalists as a pillar of the edifice they wished to destroy.

Liberalism had made no permanent gains; the constitutions unwillingly granted in 1847 and 1848 were soon withdrawn when reaction triumphed. Nor had republicanism established itself as the hope of the future. Sardinia alone had the regular troops to pit against Austria; if she was going to lead the way to unity, the new Italy would have to be a monarchy. Sardinia would have to have foreign aid; she was no match for Austria by herself. What European state, monarchies all of them up to 1870, would support republican agitation in Italy or elsewhere? The memory of the French Revolution and all that had followed from it was not yet dead enough for that.

QUESTIONS

1. Why was 1848 a year of revolutions? Why were those revolutions not more successful than they were?
2. Write short notes on the following: French National Workshops; the Vor-Parliament; the Frankfort Parliament; the Napoleonic Legend; Charles Albert of Sardinia; Louis Kossuth.

CHAPTER 37

NAPOLEON III, CAVOUR, AND ITALIAN UNITY

T HE ambition of Louis Napoleon Bonaparte was not satisfied by his election as president of the Second French Republic in 1848; his hopes were fixed upon the attainment of permanent power.

Establishment of the Second French Empire

To this end he sought to ingratiate himself with popular opinion. He embarked on vast schemes of public works, of agricultural development and industrial expansion. He wooed the army by careful attention to the well-being and comfort of the troops. Early in 1849 he tried to appease the liberals by discountenancing a proposal to limit the franchise; and he secured the favour of the Church, at least temporarily, by going to the rescue of Pope Pius IX when Mazzini endeavoured to set up a republic in Rome.

Having allowed these policies to mature for four years, Louis Napoleon asked the legislative chambers to revise the constitution so as to enable him to stand again as president immediately his term of office expired. When the chambers refused his request Louis decided to appeal over their heads to the nation at large.

On the night of 1 December, 1851, the meeting place of the legislature was occupied by troops and on the following morning the leading members of the chamber were arrested. This action was explained away to the nation by an announcement that Louis had been "compelled" into this course in order to "save" France from a serious, recently discovered "danger." Troops were moved into Paris and in the country districts all likely disaffected persons were removed from office and all critical newspapers suppressed. Opposition having been thus stifled, Louis appealed to the people of France through the ballot box. The result was a ten to one majority authorizing him to assume full powers of government and to revise the constitution.

This he did, giving himself almost absolute control of the country and robbing the legislative chambers of all their power except that of approving or rejecting his laws. A second appeal to the people in 1852 empowered Louis Napoleon to abandon his title of president for that of Napoleon III, Emperor of the French. Thus began the Second Empire.

Napoleon's prestige was built, of course, on the vision of past glories evoked by his name. As Europe was determined to prevent any repetition of the career of Napoleon I, Napoleon III had to convince Europe that he was a man of peace and France that he was re-asserting the country's international prestige.

Hinting that it was only a temporary measure, and displaying a certain sympathy for liberalism, Napoleon took all power into his own hands. The legislature rested upon imperial nomination, as he controlled both chambers, but he offered compensations—an extended banking system, freer trade, state aid to industry and agriculture, improved means of communication and state care of the poor and the insane.

Foreign Policy—The Crimean War

Such elements of the nation as remained opposed to him in spite of this bid for popularity, Napoleon hoped to conciliate by an aggressive and successful foreign policy.

The Crimean War in 1854 saw Russia championing the Greek Orthodox faith and Turkey Roman Catholicism in the struggle to gain control of the Holy places. Napoleon saw his opportunity, by taking the side of Turkey, to ingratiate himself with French Catholics, to rap the knuckles of the Tsar for having been the last of the great powers to recognize him as an emperor, and to re-assert French international influence.

Napoleon, for once, had chosen the winning side. Russia was defeated by France and Britain, and Napoleon's prestige was greatly enhanced. This early success, however, was to make his subsequent failures, in three years time when he intervened in Italian affairs, seem even more dismal.

Beginnings of Italian Unification

After 1848 the movement for Italian unification depended mainly upon the leadership of Sardinia, the state most capable of raising a good army. Sardinia, too, because of her independence and liberal constitution, seemed to the rest of Italy the embodiment of liberalism and nationalism. Moreover, she kept a check on the power of the Church within her borders, became the home of many "revolutionary" exiles, and produced men such as her king, Victor Emmanuel, Garibaldi, and perhaps the greatest of all, Cavour.

Cavour's Policy, 1850-6

Count Cavour became a member of Victor Emmanuel's council in 1850. Throughout his career, Cavour's one desire was to see the king of Sardinia on the throne of a united Italy and as a first step he set himself to the work of re-vitalizing the military and economic life of his country.

He encouraged agriculture, fostered industry by adopting a tariff policy and facilitated commerce by constructing railways, cutting canals and introducing a telegraph system. The financial advantages from these innovations he mortgaged for military development, while finding money for immediate expenses by confiscating the wealth of the monasteries.

Cavour realized that he must cultivate the goodwill of Europe if he was to win allies for the Sardinian cause. The first step was to get Europe to admit that the settlement of 1815 which provided for the Austrian rule of Italy was not final. He sent troops to aid France and Britain in the Crimean War, and thus gained a voice in the peace settlements in 1856. Sardinia's presence at this conference prevented Austria from being the sole representative of Italy, and placed Sardinia on the level of an independent sovereign state.

Next, Cavour made overtures to France, which Napoleon III welcomed, bearing in mind the first Napoleon's Italian empire. Also, by seeming to protect the interests of the Papacy he would strengthen his hold on the powerful clerical party in France. Moreover, support of Sardinia against Austria would earn popularity with French liberals and add fresh lustre to the name of Napoleon.

That some of these aims would ultimately conflict with Cavour's plans for a united Italy was obvious but neither diplomatist took the other fully into confidence and each hoped to outwit the other. It was against such a background that a compact was signed at Plombières in 1858. France was to go to the aid of Sardinia against Austria provided the latter was the aggressor. With Austria expelled by a successful military campaign from Italy, then Lombardy, Venetia, Parma and Modena were to be added to Sardinia and to be known as the Kingdom of Northern Italy. Central Italy, Naples and the Papal States were to retain their independence, while as a reward, Napoleon was to receive Savoy and Nice.

War With Austria, 1859

Cavour now set to work to provoke Austria into war. He began by persuading Victor Emmanuel to increase his army and to strengthen the defences of Piedmont. When these activities were continued in spite of repeated protests from Austria, protests gave way to an ultimatum. Sardinian forces must be reduced or Austria would declare war. Cavour now alleged that this was an infringement of Sardinia's sovereignty and he appealed to Europe for support.

Napoleon III had no alternative but to respond and the Sardinians found themselves supported by 100,000 French troops under the command of the Emperor himself. At Magenta and Solferino the Austrian invaders were decisively beaten and these two victories were the signal for the outburst of anti-Austrian feeling throughout central and northern Italy. Cavour, at the height of his success, prepared for a final assault on Austria in Venetia.

Then came disaster. Italy learned that, acting independently, Napoleon III had granted the Austrians a truce and arranged terms of peace. Napoleon had begun to fear that, if the Austrian defeat were too complete, he might not be able to control Cavour. He saw now that Cavour was aiming at much more than the creation of a mere north Italian Kingdom and that complete unification would involve an attack on the political sovereignty of the Pope. If he were party to such a development Catholic opinion in France would turn against him. He dare not take such a risk. In any case, the unification of Italy would bar the way to a re-creation of the old French empire there and establish instead a dangerously strong neighbour on France's frontier. Napoleon had to withdraw from the war and save the situation while he could.

By the Truce of Villafranca Napoleon III and Francis Joseph of Austria agreed that peace should be declared on the understanding that Lombardy and Parma be ceded to Sardinia and Savoy and Nice to France.

Cavour, feeling that he had been basely betrayed or cleverly outwitted, refused to accept the truce and offered his resignation to Victor Emmanuel if the latter would not continue the war. The king, wiser than his counsellor at this point, accepted both the resignation and the truce.

Sardinia, however, gained more than she had been offered. Parma, Tuscany and Modena by popular vote demanded union with Sardinia. Only another Austrian campaign would have reduced these states to submission and for this Austria was not prepared. In 1860, therefore, the desired union took place and a parliament representative of Sardinia, Lombardy, Tuscany, Parma and Modena met at Turin.

Garibaldi and the Conquest of Sicily and Naples

The nucleus of a united Italy had now been formed; the next step was largely the work of a soldier, Garibaldi. After returning from exile in America

Victor Emmanuel.

Count Cavour.

whence he had fled after the failures of 1848, Garibaldi waged a helpful though almost independent campaign against Austria in north Italy during the war of 1859.

The Truce of Villafranca led Cavour to turn his attention to Sicily. There, in 1860, Mazzini engineered a revolt against the tyranny of Francis II, ruler of the joint kingdom of Naples and Sicily. Garibaldi responded to Mazzini's appeal for military aid and looked for help to Cavour, now back again as head of the government in Sardinia. Cavour, thinking the enterprise too risky, officially expressed his disapproval but secretly gave it his blessing, though little more.

Undismayed, Garibaldi assembled volunteers at Genoa. Thence in May, 1860, he embarked his famous "Thousand" in two stolen steamers. Eluding the Neapolitan warships waiting to intercept him he landed his troops at Marsala. From there he marched towards Palermo, now evading, now defeating trained troops sent to capture him.

His entry into Palermo stimulated an uprising. Citizens combined with Garibaldi's Red Shirts to break down barricades erected by government troops. Finally the defending commander gave way and abandoned first Palermo and eventually the whole island. From Sicily Garibaldi crossed to Naples. The citizens again received him with open arms and in despair Francis II fled from his kingdom.

Garibaldi and Cavour

Now that Garibaldi had succeeded, Cavour was anxious to ensure that Sardinia reaped the fruits of the victory, for Garibaldi was known to favour republicanism rather than any form of monarchy. Moreover, he was proposing to march on the Papal States, a dangerous move in Cavour's opinion since it might provoke French intervention. Cavour therefore forestalled both Garibaldi and Napoleon III by announcing that a Sardinian army would be despatched to protect the political sovereignty of the Pope. Accordingly, Victor Emmanuel marched through the Papal States into Naples where the population promptly voted for incorporation with Sardinia. Sicily expressed a similar wish.

Meanwhile Garibaldi advanced on Rome. The Sardinian troops therefore retraced their steps and on their arrival in Rome Garibaldi abandoned his operations and made his submission to Victor Emmanuel. Hence on 18 February, 1861, a parliament met at Turin in which every Italian state save Venetia and Rome was represented; Victor Emmanuel took the title of King of Italy.

Cavour died in 1861. He had achieved much. Alone of all Italian patriots of the nineteenth century, he had succeeded in harnessing constitutionalism and republicanism in the cause of unity. He had induced the European powers to recognize the existence of an Italian question and to agree to a solution totally different from that laid down in 1815. He had built up the internal economy of Sardinia, exploited the ambitions of Napoleon III and reaped for Sardinia the fruits of the republican enthusiasm of Mazzini and Garibaldi. Only death robbed him of the final satisfaction of seeing Rome become what he declared it ought to be, "the national capital of united Italy."

Completion of Italian Unification, 1866-71

Most of Venetia became part of united Italy when Italian forces seized the opportunity provided by a war between Austria and Prussia. Five years later, Napoleon's war with Prussia forced him to withdraw troops from his garrison in Rome, and when Victor Emmanuel advanced on the Papal States the population declared in favour of incorporation with the rest of Italy. Rome became the capital, and the Pope was confined to his estate.

Up to the advent of Mussolini successive popes remained voluntary prisoners in the Vatican for they refused to travel through what they regarded as usurped territory.

The Austrian hold upon Italy had been the first obstacle which had stood in the way of Italian unification. It was overcome by foreign aid, and by the advantage taken of Austria's internal and international difficulties.

The second obstacle had been the political sovereignty of the Pope, and until the twentieth century the hostility of Church and state in Italy was to remain unsolved.

Third, Europe had been against the idea of a united Italy. This opposition was overcome by Sardinian participation in the Crimean War.

Fourth, the local loyalties and jealousies of the Italian states which had stood in the way of unification, had been dissolved only by the propagandist efforts of Mazzini.

Fifth, the divided aims of monarchists, republicans and liberals tended to produce intolerable diversity of aim and effort. It was Cavour's diplomacy which fused these warring elements.

Finally there was the special obstacle of France. She could not stand idly by and see a strong neighbour settle on her very doorstep; this did not fit with the "Napoleonic Legend." Cavour's outwitting of the Emperor in 1859 and Bismarck's fatal attack in 1870 provided a way of escape.

QUESTION

1. How did the great powers (*a*) help, and (*b*) hinder, Italian unification, and what were their reasons?

CHAPTER 38

NAPOLEON III, BISMARCK AND GERMAN UNITY

T HE greatest stumbling block to German unification was Austria. Germanic herself, she was unwilling to break away from the German world. Until the German states could raise or secure the help of an army equal to that of Austria, a united Germany would remain an unrealized dream.

Prussia was the strongest German state from the military point of view, but her rulers feared defeat and she had a strong anti-militaristic liberal party. This liberal outlook was strong in other German states as well.

Then, too, the princes were not eager to sacrifice their sovereign rights. Moreover, a central government uniting the Catholic south under Protestant Prussia was not an idea which appealed to the southern states.

Finally, France had not relinquished her old hopes of pushing her boundary across the Rhine. Napoleon III was quite willing to exploit the Catholicism of southern Germany for the purpose of keeping Germany disunited and therefore too weak to constitute a threat to France.

The Zollverein

The internal and external tariffs current in Germany added economic to political disunity and restricted the country's prosperity. By abolishing her internal tariffs in 1819 Prussia gained such advantages that her smaller neighbours asked to enter this customs union, or *Zollverein*. Other groups of German states founded a *Zollverein* of their own, and these were absorbed in 1836 into that of Prussia. Economic unity had been achieved, and the *Zollverein* anticipated the main lines on which political unification would be gained.

Prussia Seeks to Initiate Political Unity

In 1849 Frederick William put forward a proposal for a closer political union of Germany under Prussia. A number of smaller states responded to his invitation and when two larger states, Hanover and Saxony, agreed the League of the Three Kings was formed. Strong opposition from other large German states, however, led Hanover and Saxony first to withdraw from the League and then to join with Bavaria and Württemberg in the rival League of the Four Kings. Austria called for a meeting of the Confederal

Diet to oppose the Prussian scheme and Hesse-Cassel in 1850 provided a test case.

The Elector, in face of Austria's attitude, withdrew from the Prussian league and appealed to the Diet for support against his subjects who objected to his withdrawal. They appealed for support to Prussia. Prussia, now faced with the prospect of war against Austria and the forces of the Diet, felt too unsure of success to proceed further. Austria and Bavaria were allowed to subdue the people of Hesse-Cassel, the Convention of Olmütz (1850) dissolved the Prussian union and the authority of the Confederal Diet was confirmed. The only thing saved was the continued exclusion of Austria from the *Zollverein*.

William I, who succeeded Frederick William IV as king of Prussia in 1861, determined to develop the military might of his country and he found an outstanding army commander in Von Roon. But the liberal majority in the Prussian representative assembly, the *Landtag*, refused to vote the necessary money for the proposed military expansion. William was on the point of abdicating when he called to his councils Otto von Bismarck.

Bismarck had been Prussian representative in the Confederal Diet but his provocative attitude there towards Austria had led to his recall and subsequent service as representative at St. Petersburg and Paris. Back now in Prussia at the right hand of his king, Bismarck henceforth shaped the policy of his country in accordance with clear if ruthless principles. Unification was to be obtained, he believed, not by the absorption of Prussia in Germany but by the absorption of Germany into Prussia. This was to be accomplished by the fullest use of the absolute powers of the Prussian monarchy with no concessions to the hampering views of a liberal *Landtag*. In the last resort Prussia must be prepared for military action against foreign opposition to German unification but all the resources of diplomacy were to be employed to ensure that she would not have to fight a European coalition. Her foreign opponents must first be isolated and then defeated one by one.

It was the application of this single-minded determination which delivered William I from his dilemma of 1862. When again in 1863 the *Landtag* refused to sanction expenditure on army reform, the Assembly was prorogued, the Press censored and the necessary taxes collected on royal authority only. Not until four years later, when Bismarck's policy had begun to show successful results, did his unpopularity in Prussia tend to abate.

The Schleswig-Holstein Question

Bismarck's method of working for unification led in practice to three wars, the first and smallest of which was the war with Denmark in 1864.

To the south of the Danish peninsula were two small duchies known as Schleswig and Holstein. Nominally subject to Denmark, they retained their

331

own dukes, laws and customs. Their population was mixed and Holstein was a member state of the German Confederation.

The King of Denmark had tried to strengthen his hold on the duchies but the opposition they offered and the interest in their fate displayed by Austria and Prussia led to a meeting of the European powers in London in 1852 at which, in return for confirmation of her sovereign rights over these territories, Denmark had promised not to attempt to incorporate them.

War With Denmark

In 1863 Frederick VII of Denmark violated this London agreement and the Duchies appealed to the Confederal Diet for support. Austria and Prussia, however, agreed to settle the Schleswig-Holstein question independently of either the Diet or Europe. Together they drove the Danes out of the Duchies and over-ran Denmark itself. Defeated, Denmark surrendered all her interests in the duchies jointly to Austria and Prussia, an arrangement embodied in the Convention of Gastein, 1865. In practice thereafter Austria looked after Holstein, and Prussia, Schleswig.

Prussia and Bismarck had every reason to be pleased with the events of 1864-5. In reaching a solution of the Schleswig-Holstein question the Diet had been ignored; Austria and Prussia had imposed their own terms. The prestige of the Diet had been undermined, an essential preliminary to its ultimate destruction. Further, the joint action had been taken largely on the initiative of Prussia who now stood out in German affairs on a basis of equality with Austria. Finally, in their joint sovereignty in the Duchies, Bismarck had a potential source of conflict with Austria which he could exploit when the time was ripe.

Diplomatic Isolation of Austria

Russia was a traditional ally of Austria, and to secure her neutrality in the event of an Austro-Prussian war, Bismarck recalled the fact that Russia had been able in 1863 to suppress a Polish bid for national independence largely as the result of Prussian aid. Russia agreed to remain neutral.

France was another possible Austrian ally because of Napoleon III's aversion to German unification. With France, Bismarck was less straightforward. At an interview at Biarritz, he allowed Napoleon to conclude that, in return for French neutrality, France would later have Prussian neutrality or even support for an annexation of either Belgium or some Rhenish provinces. In the absence of a formal written agreement Bismarck knew that he could later protest that the "understanding" was in fact a "misunderstanding"— but on Napoleon's part.

To Italy, Bismarck looked for a possible ally. Bismarck suggested that while he fought Austria in Germany, Italy might reasonably hope successfully to

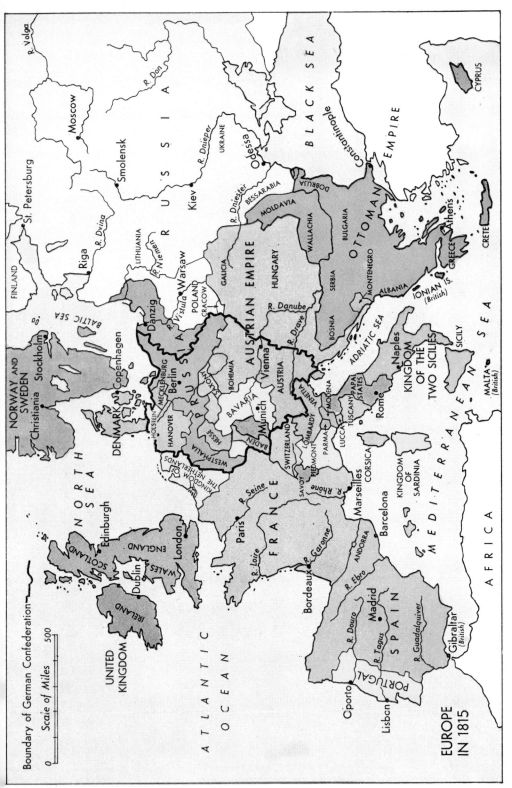

EUROPE
IN 1815

Boundary of German Confederation ——

Scale of Miles

0   500

R. Volga

Moscow

St. Petersburg

FINLAND

Smolensk

R U S S I A

Riga

R. Dvina

NORWAY AND SWEDEN

Christiania

Stockholm

BALTIC SEA

Copenhagen

DENMARK

LITHUANIA

R. Niemen

Kiev

R. Dnieper

UKRAINE

Odessa

BLACK SEA

Constantinople

O T T O M A N   E M P I R E

CYPRUS

CRETE

Athens

GREECE

IONIAN IS.
(British)

ALBANIA

MONTENEGRO

SERBIA

BOSNIA

BULGARIA

DOBRUJA

WALLACHIA

MOLDAVIA

BESSARABIA

R. Dniester

GALICIA

HUNGARY

R. Drave

R. Danube

AUSTRIAN EMPIRE

Vienna

AUSTRIA

BOHEMIA

Danzig

Warsaw

R. Vistula

POLAND

CRACOW

P R U S S I A

Berlin

MECKLENBURG

HOLSTEIN

HANOVER

SAXONY

BAVARIA

Munich

HESSE

BADEN

WESTPHALIA

KINGDOM OF THE NETHERLANDS

SWITZERLAND

PIEDMONT

SAVOY

LOMBARDY

VENETIA

PARMA

MODENA

LUCCA

TUSCANY

PAPAL STATES

Rome

Naples

KINGDOM OF THE TWO SICILIES

SICILY

MALTA
(British)

ADRIATIC SEA

M E D I T E R R A N E A N   S E A

CORSICA

Marseilles

R. Rhône

R. Seine

Paris

F R A N C E

R. Loire

R. Garonne

Bordeaux

ANDORRA

Barcelona

R. Ebro

KINGDOM OF SARDINIA

SARDINIA

SPAIN

Madrid

R. Tagus

R. Guadalquiver

R. Douro

Cporto

PORTUGAL

Lisbon

Gibraltar
(British)

A F R I C A

ATLANTIC OCEAN

NORTH SEA

UNITED KINGDOM

IRELAND

Dublin

SCOTLAND

Edinburgh

ENGLAND

London

WALES

OCL/HIST 2—X

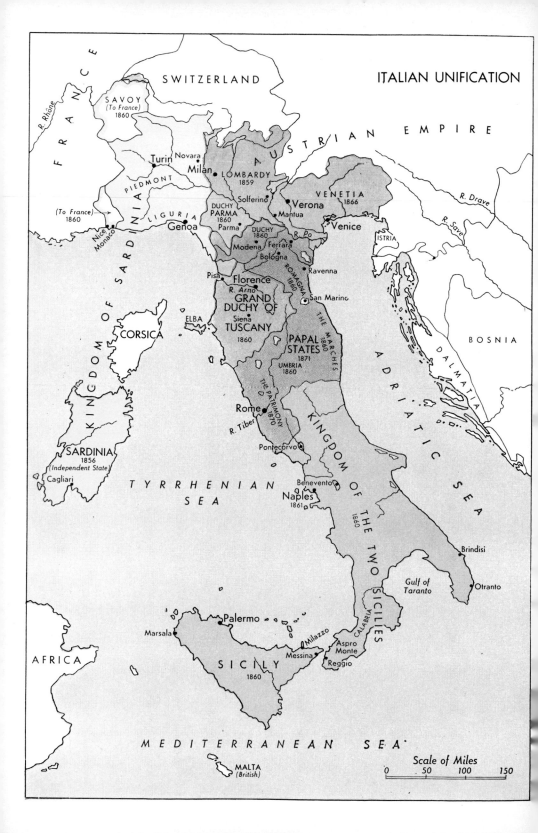

invade Venetia. In any case, he promised, the final expulsion of Austria from Italy would be the price he would be willing to pay for Italian aid in his conflict with Austria. Italy found the price right.

With Austria thus isolated, all Bismarck wanted was a reasonable pretext for war. He found it by resurrecting the Schleswig-Holstein question.

Excuse for War With Austria

In 1866 Bismarck alleged that Austria was allowing a pretender to the Duchies of Schleswig and Holstein to use the latter as a base from which to launch an attack on Prussian influence in the former. Austria, quite properly, referred the allegation to the Diet for investigation. Bismarck, however, claimed that the Convention of Gastein had taken the Schleswig-Holstein question out of the jurisdiction of the Diet and promptly sent troops to occupy both Duchies.

Austria countered by proposing in the Diet that confederal troops be sent against Prussia. Bismark accepted the challenge and the war for which he had schemed began in June, 1866, and ended by August.

In the Prussian theatre of war, Austrian troops were defeated by early July. In Italy they were more successful, but military and naval victories there could not compensate for the failure in Germany. Peace was finally concluded.

Treaty of Prague, 1866

The terms imposed upon Austria were not burdensome. Bismarck was content to see her excluded from Germany, though she had to surrender Venetia to Sardinia. The main gain from Prussia's point of view was the abolition of the Confederal Diet and its replacement by the north German Confederation under Prussian leadership. No pressure was brought to bear upon the Catholic south German states to join with the north, for such pressure might have strained French neutrality to the breaking-point and Bismarck was not yet ready for war with France.

This treaty was a model of Bismarck's skill in diplomacy. He had avoided increased bitterness with the south; he had given France no excuse to abandon her neutrality; he had put Austria under a debt of gratitude by the modesty of his demands upon her; and he had achieved his major objectives. The Prussian *Landtag* recognized his success by passing an Act of Indemnity covering the taxation Bismarck had imposed for some years past without their approval, and sanctioning his military expenditure for the immediate future.

The next step in the achievement of German unification came about as the result of war with France and led to profound changes in the French constitution. At this point therefore we may leave Germany, and return to France and her history during the ten years from 1860 to 1870.

France's Mexican Adventure

By 1860, Napoleon was suffering the consequences of absolute power. He was held responsible for the government's failures as well as for its successes. His Italian venture, contrasted with his victory in the Crimea, had been an acute disappointment. For the liberals, Napoleon had not gone far enough; for French Catholics he had gone too far. By 1860 the Catholic and liberal props of the Second Empire were weakening under the strain which Napoleon's failures were creating.

By dabbling in Mexican affairs, where the government was following an anti-Catholic policy, Napoleon hoped to overthrow the Mexican government and win the gratitude of French Catholic opinion. But when he had despatched a French force to Mexico he was faced with the prospect of war with America, who in accordance with the Monroe Doctrine of 1823 threatened to come to the aid of Mexico. Napoleon had to abandon his Mexican adventure, which had merely underlined his dismal record of foreign failure.

To offset his failure abroad, Napoleon began to follow a belated liberal policy at home. Public political meetings were permitted, press censorship was relaxed, the powers of the legislature were extended and a new constitution was drawn up making the executive responsible to the legislature. The public realized that these measures were the actions of a weak man attempting to bolster his position, and consequently had nothing but contempt for them.

By 1870 ultimate disaster was almost upon the Second Empire. Over the Rhine Bismarck was ready for that war with France which would complete Germany unity. Over the Pyrenees a crisis was developing in Spain in which Prussia was involved. These two threads woven together made the fabric of the German empire and the Third French Republic. The loom for the weaving was war.

Bismarck's Anti-French Diplomacy, 1866-70

Between 1866 and 1870 Bismarck set himself to ensure that if war came, France would find no allies among the major powers of Europe. At the end of the Austro-Prussian War he had, as we have seen, taken care to leave as little bitterness in his enemy's mind as possible. After 1866 he diverted Austrian attention from a possible war of revenge by reminding her of the conflicting nature of her interests with those of Russia in the east of Europe. He played upon her fear of Russia and left her to draw the inference that if one day she needed an ally she might look not unhopefully to Prussia.

To give reality to these Austrian fears, Bismarck encouraged Russian designs in the east. He secured in fact a promise of Russian neutrality in a possible Franco-German war by undertaking to turn a blind eye if Russia should violate her word not to send warships into the Black Sea.

With Austria diverted and Russia bribed, Bismarck turned his attention to Italy. Here his task was not difficult. In 1859 Napoleon III had forfeited all claim to Italian gratitude. Further, since 1860, it had been the presence of a French protective garrison which alone had enabled Rome to remain outside the kingdom of Victor Emmanuel. Any diversion which would compel France to withdraw that garrison would be a welcome opportunity for the completion of Italian unification.

There remained Britain and the south German states to be reckoned with, both of whom might very well support France. In these two cases, Bismarck delayed making his vital move until it was too late for France to counteract it. On the very eve of the outbreak of the Franco-Prussian war Bismarck revealed to Britain the proposals Napoleon III had made years before for the annexation of

Caricature of Louis Napoleon.

Belgium. For centuries Britain had fought to keep the low countries free from the domination of any major power and in any case, since 1839 she had been a guarantor of Belgium's neutrality. The revelation of Napoleon's idle dream was enough to ensure British non-intervention in the war of 1870.

To the south German states, Bismarck now revealed Napoleon's proposals for compensation in the Palatinate, and they saw at once that he whom they had regarded as a potential saviour of their Catholicism was at the same time a possible political despoiler. They now discovered that they were Germans first and Catholics second; nationalism triumphed over religion and Bismarck had his way.

The Spanish Succession Question

His diplomatic preparations complete, Bismarck now awaited an excuse for war. This was supplied by Spain, who offered the vacant Spanish throne to a member of the Prussian royal family, Leopold of Hohenzollern. He accepted and France took alarm. To have a strong neighbour on the Rhine was bad enough; to have a relative of that neighbour on the other side of the Pyrenees was intolerable. France was not prepared to play the role of nut between the Prussian nutcrackers.

At Napoleon III's insistence, and to Bismarck's chagrin, Leopold withdrew his acceptance of the Spanish crown, but then Napoleon pushed matters too far. He demanded assurance from William of Prussia that Prussia would never again countenance Leopold's candidature. This demand was presented by the French ambassador, Benedetti, to William I at Ems and though the interview was friendly enough, William firmly declined to make any such promise.

The Ems Telegram

William reported the Ems interview in a telegram sent to Bismarck. It was delivered while Bismarck and the army commanders Roon and von Moltke, were together at dinner. Realizing that nothing had transpired which justified the outbreak of hostilities, Bismarck proceeded to manufacture what fate had not given him. He issued to the Press an abbreviated version of the telegram which gave the impression that the interview at Ems had been much less friendly than in fact it was. At once the popular cry was raised in Berlin for war with France.

Popular opinion in Paris, on the basis of the German version of the telegram was equally bellicose. Bismarck was "trailing his coat" and Paris demanded that Napoleon accept the challenge to tread thereon. Napoleon did not dare attempt conciliation and Bismarck did not want it. The two nations went to war.

Humiliation of France

France was ill-prepared; she was without allies and her military plans and organization had to be more or less improvised on the spur of the moment. Prussia had the neutrality or sympathy of the major powers as well as the advantage of a magnificent army, precise plans of campaign and two supreme commanders in Roon and von Moltke.

The Germans undertook a threefold invasion of France. Against the invading columns marched one French force under MacMahon, a second under Bazaine and a third under Napoleon III himself. MacMahon was compelled to retire to Châlons, Bazaine to Metz. Napoleon went first to the help of MacMahon and then with MacMahon advanced to the relief of Bazaine in Metz. The relief failed. Napoleon was surrounded at Sedan, defeated, taken prisoner and himself compelled to surrender his sword.

This final ignominy was more than France could tolerate. At the news of Sedan, the republican party took control in Paris, declared the Emperor deposed and France became once more a republic.

Meanwhile the Germans advanced on Paris. The capital offered an heroic resistance for four months. Finally, its citizens wearied by cold, weakened by hunger and terrorized by bombardment, Paris surrendered. Through Napoleon I's Arc de Triomphe the German troops marched in victory. The Treaty of Frankfort followed.

Treaty of Frankfort, 1871

It was never part of Bismarck's policy to lay up for himself stores of future trouble by creating in his defeated enemies a desire for revenge. Had his counsels prevailed the Treaty of Frankfort would have been far other than it was. Over-ruled in this instance by the military authorities he had to acquiesce in terms of "peace" which twisted the knife in France's open wounds.

Alsace and Lorraine were to be ceded to Germany. France was to pay a war indemnity of £200 million and to ensure payment a German army was to remain in occupation of French territory at French expense until the indemnity was discharged.

The immediate consequences of the war were radical. With their French Catholic saviour a fallen idol, the south German states, far from resisting, actually sought incorporation within the German empire. It was in the Hall of Mirrors at Versailles that the King of Prussia was proclaimed Emperor of Germany. With that proclamation Bismarck's objectives of 1860 had been achieved by the methods he had determined.

Meanwhile, France had set up the Third Republic and while Napoleon III went as an exile to Britain, Bismarck reaped the reward of his labours by elevation to the rank and dignity of Prince.

From the outset Napoleon had been committed to an impossible task. To revive the French glory of the first Napoleon's empire was not feasible, and his foreign adventures had cost him the friendship of at least three major European powers. His concessions to liberal forces had come too late.

To all this must be added Napoleon's own limitations as a diplomatist and military leader. To have repeated in diplomacy or warfare the success of his uncle would have strained the capacity of a genius and Napoleon III was at best only a man of modest talent. Yet France must share with him the blame for the disasters of the Second Empire. National opinion encouraged Napoleon to fish in troubled waters. It was not entirely his fault if he toiled for many years and caught nothing.

QUESTION

1. Describe the methods by which Prussia succeeded in dominating a unified Germany between 1862 and 1871.

CHAPTER 39

THE EASTERN QUESTION

AT THE beginning of the nineteenth century, the Turkish empire included the Balkan Peninsula of Europe as far as the river Save in the north-west and the river Pruth in the north-east. Turkey was in fact the immediate geographic neighbour of the Austro-Hungarian and Russian empires.

The presence of Turkey in Europe created grave tensions. The Turks were Moslems; their Balkan subjects were Christians. The Turkish Sultans and governors (Pashas) tended to be despots, harsh and cruel; their western subjects sought freedom and national government. In part therefore the Eastern Question was the problem of dealing with the friction arising from these differences between rulers and ruled.

The major European powers all had interests at stake in the Balkans or the Mediterranean. Russia and Austria were rivals for the control of the mouth of the Danube which afforded its possessor access to the Mediterranean through the Black Sea. France and Britain were already Mediterranean powers unwilling to share their position with others. Thus, while all four powers sympathized with the Balkan states groaning under Turkish misrule, each was afraid lest, in the solution of the problem, any one of the other three should gain predominance in the Balkans or the Mediterranean.

As the nineteenth century advanced two rival solutions became clear. Russia suggested that Turkey was the "sick man of Europe." His death was inevitable and desirable. The process should be hastened by an attack on Turkey and a subsequent division of the spoils among the executioners. Britain, fearing that Russia would get the lion's share of the spoils, suggested instead a cure for the sick man by forcing Turkey to govern its European possessions in accordance with western European ideals.

Greek War of Independence

The first crisis developed when in 1821 Greece tried to assert her independence. The Greeks had serious grievances against their Turkish rulers. They were heavily taxed and liable to excessive punishment for political offences. They became more conscious of these burdens as they began to take a revived interest and pride in the story of ancient Greece. By 1814 a secret society had been formed at Odessa, pledged to work for Greek independence.

A rising in Moldavia in 1821 was suppressed by the Turks, but led to a more serious uprising in Morea. Turkish forts fell into the hands of the Greeks and the Turks could only reply by persecuting the Christians in Asia Minor.

Up to 1825 the Greeks owed nothing to foreign support. Russia had made no move; Austria contemplated intervention on the Turkish side; Britain sympathized with the Greeks but offered no practical help.

The threat of Russian intervention on behalf of the Greek Orthodox Christians within the Turkish empire changed the attitude of Europe, even though Egypt had by this time joined the war on the side of Turkey. Britain had no desire to see Russia act alone and reap all the rewards, and Charles X of France had strong religious convictions which impelled him to defend the Greek Christians.

Hence in 1827 Britain, France and Russia signed the Treaty of London. Greece was to pay tribute to Turkey but to be otherwise self-governing. If the Sultan did not accept this plan within a month, the signatories further agreed to recognize the full independence of Greece and to take action to force such recognition upon Turkey.

The Sultan rejected this solution and the French and British fleets were accordingly ordered to Greek waters. In an engagement in the Bay of Navarino in 1827 the Turkish and Egyptian fleets were destroyed.

Britain then withdrew from the conflict because the liberal Canning had been replaced by the reactionary Wellington, but Russia succeeded in threatening the Turks in Adrianople to the point where they were ready to compromise.

The Treaty of Adrianople in 1829 provided for the freedom of Greece with nominal Turkish overlordship, but the Greeks would not accept this. After three more years of fighting, the Turks recognized the complete freedom of Greece, and Otto of Bavaria took the newly established throne.

The Greek War of Independence marked the first real step in the break-up of the Turkish empire in Europe. The war also marked a triumph for Russian diplomacy in as much as she had played a dominant part in Greek success, and it was to this extent a rebuff for the British point of view.

Syrian Crisis, 1831-42

Egypt at this time was actually an independent sovereign state, but nominally under Turkish rule. Mehemet Ali, the governor-general, angry at not having gained Syria, which Turkey had promised him, took the territory by force in 1831. At this point he thought he saw a possibility of becoming Sultan of Turkey itself, and advanced towards Asia Minor. The reigning Sultan applied for aid to Russia, but as Britain and France threatened to ally with Mehemet Ali in order to balance the triumph of Russian diplomacy in the Greek affair, Russia backed down and the Sultan gave Syria to Egypt.

Drawn together by a common sense of defeat, Russia and Turkey now made the Treaty of Unkiar Skelessi, 1833. By this agreement Turkey undertook to close the Dardanelles to the warships of all nations except those of Russia, in return for a promise of Russian assistance in any further attack Turkey might have to meet.

In 1839 the Turks attempted unsuccessfully to drive Mehemet Ali out of Syria. This, combined with the death of the old Sultan, renewed Mehemet Ali's ambitions to secure Turkey for himself. This time, however, he lacked that European support which he had enjoyed six years earlier. Neither Russia nor Britain wished to see so ambitious a man as Mehemet Ali on the Turkish throne. Britain also disliked the fact that Mehemet Ali was receiving aid from France, who wished to advance her own interests in Egypt at the expense of Britain.

Treaty of London, 1840, and Convention of the Straits, 1841

War between Russia and Britain on the one side, and France and Syria on the other, was avoided only because Louis Philippe, to the disgust of French public opinion, withdrew his support of Mehemet Ali and thus made possible the general agreement embodied in the Treaty of London of 1840. Britain, Russia, Austria and Prussia guaranteed the integrity of the Turkish empire, recognized the rights of Mehemet Ali in Egypt but called upon him to relinquish his control of Syria. A short but decisive campaign had to be fought to compel Mehemet to accept this last provision.

A further international agreement was signed in 1841. The four signatories of 1840 agreed in the Convention of the Straits of 1841, to recognize the sovereignty of Turkey over the Dardanelles, with the proviso that in time of war these straits should be closed to the warships of all nations, including those of Russia.

The Syrian Question had wide repercussions. Louis Philippe's change of policy in face of European pressure undermined his prestige both in France and in Europe; while the diplomatic tension which preceded it poisoned the relations of France and Britain for some years.

As for Russia, by the Convention of the Straits, she lost all she had gained a few years earlier by the Treaty of Unkiar Skelessi. On the other hand, Palmerston, Britain's Foreign Minister, by securing in the Treaty of London a guarantee of the integrity of what was left of the Turkish empire, had re-imposed on Europe the British solution of the Eastern Question to the eclipse of Russian diplomacy.

The desire on the part of Russia to increase her power in the east, and British opposition to this, was one of the fundamental causes of the Crimean War. When war broke out, France and Austria were also involved because of their desire to prevent the spread of Russian influence.

In 1854 the Roman Catholic Church and the Greek Orthodox Church

Napoleon III aids the "sick men" of Europe, Turkey and the Pope.

were quarrelling over their respective rights to those areas in Palestine traditionally associated with Christianity. Napoleon III demanded that Turkey support the Catholic claims, and Nicholas I of Russia made a similar demand on behalf of the Orthodox Church.

When the Sultan rejected the Russian claim, the Tsar sent troops to occupy Moldavia and Wallachia. Turkey replied with a declaration of war, while France and Britain promised assistance to the Sultan if Russia did not show herself disposed to make reasonable terms.

Far from making terms, Russia attacked and destroyed the Turkish fleet at the Battle of Sinope (1854). Thereupon France and Britain sent fleets to the Black Sea and declared war on Russia. Meanwhile the Russian fleet retired to Sebastopol.

The Russian invasion of Moldavia and Wallachia soon collapsed. Allied fleets blockaded Odessa, Russia failed to take Silistria and Austria threatened the Russian rear. When French and British troops landed they found the Russian forces withdrawn and the principalities in Austrian occupation.

War in the Crimea

The Allies now took the war to the Russians in the Crimea. After a successful landing they defeated the Russians at the battle of Alma but neglected the opportunity afforded them to capture Sebastopol. The Russians made use of this respite to strengthen the defences of the town and there followed a nine-months' siege during which the allied troops, quite unprepared, were called upon to endure the miseries of a severe winter. They were without the necessary clothes, transport was difficult and food supplies reached the troops only with great irregularity. Of medical services for the sick and wounded there were at first none. It was as the people mainly responsible for remedying this last deficiency that Florence Nightingale and her nursing staff won everlasting fame.

The two attempts made by the Russians to break out from the siege were repelled, the first at the battle of Balaclava and the second at the battle of Inkerman (1855). It was at this point that Sardinia, for reasons we examined in an earlier chapter, entered the war on the allied side. Shortly afterwards Nicholas I was succeeded by the more pacifically inclined Alexander II and it was now possible to hope that the end of the war was in sight.

In September, 1855, the French took Malakoff, one of the key defences of Sebastopol and the British took but were unable to hold the other defensive position, Redan. The Allies made a joint effort and Sebastopol fell.

Terms of peace were finally embodied in the Treaty of Paris of 1856. The Allies agreed to restore to Russia the conquered parts of the Crimea but Russia undertook not to re-fortify Sebastopol. The Dardanelles were to remain closed to the warships of all nations but were to be open to unrestricted commercial use. Neither Russia nor Turkey was henceforward to maintain a fleet in the Black Sea and the independence of Moldavia, Wallachia and Serbia was still further increased. As a concession to Turkish dignity it was agreed that she should for the future rank as a major European power and Russia was induced to renounce her claim to protect the Greek Orthodox Church in the Sultan's empire.

Russian ambitions in the east had been foiled and her solution of the Eastern Question subordinated to that of Britain, but these were temporary advantages since much of the Treaty of Paris soon became a dead letter. Only Sardinia made any really permanent gain. Cavour of Sardinia sat at the

Florence Nightingale at the hospital at Scutari.

council table as spokesman for Italy, thus fulfilling a role formerly taken by Austria. Further, by tabling Italian affairs for discussion at the peace conference Cavour had made it impossible for the European powers later to plead the final nature of the arrangements of 1815 as a barrier to Italian unification.

Bulgarian Crisis, 1875-78

The next major development in the Eastern Question occurred in 1875 when, with the sympathic approval of Montenegro and Serbia, risings took place against Turkey in Bosnia and Herzegovina.

The European powers made strenuous efforts to avoid war. Austria, with the approval of Britain, France, Russia and Italy, presented to Turkey the Andrassy note suggesting ways in which she should reform her administration of her European empire. Turkey promised to act on the lines suggested, but the insurgents felt that Turkish promises of this kind had been broken too often in the past to be relied on for the future. They refused to recognize Turkey's acceptance of the Andrassy note as a basis for settlement unless the European powers guaranteed Turkey's fulfilment of her promise.

Faced with this firm attitude, the powers sent a second note to Turkey— the Berlin Memorandum—threatening aid to the rebels unless Turkey carried out the provisions of the Andrassy note within a period of two months. Since Britain was not a party to the Berlin Memorandum, Turkey judged it safe to ignore it.

At this point Bulgaria took up arms against Turkey. Forthwith, Turkish troops invaded Bulgaria and being irregulars they perpetrated all manner of atrocities on civilians and captured soldiers alike. The situation became more hopeful when a new Sultan, Abdul Hamid II, succeeded to the Turkish throne and having brought the war with the Bulgars to a successful conclusion appointed as his chief adviser Midhat Pasha, a man of liberal views.

Now, as a result of Russia's threat to act independently against Turkey, an international conference was held at Constantinople and suggested a reform of Turkey's administration. Turkey replied that this reform was already being carried out, but immediately the conference broke up she reverted to her traditional methods of government and Midhat was dismissed.

At this, Russia invaded the Balkans, whereupon Serbia, Rumania (the kingdom of Moldavia and Wallachia) and Montenegro declared their independence from Turkey. When the Russians threatened Constantinople, other European powers prepared to intervene, and so Russia hurriedly offered to negotiate peace with Turkey. Utterly defeated, Turkey accepted.

Treaty of San Stefano, 1878

The outcome of these negotiations was a decidedly Russian peace. By the Treaty of San Stefano of 1878 Montenegro and Serbia were not merely declared independent sovereign states but were enlarged geographically. Bosnia and Herzegovina, though remaining nominally subject to Turkey, were placed under the joint supervision of Austria and Russia. Rumania had to cede Batoum, Kars and Bessarabia to Russia in return for the Dobrudja. Finally, a new Balkan power—Bulgaria—stretching from the Danube to the Aegean was to be erected and for two years supervised in its organization and administration by Russia.

The Balkan powers were far from pleased with the Treaty. Rumania was disgruntled at the idea of surrendering the fertile Bessarabia for the barren Dobrudja, and like Serbia, Greece and Montenegro disliked the extensive boundaries proposed for Bulgaria, boundaries so drawn that groups of non-Bulgarian nationals such as Greeks and Serbs would have fallen under Bulgarian sovereignty. Albania was also aggrieved, finding the idea of ceding territory to Montenegro repugnant to her dignity.

More important than Balkan displeasure was European discontent. Both Britain and Austria were alarmed at the extension of Russian influence foreshadowed by the Treaty. The new Bulgaria under Russian tutelage blocked Austria's way to the Black Sea and British influence in the Mediterranean might some day be challenged by Russia's emergence there. Under threat of war therefore, the European powers, led by Great Britain, compelled Russia to submit the treaty for revision.

Treaty of Berlin, 1878

For this purpose, a conference of European states met in Berlin in 1878 and a new treaty was there drawn up.

Montenegro, Serbia and Rumania retained their independence, but largely lost the extension of their territories suggested in the arrangements of San Stefano. Bosnia and Herzegovina were placed under Austrian supervision alone. Russia retained Kars, Batoum and Bessarabia but as a counterbalance, Britain assumed control of the administration of Cyprus. Rumania was thus left to make the best she could of the Dobrudja.

More drastic than all these modifications was that made in the size of the new state of Bulgaria. The Bulgaria envisaged by San Stefano was now divided into three parts. One, Bulgaria itself, was to be self-governing, though owing nominal submission to Turkey. Russian supervision of this new state was cut from two years to nine months. A second part, to be known as Eastern Rumelia, was to remain a Turkish possession provided that the Governor should always be a Christian and never a Moslem. A last part, Macedonia, was to be wholly Turkish. Finally, Turkey renewed her promises of good behaviour towards such Christian subjects as still remained under her rule.

The Treaty of Berlin was another setback for Russian ambitions. Britain had again enforced her policy of opposition to the complete disintegration of the Turkish empire and had done so without recourse to war. Hence Disraeli's claim on his return from Berlin that he had brought back "Peace with honour."

Yet the treaty was far from ideal in its consequences. Russian ambitions, checked in eastern Europe, turned henceforward to the Far East where Britain found her just as inconvenient a rival. Turkey, still in Europe, continued as incapable as ever of becoming in her outlook part of Europe, for in spite of her promises of reform, there was in 1894 a fresh crop of outrages directed on this occasion by the Turks against the Armenians.

John Bull says to Mr. Turkey: "I knew my Crimean doctors would set you up": a cartoon of the period.

The nationalist aspirations of the Balkan states had been whetted rather than satisfied. Greece subsequently encouraged Crete to throw off Turkish sovereignty and Serbia, up to 1914, steadily endeavoured to bring within her orbit those Slavs who had been left under foreign rule in 1878.

If Russian ambitions in the Balkans had been checked, those of Austria had been encouraged, as was seen when in 1908 she formally annexed Bosnia and Herzegovina.

Finally, thousands of European Christians had been left still subject to Turkish rule or mis-rule. The collapse of Turkey had only been delayed. The Eastern Question was not solved by the Treaty of Berlin; it was only shelved.

QUESTIONS

1. Give an account of the causes and consequences of the Crimean War.
2. Outline events in the Balkans in the years 1875-78, and explain why the Treaty of San Stefano was modified by the Treaty of Berlin.

CHAPTER 40

INTERNAL DEVELOPMENT OF RUSSIA, 1815-1912

IN 1815 Russia stretched from the Pacific Ocean to the boundaries of the Germanic Confederation and embraced many different racial groups of which the dominant one was the Slavs. The official religion was the faith of the Greek Orthodox Church, but other types of Christian communities were well-established. Languages were equally diverse.

Socially there were only two classes; the nobility and the peasants. The former were in possession of all land and the peasants were serfs, so utterly the servants of the landowner on whose estate they worked that he even had the right of inflicting corporal punishment on them. The land of a village was divided into two parts, one for the use of the landowner, though its cultivation on his behalf was the duty of the peasants; the other part was rented by the village peasant community, the *Mir*, and farmed collectively. The peasants' standard of living was low, their income small and prospects of improvement by personal effort non-existent.

Over this nation of peasant serfs ruled the Tsar, who enjoyed absolute power. The history of Russia is in fact the history of her rulers and the line of policy pursued at any time reflects the personal character of the reigning Tsar. Thus in the nineteenth century Russia veered from liberal experiments to strict enforcement of absolutism or from a policy of "Russification" to one of "Westernization."

Eclipse of Liberalism, 1815-55

For the first fifteen years of the nineteenth century Russia had in Alexander I a liberal Tsar. The liberalism he preached in Europe he tried to practise in his own domains. When Russia acquired Poland he established there a constitution which gave the Poles a large measure of self-government.

In Russia itself Alexander made an effort to set up an efficient administration free from the corruption which had hitherto prevailed. He showed awareness of the evils of serfdom and though no radical solution of the problem was attempted the lot of some unfortunates was improved by the provision of hospitals and asylums.

Unfortunately for Russia by 1818 Alexander had fallen under the spell of

Metternich. The Austrian Chancellor brought home to Alexander the dangers of liberalism by pointing to the murder of Kotzebue, a Russian agent in Germany, and also the ingratitude of the Poles as shown by their frequent criticism of the Tsarist government. In due course such examples had the effect of convincing Alexander that by encouraging liberalism he was fanning a flame which might destroy his monarchy. As a result, the years 1820 to 1825 were marked by an abandonment of all progressive policy in Russia.

Under Alexander I's successor, Nicholas I, this reactionary policy was further developed. The Press and all forms of literature were strictly censored, religious toleration gave place to persecution, the progress of education was halted, foreign literature was excluded from Russia as far as possible, Russians were discouraged from travelling abroad and foreign visitors, if admitted, were kept under continuous police supervision during their visit. To enforce all these restrictions a force of secret police was organized with unlimited powers of arrest followed by imprisonment without trial.

Behind this reactionary policy there was also a perverted sense of nationalism. Nicholas was anxious to see Russia develop on lines in keeping with purely national characteristics. He was turning his back on that policy of Westernization which Peter the Great over a century earlier had so eagerly pursued and substituting for it a policy of "Russification."

This did not mean, however, that Russia was to adopt no reforms of any kind. It was in fact under Nicholas I that the death penalty was abolished for all offences save that of treason. He also appointed several committees to examine the evils of serfdom in the hope of alleviating the more flagrant of these. Nicholas also deserves credit for furthering the development of railway construction in Russia.

Alexander II, 1855-81

Under Alexander II, the policies of Russification gave way to Westernization. This change was partly because of his liberal nature, and partly because the Crimean War exposed the inefficiency of absolute government. He extended education and abandoned the restrictions on travel. Finally, in 1861, he turned his attention to the problem of serfdom when he issued his famous Edict of Emancipation. Henceforth, officially, all serfs were freemen. Land of which the villagers had hitherto had communal use, they now owned communally and periodically it was to be re-allocated to individual families for cultivation. The nobility were compensated by the state for their loss of ownership.

Well-intentioned as this measure was it failed to content the new freemen. Many of them were unable to appreciate the difference between communal ownership and communal use. Their freedom seemed to mean little in practice since they were still not permitted to leave the village in which they lived, and were in fact bound to the *mir* as closely as they had formerly been bound to the landowner. Periodical re-allocation meant that every time the land was redistributed the individual family received less and less yet its contribution to the compensation fund for the dispossessed landowners remained the same. As time passed the peasant found himself paying to the *mir* as much as he had ever done to the landlord while enjoying the use of less and less land. Yearly the peasant approached nearer to starvation level.

Yet in spite of its disadvantages the Edict of Emancipation was a step forward. Something had been done to curb the tyrannical oppression of the peasants by the nobility.

During the years 1864 to 1867 great strides were made in the re-organization of local government. In each local administrative district a representative body known as the *Zemstvo* was elected by the landowners and the villagers. In turn these bodies elected from among themselves representatives to a provincial *zemstvo* The function of these representative institutions was, it is true, strictly limited. They were intended merely to be the agencies through which the decisions affecting their province or district issued by the imperial government were put into execution; they were not able to initiate new developments or suggest reforms. Yet the *zemstvo*. movement is important for the way in which it served to educate the Russian villager in politics and in social co-operation.

Another aspect of Russian life which felt the reforming hand of Alexander II was the legal system. Judges, formerly removable at any time by the will of the Tsar, now held office for life, subject only to good conduct in professional and public life. Secret trial gave place to public trial and an additional guarantee of the fairness of procedure and verdict was the introduction into the Russian legal system of a jury for the trial of criminal cases.

Abandonment of Liberalism, 1867

To liberal opinion in Russia the later years of Alexander II were a great disappointment. After 1867 the enforcement of the great reforms of the earlier years became half-hearted. The secret police once more became the nightmare of Russian life and when the *zemstvos* suggested further reforms and an extension of their own powers they met with a stern imperial rebuke.

Several factors combined to produce this change in Alexander's attitude. He was personally affronted to find the peasants more alive to their difficulties under the Edict of Emancipation than to the benefits it conferred upon them. In fact both the Tsar and his subjects had underestimated the disturbance which radical reform was bound to create until the innovations had been assimilated. Moreover, the upper classes made it their business to emphasize difficulties inherent in the measures introduced in the hope that abandonment of them on grounds of impracticability would result.

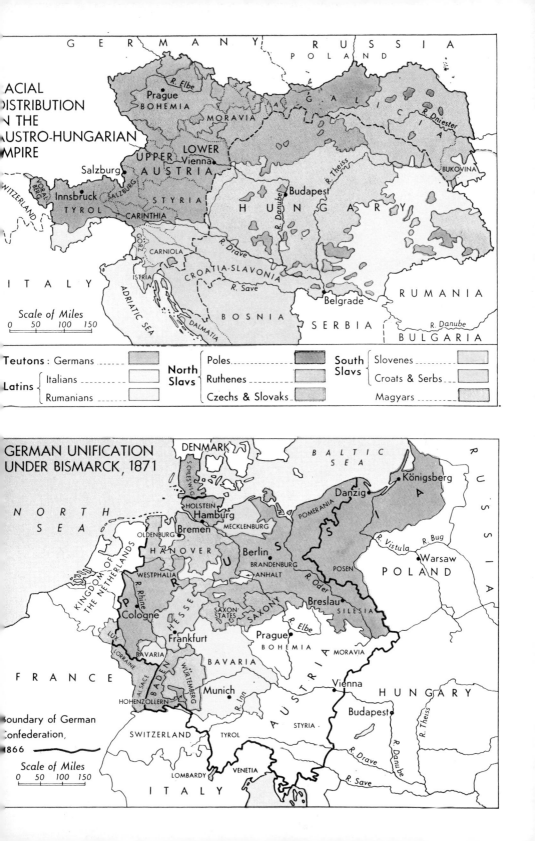

RACIAL DISTRIBUTION IN THE AUSTRO-HUNGARIAN EMPIRE

GERMANY
RUSSIA
POLAND
G A L I C I A

R. Elbe
Prague
BOHEMIA
MORAVIA

R. Dniester

BUKOVINA

UPPER
LOWER
Salzburg
AUSTRIA
Vienna
R. Theiss

Innsbruck
VORARLBERG
SWITZERLAND
SALZBURG
STYRIA
Budapest
H U N G A R Y

TYROL
CARINTHIA
R. Danube

GORZ
CARNIOLA
R. Drave

ITALY
ISTRIA
CROATIA-SLAVONIA
R. Save
RUMANIA

ADRIATIC SEA
DALMATIA
BOSNIA
Belgrade
SERBIA
R. Danube

Scale of Miles
0   50   100 150

BULGARIA

Teutons:	Germans		**North Slavs**	Poles		**South Slavs**	Slovenes	
Latins	Italians			Ruthenes			Croats & Serbs	
	Rumanians			Czechs & Slovaks			Magyars	

GERMAN UNIFICATION UNDER BISMARCK, 1871

DENMARK
BALTIC SEA
RUSSIA

S. SCHLESWIG
HOLSTEIN
Hamburg
Bremen
MECKLENBURG
POMERANIA
Danzig
Königsberg
P R U S S I A

NORTH SEA

OLDENBURG
HANOVER
Berlin
BRANDENBURG
ANHALT
R. Vistula
R. Bug

KINGDOM OF THE NETHERLANDS
WESTPHALIA
P R U S S I A
R. Oder
POSEN
Warsaw
POLAND

R. Rhine
HESSE
Cologne
SAXON STATES
SAXONY
Breslau
SILESIA

Frankfurt
R. Elbe
Prague
BOHEMIA
MORAVIA

FRANCE
LUX
LORRAINE
BAVARIA
WÜRTEMBERG
BADEN
Munich
R. Inn
A U S T R I A
Vienna
H U N G A R Y
Budapest
R. Theiss

ALSACE
HOHENZOLLERN
SWITZERLAND
TYROL
STYRIA
R. Drave
R. Danube

LOMBARDY
VENETIA
R. Save
ITALY

Boundary of German Confederation, 1866

Scale of Miles
0   50   100 150

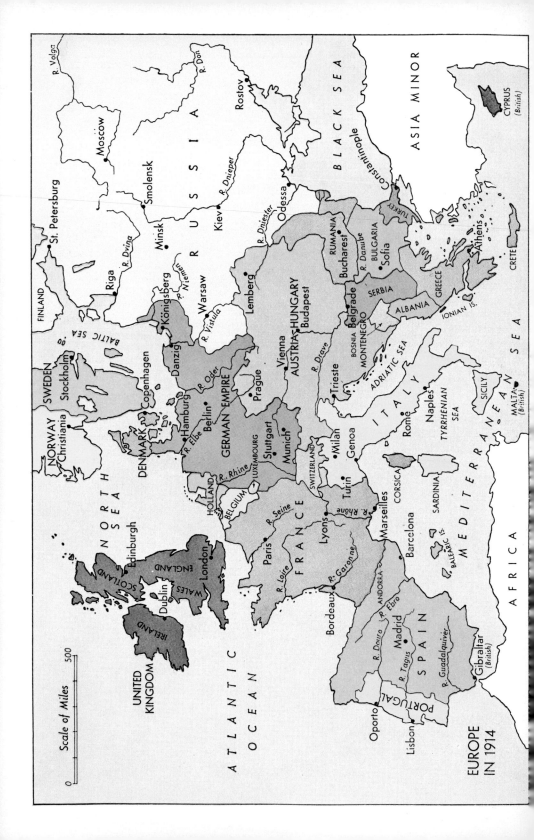

EUROPE
IN 1914

These factors were reinforced by the Polish revolt of 1863 and attempts on the life of the Tsar. Alexander resolved to make no further efforts on behalf of subjects who could not apparently appreciate the efforts already made.

The disappointment created by Alexander's change of policy led to the rise of a new form of subversive political activity known as nihilism. It was an extreme denial of the need for any kind of authority, political, religious or economic, and carried to its logical conclusion would have reduced any corporate organization to chaos.

Nihilist methods were in keeping with their destructive beliefs. Propaganda among the peasants by argument and conversation ultimately gave place to organized violence and assassination. It was this fate which finally overtook Alexander II himself in 1881.

Alexander III, 1881-94

The new Tsar, Alexander III, alarmed by the untimely death of his predecessor, intensified all the reactionary policies of the government. The functions of the *zemstvos* were curtailed; the numbers of the secret police were considerably increased in a determined effort to destroy nihilism; a frightful era of Jewish persecution followed upon the discovery that many nihilists were Jews; intellectual freedom of all kinds again disappeared and a rigorous attempt was made to turn all the subject minority groups of the empire into good Russians.

Against the rigorous reactionary policy of Alexander III must be set the consideration he displayed for the advancement of the material progress of his country. He relieved the peasants from the necessity of residing in a particular village. Consequent shift of population led to the extension of the area of land under cultivation. He also increased the industrial development of Russia by encouraging the exploitation of her rich mineral resources so that she was no longer dependent in this respect upon the west, through seeking the investment of foreign capital in new Russian enterprises such as railways.

While this industrialization of Russia was an enrichment of the country's economy and did much to raise her to the status of other European powers, it brought with it less desirable consequences. The employers reaped the benefits of an expanding volume of foreign trade and a flourishing iron and steel industry; but for the employed there was the usual lot of long hours, low wages and an unhealthy life in badly planned and hastily built cities. All this meant a discontented working class who inevitably blamed the government for their sufferings. In Russia therefore, as in Britain, France and Germany, socialism appeared.

In another way too, the industrialization of Russia created opposition to the government. It led to the rise of a new social group—a prosperous

St. Petersburg: people running to the spot where Tsar Alexander was shot.

bourgeoisie. Such a middle class, wealthy and intelligent, was not likely to tolerate indefinitely a political system which excluded it from all political power. The middle classes would never be socialists but they did provide a stiffening of the ranks of liberalism.

Nicholas II and the First Russian Revolution

When Nicholas II succeeded Alexander III in 1894 the growing forces of socialism and liberalism looked for a relaxation of the policy of oppressive reaction. They were disappointed. There ensued in fact a further tightening of the anti-liberal screw. Professors as well as students in the universities found themselves regarded with suspicion. Newspapers were more closely scrutinized than ever for signs of an anti-government point of view and liable to suppression if such a view was detected. Minority groups had to endure re-doubled efforts to turn them into good Russians. Finland is a particularly striking example of this. Its long-enjoyed constitution was virtually abolished; its army was incorporated with that of Russia proper; and its administrative services were invaded by numerous Russians who displaced Finns.

Yet in spite of all this repression, progressive forces and parties survived. The vanguard of socialism was its "intellectuals"; its rank-and-file, the landless discontented factory workers. United in a belief in class warfare, the need to destroy capitalism and the right of the workers to control the state, the Russian socialist movement was yet divided as to the means by which to achieve these objectives. A minority—the Mensheviks—were prepared to work patiently within the limits allowed by law; the majority —the Bolsheviks—advocated revolutionary, anarchist and subversive activities.

Apart from socialism another stimulus to reform was provided by middle class liberalism. This influence worked chiefly through the *zemstvos* which

354

were untiring in their petitions for the introduction of constitutional government. The opposition with which their petitions was met by the central government merely strengthened their co-operation for mutual protection and safety.

In the early years of the twentieth century the deep-seated discontent found open expression. In 1905, in sympathy with the murder of Plehve, a reactionary minister, a monster procession of workers on strike marched on the Winter Palace at St. Petersburg. This demonstration was badly handled by the government. Tsar Nicholas II was led to think that an attack on himself rather than his ministers was intended, and he authorized his troops to fire on the demonstrators. The resulting massacre destroyed the faith of the people in the Tsar as "Father of the Russians."

General insurrection followed this incident. The nobility and government officials came in for special attention. Their houses were wrecked and they themselves often enough killed. The Tsar's brother was one victim and at least one attempt was made on the life of the Tsar himself. When military defeat by Japan offended Russian national self-respect and revealed further incompetence on the part of the administration, the government thought it time to make some concessions.

The Dumas

The concessions took the form of permission for the meeting of a national representative assembly. This, the first *Duma*, met in 1906, but as the Tsar was not prepared to share his sovereignty in any way, the position reached a deadlock and the first *Duma* was dissolved. The second, in 1907, met a similar fate.

The third *Duma* which sat from 1907 to 1912, having been elected on a franchise restricted to landowners, was more amenable to the will of the

Tsar Nicholas receives a deputation of workers after the 1905 massacre.

Rasputin (second from left) surrounded by his "court."

crown, but it accomplished more. The payments still due from the peasants under the Edict of Emancipation were cancelled; individual peasant ownership of land in the *mir* was substituted for communal ownership; national defence was reorganized; further reform of local administration was effected and some measures of state socialism instituted.

On the whole, the work of the *Dumas*, sometimes called the "First Russian Revolution", must be counted a failure. All the reforms of the third *Duma* failed to touch the essential Russian problem, namely the continuance of a feudal, corrupt aristocracy dominating the court and monopolizing political power. The good which the *Duma* accomplished was indirect; it taught the middle-classes the rudiments of political science and it strengthened the conviction of the Bolsheviks that only a violent revolution would ever enable them to achieve the reorganization of society and politics on which their minds were set.

Meanwhile, Nicholas II, dominated in his later years by an ignorant, rascally peasant of strange compelling personality, the infamous Rasputin, lost all touch with the minds and aspirations of his subjects. It is reasonable as well as charitable to suppose that he did not know the full extent or nature of the corrupt and evil administration which went on in his name, but ignorance does not absolve him from all responsibility.

QUESTIONS

1. What reforms did Alexander II introduce into Russia and how far were they successful?

2. Describe the experiment of *Dumas* under Nicholas II, and explain why they failed.

CHAPTER 41

MAJOR WESTERN POWERS IN THE LATER NINETEENTH CENTURY

THE revolutions of 1848-9 in the Austro-Hungarian Empire had shown that such a patchwork of nationalities could not be held together indefinitely. The problem was to find a form of constitution which would satisfy the aspirations of the national and liberal minorities and yet avoid the dissolution of the Empire as a whole.

In the hope of harmonizing the conflicting interests, the Emperor Francis Joseph in 1860 gathered together representatives from all parts of the empire to consider the problem, but the conference did no more than restate the problem. Austro-German representatives showed a marked preference for a strong central government and the minority nationals pressed strongly for a loose federation, giving only limited powers to the central authority.

Experiments in Austria

The Emperor tried each of these alternatives in turn. That of the minorities was given its chance first. Provincial and central councils to control the financial policy of the Empire were set up and by the October diploma of 1860 their functions were extended to include a large degree of self-government for the provinces.

The experiment failed as a result of Hungarian non-co-operation. Nothing short of complete independence save for allegiance to a common crown would satisfy Hungarian opinion. The Emperor's consequent attempt to try out the centralist scheme in 1861 by creating an Imperial Diet and restricting the self-government of the provinces only intensified Hungarian discontent.

With both solutions thus shown to be impracticable the position was one of stalemate and as such it remained until 1867.

After his defeat in the Austro-Prussian war of 1866, Francis Joseph tried again, concentrating on what he thought to be the most serious danger—Magyar discontent in Hungary. He sought to please not all the minorities in the Empire but the largest of them, the Hungarians. He invited the co-operation of their leader, Deak, and together they agreed on a scheme of government which made Hungary the Imperial co-partner of Austria.

This scheme virtually divided the empire into two parts, one under Austrian and the other under Hungarian supremacy. Matters in which a common policy were essential were reserved to common ministries responsible to a cumbrously constituted central Diet. This consisted of a "delegation" from Austria and another from Hungary, each of which sat separately, both of which assembled alternately in Vienna and Budapest. Francis Joseph was henceforward Emperor of Austria and King of Hungary. Thus was the Dual Monarchy created.

Cumbrous though this constitution, known as the *Ausgleich*, was, it kept the Austro-Hungarian Empire together until the Emperor Karl abdicated in 1918. Yet it was only a settlement of the relations of Austria and Hungary, doing nothing to satisfy the ambitions of other nationalities within the Empire. War in 1914 exposed its inadequacy.

Germany After 1871

Having established the German Empire in 1871 Bismarck's problem thereafter was to ensure Prussian supremacy while avoiding undue offence to the conquered states. Equally he had to exalt the House of Hohenzollern while saving the faces and dignities of other ruling families.

The supremacy of the House of Hohenzollern having already been asserted by conferring upon the King of Prussia the title of Emperor of Germany, it was now confirmed by according him the widest powers. He alone appointed imperial ministers, decided issues of peace or war and commanded the armed forces raised from the federated states.

The supremacy of Prussia in Germany was assured by making state representation in the imperial legislative chambers dependent upon size and population. Prussia being the largest and most populous state had a greater number of representatives in both the *Bundesrat* and the *Reichstag* than any other single state. Moreover, the Prussian members of the *Bundesrat* had the right of veto on all proposals affecting the armed forces or on amendments to the Constitution.

The *Bundesrat*, composed of delegates chosen by the rulers of the German states, had the greater powers; but the *Reichstag*, elected representatives of the German people, had the important right of taking decisions concerning new, as distinct from existing, financial proposals.

The constitution did much to safeguard Bismarck's personal position, and as Chancellor he continued to control German affairs for the next twenty years.

Bismarck's Problems

Yet it would be wrong to suppose that Bismarck found everything plain sailing after 1871. The liberals in the imperial *Reichstag* continued to oppose his military policy, and every possible effort had to be made therefore to ensure the presence in the *Reichstag* of an effective pro-government majority. In the *Bundesrat* the south German states showed their dislike of Bismarck's efforts to "Prussianize" Germany and the Chancellor had to rely upon the support of the north German states to secure approval of his policies.

In addition, the Roman Catholic Church eyed with suspicion the political ascendancy in Germany of Protestant Prussia. This hostile suspicion was expressed by the formation of a Catholic party, known as the Centre, and through a national newspaper, the *Germania*. As the influence of the party and the newspaper grew, the Chancellor realized that this opposition must either be placated or suppressed. What he had to find was a suitable opportunity.

While awaiting this opportunity, Bismarck could count on the support of William I, who lived until 1888, and on the National Liberals, commercial magnates for the most part to whom a standing army needing clothing and equipment was good business. On his side also stood the thoroughly conservative Junkers, with militaristic and monarchical sympathies. Bismarck ultimately sacrificed the support of the National Liberals in the interests of the Junkers, with whom by origin he was most closely identified.

Dissension within the Roman Catholic Church in Germany afforded Bismarck the first opportunity for an attack on his opponents. In 1870 the Vatican Council reasserted the doctrine of the infallibility of the Pope when pronouncing on matters of faith and morals. Some German professors and students of theology refused to accept this ruling. Excommunicated by the Pope and expelled from all official Roman Catholic teaching posts, they formed a separate body, known as the Old Catholic party, and turned to the government for assistance. Bismarck chose to sympathize with the Old Catholic party and use it as an excuse for an attack upon the Church in Germany.

The Kulturkampf

Bismarck first sought to weaken the Church's hold on the rising generation. Schools were made subject to inspection by laymen; clergy could no longer occupy teaching posts and the Jesuits were expelled from the country. To weaken another stronghold of religion, the family, civil marriage was introduced.

More drastic still were the May Laws passed in Prussia between 1873 and 1875. Candidates for the priesthood had henceforth to take a three-year course of secular study in addition to their theological training. All appointments within the Church were subject to state approval and independent colleges maintained by the Church were to be opened to state inspection. Roman Catholic priests were forbidden to publish any sentence of excommunication and all the religious orders were dissolved.

359

To these attacks the Pope replied by declaring the May Laws invalid and by encouraging the clergy to defy them. Those who did so were imprisoned —and soon gained considerable public sympathy as martyrs for conscience's sake.

The end of the struggle came about, however, through other factors. Bismarck found another enemy advancing upon him; this was the socialist movement. He had no desire to fight a war on two fronts and he therefore ceased to press his attack on the Church so as to be free to defend himself against socialism.

His disengagement from the quarrel with the Church was made easier by the accession of a new Pope, Leo XIII, a more accommodating character than Pius IX had been. Diplomatic relations were resumed between the Vatican and Germany; quietly the May Laws ceased to be enforced; and all that Bismarck finally had to show for the conflict was state inspection of all schools and the custom of civil marriage.

Karl Marx and the Rise of Socialism

The origin of the rising tide of socialism in Germany was to be found in the writings of a German national of Jewish extraction, Karl Marx. In 1842 he had fled Germany but returned in 1847 and published his *Communist Manifesto*. During his second and permanent exile, first in Paris and then in London, he wrote and published his major work, *Das Kapital*. Marx's theory was that historical development is determined purely by economic factors; that the economic system we know as private enterprise, or capitalism, is an unsatisfactory temporary phase of human society; that as such its collapse is ultimately inevitable; and this being so, its victims everywhere should combine to hasten its disappearance and its replacement by a more just and equitable organization of society wherein all will work for the common good. Socialist parties based upon Marxist teaching, often with modifications from the similar theories of other writers such as Louis Blanc, Lassale and Engels, were established in many European countries.

Economic conditions in Germany after 1870 favoured the growth of socialism. While the period was one of prosperity for the commercial magnates of the National Liberal Party, it was one of hardship for their employees. Hence in 1875 there appeared the Social Democratic Party advocating industrial and social reform in its popular newspaper *Vorwärts*. It was the ever increasing number of seats gained in the *Reichstag* by this party which made it necessary for Bismarck to come to terms with the Catholic Centre group if his legislation was to survive the ordeal of discussion in the Imperial Legislature.

Bismarck feared socialism, not merely because of its demand for reform but because it opposed the military and imperial policy in which he fervently believed. According to the socialists, militarism and imperialism were two of the props on which the decadent capitalist organization of society rested.

In 1878 the chancellor made a pretext of two attempts on the life of the Emperor for an all-out direct attack on socialism, though neither of these attempts was socialist-inspired. Laws forbidding the meetings, the societies, and the publications associated with socialism were forced through the legislature. Summary powers for the enforcement of these laws were conferred upon the police. Then a more subtle attack was mounted. Since to popularize their views the socialists exploited the economic distress of the workers, Bismarck, to counteract such propaganda, sought to remedy the distress. In 1883

William II drops "the old pilot," Bismarck.

a scheme of state insurance for workers against sickness was established. The next year the scheme was extended to provide cover against accidents and finally in 1889 old age pensions were introduced. This system of state welfare remedied some of the worst social evils of Germany and later both France and Great Britain paid Bismarck the compliment of imitating his example, but not for some years.

Fall of Bismarck

When the aged William I died in 1888, he was succeeded by his son Frederick III, already at his accession a dying man. The same year thus brought to the throne William II, a young man of strange and ill-balanced temperament. With the arrogant ignorance of youth and inexperience, he looked upon Bismarck as a relic of the past whose services were no longer needed now that Germany had such a capable emperor as himself.

Differences of policy soon arose between the two men. The Emperor was willing to pose as the patron of socialism; Bismarck thought the experiment dangerous and said so. In foreign affairs Bismarck was anxious to preserve Russian friendship; William II was convinced it could be dispensed with safely. This was the vital point at issue in 1890.

Bismarck thought he knew the way to secure his own end; he threatened to resign. It was a card he had played often enough in the days of William I and it had never failed to win the trick. This time it was trumped. When his resignation was accepted, Bismarck in bewildered surprise sought to change his mind, only to be refused to be allowed to do so. The old "pilot was dropped" and henceforth could only watch from retirement the incompetence of those who replaced him at the helm of the German ship of state.

Establishment of the Third French Republic

Having seen what Bismarck built on the victory over France of 1871, we must now retrace our steps and see what France made of her defeat.

News of the disaster at Sedan in 1871 encouraged the republican party in Paris to seize power and establish a provisional government. An armistice was first arranged with Germany and elections were then held.

The elections somewhat surprisingly produced an Assembly in which the monarchists had a majority. Wisely this majority made no attempt to overthrow the Republic, leaving it to incur the unpopularity of what was bound to be a humiliating settlement with Germany.

The Commune

The citizens of Paris were less discreet. Disliking the government, they elected a general council as a rival authority. This council, known as the *Commune*, assumed the administration of the capital and the surrounding district and called upon other municipalities to act locally in similar fashion.

As a result of this threat to national unity, government troops laid siege to the capital and for two months the city held out. Constant bombardment, however, and the privations of hunger eventually had their effect; yet when at last government troops entered the city some days of street fighting followed before the National Assembly was in complete control of the situation.

Recovery and Reconstruction

Its authority thus re-established, the government under the presidency of Thiers directed all its energy to paying off the war indemnity and so bringing the occupation of the country by the victorious Germans to an end. By this single-mindedness of purpose France accomplished in three years what Germany and the world had expected would take a generation. By 1873 two national loans had been raised and the proceeds had discharged the war indemnity. Germany reluctantly withdrew her army of occupation. Resolved never to be at the mercy of her neighbours again, France overhauled her military organization and increased her strength by adopting the principle of conscription. By 1873 only one major problem remained: what should be the form of the future constitution of France? With the monarchists divided in their support for three rival candidates for the throne, Thiers favoured a republic, but as he could not secure the approval of the National Assembly, he resigned and left the task to others.

First Attempt to Overthrow the Republic

The supporters of Napoleon III's son abandoned his cause in the hopes of restoring a monarchy. But the Count of Chambord, to whom most of the monarchists gave their allegiance, insisted on substituting the white flag of the Bourbons for the tricolour, and as this was a denial of everything France had won at so much cost since 1789, the monarchical cause soon went by default.

With the collapse of the monarchical cause the task of drawing up a constitution for the Third French Republic was completed by 1875. A president was provided for, whose tenure of office was seven years, and whose power was strictly limited.

The Chamber of Deputies and the Senate formed the legislature. Senators were elected for nine-year periods by the members of local councils. The Chamber of Deputies was elected for four years by universal manhood suffrage and to this chamber was entrusted the control of national finance. The executive government was made responsible to the legislature though ministers were formally invited to take office by the president. In 1884 there was an addition to this constitution, declaring that no revision should ever involve the abolition of the Republic.

Second Attempt to Overthrow the Republic: the Boulanger Crisis

It took a second World War in the twentieth century to destroy the Third French Republic, but during its life-time it was attacked by enemies both within and without.

In 1886 the danger came from within. The instability of the early ministries disturbed public confidence. Sensing this, General Boulanger, Minister for War and a very popular figure in the army, gathered round him a strange group of anti-republican malcontents and denounced the incompetence and corruption of parliamentary government. He talked of summoning a national convention and of preparing for a war of revenge on Germany.

He was too slow to take advantage of the popularity he at first enjoyed. When the tide of public opinion showed signs of turning, the government charged Boulanger with conspiracy against the security of the State. At this he lost his nerve, fled to Brussels and there committed suicide in 1889. The Third Republic had survived its second attack.

Third Attack: the Panama Scandals, 1892

Yet four years later the Republic was in trouble again. A large proportion of the French investing public had put up money for a scheme, sponsored by De Lesseps, the engineer of the Suez Canal, for the construction of a Panama Canal. Through a combination of mismanagement and technical difficulties the scheme proved impracticable and had to be abandoned. The money invested was lost. Investigation was demanded.

The consequent enquiry revealed that many deputies and senators had lent their political influence to the scheme only because they had been bribed to do so. This scandal stirred into new life all the anti-republican parties, but once more the affair blew over and the Republic survived.

Fourth Attack: the Dreyfus Case, 1894-1906

By far the most serious threat to the Third Republic began in 1894 when a Jewish officer, Captain Dreyfus, was tried and condemned on a charge of

General Boulanger at work in his study.

selling military secrets to a potential enemy power. Throughout his trial and imprisonment Dreyfus protested his innocence. In 1896 it was publicly alleged that the evidence against him at his trial had been forged.

Years of controversy followed. Against Dreyfus were the forces of clericalism, monarchism and militarism, ready to believe the worst of this man because he was a Jew and because the honour of the army was to them more important than the wrongful conviction and suffering of a single individual. In defence of the condemned man were the forces of liberalism, republicanism and anti-clericalism for which men of letters were the spokesmen. Emile Zola's book *J'Accuse* was a potent agent in focusing attention on the case. The pro-Dreyfus party claimed that justice was a vital principle and they alleged that Dreyfus was being unjustly maligned to cover the crime of a non-Jewish officer, Esterhazy. Even when Esterhazy in 1899 was driven to a confession of his guilt, Dreyfus, on a retrial, was still condemned, though pardoned immediately afterwards. Not until the case was again reviewed in 1906 was Dreyfus declared innocent, re-admitted to the army, promoted and decorated with the Legion of Honour.

The Dreyfus case was of considerable importance. In the course of it the army tried hard to dictate to the government. The ultimate vindication of Dreyfus was thus a vital victory of the civil authority over the army. The long crisis also revived the sense of national unity. Socialists and republicans realized as they co-operated in defence of Dreyfus that loyalty to the nation must in the last resort transcend loyalty to party. Moreover, faith in parliamentary government, shaken by the Panama scandal, was rekindled in the effort to save the Republic from surrender to its military opponents.

State versus Church

The Church had unhappily taken an anti-Dreyfus line in the controversy of 1894-1906. Taking advantage of the growing atheism in France, the State now attacked the Church.

Use was made of an old law which prohibited the association of more than twelve persons for any common purpose. The government now legalized all associations except those connected with religion. Religious bodies required express individual sanction before they could enjoy legal protection. Such sanction was not readily forthcoming and the State further discountenanced the educational activities of the religious denominations.

At this point diplomatic relations with the Vatican were broken off and in 1905 the gulf was widened by the Law of Separation. This enactment destroyed the Concordat made with the papacy by Napoleon I and denied state recognition of any denomination as the official religion of France. Churches, chapels and cathedrals all became the property of the State. The Protestant denominations almost immediately accepted defeat and complied

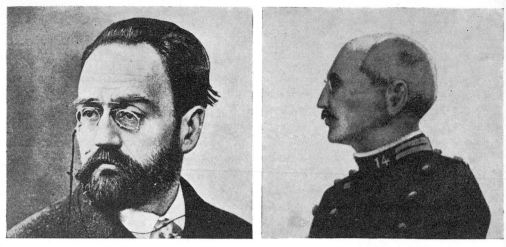

Emile Zola.   *Captain Dreyfus.*

with the law but it was not until 1907 that the state and the Roman Communion reached a compromise whereby Roman Catholic priests, as individuals, were allowed to negotiate for the use of their former buildings.

Socialism in France

The politicians who had led the attack on the Church were Waldeck-Rousseau and Aristide Briand. They had had the support in the legislature of a powerful socialist bloc for socialism grew in France as elsewhere during the last years of the nineteenth century.

The combination of Louis Blanc's doctrine of the right to work or maintenance with the teachings of Karl Marx had produced a particular brand of socialism in France known as Syndicalism. Its aim was the control of the means of production by "syndicates" or groups of the workers employed in each industry. Its methods were industrial wrecking and subversive political activity.

The socialists were for a long time ineffective because of their own internal quarrels. An indirect result of the growth of socialism, in France as in Germany, was the effort made by the State to remedy some of the grievances of the people. In 1884 trade unions were legalized; in 1906 a workman's compensation act was passed, and in 1910 a scheme of old age pensions was introduced. It was thus over a France moving like the rest of Europe into a new way of life, that the war clouds of 1914 gathered.

QUESTIONS

1. Describe the main features of Bismarck's domestic policy between the years 1878 and 1890.
2. Describe any two crises which threatened to destroy the stability of the Third French Republic between 1875 and 1914.

CHAPTER 42

EXPANSION OF EUROPE AND THE FAR EASTERN QUESTION

BEFORE we watch the destruction of much of the old Europe by the bursting war clouds of 1914, one other aspect of nineteenth-century history needs to be examined. That is the international tensions created by the expansion of some of the major powers within, but mainly without, the European continent.

For the greater part of the nineteenth century the desire for colonial possessions was by no means the overmastering political factor it had been in the previous century. History seemed to teach that dependent possessions were inevitably lost either by foreign conquest or by the assertion of independence. Thus Russia's expansionist ambitions found an outlet in Europe at the expense of Poland, rather than overseas. The gains she made in this direction by 1795 were temporarily lost during Napoleon I's victorious career, but recovered at the Congress of Vienna of 1815. Nor did the Polish rebellions of 1830 and 1863 succeed in throwing off the chains of Russian domination.

Russia had also before 1878 extended her power to the borders of Turkey-in-Europe, Persia, Afghanistan, China and Japan; while her efforts to expand in the Balkans at the expense of Turkey were the pivot of the Near Eastern Question.

Thus, colonial enterprise in the nineteenth century, prior to 1878, was left largely to France and Great Britain.

French Expansion Overseas, 1815-78

French expansionist aims, severely checked by her eighteenth-century losses to Britain, revived during the reign of Charles X when a determined attempt was made to conquer Algiers, an attempt which was only finally successful in 1847. Though Napoleon III blundered badly in Mexico, he formally annexed Algiers and put new life into the older French colonies on the west coast of Africa. His efforts to establish French influence in Egypt brought him to the brink of war with Britain, though Britain did, in fact, stand aside while French capital and a French engineer cut the Suez Canal in 1869. In the Far East France under Napoleon III was one of the European powers which tried to batter down the doors of Chinese self-sufficient isolation.

In general, French colonial acquisitions up to 1878 were made in tropical or sub-tropical lands. These offered little scope for the permanent settlement of large numbers of white people, but held commercial possibilities if they could be developed by native labour under white organization.

European Expansion After 1878

After 1878, when it seemed to be apparent that Britain's newer colonies were not going to follow the example of America, interest in the possibilities of colonial possessions revived in Europe. Colonies offered new markets and new sources of materials for the growing European industries, and colonial troops might be of service to the mother country if she were at war.

The most desirable regions of the world had already been claimed or annexed; those remaining were often either climatically unsuited to the white man or already had a teeming native population. Moreover, after 1878 Spain, Portugal, Holland, France and Britain were no longer the sole competing colonial powers; Italy and Germany claimed a place in the sun. These "newer" nations developed a sense of grievance when they found the older colonial powers not merely unwilling to share what they already possessed but still eager to add to their spheres of influence overseas.

It is not therefore surprising that colonial matters embittered international relationships in the later nineteenth century, led to a rude battering at the unwilling doors of China and Japan and produced a most undignified "scramble" for Africa.

By 1878 France, as we have seen, had already secured a footing in North Africa. Britain and the Dutch Boers were well entrenched in the south and both these powers, as well as Portugal, had coastal settlements in the east and west. Tunis and Tripoli were Turkish possessions, while Egypt was still a Turkish tributary province, though enjoying a large measure of freedom.

A succession of explorers, many of them British, such as Livingstone and Stanley, opened up the interior of Africa by following the course of rivers like the Nile, the Congo, the Niger and the Zambesi. Western knowledge of these parts was subsequently increased by the activities of missionaries sent out by Christian denominations of all kinds.

The "Scramble" for Africa

Belgium began the Europeanization of hitherto unknown Africa when in 1879 Leopold II summoned at Brussels an international conference to consider the possibility of opening up the interior of the "dark continent" to European trade and commerce. The conference led to the establishment of the International African Association which embarked upon the development

costumes and furniture of the First Empire

coach

warship

Napoleon's eagle,
emblem of the
period

Rosetta stone, found
by the French

NAPOLEONIC PERIOD IN FRANCE

Napoleon as a cadet, 1785

Egyptian campaign, 1798

Napoleon as consul, 1802

Napoleon crowns himself Emperor, 1805

retreat from Moscow, 1812

defeat of French at Waterloo, 1815

RISE AND FALL OF NAPOLEON BONAPARTE

of the Congo. Gradually the Association lost its international character and the Congo came to be a sphere of almost exclusively Belgian interest.

Other nations turned their attentions to Africa and in the hope of avoiding a dangerous conflict of interests another conference met in Berlin in 1884. Here the European powers staked out their claims with a reasonable degree of clarity and undertook to keep each other informed of any growth of their power within the defined regions. Such subsequent growth was not always achieved without the provocation of delicate international crises.

One such crisis produced the Conference of Algeciras in 1906. France had declared her interest in Morocco in 1904 and in 1906 she attempted to force on the Sultan a series of reforms designed to create a more efficient administration of the territory. The German Emperor, William II, took exception to this. He visited Tangier and publicly pledged German support for the independence of the Sultan of Morocco. He also demanded an international conference to discuss the whole issue.

For some weeks Europe trembled on the brink of war. Then America persuaded France to accept the idea of a conference. It met at Algeciras and proved a complete diplomatic triumph for France. While Moroccan independence was affirmed, the Sultan was required to admit a Franco-Spanish force for police purposes. Thus France, who had acquired Tunis at the expense of Turkey in 1882, was now given a firm footing in Morocco. Meanwhile, she had advanced southward over the Sahara to Senegal; and Madagascar had become a French island in 1896.

The Agadir Incident, 1909

Moroccan affairs were the cause of another crisis in 1909. The Sultan had been deposed in 1908 but his successor was unable completely to restore order. In response to his request a French expeditionary force was despatched to protect him in his capital of Fez. Again the German Emperor intervened, sending a gunboat to Agadir, nominally to protect German residents, but in fact in the hope of counteracting French influence by a permanent annexation of this Moroccan port.

The weight of international opinion was on the side of France, and the Kaiser had to be content with a compromise by which he received a small strip of land from France in the French Congo in return for the recognition of French predominance in Morocco.

By 1914, however, German power in Africa was by no means inconsiderable. She held in all the two provinces known as German South-West Africa and German South-East Africa as well as the Cameroons and Togoland.

By 1914 the worst of the "scramble" for Africa was over. British sovereignty reached from the Cape to Cairo, save for German East Africa, and along the west coast she held Gambia, Sierra Leone, the Gold Coast and Nigeria.

With France as a very minor sharer, Belgium was in firm possession of the Congo, in spite of the fact that in the early days of her administration she exploited the province and its people shamefully. Angola and Mozambique were administered by Portugal, while Spain had established herself on the north-west coast and on a strip of territory facing Gibraltar.

The most disappointed of the European powers in Africa was Italy. While she had made good her hold on Eritrea, she had to share Somaliland with France and Britain; and though Tripoli and Cyrenacia were hers, she failed to assert her sovereignty in Abyssinia.

Thus, with Italy disappointed and Germany smarting over two rebuffs, it was certain that the African question was by no means settled and there was one part of that vast continent, namely Egypt, where affairs were so complicated that they merit particular attention.

Egypt

When Egypt exchanged the administration of Turkey for that of Mehemet Ali, her profit was small. Mehemet's later ambitions led him into military and other enterprises which severely strained Egyptian financial resources.

To save the financial situation, the ruler, or Khedive, in 1875 offered for sale his shares in the Suez Canal. The British prime minister Disraeli, realizing the strategic importance of the canal as a short route to India, stepped in and bought the shares on behalf of Britain.

Britain now took a keen interest in Egyptian affairs. When in 1876 Egypt repudiated her foreign debts, Britain and France as two of the largest creditors worked out a scheme whereby they undertook joint supervision of Egyptian finance, a scheme which became known as Dual Control.

Within four years the scheme broke down. Mutual distrust on the part of France and Britain, combined with Egyptian opposition to foreign administration, had created difficulties from the beginning. In 1882 France refused to co-operate in the suppression of the revolt of Arabi Pasha. Britain successfully undertook the task alone and secured sole control of Egyptian affairs.

This was not to be the limit of British influence in Africa. In 1883 a fanatical Arab appeared in the Sudan, declaring himself to be the Mahdi, the prophet for whose coming the Moslems had been as expectant as had the Jews for the Messiah. The movement led by the Mahdi took on a military character and soon a "holy war" of incredible ferocity was being waged on all unbelievers and particularly on the Christian "infidels." Britain decided to withdraw all Europeans from the Sudan and entrusted this task to General Gordon and a small expeditionary force.

Gordon exceeded his terms of reference and tried to suppress the revolt. He and his troops found themselves besieged in Khartoum and before relief could arrive they were massacred. For the time being Britain appeared to accept defeat, but the Mahdist administration of the Sudan proved so harsh that in 1895 Lord (later Earl) Kitchener was sent out to suppress this sect. It proved to be a five-year task, but it was successfully accomplished and when fourteen years later Egypt became a British protectorate, the Sudan was included. It was during this war that Kitchener had to go to Fashoda (1898) to eject a French major who had set up the French flag.

The Far Eastern Question: Europe and China

Europe in the nineteenth century was also forcing her way into China and Japan, but this was a harder task since in these nations she encountered civilizations in many ways older and more cultured than her own if not militarily so powerful.

China had a philosophy and way of life centuries old, which she did not wish to change. Progress was neither a term understood nor an ideal pursued. The Chinese did not look upon themselves as a backward people desperately needing the mechanical skill or intellectual stimulus of the West. On the contrary, they regarded the West, if at all, with a condescension bordering on contempt. China's foreign policy was one of self-sufficient isolation and no bribes would induce her voluntarily to abandon it.

Opium was the discreditable means by which British traders in 1773 secured a footing in China; this doubtful offering was the one most readily accepted by the Chinese people. Their government was determined to put an end to it, but British traders refused to be discouraged.

The result of this British persistence was war. British forces captured Shanghai and Hong Kong and threatened Peking and Nanking. The Chinese, for long unaccustomed to war and a peace-loving nation, accepted defeat. By the Treaty of Nanking in 1842 Hong Kong was ceded to Britain, who thus gained a naval base in the Far East, together with five ports, among them Canton and Shanghai.

Though Britain can hardly be proud of her victory, there was more at stake in the conflict than the continued opium trade. Britain wanted to see the East treat the West as an equal and at the same time secure a firm legal basis for mutual trading relations. The war was followed by trading agreements between China on the one hand and France, Norway and Sweden on the other. The first breach had been made in Chinese isolation.

Having thus stepped over the Chinese threshold, Europe tried to move in farther. China resisted and war again followed, this time with France aiding Britain. Easy victories and a highly favourable treaty for the West were the consequences. At Tientsin in 1861, it was agreed that another eleven ports should be opened to the West. China undertook to pay a war indemnity and conceded the principle of extra-territorial rights. This meant that in future, Westerners in China were not subject to Chinese law, but if they committed any offence were tried by their own nationals under their own legal code.

The ease with which China had been overcome encouraged Europe to make less justifiable demands upon her. Encroachments were quite improperly made upon her territorial sovereignty. Russia advanced towards Korea and in Manchuria, an advance which culminated in the seizure of Port Arthur. Germany seized Kia-Chan and France claimed Kwang-Chouan.

The Boxer Rising, 1900

Contact with the West led to the introduction into China of many features of the Western way of life. A postal and telegraph system was created; railways were built, especially the trans-Siberian line which ultimately linked Port Arthur with Vladivostok and made Manchuria by 1900 almost entirely Russian-controlled. European banking houses set up branches in China and Protestant and Roman Churches both sent out Christian missions to work in this area.

All these works of the "foreign devils" China disliked; equally unwelcome to her was the penetration of her country by the Japanese. Thus, when in 1900 extreme anti-foreign opinion staged a "revolt" the Chinese government secretly encouraged it. The insurrection was marked by incidents of murder, pillage and incendiarism and the climax came when foreign legations were besieged in Peking. An international expeditionary force, representative of seven European nations and led by Germany was sent to quell this Boxer Rising and succeeded in doing so. China had to pay a war indemnity. More importantly, a policy first suggested by America in 1899 was now whole-heartedly adopted. This was the policy of the "open door," which meant that the Western powers would combine to preserve their trading rights in China

Defence of the British Legation in Peking during the Boxer rising.

but would not seek to annexe any Chinese territory. Since, however, it was unlikely that Germany would oppose any action of her ally Russia in China, Britain and Japan, both fearful of the eastern march of Russia, tended to make common cause.

Europe and Japan

Japan had also been the object of Western approaches. Unlike China, however, Japan reacted very differently towards the foreigners.

In 1853 an American ship arrived with a formal request that Japan would allow some of her ports to be open to American ships as ports of call. A year was given to Japan to make up her mind. In 1854 the American ship, this time accompanied by a small war fleet, arrived to receive Japan's answer. The Japanese government, in face of superior force, conceded the request and two ports were for the future at the service of the American navy.

Japan now made a virtue of necessity and between 1854 and 1867 concluded commercial agreements with fifteen European powers, granting them territorial rights, diplomatic and consular privileges, religious toleration and freedom to their nationals to travel unhindered in Japan. Further, as the result of a revolution in 1876, a pro-Westernizing party came into power and began an intensive development of Japanese life along European lines. The "westernization" of Japan had begun.

Japan also copied the European example of demanding right of trade with her neighbour and when China refused, declared war. The result of the war was a Japanese victory and the cession by China to Japan of Port Arthur.

Russia, however, was alarmed at the strength Japan had displayed and at once intervened to deprive her of the fruits of her victory. In 1895, on Russian initiative, Germany and France joined with Russia in forcing Japan to relinquish Port Arthur. Short of declaring war upon all three of these major powers, Japan could do nothing but yield to their pressure; whereupon Russia took possession of Port Arthur.

Yet out of this humiliation Japan seized the support of Britain, who was jealous of the growth of Russian influence in the Far East. In 1902 the Anglo-Japanese alliance was signed. Britain promised to respect Japanese sovereignty and in return Japan allowed Britain full trading rights. It was also agreed that if either power were attacked by two states jointly, either signatory would come to the aid of the other. This alliance was one of the factors which brought Japan into the First World War on the side of the Allies against Germany.

Russo-Japanese War, 1904-05

The immediate result of the alliance was to encourage Japan to try to wipe out the humiliation inflicted by Russia in 1895. The bone of contention

Chinese army cadets of the early 1900s.

was Russian supremacy in Manchuria. Japan entered into negotiations with Russia for the latter's withdrawal from the disputed territory, but finding that the negotiations were making no progress, Japan broke them off in 1905 and declared war.

To her own no less than to Russia's surprise, Japan experienced little difficulty. She captured Port Arthur, inflicted a decisive military defeat upon her rival at the battle of Mukden and a naval death blow at the Battle of Tsushima, where the Russian Baltic fleet was destroyed.

Humiliated in the eyes of Europe as well as in the opinion of his subjects, the Tsar made peace, the President of the United States of America acting as intermediary. By the Treaty of Portsmouth (New Hampshire), 1905, Japan was confirmed in her possession of Port Arthur, Russia agreed to evacuate Manchuria, and to recognize Korea as a sphere of Japanese influence.

Thus the war had resulted in a decisive check to Russian ambitions in the Far East while Japan became henceforth a competitor with Europe for power in China. From such beginnings was she able in the Second World War to intervene on terms of equality with the other participating great powers.

QUESTIONS

1. Show how the "scramble" for Africa affected the relations between the great powers between 1870 and 1914.
2. Compare the attitudes of China and Japan towards the West in the nineteenth century.

CHAPTER 43

INTERNATIONAL RELATIONS, 1871-1914

WE HAVE seen in the last chapter that rivalry in Africa and the Far East more than once brought Europe to the brink of war. Yet these problems were only some of the many which created tension among major European states between the achievement of German unity and the outbreak of the First World War. It is these other tensions that we shall try to examine in this chapter.

The Balance of Power in Europe

The Franco-Prussian War had left in the French mind a rankling bitterness and in the German mind a fear of a war of revenge. Each distrusted the other and both sought security—internally through armed preparedness and externally by a system of alliances. In the latter respect, France's task was the harder. Bismarck's diplomacy had isolated France before the war had begun and that isolation remained when the war was over. All Bismarck had to do was to see that it remained unbreached. France, on the other hand, had to try to break through the circle of suspicious neighbours with which Bismarck had surrounded her.

In the hope of strengthening that circle, Bismarck in 1872 sought to forge more binding links between Germany, Austria and Russia by the creation of the League of the Three Emperors. The objects of the league were declared to be those of maintaining the existing balance of power in Europe, suppressing movements of a revolutionary character and settling by diplomacy any international difficulties, particularly such as might arise out of the Eastern Question. Bismarck did not want to take sides with either Austria or Russia against the other over the Eastern Question, because he would then forfeit an ally to France.

By acting as an honest broker between Austria and Russia, Bismarck avoided war, but Russia resented his protective rights over Bosnia and Herzegovina. Sensing this resentment, Bismarck in 1879 concluded a secret separate alliance with Austria which provided for mutual support in case of a Russian attack on either state, and benevolent neutrality in the event of an attack by any other power unsupported by Russia. Meanwhile, in order to commit the unsuspecting Russia to the German cause, Bismarck renewed the League of the Three Emperors from time to time.

With Austria and Russia thus aligned with Germany, France's hopes could only lie in the direction of Italy and Britain. Unhappily the French clerical party were averse to an association with the State which had made the Pope a prisoner of the Vatican, while on the Italian side, the French acquisition of Tunis in 1881 was regarded as an unfriendly act. Thus in 1882, Bismarck was able to persuade Italy to join with Austria and Germany in the Triple Alliance.

As for Britain, her statesmen were deeply committed to a policy of "splendid isolation." They believed that, secure behind the shield of a powerful navy, Britain could best serve her own interests by steering clear of all Continental entanglements. In any case, Franco-British interests were in conflict in Egypt.

At last France saw brighter prospects. In 1890 Kaiser William II got rid of Bismarck, allowed the League of the Three Emperors to lapse, and France began to cultivate Russian friendship, which culminated, in 1895, in a Dual Alliance between the two countries for mutual protection in the face of aggression.

As the nineteenth century began to give place to the twentieth, British statesmen came to feel that they had been harbouring a false sense of security. Potential enemies were many. In Africa Britain was opposed by Germany over the Boer question in the south and by France on the Egyptian issue. Germany had also embarked on a policy of naval expansion. By penetration into China, Russia threatened British interests in the Far East and by the extension of influence in Afghanistan, British supremacy in India.

Sir Edward Grey, Liberal foreign minister, resolved to try to relieve these tensions between Britain and her neighbours. The overtures made to France met with a welcoming response. In 1904 the two powers reached agreement on all matters tending to cause friction and the way was thus prepared for an Anglo-French Entente. This was not an alliance, but it meant that for the future each would act towards the other on assumptions of friendship and confidence. France had not secured another ally but she had found at least another friend.

Having an alliance with Russia and an Entente Cordiale with Britain, France was able by her good offices to encourage her two associates to settle their differences. Thus by 1907 Britain and Russia agreed upon a convention defining their respective spheres of influence in Persia, recognizing the supremacy of British interests in Afghanistan and mutually promising to abstain from any penetration into Tibet. With these issues disposed of Britain had no objections to entering into a Triple Entente with Russia and France similar in character to the Anglo-French Entente.

Germany, unlike France, showed no willingness to compose her differences with Britain. In these circumstances Britain tended to be drawn into ever-closer relationship with France so that, by 1914, the European situation in practice, if not in theory, hardened into one wherein Germany, Italy and Austria stood opposed to France, Britain and Russia. The gulf between these two opposing groups widened as each new international crisis arose, and the early twentieth century saw a succession of such crises.

The first of such crises, that of 1906 which led to the Conference of Algeciras, we have already examined in its relation to the scramble for Africa, but it had European aspects also. Germany had hoped to use the occasion of the conference to drive a wedge between France and Britain while demonstrating the solidarity of her own European alliance. She was disappointed. Not only did France and Britain maintain a common front on the African issue, but Italy and Austria both took an anti-German line. It was Germany's position which was weakened, not that of France.

In 1908 the peace of Europe was again in jeopardy when a revolution occurred in Turkey. A new spirit was engendered in a group of younger politicians who deposed the Sultan and established a parliamentary government after the Western pattern. This Young Turk party sought to revive the old European empire of Turkey. The Balkan states were alarmed, and that part of Bulgaria which had been left under Turkish overlordship in 1878 now declared its independence and united with the rest of Bulgaria already enjoying self-government. Thus the Bulgaria fashioned by the Treaty of San Stefano but reshaped by the Treaty of Berlin came at last into existence. This violation of the arrangements of 1878 encouraged Austria. She promptly annexed Bosnia and Herzegovina and incorporated them in the Dual Monarchy. Serbia protested and her protest was upheld by Russia. Germany on the other hand supported Austria. Here was the stage set for war unless someone gave way.

Unwillingly, Russia advised Serbia to withdraw the protest. Serbia, left to face an Austro-German combination without an ally, accepted the Russian advice. The crisis was over, but both alliances had held fast.

The relief was only temporary, for, as we have seen, Germany tried in 1911 to exploit a delicate situation in Morocco. The Triple Entente faced the situation undivided. Britain declared she would be ready to protect her honour and dignity if these were attacked. Kaiser William II accepted both his failure to destroy the harmony of the Entente and a feeble compromise solution in Morocco. European antagonisms had been stifled, not resolved.

Fundamental Causes of the First World War of 1914-18

At the root of these antagonisms was that Franco-German hostility and fear which we noted at the beginning of this chapter. This had crystallized in the two rival alliance systems, the Triple Alliance on the one hand and the Dual Alliance with the Triple Entente on the other. British efforts to remove the inherent dangers by an Anglo-German understanding failed; Europe had to rely for the preservation of peace on this risky "balance of power."

Both Germany and France sought a second line of defence in military preparedness which each declared to be for defence in case of attack. Germany also entered into a naval armaments race with Britain. At first Britain merely watched German progress, satisfied with the lead she held. Yet as time passed and German policy in Europe and beyond seemed to become ever more menacing Britain took up the challenge and began to build ship for ship in answer to the German programme.

After the creation of the German Empire in 1871, the country underwent a rapid process of industrialization, the kind of industrial revolution in fact which Britain had experienced a hundred years earlier. Yet Germany had to rely for raw material on the colonies of other powers. Thus in the twentieth century German ambition turned in the direction of overseas expansion and it is difficult to deny the right she claimed—a "place in the sun." Yet Britain, the chief colonial power in Europe, was in no mind to strengthen German power by colonial concessions; what she had she hoped to hold. Since she held it largely by virtue of her naval supremacy it is no wonder that Germany sought in an expanded navy the only means of securing a modification of British policy on the colonial issue.

While there were those in Europe, statesmen and others, who sincerely believed that the balance of power would preserve peace, there were some who felt just as strongly that the existence of an explosive colonial issue and the continuance of an armaments race would inevitably lead to the outbreak of war. The influence of this latter school of thought resulted in the convening of two disarmament conferences, usually known as the Hague Conferences because of their place of assembly. The first, held in 1899 at the Tsar's initiative, accepted disarmament in principle and established a permanent court of arbitration to resolve international disputes. Unfortunately there was a proviso that the court could consider no international issue unless both parties to the dispute consented to submit to arbitration. This condition severely limited the likely effectiveness of the court.

The second Hague Conference of 1907 got no further than recognizing the desirability of curtailing the armaments race, and had to content itself in practical measures with the production of a convention for conducting war on more "humane" lines.

In the short-term view, the Hague Conferences must be written off as a failure; on a longer view they had the merit of bringing the powers of Europe to admit the existence of a problem—disarmament—requiring solution, and for that solution the statesmen of the world have continued to seek in spite of two intervening world wars and the evolution of ever more frightful means of waging war.

Another factor contributing to the outbreak of 1914 was the extension of German influence in the East. When, after the Bulgarian Atrocities, Britain retreated from her role of Turkey's friend in Europe, Germany stepped in, at the same time including within her patronage the newer Balkan states. It was Germany who readily found among the members of her own royal family kings for Rumania and Bulgaria.

Germany established influence and gained commercial rights in Turkey by providing capital for the country's internal development, and she evolved a scheme for the construction of a railway from Berlin to Baghdad which neccesitated territorial concessions across the Balkans. Such penetration of the Balkans and the East would have made Germany, already one of the strongest powers in Europe, incomparably the mightiest. With the agricultural and mineral wealth of these areas at her back she could have defied all European naval blockades and would have thus been, in the event of war, almost invulnerable. This would have weighted the balance of power unalterably in Germany's favour. Such an endeavour on her part seemed in the eyes of other powers a clear sign of her aggressive intentions. Her opponents sought to counteract her schemes; Germany raised the cry of "Encirclement" and another potential war factor was created.

Finally, the provocative attitude of the German Emperor must be added to the list of forces making for war. He was too fond of publicly proclaiming the might and strength of his empire; he too often declared his readiness to

Kaiser William II reviewing his troops in 1914, just before the war.

stand by his allies "in coat of shining armour." Europe's nerves were frayed by such sabre-rattling. He seemed like a man flourishing a box of matches in a munitions factory; he may have had no intention of opening the box but it was disturbing to watch him playing with it.

If the above were the deep-rooted causes of the war of 1914 we must examine the reappearance in the twentieth century of the Eastern Question to find the occasion of the immediate outbreak.

Balkan Wars and the Outbreak of War, 1914

In 1912, Rumania, Bulgaria, Serbia and Greece, alarmed at the regeneration of Turkey under German encouragement, had, on the initiative of a Greek statesman, M. Venizelos, formed a league for the purpose of conquering and partitioning the Turkish province of Macedonia. When war broke out between Turkey and the league, the latter proved an easy victor. The Bulgarians besieged Adrianople and approached within striking distance of Constantinople, while Greeks and Serbs swept through Macedonia. Failure during an armistice to agree on terms of a settlement led to the resumption of hostilities and the Bulgarians took Adrianople, the Greeks captured Janina and Turkey had to take what terms she was offered.

In the subsequent Treaty of London, most of European Turkey was ceded to the victors, but Austria and Italy intervened to insist that territory which would otherwise probably have passed into the possession of Serbia, was yielded to Albania. Crete, which was placed under the protection of the Great Powers, was subsequently incorporated in the Kingdom of Greece.

Thus the Balkan League had succeeded where the great nations of Europe had for so long tried and failed. Turkey had at last been virtually expelled from western Europe.

The unity of the Balkan League did not long survive its victory. The concessions which at Austrian insistence had been made to Albania effectively prevented the realization of Serbia's main objective in entering the war, namely, access to the sea. In these circumstances she demanded from Bulgaria compensation in Macedonia. Bulgaria refused and found herself at war once more, this time against Serbia, Greece and Rumania. When Montenegro also joined in against her, Bulgaria, realizing she was surrounded by hostile neighbours on all sides, did not wait for overwhelming defeat, but decided to make peace. At the Treaty of Bucharest there were in consequence prizes for all. Bulgaria as well as Greece and Serbia acquired part of Macedonia, though the Bulgarians had to return Adrianople to the Turks. Thus even the Turks profited.

The European importance of this refashioning of the Balkan map lay in the fears created in the Austrian mind. Austria had a large Slav population; Serbia dreamed of an all-Slav state; her acquisitions in 1913 were an immense strengthening of Serbian power; might she not soon attempt to recover Bosnia and Herzegovina whose annexation by Austria in 1908 she had so deeply resented?

Fears such as these determined the aggressive watchfulness towards Serbia which inspired Austrian policy up to the outbreak of war in 1914. The growth of Serbia as a result of the Balkan wars convinced Austria that the first excuse for an attack on Serbia which offered itself must be exploited to the full. It might even be desirable to engineer such a pretext.

Sarajevo

In June, 1914, the opportunity occurred. The Archduke Franz Ferdinand and his wife, while on a visit to Bosnia, a hotbed of pro-Slav feeling, were shot dead as they passed in procession through the streets of the capital, Sarajevo. The heir to the Austrian throne had been assassinated in Slav territory; Serbia, the chief independent Slav power, must in some way be responsible.

Though the murderer was an Austrian, the Imperial police insisted that the plot had been hatched in Serbia; that the Serbian government had known of it and done nothing to prevent it. In spite of the existence of contrary evidence the opportunity for action against Serbia was too good to lose. On the Serbian side there was the counter-suggestion that Austria had hoped for an incident when she had agreed to the Archduke's visit.

The crisis of 1908 had shown that an attack on Serbia meant reckoning with Russia. Austria found support from Germany and presented an ultimatum to Serbia which demanded nullification of Serbia's independence. Serbia suggested reference of the issue to the Permanent Court of Justice at the Hague, but Austria, confident of German support, refused and declared war.

Involvement of Russia and France

This time Russia would not give way. She had already ordered partial mobilization as proof of her intention to support Serbia, and the day following Austria's declaration of war on Serbia, Russia declared war on Austria.

Efforts by Britain to confine the struggle to the Balkans or to induce the chief contestants to submit to arbitration proved unavailing. Germany began to mobilize, well knowing that France had an alliance with Russia who was already involved. France replied with a similar mobilization. Germany thereupon declared war on France and Russia.

Involvement of Belgium and Britain

British opinion, even in the Cabinet, was divided on the question of taking up arms in defence of France. There had never been a formal alliance

Princip, assassin of Franz Ferdinand, arrested by the police.

with France, but on the strength of mutual friendship some compromising arrangements had been made. The French navy had been protecting British and French interests in the Mediterranean on the assumption that the British navy would always protect French no less than British interests in the English Channel. Moreover, staff officers of the British army had, with the knowledge of the Foreign Office, met long ago and discussed with their opposite numbers in Paris a plan of common action should Britain take up arms in support of France.

Those who knew the extent of these moral commitments were convinced that Britain was obliged in honour to rally to the side of France. Other men and ministers thought differently. Events solved the problem.

Britain demanded of both France and Germany once they were at war that they should respect the neutrality of Belgium to which both powers were by treaty committed. France agreed, Germany hedged. Then in August came the news that Germany had in fact invaded Belgium. This was something Britain could not ignore. Not only was she pledged by treaty to respect Belgian neutrality, but her own self-interest had always dictated a foreign policy based on keeping any great European power out of the Channel ports of the Low Countries. Britain therefore presented an ultimatum to Germany demanding withdrawal from Belgian territory under threat of war, and fixing midnight of the fourth of August as the time by which the withdrawal should have begun. The hour struck and no communication of any kind had been received from the German government. Britain, France, Russia and Serbia were now all at war with Germany and the Austro-Hungarian Empire.

QUESTIONS

1. Show how events in the Balkans between 1908 and 1914 affected international relations.

2. Explain how Europe came to be divided into two hostile camps by 1914.

CHAPTER 44

FIRST WORLD WAR, 1914-1918

THE outbreak of war in 1914 was to many of the people of Europe completely unexpected. The major powers had avoided war in Europe for some forty years: that a political assassination in an obscure Balkan country should have resulted in armed conflict was incredible—it could not last long; it would all be over by Christmas. This was false optimism. Yet it is doubtful if even the military experts foresaw the revolutionary character that warfare was henceforth to follow in these and succeeding years of the twentieth century.

Mechanized Warfare

From the seventh century onwards the horse had played a vital role in European warfare; it drew the transport and artillery, and the cavalry charge either scythed a path for the infantry or completed the rout of the enemy that the infantry had begun. Nobody expected things to be different in this respect in 1914. Yet when a lightning victory eluded the contestants in the autumn months of the first year of hostilities and there was no withdrawal, as in earlier wars, into "winter quarters," the mud of Flanders presented new military problems. Horses floundered in this oozy slime in which they could neither walk nor swim. Gun-carriages stuck fast, supplies could not be sent forward; the fighting forces were immobilized, watching each other from a vast network of ditch-like trenches which stretched from the Mediterranean to the North Sea.

The answer to this new problem was the invention of motorized transport which laid its own caterpillar track as it advanced. This was the "tank" which made its first appearance as an engine of war in 1916. It could cross trenches, crush barbed wire as it went and afford a degree of protection to its occupants unknown since the days of the knights in armour. This was the death of the cavalry; the man who could use a spanner was of more value than the man who could wield a sword.

There were significant changes too in the character of naval as well as military warfare. When the war began, the Central Powers, as the forces of the Triple Alliance came to be known, had the advantage of fighting on interior lines of communication. Their opponents, the "Allied Powers", had to rely on sea communications to supply their forces and on the power of the long-term effects of a naval blockade. As this began to take its toll, the Central Powers turned to underwater ships in the hope of beating the blockade. The submarine, with only its periscope to betray its presence until its deadly torpedo hit its unsuspecting target, constituted a new hazard to warships and merchant ships alike. Its appearance heralded the end of the age of supremacy of the battleship.

From the British point of view, more serious still was the development from 1914 of war in the air. Hitherto Britain had relied for its safety on its island situation. It had only to maintain its command of the sea to guarantee its preservation from invasion or from the horrors of war in its own land. The aeroplane changed all this; it could fly beyond the range of naval guns and attack Britain's industrial centres, thus interrupting the supply of munitions to forces in the field. Moreover, better than any ground-based observer it could both note military concentrations and troop disposals, and destroy them.

Another terror was added to man's means of waging war by the attempt made to introduce chemical warfare. Shells were filled not with explosives but with deadly gases which when inhaled seared and burnt men's lungs. Though used on a small scale in the First World War, this was fortunately an experiment too dangerous to pursue. A change of wind direction once the gas shells were fired could make this weapon recoil on the user. Its most effective use would have been on civilian populations from the air. Fortunately neither aeroplanes nor chemical weapons were sufficiently developed during the early years of the twentieth century to make such use possible. By the time of the Second World War science was so far advanced as to make chemical warfare of this kind out-of-date before it had been tried.

Men "called up" from their civilian occupations took the place of professional armies and navies. All countries adopted the principle of "conscription," compulsory military service. As the war progressed, so great were the casualties that the age limits for service were reduced at one end of the scale and extended at the other and increasing use was made of the voluntary services of women as cooks, clerks and nurses so as to release men for more active combat duty.

The distinction in fact between "soldier" and "civilian" was further blurred when aircraft dropped bombs on cities and towns of the "homelands."

Beginning as a European conflict, before it ended the First World War had drawn into its vortex the greater part of the world. Nations from America to Japan, from northern Europe to Australia and New Zealand, were all participants. The "western front" in Europe was paralleled by an "eastern front" and an "Italian front." The war was fought in Egypt, Africa and

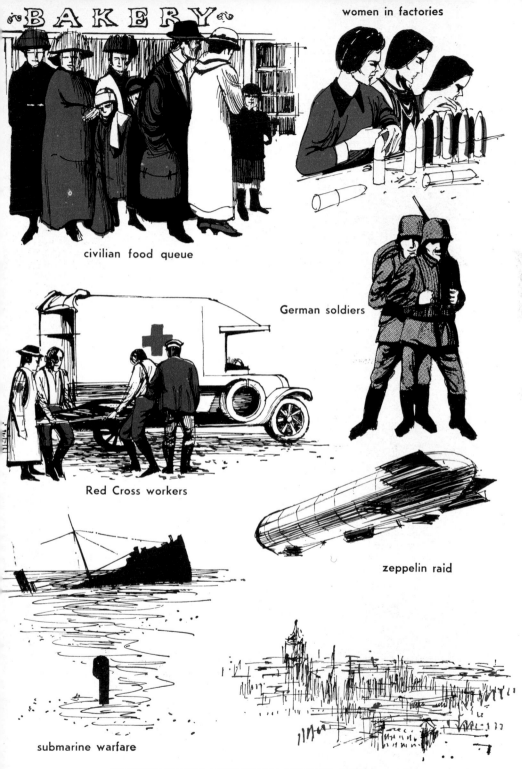

BAKERY

women in factories

civilian food queue

German soldiers

Red Cross workers

zeppelin raid

submarine warfare

SCENES FROM THE FIRST WORLD WAR

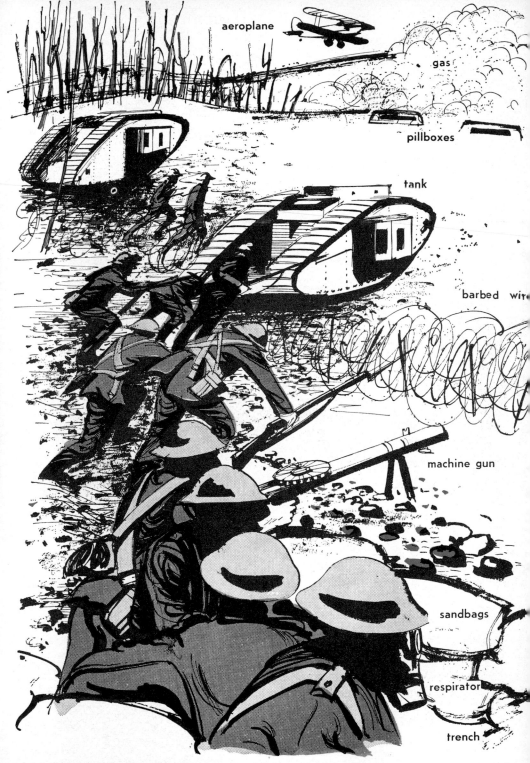

aeroplane

gas

pillboxes

tank

barbed wir

machine gun

sandbags

respirator

trench

BRITISH TROOPS GO "OVER THE TOP" IN THE FIRST WORLD WAR

Mesopotamia and troops raised in Canada, India, New Zealand and Australia served in arms far from their native shores. This was indeed the First World War.

Attack and Counter-attack, 1914-15

The German violation of Belgian neutrality which finally forced the hand of Britain was part of a plan, drawn up by the German General Staff in case of war with France. The idea was to station a strong containing force in the area of Metz, and using this as a pivot, to swing a strong, swift, encircling movement round through Belgium into France and towards Paris. Thus would the French lines be outflanked, encircled and destroyed before, it was hoped, any ally could come to their help.

This, the Schlieffen Plan, was modified in 1914 by the chief of the German General Staff, nephew of the great von Moltke who had given Germany victory against France in 1870. Fearful of a French advance into Lorraine, he weakened the right hook forces to strengthen the left. This modification, combined with the resolute delaying actions fought by the Belgians, threw the German time-table out of gear and gave time for the arrival of a British expeditionary force.

The original German plan of campaign was now drastically revised. A concerted drive was made direct for Paris but it was held short of its goal. The German bid for the Channel ports was equally unsuccessful. Antwerp fell, but a successful allied stand at Ypres prevented the German command from gaining control of the French Channel coast. Soon the German armies were in retreat to the Aisne. There they made their stand.

Checked on the western front, the Germans under General von Hindenburg had better success against Russia. At the battles of Tannenburg and the Masurian Lakes the invading Russian armies were expelled from East Prussia and Galicia. Further encouragement for Germany came when the Allies failed to persuade Turkey to remain neutral. It was this Turkish support of the Central Powers which led Britain to annex Cyprus, which she already administered. The only comfort for the Allies on the Eastern Front was the failure of the Austrian attempt to hold Serbia.

The second year of the war saw further German success in the East. The threat to Russia grew with the German advance into Poland. Bulgaria and Austria made a joint conquest of Serbia, but a joint attack by British and Australian troops on the Dardanelles failed tragically at Gallipoli. In Egypt and Mesopotamia the British advance into Turkey was held at Kut.

The climate and the nature of the ground over which they were fighting compelled both sides on the Western Front during the first winter of the war to dig themselves into long lines of trenches. Attacks, usually opened by heavy artillery bombardment which made the going more impossible for the following infantry, were launched in the areas of Neuve Chapelle, Ypres and Loos. Casualties were enormous on both sides and the territory gained amounted usually to no more than a few hundred yards.

In the second year of the war Italy renounced the Triple Alliance and declared war on Austria, as the Allies had promised her by the secret Treaty of London (1915) an extension of her northern boundaries as well as a protectorate over Albania, which would establish Italian control of the Adriatic.

Beyond diverting Austrian troops from the Russian front, Italy's defection to the Allied cause had little beneficial immediate effect and in the long run, as we shall see, proved more of a handicap than a help, even though in 1916 she extended her declaration of war to include Germany as well.

War of Attrition, 1916-17

On the Western Front in 1916 and 1917, the conflict became a war of attrition, each side seeking to wear out the patience, endurance and resources of the other. On the other fronts the war ebbed and flowed but with no decisive effect on the war in France. In the west, in 1916, the French successfully held a German attack on Verdun and the leader of the defence, General Pétain, became the hero of the day. On the other hand, the Germans equally successfully held a heavily mounted British attack along the Somme. In 1917 the great "victory" in the west was the Allied capture of Vimy Ridge, but it was offset by the failure of the main French offensive of that year and subsequent French exhaustion, so severe that it looked at one time as if France would be unable to continue the fight.

Public opinion on both sides inevitably demanded scapegoats as the war dragged on, and the obvious scapegoats were the politicians and the High Command.

Thus, in Britain, Prime Minister Asquith made way for Lloyd George; on the military side, General French, the original commander of the British

German soldiers preparing for attack on the Western Front.

A lone soldier stands guard in France during a gas attack.

expeditionary force, had already been replaced by General Haig. Prior to this in the summer of 1916, Earl Kitchener of Khartoum, Secretary of State for War, had been drowned when the ship on which he was sailing had been sunk in Scapa Flow. It was by taking the place of Kitchener at the War Office that Lloyd George was ultimately able to wrest the premiership from Asquith. He brought to the war a badly needed new sense of urgency, determination and purpose.

In Germany, change of political leadership was not possible; it was therefore the High Command who had to bear the brunt of such discontent as existed. By the beginning of 1916, von Moltke had already yielded place to Falkenhayn who in turn was replaced by Hindenburg after that British attack on the Somme, which though defeated, had come so very near to success.

In France, the French near collapse threw up a new political leader, Clemenceau, the "Tiger." His vigour and ruthlessness combined with a sense of mission matched the energy of Lloyd George. "No surrender" was the watchword which determined the policy of Clemenceau and he fired his countrymen with the same iron resolution.

On the Russian and Balkan fronts, in the years 1916 and 1917, both combatants experienced encouragement and disappointment. Rumania became a new recruit to the Allied Powers, but Russia invaded Transylvania. In Greece, Venizelos had been dismissed by King Constantine earlier in the war of 1914 because his sympathies leaned too obviously to the Allied cause. He had established a pro-Allied government at Salonica where the Allies had thus been able to make a successful landing in 1915. In 1917 Constantine abdicated, Venizelos returned to power, Greece joined the Allies and the way was opened for an Allied attack on Bulgaria.

Yet in 1917, Greece's accession to the Allied cause was offset by the increasing inability of Russia to meet the German attack. The Tsarist régime of Russia was totally unable to bear the strains and stresses of war. A revolutionary party, the Bolsheviks, seized power and began to negotiate with Germany for peace. This development enabled Germany to concentrate her military strength on the Western Front.

The most successful achievements by the Allied Powers in 1916 and 1917 were registered in Mesopotamia and Egypt. Halted at Kut in 1915, the British troops eventually entered the town only to lose it in 1916. In 1917 they recaptured it and went on to take Baghdad. In 1916 Allenby, having secured his rear in Egypt, advanced into Palestine and in the following year, on Christmas Day, victoriously entered Jerusalem.

The Central Powers did best in Italy. Austria successfully invaded northern Italy and Britain and France had to send reinforcements to contain the Austrian advance. Italy's accession to the Allied cause was at this point a liability rather than an asset.

The Final Year, 1918

There had been, prior to 1917, four main engagements between the British navy and the German High Seas fleet. In 1914, at the Battle of Heligoland, three German battle cruisers had been destroyed, but at the Battle of Coronel two British cruisers had been lost by a German attack. In the following year, at the Battle of the Dogger Bank, a German battle cruiser, the *Blucher*, after raiding the Yorkshire coast, was intercepted and destroyed. In 1917 the determining engagement occurred. This was the Battle of Jutland. Who was victor and who was vanquished in this encounter is still a matter of argument. The important point is that thereafter the German High Seas fleet never ventured forth in strength again. Germany now concentrated upon building up as quickly as possible a large fleet of submarines. If with these she could

American "doughboys" outside a cookhouse in France in 1917.

interrupt the supplies of material and food upon which Britain was dependent British control of the seas by her battleships would be destroyed. Further, the British blockade of ports controlled by the Allied Powers would be more than counter-balanced.

In 1915 Germany declared the seas round Britain to be a war zone and warned off the shipping of all nations. One of the first victims of this policy was unfortunately an American passenger ship, the *Lusitania*, sunk by German action with heavy loss of American lives. Its loss provoked strong protests from America, at the time a neutral power and hitherto more disposed to quarrel with Britain about the blockade she had established and her insistence on stopping and searching on the high seas American vessels suspected of trading with the Central Powers.

Germany was sufficiently impressed by American reaction to the loss of the *Lusitania* as to moderate her submarine policy until 1917. Then, in an all-out effort to force victory she reverted to a policy of unrestricted submarine attack. By 1917, however, the Tsarist régime in Russia had been overthrown and American unwillingness to fight alongside an undemocratic government was thereby removed. Unrestricted submarine warfare brought the United States of America into the fight against Germany.

The entry of America into the war went a long way to compensate for the withdrawal of Russia as a result of the Treaty of Brest-Litovsk. The Russian example was followed by Rumania when she signed the Treaty of Bucharest.

Elsewhere outside Western Europe, the year 1918 brought little to encourage Germany. At the battle of Vittoria, Austria was expelled from Italy. In Mesopotamia, British forces captured Damascus, occupied Syria and thus induced Turkey to sue for peace. In the Balkans a joint British and Greek force issuing forth from Salonica defeated Bulgaria who was also thus compelled to seek terms. One by one in this way the Central Powers admitted defeat, while at sea the convoy system whereby groups of merchant ships sailed together under the protection of escorting destroyers served to parry the submarine menace. This was aided by successful British naval raids on the German submarine bases at Zeebrugge.

Germany now concentrated her remaining strength on the Western Front, and by doing so came very near to victory.

Under the leadership of Hindenburg advised by Ludendorff the German armies broke through the Allied defence and swept forward as far as Amiens. This gallant effort failed, because although Ludendorff had planned the advance, he had not planned to exploit his success. He hesitated, working out tactics for the next move, and gave the Allies time to unite British, American and French forces under the supreme command of General Foch. Foch launched a counter-attack which caught the Germans unprepared. It succeeded, and German morale collapsed completely.

Civilians and soldiers join in the first Armistice Day celebrations.

Nation and army had alike made their last effort; the nation was hungry, and the army began to notice the lack of supplies and reinforcements. Strikes by the workers developed into revolution; the government, finding its overtures for a negotiated peace rejected, collapsed and the Kaiser fled to Holland and the provisional revolutionary administration had to accept what terms the Allied Powers cared to offer. Pending final peace terms an armistice came into effect at 11 a.m. on 11 November, 1918.

Despite the initial success of the German armies, their interior lines of communication, and their military preparedness, Germany met with defeat. The reasons for this are now clear.

The lightning victory on which Germany counted had escaped her, and it took her some time to form a new strategy. This gave her opponents the opportunity they needed to organize their defence. At sea, her submarine menace was successfully countered by British and Allied navies, and the Allied blockade of Germany cut off her supplies by 1918. In addition, the morale of the men in the field was undermined by news of the hardships encountered by their families at home. In the end, Germany lacked both the material means to fight, and the will to fight at all.

America's entry was the factor that turned the balance. She brought to the last two years of the war an immense wealth of men, money, ships and material; her allies could supply what she lacked in experience. American support for the Allied cause sealed Germany's fate.

QUESTIONS

1. Account for the early success of Germany in the war. Why did she fail to realize her hopes of a short war and a quick victory?

2. In what ways did the war of 1914-18 set a new pattern of warfare in Europe?

CHAPTER 45

THE PEACE OF VERSAILLES

A S EARLY as 1916 the Allied Powers had begun to discuss among themselves the lines which a peace settlement might take.

By the first months of 1918, they had agreed, with reservations, that President Wilson's Fourteen Points afforded a basis on which the task might be begun. As well as drawing in outline new national boundaries within Europe, these fourteen points provided for a reduction in armaments "consistent with national security," a new approach to diplomacy, defined as "open treaties openly arrived at," acceptance of the principle of the freedom of the seas both in peace and in war, the removal of barriers to international trade, a review of European colonial policy based on consideration of the interests of colonial populations, and the formation of a general association of nations for the peaceful solution of future international problems. When in October of the same year Germany began negotiations for the armistice it was on the assumption but without an assurance or even agreement that these terms would apply.

In practice, however, the armistice terms offered to Germany and which she was in no position to reject, were designed principally to ensure that she would be in no condition to renew the fighting. She was required to withdraw her forces from all invaded territories, to permit an Allied advance to the Rhine, and surrender her fleet to the British navy as well as considerable quantities of aeroplanes, tanks, lorries and guns to her conquerors. Above all, the Allied blockade of Germany was to continue until the conclusion of definitive peace terms unless Germany was prepared to pay for the imported food she needed.

These armistice conditions were not offered to Germany for discussion; she could only accept or reject them. With her citizen armies streaming home in disorder, her Emperor in flight, and the workers in revolt, neither the provisional republican government nor the German High Command could do anything other than accept under protest.

The Peace Conference, 1919

For the first six months of 1919 the representatives of the victorious Allied Powers were in session at Versailles drafting the final peace settlement. In contrast to the last great peace conference, the Congress of Vienna in 1815, the defeated powers were not present nor were they ever consulted.

The minor victorious powers had little decisive influence upon the course of the discussions. The Conference was dominated by Clemenceau of France. Lloyd George of Britain, Wilson of the United States and Orlando of Italy. Even of the "Big Four," as these statesmen came to be called, it was really the first three who wielded the greatest influence. Unfortunately they were driven by very different motives. Lloyd George, Clemenceau and Orlando were all practical statesmen, each with a national axe of his own to grind. Lloyd George was committed to securing the maximum economic and colonial advantage for Britain; Clemenceau was concerned only to ensure the greatest possible degree of future security for France; Orlando had his eyes set upon the acquisition of Austria's north Italian possessions in order to round off the geographical unity of his country.

President Wilson, on the other hand, was not a party politician but a scholar and a philosopher, viewing politics not in the light of what was possible but with a vision of what ideally ought to be. He was also quite unconscious of his limitations as a practical European statesman. Diplomacy should, he felt, be based upon moral principles, not upon expediency, and the achievement of world peace for the future was more important than immediate national advantage. His primary aim was the establishment of a League of Nations.

In the course of the war, bargains had been struck and promises made among the victorious powers which now had to be honoured. In 1915 Britain had lent a sympathetic ear to the offer of the Governor of Mecca, an Arab leader called Hussein, to rouse the Arabs against the Turks, and a young Englishman, T. E. Lawrence, had helped him in the execution of his successful campaigns; but in 1917 Britain, to secure the support of Jewish capital in the war against Germany, had pledged herself to create in Palestine a national Jewish state. Palestine had for centuries been Arab-inhabited though latterly part of the Turkish Empire. When the Conference of Versailles turned its attention to a settlement with Turkey what was to be done with Palestine?

Again, Italy's transfer of allegiance to the Allied cause had been secured in part at least by the promise of territorial expansion at Austrian expense. The Conference had no choice but to dismember the Austro-Hungarian Empire. In such conditions as these the Conference found some decisions already made for it.

The major task of the Conference was to reshape the national boundaries of the European nations. This involved determining the future of the Austro-Hungarian Empire, the disposal of the European provinces of the Turkish Empire, the settlement of the Balkans and some provision for the security of France and Belgium in the event of future German aggression.

A second consideration was the nature of the retribution to be demanded from Germany. Civilians in the victorious countries had suffered heavy loss of goods and property. Could these burdens be laid upon German shoulders and if so how and for how long and if Germany's colonies were not to be returned to her, what should be their future?

Yet a third issue was that of outlawing war for the future. An armaments competition had been one of the factors leading to war. By what means could it be avoided? This question resolved itself into two parts, the achievement of disarmament and the realization of Wilson's project for a League of Nations.

The complexity of these problems and the divergent motives of the negotiating powers made it inevitable that the solutions adopted should often fall short of the ideal. One single treaty could hardly embrace all these issues. In practice separate documents were signed with Germany, Austria, Hungary, Bulgaria and in 1923, Turkey. Collectively, however, they have come to be known as the Peace of Versailles and it is as such that we shall review them.

Re-shaping of Europe

Ever since her defeat in 1870, France had lived in fear of Germany. In 1914 the dreaded nightmare had turned into grim reality; in 1919 she felt she had her opportunity to rid herself of this haunting terror at last. If she could push her boundary to the Rhine, not only would an old French hope of centuries past be realized but she would have the security of a natural frontier demarcation with Germany. Once again this ambition was not realized. She had to be content with the recovery of Alsace and Lorraine, an Allied army of occupation in the Rhineland and her own occupation of the Saar valley for fifteen years. To have given France the Rhine as her boundary would have meant the incorporation of a large German population within

The Big Four: left to right, Lloyd George, Orlando, Clemenceau, Wilson.

France. Such a blatant disregard of national loyalties was more than even the elastic conscience of the architects of the new Europe could tolerate.

Perhaps the most radical re-drawing of the map of Europe originated in the dismemberment of the Austro-Hungarian Empire. Austria proper became a small, landlocked republic destined henceforth to rank only as one of the minor states of Europe. Hungary achieved the status of a republic, though she had to make territorial concessions to a new Balkan state, Czechoslovakia. At the expense not only of Austria-Hungary but also of Germany and Russia, Poland became a sovereign independent republic. A third state carved out of the old Austro-Hungarian Empire was Serbia, now enlarged by the addition of Montenegro, Bosnia, Dalmatia, Croatia, Slavonia and Herzegovina and re-named Yugoslavia. The new state of Czechoslovakia embraced Bohemia, Moravia, Slovakia and Ruthenia. Finally, the Austrian provinces of Trieste, Istria, Trentino and South Tyrol had to be ceded by Austria to Italy.

In the Balkans, Bulgaria had to yield Macedonia and Thrace, and the Turkish part of these provinces was also awarded to Greece. She had to cede the Dobrudja to Rumania and she lost her access to the Aegean Sea. Rumania also took Transylvania from Hungary along with Bessarabia and Bukovina from Russia. In the Baltic three new independent states were created, namely Lithuania, Estonia and Latvia; while North Schleswig was awarded to Denmark.

It is interesting to compare this re-alignment of Europe with that effected by the Congress of Vienna a hundred years earlier. The lines were then re-drawn in the interests of monarchs, now they were being re-drawn in the interests of peoples.

World Peace

The victorious powers accepted the principle of disarmament "consistent with national security," but they began the process with the armaments of the vanquished rather than with their own. The German fleet had already, at the time of the armistice, scuttled itself on arrival at Scapa Flow. For the future, Germany was to have no submarines and the size and numbers of other types of ships were precisely limited. Austria likewise surrendered her navy and neither Austria nor Germany were in future to build or own military aircraft. Conscription was abolished in both countries and armies of only limited size permitted. In no circumstances was the new small Austria to unite with Germany.

This disarmament of the defeated powers was to be but a preliminary to a similar reduction of armaments among the victors but this intention was never fully implemented, largely because the will to do so was lacking.

In spite of the reluctance of his foreign colleagues at the conference, Wilson insisted on the creation of the League of Nations. This was to be an

Scarcity in Berlin: German civilians wait for soup.

association open to all independent nations and the self-governing members of the British Dominions. For the time being Germany was excluded from membership.

By invoking the League of Nations an apparently honest solution was found to the colonial issues which faced the conference. Former colonial possessions of the defeated powers were entrusted to the guardianship of the League of Nations who then granted a mandate to member powers charging them with responsibility for the administration of specific colonies. The mandatory power was to administer the territory entrusted to it with primary concern for the interests and welfare of the native population. Moreover it was to give a detailed annual account of its stewardship to the League of Nations.

It thus came about that Britain was given the mandate for Palestine, Mesopotamia, Trans-Jordan and Tanganyika. France was entrusted with Syria, Togoland and the Cameroon. South Africa accepted responsibility for German South West Africa while Australia administered German New Guinea with New Zealand looking after Samoa. Germany's incentive in making war had been in part a desire for a greater place in the colonial sun. All she achieved was total eclipse.

Apart from the Balkan issue, the presence of Turkey in Europe, or the Eastern Question, as it was known, had often brought nineteenth-century Europe to the brink of war. Turkey's participation in the war of 1914 on the losing side brought an opportunity to settle the matter. The conference at Versailles proposed that Constantinople should be returned to Turkey, but the Dardanelles should be controlled by the League of Nations. Turkish Thrace and Macedonia, as we have seen, were awarded to Greece and so also was Anatolia.

Turkey, faced with defeat and this loss of territory, underwent one of her

399

Kemal Ataturk, also called Mustafa Kemal (left), the founder of modern Turkey. In Turkish, "Kemal" means "perfection."

periodical renewals of national energy, led by Mustafa Kemal. Under his leadership, Turkey declined to sign the treaty presented to her, and forcibly expelled the Greeks from Asia Minor. By 1923, the peacemakers had to accept defeat and the final Treaty of Lausanne saw Turkey re-established in Anatolia, Smyrna, Eastern Thrace and Adrianople. Thus the Eastern Question remained to complicate the diplomacy of the twentieth century.

Comments on the Peace of Versailles

The work of the Allied statesmen at Versailles has been widely criticized. The severity of the terms imposed upon Germany enabled her later, not without some justice, to claim undue victimization. In 1815 a defeated France had been admitted to the conference table; in 1919 the terms were dictated to Germany, not negotiated with her. She was required to admit her guilt for the war. This admission made no distinction between the German government of Imperial days and the German people, and it unfairly failed to recognize that factors other than German ambition had worked to cause the war of 1914. Again, the cession of Alsace and Lorraine to France included many Germans who were thus being subjected to alien rule, contrary to the conference's declared principle of respect for nationality. As for paying for the cost of the war, Germany could argue that the total was too great for any one nation to meet and especially herself, since the concessions made to France deprived her of her richest economic resources.

This reparations issue was unwise in other respects. German payment in kind by coal shipments to the victorious powers merely impoverished them by ruining their own coal industry. In Britain certainly these shipments

400

served to create unemployment. It was a decision made largely under emotional stress rather than on sound economic grounds.

It proved unwise, too, to encourage the newly created or established republics to model their constitutions after the British example of parliamentary democracy. The British system was the product of centuries of gradual development; less politically experienced nations proved unable to make the system work so that they came to distrust democracy itself and to turn to totalitarian forms of government.

The respect which the conference paid to the principle of nationalism was not wholly happy. A large German minority had to be included in the new Poland and this later proved to be an immediate cause of the outbreak of the Second World War.

The colonial mandatory system was also not without its limitations. It was little more than a disguised system of annexation. Nor did it always satisfy the colonial territories themselves. The expulsion of the Arab population from Palestine to make a national home for the Jews has never been accepted or forgiven in the Arab world and created a problem which is yet to be solved.

Finally, the failure to co-operate with Russia, the initial exclusion of Germany and the refusal of the United States to accept membership left weaknesses in the League.

The problems which faced the Allied statesmen at Versailles were immensely more complex and numerous than any that statesmen had ever had to face before, and it was not to be expected that their solutions would be perfect. Genuine idealism was not entirely lacking, and it found a practical expression in the League of Nations which lasted longer and achieved more than the earlier Concert of Europe. An attempt was made to deliver the people of colonial areas from alien rule, and to protect the rights of European minorities. Severe though the terms imposed on Germany were, the fact remained that in August, 1914, German withdrawal from Belgium would have made it possible for the diplomatists to deal with the situation, but Germany had chosen not to withdraw. The mandatory system, too, recognized that colonial territory did not exist solely for the benefit of the colonial powers, and that the latter's prime duty was to the subject peoples. Finally, if the war of 1939 arose out of the deficiencies of the settlement of 1919, at least a settlement was made; the victory of 1945 still awaits its peace treaty.

QUESTIONS

1. What were the merits and defects of the peace settlement made after the First World War?
2. Describe the territorial changes consequent on the First World War which involved the former Turkish and Austro-Hungarian Empires.

CHAPTER 46

THE LEAGUE OF NATIONS

PRESIDENT WILSON had had to work hard at Versailles to get translated into fact his ideal of an association of states pledged to avoid war for the future. For his successful insistence that it should form a part of each treaty Wilson had to agree to many details of the territorial re-arrangement of Europe in the hope that where these fell short of the ideal, they might be subsequently put right through the League. His hopes were destined to be disappointed, but he got his League.

Basis and Structure

The Covenant of the League bound all its signatories to refrain from declaring war without first submitting its case to the arbitration of the court of justice to be set up under the auspices of the League or to the League itself. Once either of these bodies had pronounced on the dispute there was to be a further interval of three months before any resort to arms. If any member state violated these undertakings, then it would be the duty of other members to take measures against the offender by breaking off trading relations, withdrawing financial support or interrupting supplies of war material. Finally, the Covenant provided a mutual guarantee of the integrity and independence of all signatory members.

The organs of the League which made decisions of policy were the Assembly and the Council. The former met yearly at the permanent headquarters in Geneva; the latter met at least three times a year. It consisted of two groups of national representatives; its permanent members represented the Great Powers and the non-permanent members were elected periodically from and by the smaller member states.

The day-to-day work of the League was carried out by an internationally recruited group of officials and secretarial staff who formed a kind of international civil service. At its head was an elected Secretary-General, who often exercised considerable influence on League policy.

While the Assembly, the Council and the Secretariat all worked from Geneva, the judicial work of the League was centred in Holland at the Hague. Here sat the Permanent Court of International Justice. It comprised eleven judges with four deputies. Its duty was to hear and determine disputes between nations and to settle the issues involved by its interpretation of existing covenants, treaties and pacts. There was the hope that the Court might build up a series of precedents similar to case law which operated in the internal legal systems of member countries.

The League's Achievements

One of the earliest tasks of the League was to supervise the carrying out of some features of the peace settlement. Thus a group of powers was appointed to act as a mandates commission to whom the powers responsible for former enemy colonies had to give an account of their administration of the territories entrusted to them. Another group, the minorities commission, was charged to keep an eye on the welfare of national minorities left under alien rule. Yet a third was the disarmament commission, whose title well defined its work.

All these special bodies had their successes varying with the complexity of the task allotted to them. Least successful was the commission charged to secure some measure of agreed disarmament. Here the effort made was immensely greater than the result achieved.

Most valuable and successful of all the League's work was its efforts to relieve human misery and distress. Special committees were set up to deal with such issues as the relief of famine and disease, the former especially prevalent immediately after the war in Austria and Germany. Slavery was an evil which still lurked in some parts of the world and the League's committee performed a valuable service by bringing it to light and doing much to mitigate it. Equally valuable was the work of another committee set up to supervise the trade in dangerous drugs.

Most successful of all perhaps was the International Labour Office— the I.L.O. as it came to be called, the permanent executive agency of the International Labour Organization. Concerned to raise the social and living standards of all workers in every nation, in the course of the years it passed resolutions on such matters as ways of lightening the hardships of unemployment, sickness and old age, the length of a working day and a working week, the desirability of pensions, and freedom for workers to organize trade unions.

The success of this body owed much to the fact that it was open to states who were not members of the League and America chose to join in its deliberations. It was also exceptional in that each member nation was represented by those who could speak for its trade unions and its employers as well as its government.

The League's Failures

Yet the League had been formed for a specific political aim—that of keeping the peace and the settlement of international disputes without recourse to war. In only one of four instances between 1919 and 1925 did the League succeed in securing respect for its decision.

The first setback came during the years 1919 and 1920 when Russia and Lithuania on the one side and Poland on the other were in dispute about the eastern boundary of Poland. This boundary had been provisionally fixed along what was known as the Curzon line. In 1919 the Poles crossed the line and seized Vilna from Russia. Russia recaptured the town and handed it to Lithuania. Poland appealed to the League for a ruling but meanwhile seized Vilna a second time. The League's protests were ignored, the dispute was taken out of the hands of the League and determined in Poland's favour by the Conference of Ambassadors still in session following the peace conference at Versailles. Poland's insistence on being judge in her own cause carried the day.

Turkey also ignored the League in her wars against the Greeks: the League could only offer aid to those Greeks rendered homeless by the Turkish victory.

Next, in 1923 Italy was in dispute with Greece. Some Italian officials had been murdered near the Albanian border but on Greek territory. Italy demanded a heavy indemnity from Greece which Greece refused to pay; instead she invoked the ruling of the League of Nations. Meanwhile Italy carried out a military occupation of the Greek island of Corfu. In this case, too, the Conference of Ambassadors acted over the head of the League, ruled in Italy's favour and ordered Greece to pay the indemnity demanded. Only when she did so was Corfu evacuated. Italy, like Poland, had shown that it paid to ignore the League and forcibly prosecute her own national interests.

Not until 1925 did the League score a success as an arbitrator in international disputes, and it was an unhappy feature of the success that Greece who had been Italy's victim should now be the loser by the League's triumph.

A series of border incidents between Greece and Bulgaria ended in a Greek invasion of Bulgarian territory. Bulgaria appealed to the League, who ordered the Greeks to withdraw their invading armies and to pay reparation. Greece, a smaller power than Italy, had to comply with the League's ruling.

A more radical weakening of the League's role as keeper of the peace was created when Canada objected to her obligation under the Covenant to defend the independence of any fellow member. This led the League to seek a more workable arrangement for creating a sense of security among European powers, by promoting a series of regional pacts. The most notable of such pacts was the Locarno Agreement of 1925. As signatories to this document, Germany, France, Italy and Belgium mutually guaranteed the Franco-German and the Franco-Belgian frontiers. Another aspect of the Locarno Agreement was the treaty of mutual assistance against German aggression made between France and Poland, and France and Czechoslovakia. These successful negotiations so far eased the tension in Europe as to permit Germany's admission to membership of the League of Nations in 1926.

Less successful by far was the Briand-Kellogg Pact of 1928, renouncing all intention of aggressive war. Although by 1930 it had been signed by all the major powers it proved ultimately to be meaningless. No nation resorting to war is ever willing, or likely, to admit that in so doing it is acting aggressively. Most intractable of the League's problems was that of disarmament. What seemed like a promising beginning was made in 1922 when France, Britain, the United States, Italy and Japan agreed upon a limitation of their respective navies. In 1930 this limitation was carried a step further but there disarmament languished. Various proposals were made but none could be agreed upon and the task was virtually abandoned when Germany first withdrew from the Commission and then from membership of the League itself in 1933.

Two years later, in 1935, Germany re-introduced conscription and made no attempt to conceal the fact that she was re-arming and by these two measures openly violated the Peace of Versailles. Britain sounded the death knell of disarmament by reaching a naval agreement with her former enemy. Thus did Britain concede to an aggressive Germany what she had denied to a peaceful, democratic Germany. Aggression was again shown to be profitable.

In 1931 an explosion occurred in the neighbourhood of the Japanese-controlled South Manchurian railway. With suspicious promptitude, Japan occupied Mukden and quickly overran the Chinese province of Manchuria.

The League of Nations in full session at Geneva in 1923.

China quite correctly appealed to the League who sent out a commission of enquiry. Though the commission pronounced against Japan it did not take the logical step of advising that she be called upon to withdraw. Instead it recommended a compromise: Manchuria should become an independent state.

Even this face-saving proposal was too much for Japanese pride to tolerate. She set up a puppet administration in Manchuria, pushed farther into Chinese territory and withdrew from membership of the League. The truth was that France, Britain and America felt that their interests were best served by Japanese expansion in the East since the alternative might well be Russian expansion there. National interest, in the last resort, still took precedence.

Finally, to compensate for her unfulfilled ambitions in Europe, Italy set her sights on Africa and in 1935 invaded Abyssinia. Haile Selassie, Emperor of Ethiopia, personally pleaded his case before the League and the League condemned the Italian action. It called upon its member states to impose economic sanctions against Italy, but carefully excluded some five basic materials without which Italy would be unable to prosecute her war effort.

Britain and France, ignoring the League's opinion, tried to reach a compromise solution by means of a scheme worked out by the British Foreign Secretary, Sir Samuel Hoare, and the French Prime Minister, Pierre Laval. This time, condonation of aggression was too much for public opinion in either country to tolerate. Hoare had to resign and the plan was dropped. Yet this was as far as public opinion could force the hands of government. The Italian conquest of Abyssinia continued unabated until the whole country passed under Italian control. Italy showed what she felt about the League by withdrawing from membership in 1937.

Events between 1937 and 1939 did not so much weaken the League, as prove that its weakness had already resulted in death. Germany in 1936 was allowed to re-occupy the Rhineland without resistance. In the same year Italy and Germany openly supported a revolution in Spain against the Spanish government. In 1937 Japan pushed farther into China, and nobody moved against her. President Wilson's dream of a world in which nations did not seek to win by war what they had failed to get by diplomacy was over.

The fundamental cause of the failure of the League was the fact that no government was prepared to surrender any degree of its sovereign right to pursue its own interests in its own way. To have imposed sanctions on the export of coal to Italy in 1935 might have saved Abyssinia, but it would have damaged Britain's export trade in coal and therefore have had unhappy effects on employment. To have closed the Suez Canal to Italian shipping in that same crisis would have hampered the Italian war effort but depleted the revenues drawn by France and Britain for the use of the canal. Germany in 1936 thought her interests would be best served by re-possession of the

Italian soldiers march through Rome on their way to Abyssinia in 1935.

Rhineland even at the risk of war, than by loyally abiding by her signature of the Locarno Pact. She put material advantage above honour and what she could not be given she was prepared to take.

A second reason for the League's failure was a certain lack of realism. It seemed to have been assumed that nations fell into dispute about ill-defined points in pacts and treaties. In fact they usually risked war from a desire to gain that to which they had no legal right and because they knew this, war was the only means of getting what they coveted. Only force can check a determined aggressor and the League had no force at its command.

This then was a third reason for failure; the League had no troops or ships or aeroplanes to enforce its decisions; it had to rely on moral influence and this was precisely what a nation bent on aggression and self-aggrandisement would not respect.

There was the fourth factor, namely, that the League never really was a League of Nations, only an association of some nations and two of the greatest, Russia and America, long remained outside it.

All the blame for failure cannot be placed on governments or statesmen. In the democracies, public opinion had been so horrified by the war of 1914-18 that, for long after, anything seemed preferable than resort to arms. Pacifism in these countries was too strong to be ignored by the politicians. To the peoples in the democracies peace without honour if necessary was preferred to war with honour. It was a policy to the errors of which they awoke too late and which provoked the very catastrophe it sought to avoid.

QUESTIONS

1. Describe the organization of the League of Nations. What strengths and what weakness had the League shown by 1933?
2. What crises threatened the peace of Europe between 1919 and 1931 and how were they dealt with?

CHAPTER 47

DEMOCRACY ON TRIAL IN FRANCE AND GERMANY, 1919-1933

WHEN one looks at the condition of France and Germany after 1919 it is difficult to see any large difference between victor and vanquished.

France

France had been the battleground of Europe for four years; her reconstruction was a formidable and expensive task. Her internal debt was enormous and in addition she had incurred a heavy international indebtedness to her allies, particularly to Britain and America.

Politically she was plagued by a multiplicity of parties. Seldom did any one of them command a strong parliamentary majority. Since the Chamber of Deputies sat for four years whether ministries rose or fell, its members had few qualms about overthrowing an administration whose policy the deputies disliked, often for quite trivial reasons.

Amongst these practical problems was an emotional one. France's victory in 1918 had done nothing to remove that distrust and fear of Germany which had been a dominating feature of French politics since 1870. In spite of her enormous debts, France found the money to construct an elaborate system of defences along her common border with Germany. This system, the Maginot line, was intended to ensure that Germany would never again be able to effect a surprise invasion of France. France was also determined to make Germany pay for the cost of the war. By doing so she would ease her own financial burden and prevent any revival of German power. France's fear was intensified as America and Britain showed increasing desire to withdraw from European involvement. She felt herself to stand alone as Europe's western bulwark against Germany.

Germany

Germany's position in 1919 was hardly less precarious than that of France. The collapse of the central government was followed by that of the princely states, the administration of these being replaced by democratic republics, It seemed as if united Germany was to be a thing of the past and all Bismarck's work undone. In addition, there was acute social distress. With her industries ruined or confiscated, unemployment was rife. Her people everywhere went hungry, and with hunger went anger—anger with themselves for allowing themselves to be defeated, anger with the victors for the harsh and humiliating peace terms dictated.

The burden of reparations amounted to £6,600 million and this huge sum Germany was committed to pay off at the rate of £100 million annually. She had asked for a reduction of the total and had been refused; she had sought a delay of two years before the first payment and had been denied this grace. France, it was clear, would exact the last penny, and there thus stretched before Germany the prospect of sixty-six years of impoverishment, even if the task was humanly possible at all.

Republican Experiment in Germany

Early in 1919 a coalition government was elected, formed of Social Democrats, Democrats, and the Centre party. To this new government fell the unenviable task of signing the Versailles Treaty. This done, its next work was to frame a new constitution for Germany.

This took the form of a republic, headed by a president served by ministers responsible to a legislative body elected by universal suffrage, the *Reichstag*. In addition to the *Reichstag*, the constitution provided for the provinces to be represented in the *Reichsrat*. The President was elected by a referendum and was to hold office for seven years. So began what was soon known as the Weimar Republic. This experiment in democratic government inherited a legacy of heavy internal and international indebtedness, social distress, and national humiliation. The resentment which the German people felt for the terms of the Peace of Versailles was transferred to the government which had signed on their behalf.

The immediate problem was that of finance and reparations. As the result of a loan raised in London, Germany made an initial payment of £50 million but by 1923 she was two years in default. France, in spite of the disapproval of her ally Britain, occupied the Ruhr, insisting that the cause of default was unwillingness to pay. This made the situation worse. The German people now felt that they had a legitimate grievance. The workers in the Ruhr made every effort to defeat French purposes. Many factories closed; many workers came out on strike. The German government persuaded the strikers to return to work and resumed payment of reparations. France for her part after two years withdrew her occupying forces and Britain, who had not liked the Ruhr occupation, proposed general cancellation of inter-Allied war debts. This proposal was a factor, along with the French action in the Ruhr, in the formulation of the Dawes plan in 1924. It was now agreed that, beginning at £50 million per year Germany should pay at gradually increasing rates until the yearly figure had reached £125 million. To make this possible, other countries, and particularly America, would both lend money to Germany and invest in her commercial enterprises.

By 1929 it was clear that this plan was too ambitious. Germany was receiving in loans and investment more than she was repaying and the Young Plan scaled down the total of reparations from the original £6,600 million to £2,000 million. This more realistic approach came too late. An economic crisis developed in America and spread to Europe. International trade and finance virtually collapsed. Reparations were suspended in 1931 and abandoned in 1932. The Weimar Republic gained no credit in Germany for the final disappearance of this financial burden. It had been removed merely as the result of a European economic crisis which brought as much distress to Germany as to any other nation.

Unstable Governments in France, 1919-32

Between 1919 and 1932 the only constant element in French political life was the frequent changes of government. Broadly speaking, they were all one of two kinds—conservative and reactionary or socialist and co-operative.

Up to 1924 the conservatives held power. By 1922 Poincare was Prime Minister. He distrusted Germany and had no sympathy for her reparations difficulties and when in 1923 Germany again defaulted on debt payment, it was Poincaré who had no hesitation in ordering the occupation of the Ruhr. Though he thus forced a resumption of payment, he was the loser. The Ruhr occupation proved more costly than profitable. France in 1924 was unable to balance her budget and the government increased taxation. This was one price the nation was not willing to pay and the government fell from power.

A new coalition of socialists and radicals came into office. In this administration the dominating figure was the Foreign Minister, Briand, both a patriotic Frenchman and a good European. For all too brief a time he was

Gustav Stresemann of Germany. *Aristide Briand of France.*

matched by a man of similar outlook in Germany, Dr. Stresemann. There seemed hope of progress towards a constructive settlement of Franco-German relationships. It was Briand who in 1925 withdrew the French troops from the Ruhr. It was Briand, Stresemann and Austen Chamberlain of Britain who negotiated the Locarno pacts. Briand responded to the American overtures which led to the Kellogg Pact. It was during this adminis-tration also that the Dawes Plan for Reparations was drafted.

The hopes aroused by the Briand-Stresemann co-operation soon faded. Despite their sound financial policy, the radical-socialists had failed to solve France's financial problems, and the government fell.

Back into power came the conservative Poincaré. The new government sought and was given power to govern by decree. Using these powers, Poincaré raised taxation to a realistic level and by this and other measures stabilized the value of the franc. But his administration had been based on a somewhat unnatural alliance of conservatives with radicals. Only a supreme crisis had brought them together and when it was over the radicals withdrew their support and the government fell.

Briand returned to office, but was not destined to repeat his former success. A new, aggressive party was on the way to power in Germany and the old French fears revived in all their old strength. In 1929 France, like the rest of western Europe, was deep in a new financial crisis. She grew increasingly resentful as it became apparent in the years 1931 and 1932 that she would have to abandon her hopes of German reparations. Briand's administration did not survive the final discontinuance of payments in 1932.

Failure of the Weimar Republic

One province in Germany, Bavaria, had retained a right-wing conservative administration based on the old autocratic tradition. The Bavarian capital, Munich, became the rallying point for many ex-officers and wealthy men who had no love for the new national constitution. In 1923 there appeared among them an ex-corporal who, by the strength of his personality and his face-saving argument that the German army had really been defeated by the Communist and Jewish enemies at home, soon established himself as their leader. Under him they set up a semi-military organization. Their companies of storm troopers adopted a brown uniform and the swastika as their emblem. They had no difficulty in attracting recruits from the ranks of the unemployed. Presently they felt strong enough to attempt to seize the government of the State by force. They failed: their ex-corporal leader, Adolf Hitler, was injured but tried and imprisoned.

His short imprisonment was anything but arduous; he had by then too many influential friends. He was allowed to occupy himself largely in literary labours, and when he was released he brought with him the manuscript of his famous book *Mein Kampf.* It was the ideas he therein expounded which became the gospel of National Socialism and the Nazi party.

The Nazi Gospel

Hitler believed in government by a leader through able subordinates—the Führer principle. He rejected the western idea of men's equality: the Aryan race, he claimed, was superior to all others and especially to the Jews. Communism he regarded as being of Jewish origin; therefore he hated it and he rejected Christianity for the same reason—a new Germany must be created, purged of all non-Aryan blood and cherishing the old German virtues of loyalty and obedience.

After the party had been re-organized in 1925 with Hitler in supreme command, Goebbels in charge of propaganda and Goering shaping its militant forces, this gospel was diligently spread through the party newspaper, edited by a rabid Jew-hater, Streicher, mass rallies, the leader's rabble-rousing speeches, and above all by the capture of the rising generation through the formation of a youth party. Money came from industrialists who saw the hope of revived prosperity through a policy of re-armament in defiance of the Peace of Versailles.

Apart from the stimulus given to the growth of the party in 1923 by the consequences of the Ruhr occupation, progress was slow. The years 1925 to 1929 were those of the Stresemann-Briand era when the Nazi appeal to discontent had only thin soil in which to feed.

The world disaster of 1929 renewed the party's opportunity. German economy was dependent upon foreign capital; the collapse of world trade and credit in 1929 exposed this serious weakness of the Weimar Republic. The numbers of the unemployed in Germany more than doubled between 1929 and 1932. German democracy could not rise to the occasion and the nation turned back to its old tradition—it looked for a leader.

Inevitably, it chose a soldier, General Hindenburg, who had brought victory so near in 1918. He was made President and with him as Chancellor was the leader of the Social Democrats, Brüning, endowed by the President with emergency powers.

The Nazis made the most of this failure of democracy. They addressed a powerful appeal to the unemployed by assuring the nation that they could find work for all. The growth of the party was startling. By 1932 they had over two hundred members in the *Reichstag* and Goering was its President. Had he been prepared to head a coalition government Hitler could have been chancellor in 1932; he preferred to wait until he could command absolute power. His opportunity came the next year. President Hindenburg, whose mental powers were failing, and von Papen, an aristocratic politician of limited experience, agreed to offer Hitler the chancellorship, in the mistaken

Nazi Youth Party members at a rally in the 1930s.

belief that such an upstart would easily fall under their control. After the elections of 1933 the *Reichstag*, with nearly three hundred Nazi members, granted Hitler supreme legislative powers and went into suspension. Hitler's first acts as dictator were to abolish all political parties but his own, to hold new elections with no candidates save Nazis and to suppress all provincial divisions. There was to be one party and one state. The Weimar Republic and German democracy were dead.

The Weimar Republic was handicapped from birth. Neither republicanism nor democracy was part of the national tradition; to many the new system was thus a foreign importation from an enemy country. It never commanded the loyalty of the army or of the civil service. In these circumstances it needed and should have had the strongest encouragement from the former enemy powers. This it never received. Europe showed itself eager to make concessions to Hitler the dictator which it had refused to make to Stresemann the European. France in particular bears heavy responsibility for her continued hostility to the Weimar Republic.

QUESTIONS

1. Show the importance between the years 1919 and 1932 of the following: (a) reparations; (b) French occupation of the Ruhr; (c) the Locarno Pact; (d) the economic crisis of 1929.
2. What were the main causes of the failure of the Weimar Republic in Germany?

CHAPTER 48

FASCISM AND COMMUNISM

HITLER and the Nazi party were at first regarded as little more than a pale imitation of the régime which had grown up in Italy by 1923. By the time Hitler became Chancellor of Germany, Italy had already had a one-party system and a dictator for thirteen years. Russia too had evolved a system of government all its own and just as alien to western Europe as the systems of Germany and Italy.

Italy and Fascism

Italy in 1919 was a disappointed nation. She had carried little weight at the Conference of Versailles and came out of it convinced that she had received less than was due to her. She did not get the port of Fiume and when former German colonies were allotted, Italy's right to be a mandatory power was ignored. Keen Italian patriots such as the nationalist poet Gabriele D'Annunzio began to preach the need for an aggressive revival of ancient Roman glory.

The parliamentary system which governed Italy from 1919 to 1923 was rife with corruption which thrived on the illiteracy of many of the voters and seemed powerless or unwilling to relieve the poverty of the mass of Italian peasants. Of several political parties, not one could establish a parliamentary majority. Social discontent found expression in strikes and riots between socialist and communist workers.

On to this scene of democratic incompetence strode Benito Mussolini, one-time teacher, then journalist. Through his newspaper, *Avanti*, he formed in Milan a party pledged to abolish parties and to establish strong efficient government. His supporters were organized in semi-military fashion with a uniform of brown shirts and short trousers. Their emblem was the fasces, the bundle of rods carried by the lictors of ancient Rome as a sign of their punitive authority.

In 1922 Mussolini had sufficient confidence in his fascist party to lead a march on Rome. There was no effective opposition: King Victor Emmanuel III yielded to Mussolini's demand to be entrusted with control of the government. Ruthlessly, Mussolini and his fascists crushed their opponents by beatings, threats, forcible dosing with castor oil, and even murder.

He successfully increased his following among the middle-classes by exploiting their fear of communism while strengthening his appeal to the wealthy industrialists by abandoning his belief in socialism. His implied readiness to revive the ancient glory of the Roman Empire drew to his cause the more fiery patriots. By 1924 he had at last a parliamentary majority. He was now free to destroy the democracy which so far he had tolerated.

Mussolini now became dictator in name as well as in fact. The new constitution was headed by the Grand Council who chose the members of the Senate, the senior legislative assembly. The lower house of the legislature did not take final shape until 1939. Trade unions had been replaced by corporations for each main industry, representing both workers and employers. It was their business to organize their particular industry in the primary interests of the State. Ultimately, these corporations chose members of the lower house of the legislature which drew the rest of its members from the ranks of the fascist party.

Much of this transformation of the political scene was possible because the Press was early made subject to government supervision. One other feature of the fascist régime was the total exclusion of women from politics and their relegation to duties exclusively domestic.

The loss of political liberty seemed to some Italians a price worth paying for what Mussolini offered. Unemployment at least diminished as he put in hand a vast land-reclamation programme, draining the Pontine Marshes, turning their waste into a productive agricultural area and easing the food shortage. A flourishing farming economy was an essential part of Mussolini's intentions since he aimed to make his country self-sufficient. That he could never wholly succeed in this aim was certain since Italy lacks coal deposits. Nevertheless fascism tried hard to industrialize the country, encouraging trade and manufactures by laying high duties on all imported goods which were in competition with native production.

Much was also done to facilitate transport. New roads were built, older ones improved. The whole railway network was electrified and for the first time in Italy's history her trains began to run to time. Skilful use was made of Italy's river system to develop hydro-electric power not only for the railways but also for industry. This off-set the lack of coal, saved expensive imports and was a further step along the road of national economic self-sufficiency. In addition, welfare was not overlooked. There was considerable expansion and development of the educational system of the country and a system of national insurance was established.

The most memorable achievement of fascism was the reconciliation of Church and State. Since 1870 successive popes had remained as voluntary prisoners in the Vatican as a protest against the incorporation of Rome into united Italy. In 1929 Mussolini arranged with the Papacy the Lateran Treaty. By this the Vatican city was recognized as having complete independence.

It was to have its own "troops," its own postal and financial systems, its own diplomatic and foreign service. It was in fact to be a state within the state of Italy. In return the Church recognized the sovereignty of the House of Savoy and Roman Catholicism became the official religion of Italy.

Mussolini despised peace and peace-lovers; the warm friendly nature of his countrymen was a weakness of national character which he was determined to remedy. It was inevitable that with such an outlook his attitude to other states was aggressive and that his aims in foreign policy were imperialistic. He saw himself as a twentieth-century Caesar, but his difficulty was to find an enemy who could certainly be beaten. He overawed a newly-created state, Yugoslavia, into ceding Fiume in 1924 and dared to assert equality with Hitler in 1934 by manning the Brenner Pass to safeguard Austrian independence from possible German encroachment. He advertised the skill of his air force by the aid he gave to General Franco in the Spanish Civil War of 1936. Thereafter he had to content himself with the conquest of an African people totally lacking modern armaments (Abyssinia) while in Europe playing a supporting role to the Hitler he had once thwarted.

Yet Mussolini in foreign affairs had a degree of success which he did not deserve. His military strength was a façade, the thinness of which a major war soon exposed. Throughout much of the inter-war years Mussolini bluffed but no one had the courage to call his bluff. The result was to encourage Hitler to risk a greater gamble and provoke world war.

In domestic affairs Mussolini's only solid achievement was the reconciliation with the Church. He improved the economy of his country but deprived his people of the full benefits of the improvement by heavy expenditure on armaments. By ultimately exposing Italy to invasion and defeat he undid what little of benefit he had accomplished. The succeeding republican government of Italy had to begin not where Mussolini had left off but where he himself had begun twenty years earlier.

Russia, 1917-35

The attempts under the Tsarist régime of Russia in the opening years of the twentieth century to establish representative government had been a failure. Revolutionary societies and leaders sprang up but they were hunted down, suppressed and their leaders exiled. The Imperial court was isolated from the people; the amiable, well-meaning but far from strong-willed Nicholas II and his wife were protected from all knowledge of the real state of the country by their entourage, while they were at the same time deceived and dominated by the evil, debauched monk, Rasputin. This rascal used their concern for the heir to the throne, delicate in health, to ingratiate himself into favour, power and influence.

Yet on the surface, Russia gave the impression of a great and strong

Mussolini and his Brown Shirts marching through Rome.

power. At the beginning of the war of 1914 Europe looked to what it called the Russian Colossus to steamroller Imperial Germany into quick defeat. It was the Russian failure during the war that exposed her hollowness and led to the crisis of revolution, which in its beginnings was mild enough. Its first leader Kerensky would have been content with a liberal monarchy which would have set about a modest programme of internal social reform. For his rival Lenin, smuggled back from exile by German connivance, this was not enough. Not even the ending of the war and the Tsar's surrender of his throne proved sufficient to save Kerensky's liberal government.

With its fall the grimmest phase of the revolution occurred. The Tsar and his family were brutally shot down; the same fate overtook hundreds of large landowners. A White Russian reactionary party, backed by France and Britain, failed to suppress the Red Russians ably led by Trotsky. At last the Bolsheviks were in power, prepared to commit their country to a new political, social and economic organization—communism.

Many minds besides those of Marx and Engels have helped to shape the doctrines of communism. It is now a complex system of ideas and where it has been put into practice different aspects have been stressed. In Russia after the revolution of 1917, it meant primarily the establishment of one-party rule, the abolition of all private enterprise and the state ownership of all that was produced and the means by which it had been produced.

As the feudal estates were broken up the land was given to the peasants who had worked on it. For the time being the *kulaks*, or farmer-employers, survived, but all their produce, apart from the minimum necessary for

417

Crowds gather outside the palace on the eve of the Russian revolution.

personal and household needs, was seized by the State and paid for at a fixed price. The kulaks replied by hiding their surplus and a shortage of food resulted. Hungry town workers and peasants were encouraged to pillage their farmer neighbours. The farmers took to cultivating only as much of their land as would supply their own needs; there was thus no surplus either for confiscation or pillage.

With the total failure of food supplies the whole economic life of the country came to a halt. The newly nationalized factories closed. Their workers fell ill through undernourishment and starvation: disease and poverty ravaged the land.

When in 1921 it looked as if even the army might mutiny, Lenin, who had for some time urged that communism would have to be temporarily modified, secured a hearing. Gradually he established himself in power. For the time being he was prepared to tolerate a certain degree of private enterprise. Cultivators were told that they would once again be allowed to sell any surplus they produced. Instead of a discouraging uniformity of reward for workers, incentives were introduced such as piece-work rates. Such concessions made the new government tolerable and gave it a second chance.

While communism was thus being modified within Russia, she also showed herself disposed to enter into peaceful relations with the hated capitalist system of Europe. The fears which Europe entertained of the new Russia began to diminish as Russia showed pacific intentions in international politics. In 1920 she guaranteed the independence of her small new neighbours in the Baltic—Lithuania, Latvia, Finland and Estonia. The next year she brought her war with Poland to an end. In 1922 by the Treaty of Rapallo she established a good-neighbour policy with Germany. By the time of Lenin's death in 1924 she was trading with most of the European powers.

418

Stalin and Communist Agriculture

Lenin's death led to a bitter contest for the leadership of the State between Trotsky, the military hero of the revolution, and Joseph Stalin, a Georgian peasant, powerfully entrenched in office in the communist party. Victory went to Stalin; Trotsky went into exile, constantly hunted and in danger from Russian agents though he escaped assassination until 1940 when he was murdered with an ice pick in Mexico.

Stalin ruthlessly and brutally addressed himself to the task of creating a completely communist régime in Russia and as Lenin's compromise régime had taken the bite out of the opposition he was largely successful. His ultimate aim was to make Russia as great an industrial nation as any in western Europe. This meant the purchase of equipment from abroad. The only export by which these imports could be paid for was grain, and he had therefore to begin by securing a vast agricultural expansion.

Collectivization of farms was the method he chose. This provoked a head-on clash with the *kulaks*, who resisted bitterly. Rather than see their holdings merged into large state-owned units they were prepared to face any penalty. Rather than accept defeat Stalin was prepared to go to any length. Many *kulaks* were killed, many of them were simply left to starve, many more found themselves condemned to forced labour in primitive camps in the wilds of Siberia.

Yet by 1930 the back of their opposition had been broken, though at a heavy cost. Determined that the State should reap as little as possible many *kulaks* had killed off their livestock and it was twenty years before the animal husbandry of Russia recovered. While the collective farms were being established Russia had less rather than more grain for export; indeed she was often hard pressed to find enough for home consumption and had to buy food abroad.

After 1930, the opposition to collective farming was weak enough to be handled more subtly. The few private farmers who were left found themselves subject to higher rates of taxes than their collective neighbours. Within the next two years over half the best agricultural land was being worked on communist principles.

Stalin could now forge ahead with his industrial designs. He began on the assumption that a communist state must be self-sufficient so that when it was sooner or later compelled to fight for its life it would not in any way be dependent for food or material upon outside sources. This was a distinct variation of the pure communist gospel which preached international socialism. Another Stalinist departure from the strict faith was his willingness to accept foreign investment and foreign technical aid.

His expediency paid dividends. Foreign aid played a vital part in the development of the new state-owned factories and the new industrial towns created under Stalin's rule. He placed the emphasis on the expansion of heavy manufacturing industries rather than upon the production of consumer goods so that the people benefited originally not from greater material comforts but by enjoying steady and full employment. The worker who could increase his rate of production might receive preferential treatment in housing; above all he was accorded public honour and esteem as a soviet hero. Stalin's justification for such non-commu-

Joseph Stalin, 1879-1953.

nist practices was that they advanced Russia farther towards the desired goal of national self-sufficiency. His degree of success was a vital factor in enabling Russia to withstand German attack in the war of 1939-45.

Social well-being was not wholly neglected. Greater strides than ever before were made in overcoming the problem of illiteracy by a large expansion of the Russian educational system and higher education, particularly of a technical character, was intensively developed; but all this rested upon basic instruction in communist principles as the only truth. There was too an improvement in the standard of living; slums were replaced by workers' flats, all state-owned, with rent controlled by the community. Homes were provided for the aged, illness was covered by free medical treatment and doctors were the employees of the State. Unemployment became a thing of the past.

Yet for all that was achieved under Stalin a heavy price had to be paid. Liberty ceased to exist: the individual was completely subordinated to the State. Christianity was frowned upon; churches were closed and often converted into museums, or flats to relieve the housing problem. No political party was allowed to exist save the communist party. Workers could not bargain about wages, hours or conditions of labour for the State was the employer. Not only was it a crime to disapprove of communism, it was equally criminal and perhaps even more dangerous to disapprove of Stalin's type of communism. Those who did met with short shrift, however prominent they might be in the communist party itself. In a series of "purges" between 1934 and 1938, many such were removed by death, sometimes without, sometimes after, trial. The secret police—*Ogpu*—were always close at hand, observing, eavesdropping and provoking.

Stalin was the main author of the constitution for the four republics which together in 1923 formed the federation of the Union of Soviet Socialist Republics. He also, in 1936, revised the constitution which now governs the republics which form the Union. Each village, town, district and province has its "soviet," or committee of elected representatives, and these bodies deal with local affairs and enforce the national decisions on internal policy. All members of the population over the age of eighteen have the right to vote but the only candidates up for election are those who have been approved by the communist party. They may not necessarily be members of the party for such membership is restricted, and is indeed an honour much prized and earned only by hard effort.

At national level stands the Supreme Soviet, consisting of two bodies, one an elected assembly containing one representative for every 300,000 people, and the other, the soviet of nationalities, containing representatives of all the republics. Since the Supreme Soviet is not in permanent session, the day-to-day work of government is carried on by a permanent council known as the Praesidium. This body chooses the Council of Ministers, or people's commissars as they are called.

The communist party has its own elaborate organization and is the real power behind the prime minister whose position is that of supreme dictator. Whoever establishes control of the party and *Ogpu* controls Russia.

Foreign aid to the enemies of her revolution in 1917 and her own inherent belief in the hostility of a capitalist world, together with her internal problems, led Russia to withdraw into diplomatic isolation until 1934. The fact that America refused until 1933 to recognize the new régime did nothing to allay her suspicions of the West. During these years of internal consolidation she regularized her relations with her immediate neighbours, the Baltic states, Poland and Germany. It was only in 1934 when she joined the League of Nations that she began to play again a major role in international politics.

QUESTIONS

1. Account for Mussolini's seizure of power in 1922 and describe his policy at home up to 1936.
2. What were the causes of the Russian Revolution of 1917? Trace the development in Russia's internal affairs from the death of Lenin to the outbreak of war in 1939.

CHAPTER 49

MINOR DICTATORSHIPS

I N THIS chapter we are concerned to trace the attempts of the peace-makers of 1919 to establish liberal democracy in their reorganized Europe. When major powers such as Italy, Russia and Germany could show their dislike of this, it is not surprising that many smaller states were not slow to follow suit.

Hungary after 1919

The Magyar aristocracy who had always dominated the political life of Hungary resented the loss of some of their choicest territory to Rumania, Yugoslavia, and Czechoslovakia. As this placed many Magyars under foreign rule, they considered the arrangements of 1919 a denial of the principle of nationalism.

At first there was little they could do; they could not even prevent the formation after revolution of a communist government. But before 1919 was over the armed forces had thrown in their lot with reaction; the communist government was overturned and the country was in the hands of Admiral Horthy, who had led the anti-communist coup.

Nominally Horthy was regent, holding the situation for the restoration of a monarchy in Hungary. In fact he remained as dictator. He regarded democratic government with grave suspicion and under him Hungary was again dominated by the narrow, exclusive Magyar aristocracy. The peasant tenantry of the large estates saw all hope of land distribution fade and their social condition was little better after 1919 than it had been before the war. Horthy and his associates never forgot their fellow Magyars living under an alien rule. The hope of re-creating an all-embracing Magyar state was never far from their dreams but they had to wait for the dismemberment of Czechoslovakia in 1939 for the opportunity to turn dreams into reality.

Yugoslavia

Yugoslavia, on the other hand, had every reason for self-congratulation. Her part in the war of 1914 had greatly helped the allied cause and she was suitably rewarded by an extension of her territory which virtually made her a new state. Her gains at the expense of Austria-Hungary and Bulgaria brought together many Slav groups and thus seemed to be an expression of

422

the principle of nationalism. Unfortunately these Slav groups were of different religion and had lived apart for too long for the ties of blood relationship to overcome the barriers of Serb Orthodoxy and the Roman Catholicism of the rest. A limited monarchy and a democratic parliament might have been expected to afford a constitutional outlet for the expression and ultimate reconciliation of these differences but it failed to do so. Yugoslavs had too long been accustomed to autocratic government to use wisely the liberty now given them.

The king, Alexander, came to the conclusion that democratic government was so unsuited to his people that it could no longer be tolerated. Accordingly in 1928 he abolished the constitution and until his death in 1934 he established a royal dictatorship.

It did not solve all Yugoslavia's problems. A Serb king through Serb ministers was ruling in a Serb capital (Belgrade) over a kingdom which included a large Croat minority. Inevitably there developed a demand for Croatian independence which became more and more difficult to ignore. By 1939 when there were signs that the Croats might resort to violence, Alexander's successor King Peter was forced to accept defeat and Croatian self-government was granted.

After Yugoslavia lost the port of Fiume to Italy, relations between the two countries improved. This was because Yugoslavia, having gained so much from the Austro-Hungarian Empire, had a sense of insecurity lest the new Austria and Hungary should seek by force to recover what the old empire had lost. There was too the fear that her discontented minorities might prove willing agents of foreign powers. She was too conscious of old enemies to neglect the opportunity of making new friends such as Italy.

Greece

Greece was far less successful than Yugoslavia in holding the territorial rewards given her at the expense of Turkey in 1919, though she tried hard, by a sternly waged war to do so. Before she had properly recovered from this effort, she found herself involved in the dispute with Italy about Corfu and the League of Nations was unable to save her.

The internal problems of Greece were an even greater handicap; she appeared unable to arrive at a satisfactory system of government; she could neither reconcile herself to her kings nor dispense with them. Constantine, whom she had deposed in the war years, she recalled to the throne in 1920, only to blame him for defeat at the hands of Turkey and so compel him to abdicate a second time. His son George II was equally the victim of a national demand for a scapegoat, this time for the Greek humiliation at the hands of Italy and the League of Nations, over Corfu. On this occasion, Greece turned from monarchy itself; after a plebiscite taken in 1924, a republican form of government was adopted and though it survived until 1935 it never ceased to be the target of monarchical plots. These finally had their effect on public opinion when by a further plebiscite the monarchy was restored in 1935.

King George II, restored in 1935, retained his throne until his death twelve years later but monarchy survived at the expense of democracy. For the first three of those twelve years parliamentary government showed itself as incompetent as ever. Then the army intervened and its leader General Metaxas assumed supreme power. Parliament was abolished: Metaxas became dictator, and mercilessly repressed those who sought to challenge him. Greece now enjoyed a degree of stability she had never experienced since 1919 but it was at the price of the loss of much liberty and freedom. Perhaps the greatest benefit the régime of Metaxas gave to Greece was not so much the modest measure of social reform introduced, as the new friendly relationship established with the old enemy, Turkey.

For such a change, circumstances were favourable on both sides. As we shall presently see, Turkey had set her own house in order in a way which, had it occurred in the nineteenth century, would have gone far towards the solution of the Eastern Question. So far as Greece was concerned, the vital development was the abolition of the old sultanate and its replacement by a republic anxious to emulate the West.

Turkey Between the Wars

In her hour of defeat in 1919 Turkey found a saviour in Mustafa Kemal, the hero who refused to accept the humiliating terms of Versailles. He led the war against Greece and compelled the European powers to acknowledge his success in the treaty of Lausanne in 1923.

It would have been too much to expect Turkey, so long accustomed to no other form of government than oriental despotism, to establish a genuine parliamentary democracy: nor did she. Her constitution was a façade behind which worked the very real dictatorship of Kemal. It is true that he gave Turkey a representative legislature, elected by universal suffrage which included even women. This was, however, but the shell of democracy, since only candidates approved by Kemal were permitted to put themselves forward for election. Yet Kemal's dictatorship had one great virtue as compared with many of those established elsewhere; it was not aggressive. On the contrary, once he had successfully challenged the Versailles settlement he showed himself anxious to establish good relationships not only with the old enemy Greece, but also with Britain. This latter friendship ultimately resulted in an alliance between the two, which greatly strengthened British security in the east.

Kemal's admiration for the West, shown by his alliance with Britain, induced him to reform the Turkish way of life. He introduced machinery into farming and thus brought Turkish agriculture up to western standards. At the same time he encouraged industry, buying equipment from abroad to install in the new Turkish factories. He encouraged the private citizen to invest his capital and to seek profits, following the pattern of western capitalism rather than Russian communism.

Kemal's most surprising success was achieved in Turkish social life. Almost every custom which marked Turkey out as an oriental nation, Kemal attacked. Men had to discard the fez and take to wearing western-style hats. The women, who had always lived in seclusion and never appeared in public save with their faces veiled, were now emancipated and compelled to throw aside their veils. Men were instructed to salute each other not with the eastern salaam but by the western raising of the hat.

Education and religion did not escape Kemal's reforming, westernizing zeal. The teaching of the old Turkish script was replaced by instruction in the western Latin alphabet. Islam was deprived of its status as the official religion of the state and polygamy was abolished. Kemal dragged a sometimes unwilling Turkey from oriental medievalism into the modern western world.

Spain

By the beginning of the twentieth century, Spain had a deeply entrenched tradition of absolutist government. It was Spanish nationalism rather than

These girls, photographed in 1926, were part of Turkey's "new look".

liberalism which had helped to defeat Napoleon. In the mid-nineteenth century Palmerston's hope of encouraging constitutionalism in Spain proved vain. When in 1870 the Spanish people rose in rebellion it was simply another monarch they found in Amadeo of Savoy and the republic they established after his three years' reign only survived for twelve months.

Under Alfonso XII who mounted the throne in 1874 and Alfonso XIII who succeeded him in 1886, Spain remained a backward, unprogressive country. Her people were unenergetic, illiterate, priest-ridden, their lives dominated by a still largely feudal nobility. There was but little industry, agricultural methods were primitive and the standard of living for all, save a privileged nobility, depressed.

Politically, power rested in the hands of the king and he was as convinced of his Divine Right as were the Stuarts in Britain in the seventeenth century. There was a representative body, the *Cortes*, but the cause of democracy which it embodied lacked both the sympathy of the Crown and the interest of the people. The royal authority was exercised through the nobility, who officered and therefore controlled the army, and through a civil service in no way subject to democratic checks and therefore often corrupt. To this system of government the state religion, Roman Catholicism, lent its support and spiritual authority.

Spain preserved her neutrality throughout the war of 1914-18 and indeed perhaps profited from the way in which the belligerents made her a hive of espionage and counter-espionage. Yet when the war was over, there remained in Spain a deposit of new ideas and new groups all serving or threatening to stir the country from its long lethargy. Socialists, communists, republicans, fascists and anarchists all disapproved of the autocratic régime in Spain though they differed in opinion on the way in which it should be reshaped. The result was a series of riots, strikes and political conspiracies but the would-be reformers lacked unity of aim and indeed were as opposed to each other as to the régime. So long as the armed forces remained loyal to the Crown, the prospects of success were negligible.

It was when this loyalty was withdrawn in 1923 that the situation began to change. General Primo de Rivera led a military coup. He demanded his own appointment as dictator after Alfonso XIII had dismissed the existing ministers. To these demands the king had to agree, for with the army supporting Rivera the Crown had no means of resistance.

Though Rivera remained in office for seven years, he was able to accomplish very little in the way of reform. He quickly found that, like the king, he was the prisoner of the army. At the time of his coup, he had carried the army with him because it wanted military reform and felt disgraced by the government's feeble conduct of a colonial war in Morocco; it had not shared its General's wish to carry out thorough reform of national life. Again, the

Church maintained its opposition to change. Politically, socialists were opposed to a strong central government unless it was socialist, republicans wished to see the abolition of monarchy, and the anarchists of Catalonia were against any kind of government at all. Recognizing his failure, in 1930 Rivera resigned and the king resumed the direction of national affairs.

Primo de Rivera had in all probability delayed the king's loss of his throne. While Rivera remained dictator, he had been blamed for the country's ills; now that he had gone all discontent vented itself on Alfonso

Primo de Rivera, Spanish dictator.

XIII. The monarchy survived the fall of its protective dictator for little more than twelve months.

Republicanism now had its opportunity to show what it could do, but at a singularly inopportune moment in history; in 1931 Europe was deeply involved in a world-wide economic depression.

The first administration of the newly established republic addressed itself to the unhealthy influence it believed the Church to exercise on Spanish life. The payments made by the State to the Church were abolished; the schools run by the Jesuits were closed. So far as the burdens of the peasantry were concerned this socialist government lightened the load by securing improved conditions of pay and tenure. For the industrial workers it did little since it lacked the necessary financial resources to institute health or unemployment insurance. By 1934, socialism had proved so disappointing that its opponents, representing the interests of the monarchy and the Church, were back in power and soon showed themselves as unwilling to promote reform as the socialists had been unable. While they remained in office it seemed that they might well overthrow the republic and restore the monarchy.

Faced with this danger, the parties of the left began to draw together and to make common cause. This alliance was led by an able trade unionist, Caballero, and was known as the Popular Front movement. The forces of the right felt compelled to act and the initiative was taken by the Fascist party, known in Spain as the Falangists, and led by Rivera's son.

The murder of a right-wing leader in the summer of 1936 was the signal for the outbreak of civil war. The army in Morocco raised the standard of right-wing rebellion against the left-wing parties anxious to preserve the republic, and General Franco placed himself at the head of the rebel army. He was deprived of the quick victory he expected by the loyalty of the naval forces and of the people of Madrid and Barcelona to the Republican cause. Thus Spain came to have two governments demanding the obedience of her people— that of the right-wing rebels at Burgos and that of the legally constituted republic in Madrid.

The right-wing parties had been in negotiation with Fascist Italy and Nazi Germany before the civil war had actually begun. For motives of their own these two powers gave a ready ear to requests for aid. Before long German and Italian armed forces were helping the Spanish rebels to destroy the republic. The republican forces were not so fortunate in their search for help. Russia intervened on their behalf but the western democracies were prepared to do no more than hold the ring and express ineffective disapproval of all foreign intervention in a civil war. All the Spanish republic got from the democracies was a number of volunteers who went out to Spain at their own risk and expense and against the wishes of their own governments.

Throughout its two and a half years' length, the war steadily moved in favour of General Franco and the rebel army. Nothing save the heroic but quixotic resistance of Madrid and Barcelona prolonged the final agony. When these last citadels of democracy fell the war ended and in 1939 Spain joined that group of European powers who had tried constitutional democratic government without success. Under General Franco there was another dictatorship in Europe differing from its prototypes in Italy and Germany only in its non-aggressive policy towards its neighbours whilst being as repressive towards its own people as were Italian Fascists and German Nazis.

QUESTIONS

1. Give an account of the importance of Mustafa Kemal.
2. How would you explain the rise of dictatorships in Europe between the two World Wars? Describe the chief features of this type of government.

CHAPTER 50

RACIAL MINORITY PROBLEMS
AND THE DRIFT TO WAR

THE major European powers were compelled to compromise with their idea of national unity. Racial groups proved to be too numerous for all to be constituted as separate nations. Areas of mixed population could not always be exactly divided along racial lines. New states were felt to need easily defendable boundaries and in some cases this meant the inclusion within their population of minority racial groups.

In the case of Austria it was felt that complete racial unity would create a state so strong as to constitute a danger to the rest of western Europe. Austrians were German by both language and historical tradition; only as the main part of the old Austro-Hungarian Empire had they been deliberately excluded from the united Germany which Bismarck had created in the nineteenth century. Now that that empire had been destroyed, logic and the principle of nationalism alike pointed to their inclusion with Germany. Also the new Austria was an incredibly small state left with the huge capital of Vienna. Its agricultural resources were in Hungary and its industrial wealth was in Czechoslovakia. It could not be self-supporting and in any case it had no outlet to the sea; incorporation with Germany seemed the obvious solution.

Before the rise of Hitler in Germany, this solution might well have been acceptable to the Austrian people. At one stage they proposed at least an economic union with Germany. This came, however, at a time when the western powers in general and France in particular felt able to insist on the treaty arrangements of 1919. Thus the proposed economic union with Germany was, on French initiative, discussed in the League of Nations, referred by them to the International Court at the Hague and by the Court forbidden. Germany had once come near to destroying national liberty in Europe; nothing could be tolerated which seemed to strengthen her resources and possibly enable her to try again.

Austria's economic insecurity was not helped by the sharp political division between the agricultural workers and those engaged in industry. The peasantry was on the whole deeply attached to their Catholic faith: the industrial workers had found a new religion in socialism. The former strongly supported the conservative Christian Socialist party; the latter formed the backbone of the radical Social Democratic party. Party feelings ran so high that street riots became frequent and fierce. When an Austrian Nazi party appeared on the scene disorder increased. Austria's troubles came to a final head in 1931 when she had to admit national bankruptcy and thus added to the universal state of economic depression.

The following year saw the Catholic Socialist party leader, Dollfuss, in office as Chancellor. Within twelve months he had suspended parliamentary democracy and made himself dictator. Small in stature, he was a man of immense courage and determination and he was firmly resolved on two things —to maintain the independence of his country against the growing threats of Hitlerite Germany and to restore firm and orderly government. Had he chosen to secure an alliance with the other parties against the Nazis he would have been in a better position to resist foreign aggression. As it was, by waging a bitter civil war against the socialists, he increased the internal opposition to his régime. To resist Hitler he had to rely upon the support of Italy, France and Britain.

In 1934 a new crisis arose. The Austrian Nazis staged an armed revolt against the dictatorship, in the course of which they burst into the Chancellery and murdered Dollfuss. Hitler might well have attempted to annex Austria at this stage, but Mussolini moved troops into the Brenner Pass and so deterred Hitler.

The Nazi revolution of 1934 thus petered out and Dollfuss was succeeded as Chancellor by Schuschnigg. Austrian opinion now seemed to veer towards the desirability of restoring the Hapsburg monarchy, but the small new nations carved out of the old Austro-Hungarian Empire strongly objected and on this point they had the support of Italy. Since Austria owed so much and relied so heavily on Italy for defence against Germany this was decisive.

·For four years the danger from Germany seemed to have receded. Indeed, in 1936, tension between the two countries was so far eased that Hitler undertook to guarantee the independence of Austria and in return Schuschnigg agreed to give the Austrian Nazi party legal recognition.

The international situation, however, began to move against Austria. Italy, her protector, quarrelled with the West over the Abyssinian question and drew towards Germany as they made common cause in the Spanish Civil War. Britain still believed that Hitler could be appeased.

Thus when the Austrian Nazis staged a second unsuccessful revolt in 1938 there was no foreign deterrent to hold Hitler back. He summoned Schuschnigg to meet him at Berchtesgaden and there compelled him under threat of invasion to hand over power in the Austrian police and foreign affairs to the Nazi party. Back in his own capital, Chancellor Schuschnigg proposed to hold a national plebiscite on the issue of independence or incorporation with

Thomas Masaryk (centre), President of Czechoslovakia, 1918-1935.

Germany. Hitler could not risk the possibility of the vote going against him. In March, 1938, Germany invaded Austria. A plebiscite was then held under Nazi auspices conducted by methods designed to give a predetermined result; the verdict was for incorporation with the occupying military power. Once again parliamentary democracy had failed to take root.

Czechoslovakia

Czechoslovakia after Versailles was the supreme example of the principle of nationalism. This new state had been carved out of the old Austro-Hungarian Empire by the union of two racial groups—the Slavs proper and their cousins the Czechs. It was a sensible arrangement; the two groups had a common history and they had made common cause against alien Austrian rule; they had long sought independence.

It was, however, also felt essential that Czechoslovakia should be given easily defendable natural frontiers, lest a future Austrian revival or German resurgence should put the independence of the new state in danger. Thus the Carpathian foothills were included within her boundaries. Here the population was unfortunately largely German but this in 1919 was considered no bad thing. United Germany had come near to dominating Europe; a little clipping of her wings would limit her aspirations for the future.

For some years it seemed as if the making of this new state was one of the best aspects of the settlement of 1919. A democratic constitution was welcomed and under the presidency of Thomas Masaryk worked well up to his death in 1935. Edward Benes who followed him continued in the Masaryk tradition. Whilst both were great patriots both were good Europeans with a strong leaning to the western pattern of political life. The minority racial

431

groups seemed likely to become reconciled to their inclusion with the Slavs; their rights were both respected and protected by the ruling majority group.

Such dangers as threatened Czechoslovakia were external. As well as a German minority she had also a Polish minority and Poland longed to see these separated brethren reunited with the family.

A more serious situation threatened the Czechs and Slovaks with the rise of Hitler. His fanatical cry of "one people, one state" held ominous overtones. Yet Czechoslovakia felt that she had her defences. She was glad now of her mountain barriers. Without them she might well have had less of a minority problem, but her industrial resources and her armaments factories might well have tempted a strong neighbour intent on aggression elsewhere in Europe. She had too a small but highly efficient, well-trained and well-equipped army. This might be able to hold the fort while France and Russia could come to her aid; and though she had no alliance with Britain, sympathy between the two countries was strong.

One by one, as Hitler's appetite grew and his threats became more menacing, these defences were stripped away. The German annexation of Austria removed the northern mountain barrier. Discontent was fomented among the German minority by the formation under Konrad Henlein of a German Sudeten party. Over the border, the government-controlled German press grew increasingly hysterical about alleged Czech atrocities committed against the German minority. This propaganda campaign reached the point where in 1938 Henlein demanded legal recognition of the Czech Nazi party and self-government for the German-speaking Sudetenland. Ominously Hitler began to strengthen the defences of his western frontier.

The possibility of a German attack on Czechoslovakia threatened to produce a grave international situation in view of the Franco-Czech alliance. Britain attempted to mediate between the Czechs and Hitler; yet while the British mission was still examining the possibilities of compromise Hitler's threats against the Czechs steadily mounted. Lord Runciman, head of the British mission, could only report that in his opinion no compromise was possible; the Sudetenland would have to be transferred to German sovereignty without delay.

The British Prime Minister, Neville Chamberlain, still stood by his policy of appeasement; he could not bring himself to believe that any statesman, not even Hitler, would deliberately provoke war. At this juncture, he flew to meet Hitler at Berchtesgaden.

He returned convinced that he had found a basis for a settlement. Czechoslovakia was to surrender at once all areas in which fifty per cent of the population was German. Other German-speaking areas were to decide by popular vote to which country they wished to belong. Finally, Czechoslovakia was to abandon her alliances with Russia and France. Britain and

1938: Chamberlain reads the terms of the Munich Agreement.

France joined in telling President Benes that his government must accept these terms.

Rather than betray his country as he had been betrayed by his friends, Benes resigned and with him his cabinet. President Hacha succeeded him, but the crisis was not yet over. Chamberlain now found that Hitler was putting forward demands for the cession of Czech territory to Hungary and Poland; this was too much even for Chamberlain, and London, Paris and Moscow all prepared for war. At the eleventh hour and at the expense of Czechoslovakia, peace was saved. Mussolini urged Hitler to submit the issue to an international meeting of Italy, France, Britain and Germany, and none too willingly Hitler agreed. The meeting took place at Munich; the Czechs were called in only to be told the terms they must accept and those terms gave Germany all she had demanded.

Six months later Hitler summoned President Hacha to Berlin and under threat of immediate war compelled him to agree to the extinction of Czechoslovakia as an independent state. Germany, Hungary and Poland divided the spoils between them. The parliamentary democracies of the West had sacrified to the German dictator the only outpost of parliamentary democracy in the Balkans.

Poland and the Final Crisis

Poland, like Czechoslovakia, had been the creation of the settlement of 1919 and it had had conferred upon it the blessings of parliamentary democracy which it failed to appreciate. Its first president, a musician, Paderewski, was in office only a few months before being succeeded by a military man, Marshal Pilsudski. The Marshal established a dictatorship and remained in power until his death in 1936.

Poland also had a minority racial problem. In order to give her access to the sea, a strip of East Prussian territory running to Danzig was included within her boundaries. Inevitably this placed many Germans under Polish sovereignty and Germany never became reconciled to this "Polish Corridor." Since Danzig too was largely German in population, it became a "free" city under the auspices of the League of Nations. To make assurance of a sea outlet doubly sure, Poland built in the post-war years, a new port, Gdynia, and entered into alliance with France. In 1925, she further sought to strengthen her security by negotiating an accommodation with her most likely enemy, Germany.

It was as well that Poland had built Gdynia, because from 1936 onwards, Danzig became more and more actively pro-German. Yet vulnerable as she was, Poland in 1939 could not resist the temptation, as we have seen, to join with Germany in the dismemberment of Czechoslovakia.

Within a matter of weeks, Poland found herself the object of Hitler's next ambition. "Disturbances" suddenly began to grow in number and frequency in Danzig; Hitler's heart was "moved with compassion" for his fellow country-men living under the "harsh and alien" Polish rule; he made it clear that he conceived it his mission to "liberate" them. The international climate had now grown chillier to his adventures. Britain, as a warning of her seriousness of intention, gave a guarantee of support to Poland, Greece and Rumania should any of them find their independence under attack. Hitler replied by renouncing Germany's signature to the naval pact made with Britain in 1935.

Germany and Britain both now made overtures to Russia, the former in the hope of avoiding a war on two fronts, the latter in the hope of securing a near neighbour of Poland's as a reinforcement for Polish independence. Russia, however, had lost faith in the western democracies as the result of their betrayal of Czechoslovakia; in any case Hitler was prepared to offer terms that France and Britain could not match. The result was that the British negotiators returned from Moscow empty-handed; Hitler's envoy brought back a promise of Russian neutrality in return for the promise of eastern Poland and the Baltic republics for Russia.

Hitler was now sure that the last red light against him on the road to Poland had turned to green. He summoned the Poles to send representatives to Berlin to reach a settlement of the Polish Corridor question. Remembering what had happened to President Hacha of Czechoslovakia in Berlin the Poles refused to go. Thus on 1 September, 1939, German troops and aircraft began to batter Poland into surrender and by 5 October Hitler was riding through the streets of Warsaw. Russia had meanwhile crossed the Polish frontier only two weeks after Hitler so that in late October it was possible for Germany and Russia to sign an agreement partitioning Poland between them. France and Britain, however, had declared war on Germany on 3 September and to Hitler's astonishment his success in Poland did not lead them to change their minds. The Second World War had begun.

Causes of the Second World War

Hitler was fond of pointing to the evils of the Versailles Treaty as the source of all the difficulty and saying he was only trying forcibly to cure the injustices which Europe had refused, when approached reasonably, to recognize. He always ignored two things—one, that Germany had begun the war of 1914; and two, that she had lost it. The Treaty of Versailles could have been rearranged by normal diplomatic negotiations, given time and goodwill. On the other hand, France must take some responsibility for the rigidity with which she insisted on the strict maintenance of the settlement. Britain's attitude to the Versailles settlement was but little better than that of France. Britain had a guilty feeling of sympathy towards Germany but lacked the courage to urge clemency on her French ally.

Similarly no British government before that of Baldwin in 1936 was willing to accept the necessity of rearmament; even then a strong pacifist opinion in the country condemned the policy while clamouring for resistance to German and Italian aggression.

The Chamberlain government which succeeded that of Baldwin was sadly at odds with itself on foreign affairs. Sir Anthony Eden, the Foreign Minister, sought to take a firm stand against aggression; Chamberlain, as Prime Minister, speeded up British rearmament but steadfastly believed that Hitler could be "appeased" and he gave guarantees of security to countries Britain could only reach by air over what would clearly be possible enemy territory. The indecisiveness of British foreign policy helped to destroy the peace it sought to promote.

The forces of peace were further weakened by America's withdrawal from Europe after 1919, and her refusal to recognize her president's parentage of the League of Nations went far to ensure the failure of that ideal. A country of freedom and idealism, she was not going to expend her wealth and blood a second time to save the western imperialist nations. Not until her own fleet blazed in Pearl Harbour in 1941 from a Japanese air attack did she accept the fact that she could not live by herself alone.

To Russian communism the West represented capitalism, and war to the death between the two rival economic systems was a fundamental article of the communist creed—the capitalist West had tried to suppress the communist revolution, and was not to be trusted. Thus Russia withdrew from Europe until first, economic necessity, and then Nazi temptation aroused her national self-interest. Her promise of neutrality set the seal on Hitler's resolve to go to war.

That resolution was strengthened by Hitler's knowledge that he had two committed armed allies. Italy's estrangement from the West by her aggression in Abyssinia and Albania had driven Mussolini into the arms of the German dictator. It was because he was locked in this fateful embrace that Mussolini was unable in 1938 to prevent the annexation of Austria by moving troops into the Brenner as he had done in 1934; he was by 1938 no longer a free agent so far as Germany was concerned; the Rome-Berlin Axis had been forged. In 1936 that Axis had been strengthened by the addition of Japan, another aggressive power seeking at that time to conquer her Chinese neighbour.

Adolf Hitler, Nazi dictator of Germany

Opposed to the Rome-Berlin-Tokyo Axis was the much looser association of France and Britain. Both sides by 1939 were feverishly building up their armaments, though the Axis powers had the longer start and the Allies lagged well behind. The adhesion of Russia or America to the Allied camp might well have restored a deterrent balance which would have preserved an uneasy peace. As it was the Axis powers in 1939 felt confident of victory; their opponents felt with equal conviction that they could not, in the last resort, let the causes of personal liberty and racial tolerance go by default.

Whatever may have been the mistakes of other powers, the precipitating factor in the outbreak of war in 1939 was undoubtedly the aggressive violence of Mussolini and Hitler. The former set the pattern, but the latter bettered by far the Italian example. The rearmament of Germany in spite of the Treaty of Versailles, withdrawal from the Disarmament Conference in 1933, the reintroduction of conscription in 1935, the fortification of the Western Front between 1936 and 1938, the beguiling Anglo-German naval treaty of 1935 unilaterally renounced in 1939, the unchallenged re-occupation of the Rhineland in 1936, the successive and unwarranted annexations of Austria in 1938 and Czechoslovakia in 1939 reached their inevitable climax in the attack on Poland. In the war of 1939-45 Europe paid dearly for her forbearance; a divided Germany still pays.

QUESTIONS

1. What was the importance in international affairs between 1936 and 1939 of the following countries: Spain, Austria, Czechoslovakia?
2. Account for the outbreak of war in 1939.

REVISION SUMMARY

THE FRENCH REVOLUTION, 1789-95

REACTION, 1815-25

THE REVOLUTIONS OF 1848

MAJOR WESTERN POWERS IN THE LATER
NINETEENTH CENTURY

THE PEACE OF VERSAILLES

SPECIMEN EXAMINATION PAPER

Syllabus: "Outlines of European History, 1494-1939." Five questions to be answered, chosen from not fewer than two sections of the paper. Time: 2½ hours.

SECTION I (1494-1648)

1. Why was Italy the battlefield between France and the Hapsburgs in the first half of the sixteenth century?

2. "The Emperor Charles V had too many problems to deal with." Explain what these problems were.

3. What factors contributed to the success of Luther in Germany?

4. Describe the main features of the Calvinist Reformation in Geneva.

5. What factors, other than religion, caused the Civil Wars in France, 1558-98?

6. Why did Philip II fail to suppress the revolt of the Netherlands?

7. What steps were taken by: **a.** Henry IV, and **b.** Richelieu, to restore and strengthen the power of the monarchy in France?

8. Describe the motives of, and the part played by, Gustavus Adolphus in the Thirty Years' War.

9. Give an account of the overseas expansion of the Continental European Powers in the sixteenth century.

10. Write briefly about *three* of the following: **a.** Erasmus; **b.** Zwingli; **c.** Machiavelli; **d.** Julius II; **e.** Coligny; **f.** Wallenstein.

SECTION II (1648-1789)

11. Describe the services of Colbert to France.

12. Describe the main aspects of the reforms of Peter the Great, discussing in your answer as many of the following topics as you can: Military Reform; Subordination of the Nobility; Financial Reform; Industry; Communications; Foreign Trade; Agriculture; Administration; Education; Religion.

13. Account for the rise and decline of Sweden during this period.

14. What were the causes of the War of the Spanish Succession and how far were they removed by the terms of the Treaties of Utrecht and Rastadt?

15. Show how the Turkish threat to Europe was checked during this period by: **a.** Leopold I of Austria, and **b.** Catherine the Great of Russia.

16. What was the importance of Silesia to Prussia? Outline the course of the struggle between Maria Theresa and Frederick the Great for possession of Silesia.

17. What were the characteristics of an "Enlightened Despot"? Does Joseph II of Austria deserve this title?

18. For what reasons is Catherine II of Russia called "The Great"?

19. What was the importance of the outcome of the Seven Years' War for Great Britain, France, Prussia and Austria respectively?

20. What were the grievances of: **a.** the Bourgeoisie, and **b.** the Peasantry, of France on the eve of the French Revolution?

SECTION III (1789-1878)

21. Trace the course of events in France between the meeting of the States-General in 1789 and the execution of the King in 1793.

22. Why were the European powers unsuccessful in their efforts to defeat the armies of the French Revolution but successful against Napoleon's forces?

23. "Napoleon, child of the Revolution and heir of the Ancien Régime." How does Napoleon's career justify this description?

24. "A settlement of Europe made in the interests of governments, not in the interests of nations." Examine the decisions of the Congress of Vienna from this point of view.

25. What was the "Concert of Europe"? Why did the Congress System to which it gave rise fail?

26. Show how *either* Greece *or* Belgium achieved independence.

27. Show how revolution seemed likely in 1848 to lead to the break-up of the Austro-Hungarian Empire. Why did the revolutionary movements fail?

28. Explain Bismarck's diplomacy preparatory to the wars with (a) Austria, (b) France.

29. Why did Sardinia become the successful leader of the movement for Italian Unification?

30. Write briefly about any *three* of the following: **a.** The Carlsbad Decrees; **b.** Mehemet Ali; **c.** The policy of Alexander II of Russia during the years 1855-66; **d.** Bismarck and the Kulturkampf; **e.** The Ausgleich in the Hapsburg dominions; **f.** The Treaty of San Stefano.

SECTION IV (1878-1939)

31. Trace the growth of socialism and anti-clericalism in the Third French Republic.

32. Trace the growth of French, German and Italian power in Africa up to 1914.

33. "By 1914 Europe stood divided into two armed camps." Explain how this system of rival armed alliances had come about.

34. Explain why Germany came so near to success in 1914, and why she met defeat in 1918.

35. To what extent were President Wilson's Fourteen Points applied in the Treaty of Versailles of 1918?

36. Explain the main achievements in domestic policy of *either* Kemal Ataturk *or* Mussolini.

37. Indicate the main acts of aggression of Hitler between 1935 and 1939.

38. What were the main features of the domestic and foreign policy of Lenin between 1917 and 1924?

39. Trace the steps by which Japan emerged as a Great Power in the Far East in the face of the European Powers.

40. Explain *two* of the following carefully:

    (a) The reasons for, and the consequences of, the fall of Bismarck.

    (b) The weaknesses of the League of Nations.

    (c) The reasons for the Russian Revolution of 1917.

    (d) The causes of the World Economic Crisis of 1929-32.

    (e) The causes of the Spanish Civil War of 1936-39.

OUTLINE ANSWERS TO TEXT QUESTIONS

CHAPTER 1

1. **End of fifteenth century:** the **Renaissance, Reformation, Voyages of Discovery** and the **Rise of National States** brought changes in methods of government, structure of society, men's ideas and beliefs, which made the century more akin to those which followed it than those which preceded it. **Renaissance—humanism—secular writing** in languages other than Latin—**new styles** and subjects in painting and sculpture—new techniques in building—**new theories** of the universe. **Reformation—decline in the power of the Pope**—new religions and a diversity of theological ideas. **Voyages of Discovery**—revised ideas about the shape of the earth—**knowledge of new lands**—introduction of new products—import of precious metals. **Rise of National States**—increase in the power of national monarchs and decline in that of the Emperor—decay of feudal society.

2. **Columbus**—1492 to 1502 made four journeys across the Atlantic, landed on islands in the Caribbean—claimed them for Spain—named them West Indies. Believed that he had reached India by going west. Voyages led to **discovery of America—switched trade from Mediterranean to Atlantic. Vasco da Gama**—1496 sailed from Portugal via west coast of Africa over Indian Ocean to Calicut. **Opened up sea route to east.** Valuable as land trade was impeded by Turkish taxation.

CHAPTER 2

1. **Italy: disunited**—several independent states—none strong enough to force unity. Refused to help each other. **Easy prey for invaders. Milan**—north-west—despotically ruled by Sforza. **Venice**—north-east—nominally a republic—wealthy families held the power. **Florence**—city and surrounding area—republican constitution but dominated by the Medici. **Papal States**—Rome and parts of central Italy—sovereignty of Pope. **Naples**—southern Italy and **Sicily**—badly ruled by a branch of the Spanish Royal Family.

2. **Charles VIII—1494 joined Milan in attack on Naples**—success following submission of Florence and Papacy. Isolated by withdrawal of Milan confronted by League of Venice forced to leave Naples. Fortunate in **victory at Fornova** (1495)—enabled him to reach France. Nothing to show for much expense. Showed Italian vulnerability to Europe. **Louis XII—1499 joined Venice**, took Milan, beat off Sforza's counter attack Novara (1500). **1500 captured Naples** with aid of Ferdinand of Spain—quarrelled and forced to surrender share of spoil. 1508 joined League of Cambrai against Venetians—defeated them at **Agnadello** (1509). 1511 faced the Holy League of Julius II—**victorious at Ravenna** (1512) but driven from Milan and **defeated at Novara** (1513). Like Charles had nothing to show for an expensive intervention.

CHAPTER 3

1. **Charles V: Flanders, Burgundy** and **Netherlands** (1506) from father Philip the Fair who had inherited from his mother Mary; **Spain, Naples** and **Sicily**, possessions in Africa and America (1516) from his maternal grandfather Ferdinand of Spain;

Austrian Empire (1519) from his paternal grandfather Maximilian of Austria; **Holy Roman Empire** (1519) by a successfully contested election.

2. **Francis:** was jealous of Charles' success in election—anxious because he was encircled by Hapsburg territory and furious because Spain had not given back Navarre as promised at Noyon (1516). Francis unable to hold Navarre because of treachery of Bourbon—lost advantage in Italy as his army was weakened by plague and supply shortage and he fell out with Andrea Doria—after Landriano (1529) he was driven from Milan.

CHAPTER 4

1. **Church:** compared unfavourably with that of earlier times. Calls to reform went unheeded as those in authority were profiting from the prevalent abuses. **Papacy** —too much emphasis on worldly power and collection of money—**wrong type of man** achieving office. **Clergy. Pluralism**—simony—absenteeism—broken vows of celibacy—much neglect of duty. **Monasteries**—rules ignored—monks surrounded themselves with luxuries.

2. **Luther:** born at Eisleben (1483). Became an Augustinian Friar (1505). Deeply shocked by visit to Rome (1511). **Professor of Theology at Wittenberg (1512). 95 Theses (1517). Excommunicated (1520).** Diet of Worms outlawed from the Empire—hid in Wartburg Castle—**translated the Bible (1521).** Married Catherine von Bora (1524). Refused support for Peasants' Revolt (1525). Failed to come to terms with Zwingli (p. 41). Confession of Augsburg—no conciliation with Catholics (1530). Died at Eisleben (1546).

CHAPTER 5

1. **Turks:** after the succession of **Suleiman** (1520) Turks threatened Europe by land and sea. **Belgrade captured (1520);** after victory at Mohacs (1526) dominated Hungary. Successfully resisted Charles' attempts to put brother on Hungarian throne and besieged Vienna (1529) but repulsed. Pirates menaced shipping in Mediterranean and they held Tunis (1533)—driven out by Charles. Prevented Charles taking Algiers (1541) allied with Francis I. In order to attack Persia came to terms with Charles (1545) but started to molest his ships again as his fortunes in Europe declined.

2. **Charles V:** Charles' plan to rule Europe seemed fulfilled (1547). Then **Maurice of Saxony changed sides**—Henry II sided with Princes—**Turks became active** in Mediterranean. Charles gave up. He gave the Netherlands to Philip (1555) and Spain and Italian possessions (1556). His brother received Imperial authority (1556) and was elected Emperor (1558). Charles went to live in Spain where he died (1558).

CHAPTER 6

1. **Luther: Justification by Faith**—accepted anything not forbidden in Bible. God as the **God of Love.** In his teaching about Communion—denied Catholic miracle wherein it is held that the elements are changed but accepted the spiritual presence of Christ (Consubstantiation). **Calvin: Justification by Faith—Predestination**—accepted those things specifically mentioned in the Bible—**God as the fearful judge**—in his teaching about the Communion held a position between that of Luther and the Zwinglian contention that the service was purely commemorative.

2. Calvin: born at Noyon (1509). Started to study theology—turned to law and then literature. Severed connections with Church (1534). Published ideas in Institutes of Christian Religion (1536). Took over the direction of religious and secular affairs in Geneva with Farel (1536). Became unpopular and banished from city (1538). Returned and directed churches there and in rest of Europe till his death (1541). Died (1564). By creating an administrative system and laying down rules for Protestant Church made it a strong organization capable of combating Catholicism.

CHAPTER 7

1. Loyola: entered military career—badly wounded in battle (1521)—during convalescence experienced conversion. Entered the University of Paris (1528). **Founded the Jesuits as crusading order (1534).** Ordained (1537). Movement formerly approved by Pope (1540). Loyola became its first general, an office he held until his death (1556). When planned crusade proved impractical **Jesuits set out to attack heresy in Europe.** Won converts through their preaching—through their schools influenced youngsters and ensured a supply of priests—as confessors to kings and statesmen greatly influenced European politics.

2. Counter-Reformation: movement was **launched too late. Strength of Calvinism.** Lost support through narrowness of doctrines put forward at Trent. Catholicism became associated with political aggression in France, Spain and the Empire—Catholics involved in assassination and conspiracy. As an international movement, could make little headway against **growing strength of nationalism.**

CHAPTER 8

1. Philip II: achieved **absolute power in Spain.** Failed in attempts to dominate Europe—though he annexed Portugal he **could not prevent Dutch independence**—was unsuccessful against England and driven from France. Plans to destroy Protestantism succeeded only in his own dominions.

2. Though the **Moriscoes** had turned from the Moslem creed to Christianity, Philip made them conform to Spanish customs—must speak Castillian—wear Spanish clothes—use Christian names. Their efforts to object were suppressed by Don John. Restrictions on their movements led to complete expulsion after Philip's death. All parts of Philip's fetish for uniformity. The **Turks** were a menace to shipping in the Mediterranean. Successfully stopped by Don John of Austria who defeated them at Lepanto (1571) with aid from Venetians and Papacy. The **Portuguese** provided Philip's greatest success in foreign policy. Claimed throne (1580) despite competition from better claimants and Portuguese hatred of Spain he triumphed. This brought the whole peninsula under one king. Philip joined the **French Catholic Section** at Joinville (1585) ostensibly to prevent Protestant succession in France—privately with hope of becoming king himself or at least keeping France divided and weak. Completely unsuccessful. Though an orthodox Catholic Philip was prepared to challenge the plans of **Pope** if they conflicted with his own.

CHAPTER 9

1. Netherlands: the influence of Spain upon the Regency and the policies which were followed were seen as a threat to Dutch privileges, economy and religious beliefs. The people were inspired by **leadership of William of Orange** and incensed by the

461

brutality of Alva. While other interests prevented Philip and his successors from focusing their full attention upon the Dutch, the death of Parma and the brilliance of Nassau gave the Dutch military superiority. Later they attained economic superiority.

2. **Dutch Independence:** this can be followed in the text pages 62-65.

CHAPTER 10

1. **Admiral Coligny: Calvinist—Admiral of France**—and outstanding character of French Court. **Joined Condé against Catholics** and was responsible for death of Duke of Guise. Later as a member of Council pressed for the Union of France in order to present a strong front against Spain. Union to be strengthened by the marriage of Margaret and Henry of Navarre. Catherine grew increasingly alarmed at the influence he wielded over Charles IX. Her plan to assassinate him failed. She ensured his destruction through the **Massacre of St. Bartholomew. Catherine de Medici:** seized power on death of Henry II (1559) and until her death (1589) did her best to retain it. From the **Edict of 1562**—the **Peace of Amboise (1563)**—**Peace of St. Germain (1570)**, **Massacre of St. Bartholomew (1572)** and **Peace of La Rochelle (1572)** it can be seen that she **frequently changed policy** in order to maintain a balance between the warring parties thus keeping them weak and incapable of challenging her authority.

2. After 1574 the wars became a political as well as a religious struggle. Holy League under **Henry of Guise** opposed possible accession of a Huguenot and sought help from Spain. Henry III opposed the League and was driven from Paris. To save his power he had the Duke of Guise murdered. To defend himself from Catholic retaliation he allied with Navarre and the Huguenots.

CHAPTER 11

1. **Henry IV:** ruled as an **absolute monarch**—ignored the States-General and removed the power that nobles had assumed in the wars. When necessary he bribed them by offering titles, pensions, etc. **Sully** reformed tax-collection. Nobles were ordered to run their estates more efficiently—**marshes were drained**—**new crops and techniques introduced**—peasants protected and helped to prosper. **Commercial treaties were made** with England and Holland—a charter was issued to **French East India Company**—Champlain colonized shores of St. Lawrence.

2. **Edict of Nantes: Huguenots to enjoy civil rights**—no exclusion from office—trial by special tribunals, allowed to hold own meetings and build schools, etc. Might worship freely in all places used before but not in Paris. Offered certain strongholds as a security. **Edict brought an end to religious squabbles** and allowed progress which wars had prevented but failed to unite France and thwarted the absolutist designs of later statesmen, who gradually removed it.

CHAPTER 12

1. **Thirty Years' War:** war started as a dispute between Emperor and Bohemia— Emperor continued it to strengthen his own power. Others joined in to defend their own interests and possibly increase them, e.g. Palatinate, Bavaria, Protestant princes, Wallenstein, Danes and Swedes. Richelieu introduced other powers and latterly France to keep the war going and thus weaken the power of the Hapsburgs.

2. **Treaty of Westphalia:** certain features brought the end of the old order. Decline in the power of the Pope and the Emperor and of ecclesiastical influence in politics. Others heralded the arrival of something new. Ascendancy of France, Sweden and Brandenburg. The independence of Switzerland and the Netherlands.

CHAPTER 13

1. **Richelieu:** a man of great ambition with a fine intellect and a dominating personality (Day of Dupes). He had a great love of France—as her ruler showed that he had diplomatic skill but he was also cruel and unscrupulous. He was a cold and friendless man, who suffered from fits and delusions. To strengthen the monarchy, **he removed the political power of the Huguenots** and **weakened the power of the nobility** by destroying castles, prohibiting duelling and increasing the power of the Intendants.

2. **Foreign policy: return to anti-Hapsburg policy** of Henry IV. Unsuccessful in regaining complete control of the Valtelline but saw a French candidate assume control in Mantua. Greatest success prolonging the Thirty Years' War by Swedish then French intervention to the detriment of the power of the Hapsburg Emperor.

CHAPTER 14

1. **Gustavus Vasa:** nominated king after successful revolt against Denmark (1523)— **strengthened the monarchy by declaring it hereditary** and suppressing opposition harshly. He made it rich by seizing the wealth of the Church and made the country prosperous by developing natural resources, trade, industry and commerce. **Charles IX: strengthened the power of the Government** so that foreign powers could be dealt with. He curbed power of the nobles—**improved administration—encouraged trade** to improve revenue and **built up an efficient army.**

2. **Gustavus Adolphus** entered the Thirty Years' War because, the **Protestants needed help**, he feared for his trade, **France subsidized him** and he felt that he could attain his ambition of making the Baltic into a Swedish lake. Defeated Tilly at **Breitenfeld (1631)** and again at **Lechfeld (1631)** where Tilly was killed. Seized Munich. Routed Imperial Forces at **Lützen (1632)** but was killed. Without him his army was not so effective and was defeated at **Nordlingen (1634):** see p. 83.

CHAPTER 15

1. **Colbert's contribution: overall object** to mobilize wealth and resources of France to enable Louis to carry out policy of domination. Secured Fouquet's dismissal and drew attention to widespread corruption of finances but could not alter unfair system of taxation. **Accepted mercantilist theory of trade;** i.e. government's duty to regulate economic activities to increase country's share of bullion. **Developed trade** by improving internal communications, creating merchant fleet like that of Dutch, creating trading companies and by establishing anti-Dutch tariffs. **Fostered industry** by use of protective tariffs against foreign goods, encouraging new industries. **Success jeopardized** by irritation of manufacturers with regulations, persecution of Huguenots, failure to attract full financial support of middle class, unwillingness of privileged orders to give up their immunity from taxation, and ruinous wars due to aggressive economic nationalism implied in mercantilist theory.

2. **Religious policies of Louis XIV:** intolerant of any religious institution detracting from own glory. **Conflict with Pope** about respective powers of Church and State over *Régale*. This ended in compromise. **Persecuted Jansenists** because they attacked moral laxity of Court and because their rivals, the Jesuits, influenced Louis. Louis secured Bull Unigenitus condemning Jansenists. **Ended toleration of Huguenots** by revoking Edict of Nantes. Emigration of Huguenots struck blow at French economy. Louis' hatred of Dutch in part due to their being Protestant. **His support of Stuarts** (p. 139) arose from desire to restore Roman Catholicism in England. But Louis was prepared to fight Catholic powers such as Austria. Religious considerations not the only motives.

CHAPTER 16

1. **Louis XIV's foreign policy:** "*La belle gloire*" . . . self-glorification identified with extension of French influence into Europe. **Asserted dynastic claims to Spain, supported Stuarts** in England to make them dependent upon him in their struggle with Parliament, **asserted French commercial and naval power at expense of rivals,** especially Dutch Republic. **War of Devolution, 1667,** between Spain and France when Louis asserted his queen's rights to Spanish Netherlands. England, United Provinces and Sweden formed Triple Alliance against France. **Dutch War, 1672.** Louis' object to crush Dutch who were obstacle to his expansion. **He achieved break-up of Triple Alliance** when England signed Treaty of Dover. Sweden was bribed to back France. Reforms took place in French army. 1672, French invaded Holland. Dutch republic overthrown by William of Orange. War of sieges, mostly in favour of France. William created Grand Alliance, anti-French and including United Provinces, Empire, Spain, Denmark. By Treaty of Westminster England made peace with Dutch. Marriage of **William of Orange** and **Mary (Stuart)** improved Anglo-Dutch relations. Louis isolated. **Peace of Nymegen, 1678.** Louis gained territory from Spain but alienated Europe. **Grand Alliance resulted from Louis' aggressive policies.**

2. **Anglo-Dutch Wars, 1652-54 and 1665-67:** same causes for both wars, **economic and naval rivalry.** Both countries believed in mercantilist theory or prosperity at expense of rivals. Competition for trade in East and West Indies. Navigation Act of 1651 aimed at Dutch carrying trade. Both wars essentially naval. **First war** brought hardship to Dutch and resulted in rise to power of **de Witt.** He negotiated Treaty of Westminster with **Cromwell** but treaty failed to settle fundamental rivalries. Hence **second war** broke out following re-enactment of Navigation Act and seizure of New Amsterdam in North America by English colonies. **War ended by Peace of Breda,** precipitated by common threat from Louis XIV. Hereafter Anglo-Dutch relations improved.

CHAPTER 17

1. **Duke of Marlborough:** with death of William III in 1702 **Marlborough assumed leadership of Grand Alliance** and used it to inflict crushing defeat on Louis. **Blenheim, 1704.** Secret planning enabled Marlborough to move army down Rhine and meet reinforcements. Victory at Blenheim saved Empire and Grand Alliance, destroyed French reputation for invincibility, and forced French to withdraw from Germany. **Ramillies, 1706.** French evacuated Netherlands, northern Italy, and cancelled advances on Germany. **Oudenarde and Malplaquet** forced Louis to sue for peace. **Influence of Marlborough declined when Tories**

came to power and **Sarah,** his wife, lost favour with Queen Anne. Tories sacrificed full fruits of Marlborough's victory by opening separate peace negotiations with France and splitting Grand Alliance. Marlborough's defeat of Louis resulted in destruction of French trade and expansion of British trade, and removal of threat of invasion of Britain.

2. **Treaties of Utrecht and Rastadt: Philip V** acknowledged King of Spain and Indies. **Louis' object of Bourbon on Spanish throne realized** but union of Spanish and French thrones would upset balance of power so **Philip had to renounce French throne. Emperor Charles VI** was compensated for loss of Spanish throne with Spanish territory in Italy. **Anglo-Dutch barrier treaty renewed** to stop French aggression but caused friction between Dutch and Austria. Closure of river Scheldt and Antwerp to foreign shipping. **Britain acquired valuable land in North America** from French; **Louis XIV recognized Hanoverian claim to British throne.** Treaty ushered in comparative peace for Europe until 1740.

CHAPTER 18

1. **Policy at home and abroad of Duke of Orleans: Orleans hoped to succeed to French throne** in event of Louis XV's death. Sought support of Parlement of Paris, nobles deprived of political power by Louis XIV, and Britain (Triple Alliance) which was a diplomatic revolution. **Ended persecution of Jansenists** and tried unsuccessfully to end persecution of Huguenots. **Adopted Law's financial schemes** based on principle that credit creates wealth. Law thought that plentiful supply of paper money would stimulate commercial development. Law's bank became government institution, but failed and ruined thousands. **Regency period marked temporary end of absolutism in France.**

2. **Main threats to peace, 1713-31: 1713-20, conflicting ambitions of Spain and the Empire. Alberoni** wished to restore Spanish territory lost to Hapsburgs, while **Emperor Charles** wished to secure Hapsburg power in Italy and acquire Spanish throne from **Philip V.** 1717, war broke out; peace restored by "Quadrilateral Alliance." Philip accepted **Stanhope's** scheme to resolve differences between Spain and Empire. **1720-29, Pragmatic Sanction.** Charles' efforts to ensure his daughter's succession rights challenged by electors of Bavaria and Saxony. **Ostend East India Company** scheme of Charles, proposing to develop trade of Netherlands, offended Britain and Holland. **Gibraltar** caused trouble between Spain and Britain. **First Treaty of Vienna** between Spain and Empire **threatened possibility of marriage between Hapsburgs and Spanish Bourbons.** League of Hanover formed to counter threat. **Fleury** and **Walpole** averted war. **1729-31, Emperor tried to sieze Parma;** war averted by Walpole negotiating Second Treaty of Vienna.

CHAPTER 19

1. **Aims and achievements of Peter the Great: Peter wished to make Russia a strong power by ending isolation from West.** Introduced "Western" reforms, extended boundaries of Russia to Baltic and Black Sea. At Azov, 1696, Peter learned lesson of sea power. Tour of western Europe, 1697-98. **Reforms begun on social customs, army, navy.** After war with Sweden and early disaster of Narva Peter remodelled army on Swedish lines. **Poltava victory, 1709. Russian supremacy in Baltic confirmed** at Nystadt, 1721. Struggle with Turkey, 1711. **Administrative reform; new capital at St. Petersburg; Senate, 1711; Colleges, 1715. Provincial government**

reformed. **Church subordinated to State.** New "nobility of service" created. No restriction on noble's power over peasants. **New taxes and new industries introduced,** stimulated by war.

2. **Struggle between Peter the Great and Charles XII: both wanted Baltic supremacy at expense of each other.** Peter had limitless resources, allies, but untrained army. Danger to Russia if Turks attacked. Charles had trained army, limited resources, no allies. He hoped to use Turks against Peter. Peter entered war at untimely moment, 1700. **Victory of Charles at Narva, 1701.** Charles overran Poland but Peter overran Livonia, Estonia, Ingria and Karelia. **Charles' Russian campaign ended at Poltava, 1707-9.** Charles wounded at Poltava; Russians won battle. Triumph for Peter's reforms and leadership, and blow to Sweden from which she never recovered. Charles went to Turkey, induced Turks to attack Peter. **Success of Turks against Peter** marred victory at Poltava. Peter campaigned in Poland, Pomerania, while Charles in Turkey. With death of Charles, Swedish nobles came to power and **Sweden made peace with Russia,** losing her Baltic empire.

CHAPTER 20

1. **Services rendered by Great Elector to Brandenburg-Prussia:** to extend territories, Frederick William **created powerful national army and efficient, honest civil service.** Had to impose common sense of unity amongst scattered dominions. **Extended his possessions** at Treaty of Westphalia and Treaty of Oliva. Imposed taxes to finance army, which distinguished itself at battle of Fehrbellin (1675) against Swedes. No strong middle class to challenge Elector. **Promoted trade and industry. Encouraged settlement of Protestant refugees. Gained loyalty of nobility.**

2. **Domestic policies of Frederick William I and Frederick II: both believed in personal rule.** Respective characters determined character of their rule. **Frederick William created national directory** which Frederick II enlarged to extent of undermining its authority. **Frederick II allowed ministers slightly more scope.** Frederick II influenced by Enlightenment, sponsored more legal reforms. Both Frederick William and Frederick II encouraged participation of nobility in government. Ruinous wars in which Frederick II indulged forced him to develop agriculture, industry, more than his father. **Greater economic development under Frederick II.** Both Frederick William I and Frederick II believed in mercantilist theory of trade.

CHAPTER 21

1. **Describe Turkish threat to Europe during latter half of seventeenth century: revival of Turkish power after 1656.** Transylvania overrun, Hungary and Austria invaded. **Emperor Leopold I** appealed to crusading spirit of European rulers. **Hapsburg army created,** including **Louis XIV, Philip IV, The Great Elector, Pope Alexander** and German princes. **Turkish army shattered,** made Peace of Vasvar. Twenty years later Hungarian Protestant rebels, to whom Turkish threat preferable to Catholic Hapsburgs, intrigued with Turks. **Vienna besieged (1683).** Leopold again appealed to crusading spirit of Europe, and **Christian League formed.** Relief army of **John Sobieski,** King of Poland, saved Vienna and Europe. **Turkish power receded** and peace made at Carlowitz (1697). Turks lost Hungary. European rulers had forgone differences and united under common threat to Christianity. **Prestige of Hapsburgs increased.**

2. **Reforms of Emperor Joseph II,** 1780-90: death of Maria Theresa enabled Joseph to prove himself **enlightened reformer. Religious reforms** with Patent of Toleration (1781). Freedom of worship for all subjects. **Legal reforms:** judges chosen for integrity, cost of legal advice lowered, more humane criminal code and modern civil code. **Administrative reforms:** centralization of authority under Joseph which caused dissent in Netherlands and Hungary. German replaced Latin as official language. **Legal reforms were most lasting.** Other reforms were too premature and tactlessly introduced.

CHAPTER 22

1. **Reasons leading Britain to declare war on Spain:** ill-treatment of **Captain Jenkins** by Spaniards, who cut off his ear, used by parliamentary opposition to **Walpole** as excuse for war with Spain. **Real causes for war: trade rivalry between Spain and Britain.** Limited trading rights in Spanish America granted Britain by Asiento Treaty whetted Britain's appetite for more. Spanish trade laws prevented British merchants from trading with Spanish colonists, who welcomed British goods. Smuggling resulted, so Spanish *guarda costas* patrolled coasts. Unofficial war between these and merchant ships.

2. **European powers engaged in War of Austrian Succession and motives: war aims of anti-Hapsburg powers:** Prussia seized Silesia from Austria, Austria's defeat at Mollwitz induced France to form anti-Hapsburg alliance (Treaty of Nymphenburg, 1741) aimed at destruction of Hapsburg power in Germany and Italy. Mutually incompatible aims of countries involved. **Prussia** wanted extension of Hohenzollern power in Germany; **France** wanted influence in Germany and extension of colonial trade at expense of British; **Charles Albert of Bavaria** wanted Imperial title and refused to recognize Maria Theresa's claim; **Saxony** wanted Moravia; **Sardinia** and **Spain** wished to exclude Hapsburgs from northern Italy. **Hapsburg allies: Austria** under **Maria Theresa** wanted recognition of her Imperial title and return of Silesia. **Britain** Austria's only ally. **George II** was Elector of Hanover and wished to safeguard it. Treaty-bound to support Hapsburgs, yet wished to expand trade, colonies, at expense of Bourbons of France and Spain. George and ministers Carteret and Newcastle favoured renewal of Grand Alliance against Bourbons, and formed Pragmatic Army.

CHAPTER 23

1. **Anglo-French rivalry in North America and India: North America:** British colonies seeking to extend frontiers west and north. Conflicted with French colonies seeking expansion. Principal areas in dispute: **St. Lawrence, Ohio Valley,** and **Hudson Valley** and **Great Lakes.** French had inferior numbers but greater unity than British colonists. Outbreak of Seven Years' War, 1756. **India:** struggle for trade between rival East India companies. Struggle centred first on Carnatic. **British at Madras, French at Pondicherry. Dupleix** developed scheme for interfering in native rulers' disputes to secure privileges. Threatened British at Trichonopoly. **Clive** saved situation at Arcot, 1751. Decline of French. British secured Bengal (1756) and gained Calcutta (p. 215).

2. **Diplomatic Revolution:** change in alliances of major powers (1756-57). **Break-up of traditional alliance of Austria and Britain; alliance of Britain and Prussia** (convention of Westminster, 1756) which brought about **alliance of traditional enemies France and Austria** (Treaties of Versailles, 1756, 1757). Original idea of

Hapsburg-Bourbon alliance that of **Kaunitz.** Because Britain preoccupied in colonial struggles, he turned to France for aid in recovering Silesia from Prussia. **George II** feared French attack on Britain. To maintain defence, preservation of peace in Germany was necessary. Hence negotiations with Russia and Prussia. After **Convention of Westminster** France felt isolated. Austria, whose old ally Britain was now ally of Prussia, formed defensive alliance between Austria and France. France now committed to help Austria at detriment to herself. French policy dominated by Kaunitz.

CHAPTER 24

1. **Frederick the Great and the Seven Years' War:** Frederick inspired subjects in face of hopeless odds. **Master of defence and strategy;** "oblique attack." Was helped by **short supply lines, discipline of army. Aided by Britain,** as Pitt subsidized Prussian army and revived Hanoverian army under Frederick the Great in order to distract France from colonial struggle. Frederick felt betrayed when British subsidies withdrawn. **Anti-Prussian alliance between France and Austria was disunified.** France had nothing to gain by fighting Prussia. **Third Treaty of Versailles, 1759:** France reduced military and financial support of Austria. Russia failed to follow up victories against Prussia due to **jealousy between Austria and Russia** and because of Peter III's pro-Prussian outlook. At Peter's death, Catherine refused to renew war. By **Peace of Hubertsburg** Frederick retained Silesia.

2. **Anglo-French conflict in North America: early disasters for British:** forts lost. Disasters due to **colonial disunity, able French leadership** under Montcalm. **Final French defeat:** result of outstanding leadership of **Pitt,** whose primary object was conquest of Canada and ruin of French trade. **Pitt's support of Prussia** occupied French armies in Europe; "Canada won on banks of Elbe." **Three-pronged attack on Canada:** St. Lawrence, Hudson, Ohio. **British sea power and manpower greater than French; 1758, Wolfe, aided by Amherst and Boscawen, captured Louisburg; Forbes captured Fort Duquesne. 1759, Wolfe captured Quebec; Amherst captured Ticonderoga and Crown Point. 1760, Amherst captured Montreal.**

CHAPTER 25

1. **How Catherine became Empress of Russia: Empress Elizabeth died 1761, Peter III proclaimed Emperor.** Because of personal qualities, anti-clerical activities, and support of Prussia Peter had alienated all classes in Russia. Catherine was intelligent, ambitious, and had always aimed at the Crown. Had love and respect of subjects and essential support of the Guards. **Tradition of Court uprisings in Russia was strong; Orlov uprising** which brought Catherine to power in 1762 not exceptional. Orlov hoped to marry Catherine and share Crown. **Dangers to Catherine:** her illegal position; two deposed emperors living at time of her accession. Peter III murdered by Orlov. Ivan VI murdered, 1764. **Pugachev revolt** of peasants, 1773, also dangerous to Catherine. Revolt put down after peace with Turkey, 1774. **Measures taken by Catherine to strengthen position:** favours granted to influential subjects; refusal to weaken power of nobility over peasants; posing as enlightened ruler (*Nakaz*); brilliant court life to show herself as great ruler.

2. **Enlightened despotism and Catherine:** term enlightened despotism describes work of late eighteenth-century rulers whose ideas on government were influenced by

philosophers of the "Enlightenment." **Examples of enlightened despots:** Catherine of Russia, Joseph of Austria, Frederick of Prussia. They exercised power for best interests of subjects, without at same time weakening own authority. **Attempt made to reconcile respect for rights of individuals (enlightenment) with negation of this respect (despotism). Catherine as enlightened despot: corresponded with Voltaire,** friend of Diderot; established *Nakaz* (set of instructions to govern legislative commission), containing Western ideas adapted to Russian society; **was patron of the Arts and science.** Despite loathing serfdom, Catherine made no attempt to abolish it at expense of her own power. **Brilliance of court life at expense of subjects.** Posed as humane ruler, but her power to reform conditions was limited as a despot cannot afford to alienate influential nobility; Catherine was realistic, saw what happened to Joseph and his reforms. She **effected administrative reforms to strengthen her authority in provinces.**

CHAPTER 26

1. **Underlying weaknesses of Poland: internal weaknesses, political defects:** "Poland" geographical term for large area lacking any national consciousness. No strong government to give necessary lead. Elective monarchy; king dominated by nobles, answerable to Diet, lacking in money and strong army. Diet's *liberum veto* paralyzed its effectiveness, *rights of confederation* legalized civil war. **Social and economic defects:** all landowners jealous of each other. Agriculture backward, trade non-existent, lack of population. **Religious divisions:** Catholics against Dissenters. **Lack of cultural achievements; no natural barriers to country** apart from Carpathians. **External dangers:** Poland surrounded by strong aggressive states, Russia, Prussia and Austria, who wished to extend their territories by maintaining weak Polish state.

2. **First partition of Poland:** death of Augustus, 1763. Question of succession. **Stanislas Poniatowski** elected king by **Russian-Prussian alliance, 1764. Poniatowski led reform movement** to end *liberum veto*. Russia stirred up civil war, stimulated religious strife by supporting Dissenters, as Catherine feared revival of Polish power. **Russo-Turkish war, 1768-74:** France, supporting Polish Catholics, induced Turkey to declare war on Russia to distract Russian armies. Success of Russians in Balkans alarmed Austria. **Austria threatened to help Turkey. This would force Prussia to help Russia. Frederick proposed to partition Poland,** because **peace essential to Prussia** to enable her to consolidate Silesia (gained from Austria) and to recover from wars. **First Partition Treaty, 1772:** Russia acquired Lithuania; Austria acquired Galicia; Prussia acquired West Prussia. **Effects of partition:** made later partitions inevitable; not really in interests of large powers to partition Poland in long run (Austria gained troublesome new race); Sweden and Turkey saved from dismemberment by fate of Poland; partition stimulated rebirth of Polish national consciousness.

CHAPTER 27

1. **Partition of Poland, 1772-95:** rebirth of Polish nationalism after first partition. **Factors helping Polish reform movement, 1788-91:** Russian-Prussian alliance gone, since Russia and Austria now preoccupied in war with Turkey. Austria favoured reformed Catholic Poland to block Russia and Prussia. Poles inspired by French revolution. Polish constitution, 1791. Hereditary monarchy, abolition of *liberum veto*, religious toleration. Russia against reformed Poland but involved

in Turkish war. Prussia after 1791 no longer a Polish ally, and also against idea of a strong Poland. **1792, Russia at peace with Turkey, able to invade Poland.** Polish appeals for help ignored by Austria and Prussia. Poland overrun by Russia. **Second Partition, 1793:** Russia acquired eastern Poland, Prussia acquired Danzig, Thorn, Posen. Austria gained nothing. **Polish Rising, 1794:** Poles resented partition; rising led by **Kosciusko.** Rebellion put down by combination of Prussian and Russian armies. **Third Partition, 1795:** Catherine dictated terms, giving Austria greater share as she distrusted Prussia. Polish State completely disappeared, divided among Russia, Austria and Prussia. Partitions were inevitable. Russia could not afford to see emergence of a strong Poland. Shamelessness of all powers in treatment of Poland.

2. **Catherine's relations with Turkey, 1774-91: Catherine's ambition**—make Russia a Black Sea and Balkan Power at expense of Turkey. **Treaty of Kutchuk Kainardji, 1774.** Ended Russo-Turkish war, 1768-74. Russia acquired protectorship of Christians in Turkish Empire; free navigation in Turkish waters; Crimean independence recognized by Turkey. Terms of treaty had been modified by Catherine to avoid European war. Russia compensated by gaining part of Poland. **Annexation of Crimea, 1783:** annexation recognized by Turkey, 1784, by Treaty of Constantinople. Allowed Russia to use Sebastopol as naval base. **Greek Project:** climax of Catherine's ambitions, involving division of Turkish Empire in two parts, both under Russian influence. (Kingdom of Dacia under Potemkin; revived Byzantine Empire under Catherine's grandson.) To fulfil ambition, Catherine made Austro-Russian alliance, and provoked Turkey into war, 1787, by mobilizing army. War of 1787-91: Austrian withdrawal, 1790, forced Catherine to make peace with Turkey to deal with Polish question. **Peace of Jassy, 1791:** earlier Russian gains confirmed. Catherine's Greek project not realized. Other powers hostile to idea of extinction of Turkey; Turkey survived to become part of "Eastern Question" which troubled diplomatic relations until 1919.

CHAPTER 28

1. **Scientific Revolution:** seventeenth-century appeal to reason, which undermined Church teaching on nature and universe. Weakening of Church's authority following Renaissance, Reformation. Copernicus was first successful challenge. **Astronomy: Galileo**—telescope, theory of Milky Way. **Physical sciences: Newton** —gravitation. **Boyle. Viviani**—density of fluids. **Linnaeus**—classification of plants, animals. **Leibnitz**—infinitesimal calculus. **Medical sciences: Harvey**— circulation of blood. **Haller** and **Willis**—physiology of body. **Philosophical thought: Descartes**—New methods of reasoning (*"cogito ergo sum"*). **Leibnitz. Social Sciences: Locke**—Contract theory to justify constitutional rule. **Hobbes**— Contract theory to justify absolute rule. Divine Right as theory of government challenged in seventeenth-century Britain. Scientific revolution used deductive reasoning in contrast to Church's "revealed truths." Shook stability of medieval world.

2. **Work and importance of following writers: Voltaire,** leading figure of Enlightenment. Satirist, champion of toleration. Admirer of freedom he found in England, *"Lettres sur les Anglais."* He particularly attacked intolerance of Catholic Church; championed Calas. Yet not a democrat. Corresponded with European rulers. **Montesquieu:** admirer of British political system, advocate of constitutional monarchy based on rule of law. *"L'Esprit des lois."* Believed in separation

of powers, and in influence of environment on constitution. Ideas incorporated in American Constitution and in constitution of French Revolution in 1791. **Diderot:** editor of Encyclopaedia (1751-72) to which all philosophers contributed. Believed in man's progress through acquisition of knowledge based on reason. **Quesnay:** founder of Physiocrats. Economic ideas contained in *"Tableau Économique."* Primacy of agriculture over industry as source of wealth; existence of natural economic laws. Attacked mercantilism, advocated *"laissez-faire,"* or free economy. Influenced Turgot in France, Adam Smith in Britain. **Rousseau:** appeal to emotions as well as reason. Attacked artificial French society, pleaded for return to state of nature. *"Contrat social"* dealt with problem of relationship of freedom and authority. Confusion over term "general will." *"Émile"*—concern for individual, character developed through education. *"Julie"*—emotion over intellect. Began Romantic movement in literature. All these men led Enlightenment in France. Common belief in rights of individual; criticism of Ancien Régime. Collectively influenced thought throughout Europe, provided stimulus for French Revolution.

CHAPTER 29

1. **Decline of Bourbon monarchy under Louis XV: problems bequeathed to Louis XV—** financial deficits, inefficient system of taxation, religious quarrels, Jansenist controversy, administrative defects of royal bureaucracy. Louis XV's policies aggravated these problems. **Criticism of philosophers and Parlements** undermined authority of Louis' administration. **Character of King important** in absolute monarchy; Louis idle and irresponsible; failed to exercise his power to tackle problems. **Rival court factions** and constant changes of ministers discredited government. **Failures in foreign policy** such as loss of overseas empire and ruin of trade during Seven Years' War. **Domestic crises:** attacks on Church and thus on religious foundations of monarchy. Jansenist controversy. Failure of Louis to solve financial problems. Exemption of privileged classes from taxation was root of national grievances. Louis made no attempt to change this.

2. **Jesuit Order:** Society dissolved in 1773 by Pope Clement XIV, Bull *Dominus ac Redemptor.* **Jesuits in Portugal:** Prime Minister **Pombal** objected to Jesuit opposition to his reforms which undermined their trading activities. Took advantage of attempted assassination of King to expel Jesuits from country, 1760. **France:** Jesuits opposed by philosophers, Parlements, Jansenists, many of the people, **Mme de Pompadour, Duke of Choiseul.** Lawsuit against bankrupt Jesuit sugar enterprise in Martinique resulted in Society appealing to Parlement of Paris. Parlement declared Society's constitution incompatible with allegience to King. Louis XV forced to expel order, 1762. **Spain:** Jesuits at root of disturbances against reforms of **Charles III** and his ministers **Squillacci** and **Count d'Aranda.** Count d'Aranda an admirer of Voltaire. 1767, order expelled. **Austria: Maria Theresa** forced to expel Jesuits in 1773 through influence of **Joseph II,** and action of other Catholic rulers. **Jesuits an international organization** with loyalty to their General rather than to ruler of a particular country. Thus were challenge to temporal authority of even Catholic sovereigns. **Political interference of Jesuits** was resented by rulers. **Jesuits opposed Enlightenment.** Those advisers closest to rulers of Europe were anti-Jesuit. **Jesuits lost support of Catholic Church.** Order criticized, for its worldly activities undermined its spiritual work.

CHAPTER 30

1. **Reasons for revolution in France: fundamental causes** incompetence of governments under **Louis XV** and **Louis XVI** in domestic and foreign policies. Criticism stifled. Growing gulf between nobility and peasants. Efforts at agricultural reform threatened peasants with dispossession of their land. Constantly increasing national debt due to wars, system of taxation. Criticism of philosophers who called attention to grievances and suggested remedies. Role of Parlement of Paris in challenging king's government. **Immediate causes:** essentially contradictory policies of king and his ministers. **Vergenne's** foreign policy resulting in French support of American Revolution. Frenchmen inspired to seek liberty by example, and financial situation worsened still further. Failure of Louis' ministers of finance, **Turgot, Necker, Calonne,** to reduce national debt because of refusal of privileged classes to forgo immunity from taxation. Louis forced to summon Assembly of Notables which advised him to summon States-General. Meeting of States-General, 1789, marked outbreak of revolution. Paris filled with discontented thousands as result of famine, unemployment of years 1787-89.

2. **Attempts made by Louis to solve financial problems, and reasons for failure:** inherited financial situation too acute for Louis or ministers to cope with. **Turgot, 1774-76:** policy of rigorous economy. Met with opposition to proposed scheme of taxation of nobility. Was dismissed. **Necker, 1776-81:** engaged in war of American Independence. Policy of borrowing, but forced to adopt high rates of interest. *"Compte Rendu"* falsified actual financial state, made him popular. This created jealousy which led to his dismissal. **Calonne, 1783-87:** continued policy of borrowing at high rates of interest. Made no attempt to curb Court expenses. Proposed land and stamp tax from which no one was to be exempt. Advised summoning of Assembly of Notables, whose opposition resulted in his dismissal. **De Brienne, 1787-88:** failed to get Parlement's support for proposed land and stamp tax, dismissed. **Necker recalled, 1788-89:** advised King to summon States-General to offer concessions to "reformers." States-General refused to grant necessary taxes until fundamental reforms had been effected. The Revolution had begun. **Reasons for failure to solve financial problems:** weakness of Louis XVI, who failed to back ministers against opposition of landed classes. Selfish refusal of privileged classes to undergo taxation. Disastrous government policies: foreign policy of aggression; policy of Necker and Calonne's of borrowing at high rates of interest.

CHAPTER 31

1. **National Assembly and the Convention:** see text, pp. 287-88; 291-92.

2. **Attempts at limited monarchy:** see p. 290.

CHAPTER 32

1. **French revolutionaries:** see pp. 293-94.

CHAPTER 33

1. **Decline of Napoleon's power after 1807:** Failure to defeat Britain, by either invasion or economic war. Spanish rebellion, Peninsular war, Austrian diversion, Moscow campaign. Expulsion from Spain and invasion of France. Resentments created in subject peoples by effects of Continental system. Spirit of nationalism aroused. Provocation of Spanish nationalism, success of the British navy,

Russian winter. Prussian reform and revival, which created a Continental army to rival the Grand Army. Exhaustion of French manpower. Decline of Napoleon's mental powers and health.

CHAPTER 34

1. **Main ideas of Congress of Vienna:** Legitimacy, balance of power, containment of France, political reorganization of Europe by dismantling of Napoleonic empire, rewards for the victors, preservation of peace. (For explanation of these points see text, pp. 306-8.)

2. **Aims of Metternich:** see pp. 309-10. **Influence of Metternich:** Survival of Austrian empire due to Metternich. He delayed Italian and German unification, and he delayed development of Prussian supremacy in Germany. He suppressed liberalism and nationalism by means of the Congress System.

CHAPTER 35

1. **Reasons for lack of opposition to Belgian and Polish revolutions of 1830. Belgian revolution:** Withdrawal of Britain from the Congress of Verona, 1822, marked the end of the Concert of Europe. Austria no longer had power to express opposition to change in Europe. **Liberalism** stirring in Parma, Modena, and Papal states, and Austria wished to concentrate on those areas. **Britain** had traditional policy of encouraging small independent powers in the Low Countries as a measure of safety against invasion. Palmerston was Foreign Secretary, and champion of small states and liberalism abroad. **France** disliked union of Holland and Belgium which had been expressly designed to prevent French expansion. Louis Philippe, on throne he owed to a revolution, could hardly oppose revolt in Belgium. He feared to lose support of French liberalism if he aided reactionary Holland. **Russia** was too busy suppressing revolution in Poland. **Prussia** was deterred by French threats to herself, and by watching growth of liberalism in her own territory. **Polish revolution:** strong reactionary views of Tsar Nicholas I. He only supported liberalism and nationalism outside Russia when the interests of traditional Russian policy of expansion seemed likely to be served by so doing. Other powers reluctant to intervene. Poland was part of the sovereign domains of Nicholas I, and to support Poland would have been to risk war with Russia.

2. **Causes of revolts of 1830:** revolts were either liberal (France) or national (Belgium) or both (Poland and Greece). The arrangements of the Vienna settlement in 1815 had been reactionary, and in some cases so unsuitable as to make revolt ultimately inevitable (e.g. Protestant Holland given Catholic Belgium, autocratic Russia given Poland, constitutionally averse to strong central government). Factors other than the Vienna settlement were the reactionary policies of Metternich, Charles X, and the Russian desire to dismember Turkey-in-Europe (see p. 341).

CHAPTER 36

1. **1848, year of revolutions:** forces of reaction of 1830 had not destroyed **liberalism and nationalism,** which had continued to exist underground and in exile. **Britain's** sympathy for liberalism and nationalism made her a base from which exiles of reactionary countries could propagate ideas. **Middle-class intellectuals** even in reactionary central Europe remained liberal and nationalistic. As landlords,

clergy and professional men their influence was effective. Some rulers were losing their fears of liberalism. They looked to French example. Revolution in one area kindled sparks which fired neighbours. Revolutions not more successful because of lack of adequate co-ordination of effort in Austria and Hungary. Conflicting aims and interests of nationalism and liberalism, e.g. in Germany. **Indifferent leadership,** e.g. Germany. Reactionary governments more mutually helpful to each other than were the revolutionary movements.

2. **National workshops:** inspired by socialism of Louis Blanc. "To the able-bodied citizen the State owes work." Proposal—system of co-operative factories, state-owned and guaranteed but managed by workers. Provisional government after revolution of 1848 hurriedly put the unemployed to work on public improvements in Paris. **Vor-Parliament:** German liberals and nationalists, encouraged by the outbreak of 1848 revolution in France, gathered unofficially at Heidelberg to consider future of Germany. Members drawn from almost all German states. Drafted scheme for election of a national parliament to be elected on basis of universal suffrage. German-speaking provinces of Austria to be included, which would have meant dismemberment of Austrian empire. Looked to liberal Frederick William IV of Prussia to give support to scheme. **Frankfort Parliament:** Diet of German Confederation induced to authorize popular election of German National Assembly in Frankfort. Prolonged debates at Frankfort on fundamental rights of German people allowed Austria time to suppress movement. **Napoleonic Legend:** Originated after 1830. Propagated by Bonapartists in opposition to government of Louis Philippe (see pp. 316-17). Importance of Legend was factor in rise of Napoleon III but his failure to live up to legend was factor in his loss of his throne. **Charles Albert of Sardinia:** see pp. 322-23. **Louis Kossuth:** Hungarian nationalist (born 1802, member of National Diet at Pressburg, 1825). Political programme—separation of Hungary from Austria and establishment of sovereign Hungarian republic. Abolition of feudalism and annexation of Transylvania. Part in revolution of 1848; Austria conceded to Hungary her own ministries: Hungarian Diet established at Pesth (Appointed minister of national defence.) Resisted Slav demand for independence from Magyars. His failure, Austria exploited differences between Slavs and Magyars. Opposition of liberal moderates in Hungary and external opposition by Russia after Kossuth proclaimed Hungarian independence. Flight of Kossuth and submission of Hungary.

CHAPTER 37

1. **Contribution of European powers to Italian unity:** Europe recognized existence of "Italian Question" at Paris Conference of 1856. Palmerston sympathetic to cause of Italian unity, encouraged support of Cavour. **Britain** pressed Francis II of Naples to support liberalism in Naples and nationalism in Italy. Britain and Russia sought to induce Austria to make concessions to Cavour, 1859. **France** under Napoleon III, compact of Plombières and war with Sardinia against Austria, 1859 (see text, pp. 326-27). **Prussia** awarded Venetia to Italy after Austro-Prussian war of 1866 as price of Italian alliance with Prussia against Austria. Prussian attack on France in 1870 forced France to withdraw her garrison in the Papal States. **Hindrance of European powers to Italian unity:** reactionary attempts to enforce settlement of 1815, especially by Austria up to 1848. **Austrian** suppression of risings in Naples and Piedmont, 1820, and risings in Parma, Modena

and Papal States in 1831. Restoration of political power of Pope in Papal States by **France,** 1849. **Austrian** suppression of revolt in Lombardy, Venetia, and Piedmont in 1848 and defeat of Sardinia. **Napoleon's** betrayal of cause of Italian unity at truce of Villafranca in 1859, maintenance of a French garrison in Rome until 1870 to protect political security of Papal States.

CHAPTER 38

1. **Prussian methods of securing domination of a united Germany: autocracy established** in Prussia. Bismarck refused concessions to liberals and assured himself of support of conservatives. Enabled a policy of military expansion and reform, and gave Bismarck financial means to do this. Absolute financial and military control. **Authority of Confederal Diet undermined:** Prussia refused to co-operate in scheme, 1863, by which Confederation would be run as Directory under Austrian supremacy. 1864-5, Prussia negotiated privately with Austria over Schleswig-Holstein question and ignored Confederal Diet. Finally Prussia withdrew from Confederation, 1866. **Prussia diplomatically isolated powers** likely to oppose unification and attacked them one by one: e.g. Denmark, 1864; Austria, 1866; France, 1870. Prussia exploited differences between minor German states, to form North German Confederation. Weaning of south German states from reliance on French protection by revelation of Napoleon's demand for Rhine Palatinate.

CHAPTER 39

1. **Causes of Crimean War: Basic factor**—presence of **Turkey-in-Europe.** Turkish misgovernment of her European subjects was excuse for Russia to seek expansion through Balkans and Black Sea to Mediterranean. Russian expansion unwelcome to Britain, who saw it as threat to British power in east. **Immediate issue:** disputed guardianship of Holy Places in Palestine between monks of Greek and Latin churches; French support for Latin Church; Russian support for Greek Church. Refusal of Turkey to accept diplomatic resolution of issue. Russian invasion of Moldavia and Wallachia. **Consequences of Crimean War:** For **Britain,** triumph for her solution of the Eastern Question as against that of Russia, but not final solution. Revelation of serious weaknesses of British army, consequent army reforms and beginning of adequate military and civil nursing system. For **France,** triumph for Napoleon III and increase of popularity, but created expectation of continued success which he could not live up to. For **Sardinia,** recognition of her place among independent major powers and her equality with Austria, and leadership of Italian affairs. For **Turkey,** European guarantee of the integrity of her empire. For **Austria,** safeguarded her position on Danube but barred extension of her territories by creation of independent Moldavia and Wallachia. Defeat in Italy by recognition afforded Sardinia. For **Russia,** defeat of her policy towards Turkey-in-Europe. Defeat for her aims of expansion in Balkans and Black Sea. Latter declared open to merchant ships of all nations, closed to all warships.

2. **Treaty of San Stefano:** see pp. 345-47.

CHAPTER 40

1. **Reforms of Alexander II:** Edict of Emancipation, reform of local government, legal reform (see text, p. 350). Other measures, **increased liberty of individual** by relaxation of restrictions on press, universities, and foreign travel. **Reform of**

national economy, financial abuses reduced, trade and industry encouraged, natural resources developed and communications system improved by railway construction. **Degree of success:** Edict of Emancipation did not solve the problem of serfdom. Peasants still tied to *mir* as closely as they had been to the landowner. Discontent aroused by constant reduction of size of land-ownings, compensation fund to former landed proprietors burdensome to freed serfs. Change of Alexander's policy after 1867 limited effectiveness of reforms. Social reforms entrusted to inept upper classes. Renewed activity of secret police. Press censorship reintroduced. Deportation of political agitators resumed. **Ineffectiveness of reforms** shown by growth of nihilism and attempts on Tsar's life.

2. **Dumas experiment:** see pp. 355-56. **Reasons for failure:** unwillingness of Crown to share sovereignty. Autocracy of Crown remained untouched by any representative body. **Restricted franchise** on which the third Duma was elected limited its representative character. It thus reflected views of the landowners rather than those of the people. It was not strong enough to break the monopoly of political power held by the corrupt aristocracy. Tsar remained a tool in the hands of his advisers, especially Rasputin. **Police system** and deportation of "agitators" eliminated the anti-government leaders but left Opposition forces to secret leadership of the more extreme and revolutionary opinion.

CHAPTER 41

1. **Main features of Bismarck's domestic policy: Settlement of conflict with Church.** Agreement with Pope Leo III. Regulations of 1873-75 imposed on priesthood ceased to be enforced. Germany again diplomatically represented at Vatican. Roman Catholic orders allowed to resume operations in Germany, but state inspection of all schools and custom of civil marriage retained. **Efforts to combat socialism,** by repression of it in any form other than state socialism (see text, pp. 360-61). **Development of German economy** with state aid to industry and adoption of protectionist policy.

2. **Crises threatening stability of Third French Republic:** describe any two of the crises narrated on pp. 363-65.

CHAPTER 42

1. By 1878 **France and Britain** were well established in Africa; **Italy** less so and therefore anxious to expand; **Germany** and **Belgium** keen to participate. But expansion and participation both involved possibility of border conflict with the established powers. Hence **Congress of Berlin, 1884,** to determine spheres of interest and avoidance of trespass in North Africa: **Britain**—Kenya, Uganda, Rhodesia, Nigeria, Gold Coast; **France**—West Africa less Gold Coast, Madagascar; **Germany**—Tanganyika, South-west Africa, Togoland, Cameroons; **Portugal**—Angola, Mozambique; **Belgium**—Congo Free State. Africa north of Sahara a source of conflict: France *versus* Britain re **Egypt.** French enterprise had built the Suez Canal, Britain was the main user; **Disraeli's** purchase of canal shares. 1876, **Dual Control** established and renewed 1879, abandoned, 1882, after French failure to support British suppression of Arabi Pasha's independence revolt. France *versus* Britain re **Sudan.** 1896, British conquest of Sudan; 1898, Fashoda incident and Anglo-French estrangement. **Moroccan crises:** the Tangier crisis and the Conference of Algeciras, 1906 (see p. 371); the Agadir crisis, 1909 (see p. 371). **Italy:** essentially a **Mediterranean power** but entered the scramble

for Africa too late to secure what she considered a fair share. By 1912 in **Eritrea, Somaliland, Libya** but remained unsatisfied. Designs on Abyssinia. Hence she threw in her lot with the other dissatisfied powers and joined Germany, Austria in **Triple Alliance** in opposition to France, Russia, Britain. Hence Africa a factor in producing the Anglo-French Entente, the crises of 1906 and 1909, and the shaping of the rival alliance system which led to war of 1914.

2. **Oriental attitudes to West. Prior to Western approaches,** both Japan and China content with own way of life. Japan indifferent, China actively opposed to Western contact. **After Western approaches,** Chinese hostility intensified. No desire to adapt or adopt to West. Accepted military defeat. Japan in defeat adopted Western ways to meet West on equal terms. Became military power, industrialized, aggressive.

CHAPTER 43

1. **Crisis of 1908:** revolt in Turkey. Turkish revival. Hence Austrian annexation of Bosnia and Herzegovina in contravention of Treaty of Berlin of 1878. Serbian protest. Russia supports Serbia, Germany supports Austria. Russia withdraws. Possible war threat passes. **Crisis of 1912:** Turkey defeated by Balkan league of Bulgaria, Greece and Serbia. Intervention of Powers. Treaty of London. Austria and Italy insist on limiting the gains of Serbia. Creation of a new state, Albania. Second Balkan War follows, 1913. Serbia enlarged; opposition of Austria in fear of Serbian championship of Slavs in Austria-Hungary. Austria anxious for excuse to attack Serbia. **Crisis of 1914:** murder of Austrian Archduke Francis Ferdinand and his wife at Sarajevo. Austrian ultimatum to Serbia, German support for Austria, Russian support for Serbia. No withdrawal, so war of 1914.

2. **Italy and Germany** drawn together as dissatisfied colonial powers desiring expansion in Africa and therefore opposed to Britain and France, both colonial powers and in possession of lion's share in Africa. **Armaments rivalry:** Britain *versus* Germany re naval armaments; France *versus* Germany re military armaments. **French desire to avenge defeat** of 1870; German fear of such French desire. Mutual distrust. **Austro-Russian conflict** in Balkans over control of mouth of Danube. **Anglo-Russian mistrust** over Russian Mediterranean expansion with possible threat to British trade routes and influence in India. **Anglo-French-Russian** *détente* consequent upon British abandonment of "Splendid Isolation." Failure of Germany to respond to British overtures for settlement of outstanding differences. Failure of the Hague disarmament conferences. Hence **Triple Alliance** of Italy, Austria, Germany and **Dual Alliance** of France and Russia and Anglo-French Entente.

CHAPTER 44

1. **Reasons for early German success: Superiority of German preparation.** The conception of a lightning campaign. The Schleiffen Plan. Conscript army well trained and with strong reserves. Organization of industry for war production, interior lines of communication. **Unexpected nature of the German attack:** Franco-Belgian border comparatively undefended as compared with Franco-German frontier, in reliance on respect for Belgian neutrality as provided for in Treaty of London, 1839. German violation of Belgian neutrality. Unified German Command as compared with separate commands of French, Belgian and British armies. **Reasons for German failure** to achieve quick victory:

Unexpected determination of Belgian resistance gave time for British mobilization and landing of troops on the Continent. British participation. Successful French defence of Channel ports and consequent German failure to cut British communication by sea with the Continent.

2. New pattern of warfare: see pp. 385-86.

CHAPTER 45

1. **Merits and Defects of peace settlement:** see pp. 398-401.

2. **Turkish and Austro-Hungarian Empires:** see p. 398.

CHAPTER 46

1. **League of Nations:** see pp. 402-5.

2. **Crises in Europe, 1919-31:** see pp. 404-5.

CHAPTER 47

1. (a) **Reparations:** Soured relations between Great Powers, e.g. Germany and France, the latter refusing to admit former's inability to pay; Britain and America, the latter insisting on repayment of monies borrowed though Britain had reduced her demand on her Continental debtors. Led to the French occupation of the **Ruhr.** Coolness between France and Britain. Latter more ready to make concessions to Germany than former. Britain also disagreed with French reoccupation of Ruhr. Payment in kind (German coal) a factor producing world economic crisis of 1931-32. (b) **Occupation of the Ruhr:** Soured Franco-British relations. Increased the difficulties of Stresemann Government in Germany. Stimulated German economic chaos and created favourable climate for growth of ultra-nationalist party in Germany. Led to international examination of inter-Allied war debts. This soured British-American relations. Led to the Dawes Plan. (c) **Locarno Pact, 1925:** Raised hopes of possibility of achievement of disarmament. Led to admission of Germany to League of Nations and her restoration to Great Power status by award of a permanent seat on Council of League. Possibly the last chances of smoothing out international post-1918 relations without recourse to Second World War. (d) **Economic Crisis, 1929:** Led to the abandonment of attempt to enforce reparations from Germany. Contributed to the fall of Briand's administration. Ended prospects of Franco-German reconciliation. Opened the way for the advent of power in Germany of the Nazi party by revealing full extent of dependence of German economy on foreign capital. Hence a factor in the fall of the Weimar Republic.

2. **Weimar Republic:** see pp. 410-13.

CHAPTER 48

1. **Reasons for Mussolini's seizure of power:** (Expand by reference to text the following points) Italian disappointment at Versailles. Subsequent growth of Italian colonial ambitions. Weakness of parliamentary government in Italy, 1919-22. Social unrest. Breakdown of law and order. Powerlessness of the monarchy to take effective action. Growth of revolutionary forces. Leadership and organizing ability of Mussolini. Brownshirts' intimidation of opponents and rivals. **Domestic policy:** see pp. 415-16.

2. Causes of revolution of 1917 in Russia. Basic causes: Autocratic aristocracy dominated by central government, corrupt and inefficient. Failure of attempts at constitutional reform. Well-meaning Court but isolated from subjects and dominated by unscrupulous advisers. Tyranny of secret police. Failure of Government to distinguish between desire for reform and revolution. Exile of moderate reformers. Secret growth of revolutionary ideas and parties. **Immediate causes:** Defeat due to inefficiency of military organization. **Russian internal development to 1939:** see pp. 419-21.

CHAPTER 49

1. Mustafa Kemal: Saved Turkey from the consequences of defeat in war of 1914-18. Abandoned the old Turkish European imperialism after war with Greece; concentrated on development as a nation. Brought Turkey into the community of Western Europe by abandoning Balkan ambitions, thus terminating the Eastern Question, by policy of peace, by policy of Westernization of Turkish social life. Reconstruction of Turkish national life by reforms, see pp. 424-25.

2. Reasons for rise of dictatorships: Creation of parliamentary democracies in Europe on British pattern after 1918 was unwise—such a form of government had only succeeded in Britain as a result of a long process of historical development. Deficiencies and grievances real or imagined arising from the Versailles settlement. Failure of League of Nations to remove these grievances legally. Hence rise of national parties prepared to achieve revision by unilateral action and by force. Popular acceptance, e.g. Italy and Germany, of "Leadership" principle. Economic chaos resulting from disruption of national economies by war, war debts, reparations, world economic depression leading to discrediting of existing national systems and growth of social unrest. **Chief features:** One-party system. Leadership principle. Aggressive foreign policy. Extreme nationalism. State regulation of the economy (wages, prices, conditions of labour). State police systems—persecution of minority opinions—suppression of personal liberty—subordination of the individual to the State. Subordination of Church to State—attack on religion of all forms.

CHAPTER 50

1. Spain: The trial battleground of Communism and Fascism. Served to forge the Rome-Berlin Axis. Exposed the ineffectiveness of the League of Nations, sanctions, and of collective security. Convinced Germany and Italy of the pacifism of France and Britain and planted doubts in the Russian mind on the same issue. Hence a factor in ultimate Russo-German pact (p. 435). **Austria:** see pp. 429-31. **Czechoslovakia:** see pp. 431-33.

2. Outbreak of War, 1939: see pp. 435-36.

OUTLINE ANSWERS TO EXAMINATION QUESTIONS

SECTION 1 (1494-1648)

1. **Hapsburg-Bourbon rivalry:** Mention *briefly*:
   (*1*) Their respective claims to Milan and Naples.
   (*2*) Personal rivalry of Charles V and Francis I.
   (*3*) French fears of territorial encirclement by Hapsburgs.
   (*4*) Importance to the secular powers of being able to influence Papal policy and diplomacy.
   (*5*) The threat to the Balance of Power by the extent of the Hapsburg possessions.
   Explain *at greater length*:
   (*6*) The vulnerability of Italy to invasion by reason of her disunity, inter-state rivalry, reliance on mercenaries for defence.
   (*7*) The attraction of her wealth.
   (*8*) Geographic importance of Italy as a link between Austria and Spain.

2. **Problems of Charles V:**
   (*1*) Rivalry with France.
   (*2*) Luther and Lutheran movement in Germany.
   (*3*) Opposition of German princes to the Central Imperial authority and their desire to increase their own sovereign independence.
   (*4*) The Turkish threat. (The readiness of Charles' Christian enemies to exploit it.)
   (*5*) Lack of permanent Imperial army. Employment of German mercenaries.
   (*6*) Inadequate Imperial finance and Spanish unwillingness to allow national resources to be used for Imperial ends.

3. **Factors contributing to Luther's success:**
   (*1*) Anti-clerical feeling in Germany.
   (*2*) Readiness of the nobility to lay hands on the wealth of the Church.
   (*3*) Luther's appeal to German nationalism.
   (*4*) Desire of German princes to increase their sovereign independence at the expense of the Emperor.
   (*5*) Initially the social and economic implications of Lutheranism. (This factor, however, diminished after Luther's opposition to the Peasants' Revolt.)
   (*6*) Charles V's many tasks elsewhere; the readiness of his enemies to encourage Lutheranism even though they did not share Luther's views.

4. **Calvinist Reformation in Geneva:**
   Doctrine and Ritual:
   (*1*) Abolition of the Mass. Communion in both kinds. Belief in Spiritual Presence received by faith.
   (*2*) Predestination.

(*3*) Demand for Scriptural proof of all doctrine.

(*4*) Removal of images and organs.

Church Organization:

(*1*) Four orders—Doctors for teaching; Pastors for the Spiritual ministry (Clerics); Elders for Discipline; Deacons for the relief of the poor—Laymen.

(*2*) Independent congregations. Large element of lay control.

(*3*) Church dominates the State: Geneva Theocracy.

Discipline:

(*1*) Enforced by the Consistory under joint Lay and Clerical control.

(*2*) By means of penance, public confession and excommunication.

(*3*) Intolerance towards non-Calvinist views.

(*4*) Sin treated as a crime (Sumptuary Laws).

(*5*) State required to enforce decisions of the Consistory.

5. **Non-religious causes of French Wars of Religion or Civil Wars:**

(*1*) Cessation of Italian Wars. Warlike tradition of French nobility. Now left without employment.

(*2*) Territorial division of the country between Guise, Montmorency and Bourbon. Feudal rivalry of the three.

(*3*) Feudal opposition to the growth of the centralizing power of the French monarchy.

(*4*) Opportunity for assertion of feudal independence by reason of the weakness of French kings after Henry II and before Henry IV, and unpopularity of Catherine de Medici as a foreigner.

(*5*) Social discontent:

    (*a*) Lesser nobility—division of estates. Diminishing wealth. Rising prices.

    (*b*) Industrial workers—rise in wages outstripped by the rise in prices.

    (*c*) Peasants—heavy burden of taxation.

6. **Reasons for the failure of Philip II to suppress Dutch revolt:**

(*1*) Leadership of House of Orange, especially William and Maurice.

(*2*) Foreign aid to rebels, especially from England.

(*3*) Philip's other preoccupations—France, England.

(*4*) Overstrained Spanish finances.

(*5*) War stimulus to the Dutch economy—development of industry, fishing and carrying trade. (Made possible by the use of mercenaries for army while the native population continued in commercial activities.)

(*6*) Nature of Dutch terrain—canals natural defence lines. Dykes could be cut and an invader defeated by subsequent flooding.

(*7*) Effect of Dutch privateers—raids on enemy commerce, growth of wealth of the Dutch ports.

7. **Revival of Monarchical power by Henry IV and by Richelieu:**

a. **Henry IV:**

(*1*) Reconciliation of both religious parties to the crown, Protestants by Edict of Nantes, Catholics by his conversion.

(*2*) Bribery of nobility and maintenance of a standing army to meet threats to the crown from ambitious nobles.

(*3*) Creation of Treasury surplus to establish financial independence of the Crown. Limitation of powers of provincial administrators to raise money on their own initiative. Stringent economy.

b. Richelieu:

(*1*) Peace of Alais—preserved religious toleration for the Huguenots but deprived them of their political privileges which might have enabled them to resist the Crown.

(*2*) Weakened feudal strength of the nobility by destruction of castles and fortified houses not needed for defence against foreign invasion.

(*3*) Creation of *Intendants*, who took over administrative provincial functions including responsibility for the militia, thus weakening further the political power of the nobility who were the provincial administrators. Intendants drawn from the middle class. (Wholly dependent upon Crown for their status and employment. Hence not likely to resist the Crown).

(*4*) Ceased to summon Estates-General.

8. **Gustavus Adolphus and the Thirty Years' War:**
   Motives for intervention:

   (*1*) Desire to make Sweden the supreme Protestant power in northern Europe.

   (*2*) Desire to make the Baltic a "Swedish Lake." A Germany at war would afford him opportunity, and weaken a possible rival.

   (*3*) Success against Russia (1617) and Poland (1621-29) would be completed if mastery of the North German coast of the Baltic could be established.

   (*4*) Richelieu's offer of money and material for intervention in Germany.

   Part played:

   (*1*) (Landing in Pomerania, 1630.) Negotiations for an alliance with Brandenburg and Saxony.

   (*2*) Imperialist capture of Magdeburg, 1631.

   (3) Swedish advance through Saxony. Victory over Tilly at Breitenfeld near Leipzig.

   (*4*) Southern advance in hopes of a joint front with the Calvinist states of the Rhine Valley. (This move opposed by Richelieu who feared for the independence of the Catholic Archbishoprics of Cologne, Trier and Mainz.)

   (*5*) Invasion of Bavaria: death of Tilly at Lechfeld, 1632. Sweden prepares to invade Austrian hereditary dominions. Emperor recalls Wallenstein.

   (*6*) Battle of Lützen, 1632. Swedish success but Gustavus Adolphus killed.

9. **Continental overseas expansion in the sixteenth century** (*N.B.:* Terms of question *exclude* England):
   Portugal:

   (*1*) The work of Alphonso Albuquerque—Goa, Cochin on Indian coast, Ormuz in Persian Gulf.

   (*2*) Colonization of Malabar coast.

   (*3*) In the Far East—trade through Canton from 1517. Island of Macao colonized.

   (*4*) Trading post in Japan, 1542. Support for missionary work of St. Francis Xavier. No colonization.

   (*5*) Trade opened with Sumatra, Java and the Spice Islands.

   (*6*) Trading posts in Africa at Mozambique, 1520, and Loanda, 1576.

   (*7*) Protectorate established over Abyssinia.

   (*8*) Colonial Empire established in Brazil. Settlements at S. Paulo, Pernambuco and Bahia. Governor-General appointed, 1549. Rio de Janeiro conquered from France, 1567.

Spain:

(*1*) First colony established at San Domingo. Followed by conquest of Caribbean islands.

(*2*) Conquest of Mexican Aztec Indians by Cortez, 1519-20.

(*3*) Conquest of Peru by Pizarro, 1531-35. Lima as capital of Spanish empire in South America, 1535.

(*4*) Foundation of Buenos Aires, 1545, and Asunción, 1536, by Mendoza.

(*5*) Philippines annexed, 1542.

(*6*) Extension along Chilean coast, and foundation of Santiago de Chile, 1541.

(*7*) Foundation of future Ecuador, 1535.

(*8*) Penetration into Colombia, 1538.

(*9*) Organization of Empire into New Spain (Mexico, West Indies, Central America, northern South America, Philippines) and Peru (Peru, Chile, Ecuador and Argentine) under two Viceroys.

(*10*) Introduction of Spanish language, customs, University education, Catholicism and Diocesan organization of Church. Exploitation of deposits of gold and silver.

(*Note:* 1580, Union of Spain and Portugal united the Spanish and Portuguese colonial and trading empires for the next sixty years.)

10. **Erasmus:**

(*1*) Essential biographical details.

(*2*) Achievements as a Humanist.

(*3*) Attack on Church from Humanist point of view.

(*4*) Relations with reformers.

Zwingli:

(*1*) Essential biographical details.

(*2*) Contribution to reformation in Switzerland.

(*3*) Differences of teaching from Luther's and Calvin's.

(*4*) Involvement in Swiss politics leading to death in battle.

Machiavelli:

(*1*) Essential biographical details, especially his political service.

(*2*) *The Prince*—political views. Their relations to Machiavelli's practical experience of political service.

(*3*) Influence in political thought.

Julius II:

(*1*) Julius as founder of political power of Papal States (as distinct from his predecessors, Sixtus IV and Alexander II, who sought to turn the papacy into a family dynastic possession).

(*2*) The unsuccessful would-be Liberator of Italy. Papal States to be strong enough to unite Italy and expel foreigners. Hence his organization of the League of Cambrai and the Holy League. (But he failed in his objects inasmuch as Cambrai established France in Milan and Holy League established Spain in Naples. Net result, the permanent strengthening of foreign domination of Italy and postponement of Italian unification.)

(*3*) Julius and the Church. Recognized the need for reform. (Tried to reduce the influence of simony at papal elections. Called the Lateran Council, 1512, to effect reform, but reform shelved in pursuit of his political schemes.)

(*4*) Julius and the Renaissance. Desire to reconcile classical culture and Christianity. Patronage of Bramante, Raphael, Michelangelo, Builder of Renaissance palaces and St. Peter's.

Coligny, 1519-72:
(*1*) His religious and political connections.
(*2*) Career up to the death of Condé. Welcomed the murder of Guise, 1563. Criticized Pacification of Amboise, 1563 (inadequate safeguards for Protestants). Escaped an attempt on his life by Catherine de Medici, 1568, after a Catholic defeat in the second civil war and death of Montmorency. (Succeeded Condé as leader of the Huguenots on the murder of Condé after the battle of Jarnac, 1569).
(*3*) Leader of the Huguenots. Military command in the third civil war. Growth of influence with Charles IX after Peace of St. Germain. Charles' plans to join Coligny in war against Spain. Catherine de Medici jealous of Coligny's influence over Charles. Catherine secures Charles' consent to Coligny's death by the story of fear of Huguenot revenge. Coligny's murder at the beginning of the Massacre of St. Bartholomew.

Wallenstein:
(*1*) Rise—Dessau—Lutter—Defeat of Denmark—Treaty of Lübeck.
(*2*) Opposition to Wallenstein. Fear of over-strong Imperial power. Personal jealousy. Resentment of his enforced contributions to the Imperial army.
(*3*) Temporary eclipse. Conflict with the Emperor over the Edict of Restitution, 1629. Catholic League demand for his dismissal, 1630.
(*4*) Conflict with Gustavus Adolphus.
(*5*) Fall. (His policy of peace and religious compromise. Opposition to him at the Imperial court. Desertion of his officers. His assassination at Eger, 1634.)

SECTION 2 (1648-1789)

11. **Colbert:** See pages 115-18.

12. **Peter the Great's reforms:** See pages 161-62, 167-69.

13. **Rise and fall of Sweden.**
   Factors accounting for predominance:
   (*1*) The first of the Baltic powers to achieve national consolidation, independence and religious stability.
   (*2*) National resources well developed by the end of the sixteenth century.
   (*3*) Military organization, absence of comparable national armies.
   (*4*) Ambition of Charles X and XII.

   Factors accounting for decline:
   (*1*) Rise of Russia and Prussia. Their greater resources, once mobilized.
   (*2*) Sweden's own resources too small to enable her to hold what she had temporarily gained during her neighbours' weakness.
   (*3*) Financial and economic exhaustion by 1718.
   (*4*) Supremacy too dependent upon character and ability of two particular rulers. National disunity after 1721. Hats versus Caps.

14. **Causes of the War of the Spanish Succession:** See pages 130-33.

15. **Turkish threats to Europe:**
   a. **Leopold I:** See pages 181-82.
   b. **Catherine the Great:** See pages 231-34.

16. Importance of Silesia to Prussia:

(*1*) Its acquisition in line with Frederick's policy of territorial extension.

(*2*) By its command of the valley of the Oder, Silesia would afford protection to Brandenburg.

Frederick versus Maria Theresa over Silesia:

(*3*) First contest, 1740-42.

(*4*) Second attempt, 1744-45.

(*5*) Relevant terms of Peace of Aix-la-Chapelle, 1748.

(*6*) Influence of Silesian question on Diplomatic Revolution.

(*7*) Austrian recovery and final loss of the province in Seven Years' War. Relevant terms of Peace of Paris, 1763.

17. Characteristics of an Enlightened Despot:

(*1*) An absolute monarch.

(*2*) A ruler who sought the welfare of his subjects according to his own conception of their interests.

(*3*) Personal interest in and conscientious discharge of his duties as Head of Government as well as Head of State.

Joseph II:

(*4*) Describe his religious, social, legal and economic reform policy.

(*5*) Point out his limitations, e.g. revocation of reforms, 1790.

(*6*) Illustrate his absolutism—centralization of administration—distrust of and opposition to representative institutions.

18. Catherine the Great: See pages 222-26.

19. Importance of Seven Years' War:

For Britain:

(*1*) Colonial empire acquired. Final defeat of France in the long colonial struggle.

(*2*) Establishment of British imperial power in India at the expense of France.

(*3*) Contribution to the revolt of the American colonies by removal of the French threat.

(*4*) Left France and Spain defeated but not reconciled to their defeat. Hence their later support for the revolt of the American colonies.

For France:

(*1*) Loss of colonial empire and command of the seas.

(*2*) Expense of war added to internal stresses.

(*3*) Failure of the Austrian alliance confirmed its unpopularity.

(*4*) A factor contributing to the French Revolution.

For Prussia:

(*1*) Retention of Silesia. Final victory over Maria Theresa.

(*2*) Step towards territorial integration of Prussia.

(*3*) Prussia in North Germany now the equal in influence of Austria in South Germany. Beginning of the duel between the two for supremacy within Germany.

For Austria:

(*1*) Final loss of Silesia.

(*2*) Henceforward challenged for the leadership of Germany by Prussia.

20. Grievances of Bourgeoisie and Peasants on Eve of French Revolution:
a. **Bourgeoisie:** See page 263.
b. **Peasants:** See pages 263-64.

SECTION 3 (1789-1878)

21. Events in France, 1789-93: See pages 285-88 and 290. Concentrate attention on:
(*1*) Transformation of States-General to National Assembly.
(*2*) Oath of Tennis Court and Court withdrawal to Versailles.
(*3*) Main measures of National Assembly.
(*4*) Court's return to Paris. Measures of Constituent Assembly.
(*5*) Flight of royal family to Varennes, 1791.
(*6*) Growth of Republicanism.
(*7*) Court's appeal for foreign aid—invasion.
(*8*) The Convention and triumph of Jacobinism.
(*9*) September massacres, 1792, and execution of the King, 1793.

22. European powers v. the armies of the French Revolution and Napoleon:
(*N.B.:* This question does not seek a statement of the causes of the failure in 1793 followed by an unrelated statement of the causes of success in 1815. It seeks a continuous comparison of the relevant factors in both cases.)
(*1*) 1793-1802, crowned heads and upper classes monopolizing control of government, fighting to maintain their position and power against a movement which by inviting rebellion threatened their existence. Popular opinion in European countries not unanimously opposed to revolution in France (e.g. Fox v. Burke in Britain). But, 1807-15, peoples conscious of domination by a foreign tyrant for his own ends, fighting for their national liberty.
(*2*) Hence, 1793-1802, fervour and conviction in French armies, but such a spirit non-existent in opposing armies before 1807-15.
(*3*) 1793-1802, France fighting to determine her own internal destiny against enemies who sought to thwart the national will. 1807-15, Europe fighting to resist French domination and aggression.
(*4*) 1793-1802, Allied governments fighting for particular narrow national interests. When these were achieved or seen to be impossible of attainment, they left coalitions. 1807-15, necessity for destroying Napoleon's power over-rode all narrower particular interests.

23. Napoleon, "Heir of the Ancien Régime":
(*1*) Restoration of autocracy in France.
(*2*) Restoration of a form of monarchy.
(*3*) Restoration of highly centralized government.
(*4*) Restoration of class distinction—creation of a new nobility.
(*5*) Reversion to an aggressive foreign policy which sought the traditional object of a Europe dominated by France.
"Child of the Revolution":
(*1*) Preservation of civic equality for all before the law.
(*2*) Preservation of the Revolutionary approach to property: corporate property vested in State; equal division of private estates on death of owner between family.
(*3*) Retention of public trial-and-jury system.
(*4*) Retention of subordination of the Church to the State (Concordat), and religious toleration.

24. Congress of Vienna:
In principle:
(*1*) Obsession with Legitimacy to neglect of Nationalism.
(*2*) No provision for liberal constitution except for France.
(*3*) Obsession with building frontier barriers against future French aggression.
Hence weaknesses of a detailed settlement:
(*1*) Union of Belgium under Holland with no safeguards for Belgian nationalism. Only justification, barrier against France. Economic and political advantage to Holland only.
(*2*) Prussian gains offset by Austrian Presidency of Germanic Confederation. Preservation of Austrian prestige but not in the interests of Germany.
(*3*) Division of Italy by restoration of Austria, the Papacy, Savoy and Hapsburgs in interests of former ruling families, not of Italy or Italians.
(*4*) Union of Norway with Sweden as reward to latter for her part in defeat of Napoleon, rather than out of regard for wishes or interests of the Norwegians.

25. Concert of Europe:
(*1*) Arose out of Russia's "Holy Alliance" project.
(*2*) This transformed itself into the Quadruple Alliance.
Reasons for failure:
(*1*) Objective of preserving peace of Europe transformed into determination to preserve unchanged the detailed settlement of 1815.
(*2*) Domination of Congresses by Austria under reactionary Metternich.
(*3*) Failure to distinguish between international issues and internal domestic issues. Intervention in domestic crises of Italy, Spain and Greece.
(*4*) Opposition of Britain and her withdrawal from the system.
(*5*) Influence of the Monroe Doctrine.

26. Belgium Independence: See pages 314-15.
Greece Independence: See pages 340-41.

27. Revolution in Austria-Hungary in 1848: See pages 318-20.

28. Bismarck's policy: See pages 332, 335-37.

29. Reasons for Sardinian leadership towards Italian Unity:
(*1*) Abdication of Charles Albert after failure in 1848. His successor not tainted with failure.
(*2*) Republicanism and liberalism alike discredited as a means of achieving unity after 1848. Hence leadership of Sardinian monarchy acceptable.
(*3*) After 1848, strong anti-clerical feeling in Italy because of "betrayal" of national cause by Pius IX. Sardinia alone pursued in domestic affairs an anti-clerical policy.
(*4*) Foreign aid essential. European powers more likely to afford such aid to a monarchy than to a republican party.
(*5*) Military effort the next alternative on the failure of liberalism. Sardinia alone had the necessary military nucleus.
(*6*) Assertion of Sardinia's right to speak for Italy, rather than Austria. established at Conference of Paris, 1856.

30a. Carlsbad Decrees: See pages 309-10.
  b. Mehemet Ali: See pages 341-42.

c. Alexander II: See pages 349-50, 353.
d. Kulturkampf: See pages 359-60.
e. The Ausgleich: See pages 357-58.
f. Treaty of San Stefano: See pages 345-46.

SECTION 4 (1878-1939)

31. Socialism, growth stimulated by:
(*1*) The Paris Commune of 1871.
(*2*) National Federation of local workmen's clubs, 1886.
(*3*) National Federation of Friendly Societies, 1892.
(*4*) Union of the two National Federations, 1895.
(*5*) By 1898 five socialist groups organized.
(*6*) United Social Party, 1898-1901.
(*7*) Split in socialist organization, 1901, on the issue of Millerand, a socialist, accepting Cabinet appointment as Minister of Commerce in Waldeck-Rousseau's government. Millerand the first instance of appointment of a socialist in a European cabinet.
(*8*) Formation of Confédération Générale de Travail, 1905.
(*9*) Growth of Socialist representation in parliament 1905-14, four national newspapers established, socialist in policy.
(*10*) 1919-29, Socialism weakened by growth of Communism at socialist expense.
(*11*) 1936, Popular Front Government under Socialist Blum.
Socialist legislation:
(*1*) 1888, Workmen's compensation introduced.
(*2*) 1889-1902, Labour Department established. Trade Unions (*Syndicats*) encouraged.
(*3*) 1906, Factory legislation. Progressive introduction of a ten-hour day. Protected conditions for women and children.
(*4*) 1906-10, Social unrest. Strikes. Repressed by the use of the military.
(*5*) 1910, Old Age Pensions.
(*6*) 1936-37, paid holidays for workers. Forty-hour week. Improved wage rates.
Anti-clericalism: See pages 365-66.

32. Growth of European power in Africa: See pages 367-68, 371-72.

33. System of rival alliances: See pages 377-79.

34. Reasons for early German success:
(*1*) Greater preparedness.
(*2*) The Schlieffen Plan.
(*3*) United command.
(*4*) Element of surprise.
(*5*) Interior lines of communication.
Reasons for final failure:
(*1*) Failure to finish the war in 1914. This gave time for Germany's opponents to organize their defence.
(*2*) British and American intervention.
(*3*) British naval supremacy. Blockade. Confinement of German High Seas

fleet to port. Maintenance of sea communications with land forces. Defeat of U-boat campaign.

(*4*) German involvement on two fronts.

(*5*) Unexpected weakness and collapse of Germany's allies.

(*6*) Allied air superiority by 1918.

35.

Wilson's Points:	Treaty of Versailles:
(*1*) Open covenants of peace openly arrived at.	(*1*) Terms of Versailles dictated, not negotiated with Germany.
(*2*) Freedom of the seas.	(*2*) Right of blockade retained.
(*3*) Removal of economic barriers to international trade.	(*3*) No provision for abolition of tariffs.
(*4*) Reduction of armaments.	(*4*) Only the defeated powers compelled to disarm. Allied promises to do so not fulfilled.
(*5*) Adjustment of colonial issues in interest of colonial peoples.	(*5*) Mandate system. Rewards for major victors. But perhaps some gain to colonial peoples.
(*6*) Russia to be free to develop her own constitution and join the League of Nations.	(*6*) Nothing to prevent European opposition to Russian Communism. Russia declined to join the League.
(*7*) Belgium to be evacuated.	(*7*) Implemented.
(*8*) Alsace Lorraine to France.	(*8*) Implemented.
(*9*) Italian frontiers to be readjusted on lines of nationality.	(*9*) Austrian Italy to Italy. Italian claim to Fiume unsettled. Italian claim to Slav area of Dalmatia rejected.
(*10 & 11*) Peoples of Austria-Hungary to be independent.	(*10 & 11*) Dismemberment of the Austro-Hungarian Empire. Czechoslovakia and Yugoslavia independent states. But minority national problem created in both new States.
(*12*) Nationalities under Turkish rule to be independent. Dardanelles open to all.	(*12*) Greece given Thrace, Macedonia, Smyrna and Anatolia. Dardanelles under the League of Nations.
(*13*) Poland independent with access to the sea.	(*13*) Independence granted but Danzig made a Free City. Polish corridor created and Poland to enjoy free navigation of all waterways to secure access to the sea.
(*14*) Association of Nations to be formed.	(*14*) League of Nations established.

36a. Kemal Ataturk: See pages 424-25.
   b. Mussolini: See pages 414-16.

37. Hitler's aggression: See pages 430-34.

38. Lenin's domestic policy:
War Communism:
(*1*) Industrial nationalization, 1918-20.

(2) Fixed prices for grain. Peasants refuse to produce surplus.

(3) Inflation. Collapse of industry and transport. Famine, sickness.

New Economic Policy, 1921:

(1) Modified communism as temporary measure.

(2) Surplus produce allowed to be sold on the open market.

(3) Restoration of private trading.

(4) Small factories restored to private ownership.

(5) Resumption of foreign trade.

Foreign policy:

  War with Poland:

(1) The Curzon-line boundary dispute.

(2) Polish victory on the Vistula and at Vilna.

(3) Treaty of Riga.

  Re-entry into European power system:

(1) 1920, treaty recognizing independence of the Baltic States.

(2) 1921, commercial treaty with Britain.

(3) 1922, treaty of Rapallo with Germany.

39. Emergence of Japan:

  a. Before 1905: See pages 375-76.

  b. After 1905:

(1) 1921-22, Washington Naval Conference. Japan on equal terms with major Western powers (U.S.A., France, Britain, Italy).

(2) 1927, adoption of policy of aggressive military expansion.

(3) 1931, Mukden Incident. Failure of the League to defend China. Japanese conquest of the province.

(4) Japanese withdrawal from the League of Nations.

(5) 1932-37, pressure on China.

(6) 1936, Rome-Berlin-Tokyo Axis formed.

(7) 1937-40, invasion of China. Conflict absorbed in the Second World War after Japanese attack on Pearl Harbour, 1941.

40a. Fall of Bismarck: Reasons:

(1) Accession of William II.

(2) Desire of William II to control policy.

(3) Divergence of views between Bismarck and William on Russian alliance.

(4) Bismarck offers resignation in hope of forcing William to agree with him. Resignation accepted.

Consequences:

(1) Treaty with Russia allowed to lapse.

(2) Succession of subservient Chancellors.

(3) Collapse of Bismarck's system of protective alliances.

(4) Adoption of aggressive foreign policy.

  b. Weaknesses of the League of Nations:

(1) Non-participation of Russia and America.

(2) Initial exclusion of Germany.

(3) Identification with the Versailles system.

(4) Lack of effective means of enforcing decisions.

(5) Based on false assumption of willingness of members to accept limitation of their national sovereignty.

c. Reasons for Russian Revolution, 1917:

(*1*) Autocratic monarchical régime. Evil monarchical advisers.

(*2*) Gap between Court and aristocracy on the one hand and the people on the other.

(*3*) Oppressive feudal social system.

(*4*) Failure of efforts for constitutional reform in the late nineteenth century.

(*5*) Underground growth of subversive forces and ideas—Nihilism, Anarchism.

(*6*) Incompetent war leadership leading to defeat and suffering of ill-equipped troops. (Involvement of Tsar as Commander-in-Chief.)

d. Causes of World Economic Crisis, 1929-31:

(*1*) Exhaustion of artificial and uncontrolled boom following the return to peace economy after the war of 1914-18.

(*2*) Effect of reparations on world trading and monetary systems.

(*3*) American insistence on repayment of war debts by her allies.

(*4*) Fall in price of primary products. Agricultural nations too poor to buy products of industrial nations.

(*5*) Depression and unemployment.

(*6*) Series of financial crises in European countries, reacting on America.

e. Causes of the Spanish Civil War, 1936-39:

(*1*) Social discontent. Illiteracy. Primitive agriculture. Conservative influence of Church and Army.

(*2*) Exposure of the Monarchy to criticism on the fall of de Rivera's dictatorship.

(*3*) Inability of Republican government to achieve adequate degree of reform owing to world economic depression.

(*4*) Fear of overthrow of Republican constitution by reactionary groups.

(*5*) Foreign encouragement of reactionary rebels.

INDEX

ACKNOWLEDGEMENTS

The publishers wish to thank the following for the use of photographs on the pages indicated: J. Allan Cash, 8 (top). Giraudon, 313. Trustees of the Imperial War Museum, 8 (bottom). Mansell Collection, 13, 14, 23, 33, 40, 47, 49, 57, 59, 63, 66, 74, 83, 89, 93, 95, 113, 117, 128, 146, 151, 167, 175, 227, 234, 235, 241, 247, 265 (Marie Antoinette), 297, 301, 305, 310, 319, 322, 327, 337, 343, 344, 347, 354, 355, 356, 361, 364, 366· National Maritime Museum, 192. Paul Popper Ltd., 189, 259. Radio Times Hulton Picture Library, 77, 125, 155, 194, 205, 215, 221, 224, 229, 253, 265 (Louis XVI), 267, 289, 295, 374, 376, 381, 384, 390, 391, 392, 394, 397, 399, 400, 405, 407, 410, 413, 417, 418, 420, 425, 427, 431, 433, 436.